Classifying Christians

Classifying Christians

*Ethnography, Heresiology, and the
Limits of Knowledge in Late Antiquity*

Todd S. Berzon

UNIVERSITY OF CALIFORNIA PRESS

University of California Press, one of the most distinguished university presses in the United States, enriches lives around the world by advancing scholarship in the humanities, social sciences, and natural sciences. Its activities are supported by the UC Press Foundation and by philanthropic contributions from individuals and institutions. For more information, visit www.ucpress.edu.

University of California Press
Oakland, California

© 2016 by The Regents of the University of California

First Paperback Printing 2021

Library of Congress Cataloging-in-Publication Data

Berzon, Todd S., author.
 Classifying Christians : ethnography, heresiology, and the limits of knowledge in Late Antiquity / Todd S. Berzon.
   p. cm.
 Includes bibliographical references and index.
 ISBN 978-0-520-28426-5 (cloth, alk. paper); 978-0-520-38317-3 (pbk. : alk. paper); 978-0-520-95988-0 (ebook)
 1. Christian heresies—History—Early church, ca. 30–600. 2. Church history—Primitive and early church, ca. 30–600. I. Title.
 BT1319.B47 2016
 273—dc23   2015030384

For my parents

CONTENTS

Acknowledgments ix
List of Abbreviations xiii

Introduction: Writing People, Writing Religion 1

1. Heresiology as Ethnography: The Ethnographic Disposition 27

2. Comparing Theologies and Comparing Peoples: The Customs, Doctrines, and Dispositions of the Heretics 58

3. Contesting Ethnography: Heretical Models of Human and Cosmic Plurality 98

4. Christianized Ethnography: Paradigms of Heresiological Knowledge 127

5. Knowledge Fair and Foul: The Rhetoric of Heresiological Inquiry 156

6. The Infinity of Continuity: Epiphanius of Salamis and the Limits of the Ethnographic Disposition 186

7. From Ethnography to List: Transcribing and Traversing Heresy 218

Epilogue: The Legacy of Heresiology 247
Bibliography 259
Index 285

ACKNOWLEDGMENTS

As I look back upon the experience of writing this book, which began as my dissertation in the Department of Religion at Columbia University, I am overwhelmed by the number of people who spared so much time and energy to answer my questions, offer bibliographic suggestions, and read my work. First and foremost, I benefited enormously from the advice and insights of the members of my dissertation committee: Adam Becker, Courtney Bender, Beth Berkowitz, and Seth Schwartz. Their comments over the years have enabled me to produce a far more lucid and coherent final product. Seth and Courtney in particular expended a remarkable amount of time conversing with me about the contours of the project. I am enormously indebted to them both. Celia Deutsch, Wayne Proudfoot, Robert Somerville, and Gareth Williams were tremendously helpful interlocutors during my time at Columbia. Jack Hawley always held his door open to offer me encouragement and guidance when I most needed them. My deepest gratitude is reserved for my advisor, Elizabeth Castelli. Words cannot express just how much I have learned from her. No matter the occasion, she has always made time to listen to me and temper my unceasing anxiety. She has patiently and empathetically answered every question I have ever asked. Our conversations about everything, from Italian food to Joni Mitchell, are among my most cherished memories. Her wit, generosity, humility, engagement, and kindness have inspired me both professionally and personally. And her incisive and detailed comments on the manuscript have made it immeasurably better. Without her constant and unwavering support, this book would have been impossible to write. She is my mentor, my confidante, and most important, my friend.

I presented versions of several chapters to forgiving audiences at the Society of Biblical Literature, the American Academy of Religion, the North American

Patristics Society, Brown University, Columbia University, and Bates College. The readers for the University of California Press—revealed to be Andrew Jacobs and Jeremy Schott—were both critical and constructive with their comments and questions. Their insights and suggestions have vastly improved the final product. Likewise, numerous colleagues beyond Bowdoin College have been stimulating conversation partners as this project took shape and came together. I thank Yoni Brafman, Liane Carlson, Catherine Chin, Nilo Couret, Charlotte Fonrobert, Kali Handelman, Sajida Jalalzai, Jocelyn Killmer, Jennifer Knust, David Maldonado-Rivera, Christine Luckritz Marquis, Ellen Muehlberger, Daniel Picus, Annette Yoshiko Reed, Greg Robbins, Nate Schumer, Drew Thomases, Anand Venkatkrishnan, Phil Webster, Heidi Wendt, and Ryan Woods. At the University of California Press, Eric Schmidt, Maeve Cornell-Taylor, and Cindy Fulton have been in equal measure encouraging and patient. My sincerest thanks to them for making this book a reality. Paul Psoinos was a scrupulous, engaging, and witty copyeditor, who saved me from many infelicities. Working with Paul was a genuine pleasure (and not just because of his boundless knowledge and wonderful stories). My thanks also to Roberta Engleman, who compiled the index. I must single out—and profusely thank—Abby Kluchin, who read every word of this manuscript multiple times. Her editorial hand not only honed my prose (and strengthened my resolve!) but also vastly improved the clarity and scope of my argument. Readers can blame her for excising my repeated use of the word "potamological." All remaining mistakes and omissions are my own.

I began the revisions for this book at Iliff School of Theology, where colleagues patiently listened to my extended monologues (i.e., rants) about heretics. My students in the course "A History of Heresy" provided me a useful sounding board for many of the ideas in this book. At Bowdoin College, Robert Morrison, Elizabeth Pritchard, John Holt, and Jorunn Buckley have warmly welcomed me into the Department of Religion by offering advice, support, and friendship. Lynn Brettler, our departmental administrator, has helped me to navigate every aspect of Bowdoin. I must also thank the students in my first-year seminar entitled "Heresy and Orthodoxy"—Sydney Avita-Jacques, Angela Dahl, Aidan French, Matthew Melanson, Sara Poole, and Conor Walsh—who listened to and challenged my ideas about heretics and heresiology. Librarians at Columbia University, Union Theological Seminary, Iliff School of Theology, University of Denver, and Bowdoin College eagerly helped me track down obscure references and volumes.

My friends and colleagues in Maine, Jenny Baca, Matt Botsch, Alanna Hoyer-Leitzel, Jan Kotowski, Sarah Mak, Ryan McConnell, and Kathryn Sederberg, were encouraging, reassuring, and, most important, entertaining. Monica Asher, Jacob Hupart, Evan Mayo-Wilson, Abby Rubenstein, Jim Sherwin, David Singerman, Linda Saferin, Steven Saferin, Jamie Kessler, Dan Kessler, and especially Jacob Kessler kept me engaged in the world beyond my work. I am exceedingly fortunate to have such caring friends and family. Finally, I thank my parents, Susan and David Berzon, who have been tireless in their support of everything that I have done. I will never be able to repay them for their generosity, advice, and support over these many years. As a small token of my gratitude for all that they have enabled me to do, I dedicate the ensuing pages to them.

A précis of this book project appeared as "Heresiology as Ethnography: Theorising Christian Difference," in *Religious Competition in the Third Century CE: Jews, Christians, and the Greco-Roman World*, ed. Jordan D. Rosenblum, Lily C. Vuong, and Nathaniel P. DesRosiers (Göttingen: Vandenhoeck & Ruprecht, 2014), 180–92. An earlier version of chapter 6 was published as "Known Knowns and Known Unknowns: Epiphanius of Salamis and the Limits of Heresiology," *Harvard Theological Review* 109.1 (2016): 75–101.

ABBREVIATIONS

ACW	*Ancient Christian Writers*. Mahwah, N.J.: Paulist Press, 1978–
AJP	*American Journal of Philology*
ANF	Ante-Nicene Fathers
ANRW	*Aufstieg und Niedergang der römischen Welt*
Aug	*Augustinianum*
AugStud	*Augustinian Studies*
CCSL	Corpus Christianorum: Series Latina. Turnhout: Brepols, 1953–
CH	*Church History*
CP	*Classical Philology*
CQ	*Classical Quarterly*
CSEL	Corpus Scriptorum Ecclesiasticorum Latinorum. Vienna: Akademie-Verlag, 1866–
FC	Fathers of the Church: A New Translation. Washington, D.C.: Catholic University of America Press, 1947–
FGrH	*Die Fragmente der griechischen Historiker*. Ed. Felix Jacoby et al. Leiden: Brill, 1923–
GCS, n. F.	Die griechischen christlichen Schriftsteller der ersten drei Jahrhunderte. Neue Folge. Leipzig: Hinrichs, 1897–1969
GR	*Greece and Rome*
HTR	*Harvard Theological Review*
Irén	*Irénikon*
JAAR	*Journal of the American Academy of Religion*
JECS	*Journal of Early Christian Studies*
JEH	*Journal of Ecclesiastical History*

JHI	*Journal of the History of Ideas*
JJMJS	*Journal of the Jesus Movement in Its Jewish Settings*
JMEMS	*Journal of Medieval and Early Modern Studies*
JRS	*Journal of Roman Studies*
JTS	*Journal of Theological Studies*
LCL	Loeb Classical Library. Cambridge, Mass.: Harvard University Press, 1912–
MTSR	*Method and Theory in the Study of Religion*
NPNF	*A Select Library of the Nicene and Post-Nicene Fathers of the Christian Church*. Ed. Philip Schaff et al. Buffalo: Christian Literature Company, 1886–90.
PL	*Patrologia Cursus Completus, Series Latina*. Ed. J.-P. Migne. 217 vols. Paris: 1844–64.
PG	*Patrologia Cursus Completus, Series Graeca*. Ed. J.-P. Migne. 162 vols. Paris: 1857–86.
RÉAug	*Revue des Études Augustiniennes*
RevScRel	*Revue des Sciences Religieuses*
SC	Sources Chrétiennes. Paris: Cerf, 1943–
SCH	*Studies in Church History*
SecCent	*Second Century*
StPatr	*Studia Patristica*
TAPA	*Transactions of the American Philological Association*
VC	*Vigiliae Christianae*
ZAC	*Zeitschrift für Antikes Christentum*

Introduction

Writing People, Writing Religion

> *A survey of our globe shows the continents inhabited by a great diversity of peoples different in appearance, different in language and in cultural life. The Europeans and their descendants on other continents are united by similarity of bodily build, and their civilization sets them off sharply against all the people of different appearance. The Chinese, the native New Zealander, the African Negro, the American Indian present not only distinctive bodily features, but each possesses also his own peculiar mode of life. Each human type seems to have its own inventions, its own customs and beliefs, and it is very generally assumed that race and culture must be intimately associated, that racial descent determines cultural life.*
>
> —FRANZ BOAS

The opening of Franz Boas's watershed anthropological text, *The Mind of Primitive Man*, describes the long-held theory that "primitive" was both a racial and a cultural designation.[1] Insofar as the latter was a derivation of the former, racial typology served as the foundation for hierarchical classifications of culture. The modes of life that ethnographers, missionaries, and travel writers had described were reflections of racial differences, where race, as a hereditary biological unit, was governed by phenotype, aptitude, and anatomy. Over the next almost three hundred pages, Boas sharply contests this supposed correlation between race, culture, and civilization. In arguing that "there is no necessary relationship between the 'race,' the language, and the cultural forms and expressions of a people," Boas imagined "cultures transcending racial classifications, and racial groups crossing cultural boundaries."[2] Boas's major contribution to the history of anthropology was to combat the science of racism and eugenics, to reject not only the idea of race as a biological category but also the very idea of evolutionist

---

1. The epigraph to this chapter is quoted from Franz Boas, *The Mind of Primitive Man*, rev. ed. (New York: MacMillan, 1938), 1.
2. Susan Hegeman, "Franz Boas and Professional Anthropology: On Mapping the Borders of the 'Modern,'" in *Victorian Ethnographies*, ed. James Buzard and Joseph Childers (Bloomington: Indiana University Press, 1998), special issue, *Victorian Studies* 41.3 (1998): 455–83, at 471.

ethnology.³ He was emphatic that human beings were ultimately "subjugated to the tyranny of customs" and that those customs—many of which we were barely even aware of—were the foundations of culture.⁴ But it was only at the end of Boas's lengthy career that he actually proffered a coherent definition of culture. And in fact, it was his students—Margaret Mead, Ruth Benedict, Edward Sapir, Robert Lowie, Alfred Kroeber, among others—who have been credited with defining culture "as a complex set of life ways of a given group of people."⁵

Boas's contributions to the development of professional anthropology and critical ethnography, combatting the cultural prejudices of his Victorian predecessors, the biblicism of ethnologists, and the overt racism of eugenicists, is part of a long, complex, and diverse intellectual genealogy.⁶ The intense preoccupation with the roots and causes of human difference was a fixture of centuries of critical and uncritical ethnographic writing alike. The unspoken counter term of much of Boas's argument, implied by his persistent use of the term "Europeans," is Christianity, the dominant ideological framework for centuries of ethnographic representation, ethnological theorization, and cultural hierarchization.⁷ As the anthropologist Kenelm Burridge has noted,⁸

> Through the Bible and its interpreters all kinds of different European communities were brought onto common ground, came into contact with, and knew, the word of God as it was expressed in the myths, history, figures, and customs and activities of a strange non-European people. . . . It was through the variety of images of other kinds of man that European peoples were invited to seek the dimensions and mystery of God and of themselves.

---

3. See George W. Stocking, Jr., "Franz Boas and the Culture Concept in Historical Perspective," *American Anthropologist* 68 (1966): 867–82.

4. Ibid. 876–78.

5. Hegeman, "Franz Boas and Professional Anthropology," 463.

6. See Margaret T. Hodgen, *Early Anthropology in the Sixteenth and Seventeenth Centuries* (Philadelphia: University of Pennsylvania Press, 1998); Michael Herzfeld, *Anthropology through the Looking-Glass: Critical Ethnography in the Margins of Europe* (New York: Cambridge University Press, 1987); Aron Gurevich, *Historical Anthropology of the Middle Ages* (Chicago: University of Chicago Press, 1992); Claire Sponsler, "Medieval Ethnography: Fieldwork in the European Past," *Assays* 7 (1992): 1–30; Anthony Kaldellis, *Ethnography after Antiquity: Foreign Lands and Peoples in Byzantine Literature* (Philadelphia: University of Pennsylvania Press, 2013); Mary Baine Campbell, *The Witness and the Other World: Exotic European Travel Writing, 400–1600* (Ithaca: Cornell University Press, 1988); and Shirin A. Khanmohamadi, *In Light of Another's Word: European Ethnography in the Middle Ages* (Philadelphia: University of Pennsylvania Press, 2014).

7. For further discussion on the relationship between Christianity and anthropology, see E. E. Evans-Pritchard, "Religion and the Anthropologists," in his *Essays in Social Anthropology* (New York: Free Press of Glencoe, 1963), 29–45; and the essays in *The Anthropology of Christianity*, ed. Fenella Cannell (Durham: Duke University Press, 2006).

8. Kenelm Burridge, *Encountering Aborigines: A Case Study—Anthropology and the Australian Aboriginal* (Elmsford, N.Y.: Pergamon Press, 1973), 14.

Christian theology—and a belief in the fundamental unity of the human species—was the foundation of European ethnology and ethnography.[9] In that sense, Boas was seeking to overhaul both an ethnocentric and a theological anthropology. Tomoko Masuzawa, David Livingstone, and George Stocking, Jr., among others, have emphasized that Christian writers—uncritical ethnographers, theologians, missionaries, philologists, and so forth—relied upon their own theological orthodoxy to elaborate the contours of racial, cultural, religious, and geographical differences.[10] Comparative philology, ethnography, and theology were all part and parcel of the discourse of world religions and of religion itself.[11] The intersection of these disciplines constructed a scientific scheme of religious classification: "Religion," as Masuzawa puts it, "offered European scholars a powerful, far-reaching, and comprehensive categorical framework by virtue of which they could hope to explain the characteristic features of a given non-European society."[12]

Shrouded in the language of evolution and devolution, the science of religion was guided by the comparison of ethnographic and hermeneutical data. The organization and analysis of these data created taxonomies of religions and provided verifiable models of religious and ethnological difference and behavior.[13] Uncritical ethnography was as much about theology as about customs, habits, and dispositions. Early modern ethnological theories—theories about the causes and nature of human difference—took Genesis as their starting point and, indeed, as their end point. Although the authors of Genesis had enumerated an explicit correspondence between nations and languages (and perhaps also cultures), their narratives were hardly comprehensive. As the historian Colin Kidd observes:[14]

> Of course, Old Testament anthropology runs into the sand. There is a huge gap—or perhaps not so huge, depending upon one's scheme of chronology—between the facts of ethnicity set out in Genesis and the appearance of ethnic groups in the

---

9. See ibid. 8–42.

10. Tomoko Masuzawa, *The Invention of World Religions; or, How European Universalism Was Preserved in the Language of Pluralism* (Chicago: University of Chicago Press, 2005); David N. Livingstone, *Adam's Ancestors: Race, Religion, and the Politics of Human Origins* (Baltimore: The Johns Hopkins University Press); and George W. Stocking, Jr., *Victorian Anthropology* (New York: Free Press, 1991).

11. See Masuzawa, *The Invention of World Religions*; Maurice Olender, *The Languages of Paradise: Race, Religion, and Philology in the Nineteenth Century*, trans. Arthur Goldhammer (Cambridge, Mass.: Harvard University Press, 2009); Richard King, *Orientalism and Religion: Postcolonial Theory, India and 'The Mystic East'* (New York: Routledge, 1999); and now David Chidester, *Empire of Religion: Imperialism and Comparative Religion* (Chicago: University of Chicago Press, 2014), esp. 59–89.

12. Masuzawa, *The Invention of World Religions*, 18.

13. See Arie L. Molendijk and Peter Pels, eds., *Religion in the Making: The Emergence of the Sciences of Religion* (Boston: Brill, 1998).

14. Colin Kidd, *The Forging of Races: Race and Scripture in the Protestant Atlantic World, 1600–2000* (New York: Cambridge University Press, 2006), 21. See also Guy G. Stroumsa, *A New Science: The Discovery of Religion in the Age of Reason* (Cambridge, Mass.: Harvard University Press, 2010), 77–100.

historical and ethnographic works of Greece and Rome. From which of Noah's sons came the Scythians, say? A great deal of early modern anthropology involved the reconstitution of the lineages of peoples between the petering out of scriptural ethnography and the start of the classical record.

Early modern anthropologists sought to manage, to borrow Stocking's phrase, the "ethnological problem" of monogenism: they sought to demonstrate the fundamental unity of the human species and the transmission of original sin despite evidence to the contrary.[15] The work of Christian ethnographers and theologians was thus to fill in the gaps of the biblical narrative and to maintain its ethnological integrity. In certain cases, however, ethnological theories that were said to undermine the integrity of the biblical narrative led to accusations of heresy. The arch-heresiarch, so to speak, of Christian anthropology was Isaac La Peyrère (1596–1676), who had argued in his *Prae-Adamitae* (*Men before Adam*, published in Latin in 1655) that a careful reading of Romans 5.12–14—Paul's discussion of sin, law, Adam, and Moses—indicated that there were human beings before Adam.[16] La Peyrère, though a Calvinist, was brought before Pope Alexander VII to answer for his heresy, after which he recanted but remained subject to intense opprobrium from scores of theologians and ethnologists.[17] By 1656, according to Anthony Grafton, there were already nineteen published refutations of his treatise.[18]

With the accusation of heresy swirling, debates over ethnological theories illustrated the centrality of orthodox thinking to questions of human difference. The language of heresy was not only an accusation to be hurled against blasphemous ideas or interpretations—a charge by clerics—but was itself an important theological force in the history of both human and religious diversity. The development of a hierarchy of culture and nations as a hierarchy of religion follows not only from biblical interpretation but also from the development of the Christian discourse of heresy. Whereas it is true, as Kidd notes, that the narrative of Genesis 11

---

15. Stocking, *Victorian Anthropology*, 51.

16. In the words of Richard H. Popkin, *Isaac La Peyrère (1596–1676): His Life, Work and Influence* (Leiden: Brill, 1987), "[La Peyrère] was regarded as perhaps the greatest heretic of the age, even worse than Spinoza, who took over some of his most challenging ideas. He was refuted over and over again by leading Jewish, Catholic, and Protestant theologians" (1). On the specifics of La Peyrère's biblical anthropology, see Livingstone, *Adam's Ancestors*, 32–37. If the law to which Paul was referring in these verses was, as La Peyrère argued, a primeval law given to Adam, and sin exists before law, there must have been people before Adam who had sinned. Adam was thus described not as the father of humanity but as the father of Judaism. See Matthew R. Goodrum, "Biblical Anthropology and the Idea of Human Prehistory in Late Antiquity," *History and Anthropology* 13.2 (2002): 69–78.

17. Livingstone, *Adam's Ancestors*, 37–38. For the details of La Peyrère's recantation before Pope Alexander VII, see Popkin, *Isaac La Peyrère*, 13–22.

18. Anthony Grafton, *Defenders of the Text: The Traditions of Scholarship in an Age of Science, 1450–1800* (Cambridge, Mass.: Harvard University Press, 1991), 204–13.

did not offer a comprehensive genealogy of all peoples everywhere, the New Testament supplied an important conceptual addendum: it laid the foundation for the Christian discourse of heresy, which would, over time, supplement the narrative gaps of Genesis 11 while also creating its own problematic narrative of theological diversity.[19] A central piece in the foundations of theological anthropology belongs, then, to a much earlier set of debates, theories, and writings: the discourse of early Christian ethnography.

For those who study the ancient world, ethnography is an absorbing yet elusive subject. In contrast to the modern concept, which denotes both the practice of fieldwork and a genre of writing, there were no established methods or a fixed generic form in the ancient Mediterranean world. Few ancient authors undertook anything approximating modern fieldwork. Greeks and Romans—from Homer to Pliny, and Herodotus to Tacitus—did write profusely about foreign dress, myths, dietary habits, histories, cosmologies, and religious customs. But they "wrote peoples" (*ethno-graphy*) primarily as a counterpoint, both positive and negative, to their own cultural conventions.[20] Building upon the work of classicists, scholars of religion, anthropologists, and literary critics, this book posits that ancient ethnography, specifically Christian ethnography, attests a complex set of negotiations between attempts to understand the surrounding world by inventorying its people, explaining their history and origins, and by establishing a position within it.[21] Ethnography in the ancient world functioned descriptively, though tendentiously, through the chronicling, stylizing, and essentializing of human customs, communities, and institutions. It operated as a discursive activity in which people were created as textual objects with discrete and precise characteristics, origins, histories, and customs. While ethnographers moved to study the changing world—not only to orient themselves within their evolving social and cultural surroundings but also to articulate the terms of these changes from their own cultural perspective—they supplied a certain fixity and predictability to the diversity of people

---

19. On the New Testament and the discourse of heresy, see Robert M. Royalty, Jr., *The Origin of Heresy: A History of Discourse in Second Temple Judaism and Early Christianity* (New York: Routledge, 2012), 53–171.

20. See, for example, Benjamin Isaac, *The Invention of Racism in Classical Antiquity* (Princeton: Princeton University Press, 2004); Greg Woolf, *Tales of the Barbarians: Ethnography and Empire in the Roman West* (Malden, Mass.: Wiley-Blackwell, 2011); Joseph E. Skinner, *The Invention of Greek Ethnography: From Homer to Herodotus* (New York: Oxford University Press, 2012); François Hartog, *The Mirror of Herodotus: The Representation of the Other in the Writing of History*, trans. Janet Lloyd (Berkeley and Los Angeles: University of California Press, 1988); and Christian Jacob, *Géographie et ethnographie en Grèce ancienne* (Paris: Armand Colin, 1991).

21. As Burridge, *Encountering Aborigines*, argues, "The heirs of Herodotus, traveler and recorder, and of St. Paul, prototypical Christian missionary, have provided the materials for the growth" of anthropology (39). Anthropology, he contends, "derives from the Graeco-Christian synthesis" (ibid. 38), a sense that the world can be studied as an objective reality and that the world's people are fundamentally united.

who inhabited and would come to inhabit it. They sought not just to report information but also to organize and theorize it, to try to understand the root causes and implications of their knowledge about the world's peoples.[22] Ethnography constituted a *process* of analysis about the possibilities, implications, and limits of comprehending the surrounding world and its people.

The chapters that follow aim to assess the conceptual paradigms and epistemological implications of ethnography for the construction of Christianity in late antiquity. I investigate how Christians harnessed the vernacular of ethnography, the process of describing and classifying peoples, to advance theories of human difference and the boundaries of human knowledge: how, in other words, late antique writers depicted and organized the world and its peoples in distinctly Christian terms and thus constructed the contours of Christianity itself. I concentrate on one particular set of Christian ethnographers, the heresiologists, who wrote the heretics via their customs, habits, beliefs, and dispositions.[23] I will focus my attention on the writings of six heresiologists: Irenaeus of Lyons (ca. 130–202 C.E.), Hippolytus of Rome (170–235 C.E.), Tertullian of Carthage (ca. 160–220 C.E.), Epiphanius of Salamis (ca. 315–403 C.E.), Augustine of Hippo (354–430 C.E.), and Theodoret of Cyrrhus (393–457 C.E.).[24] Not only do their texts reflect different stages, geographies, and styles of heresiology; they also list different numbers of heretics and employ different strategies to theorize the diversity of the

---

22. Although ethnographers in the ancient world occasionally drew upon their own experiences to write people—via travel and social exchange—they tended, more often than not, to recapitulate earlier sources. But these acts of recapitulation often worked in different ways: writers used the same data, stereotypes, and tropes to make different arguments about cultural, dispositional, phenotypical, and religious diversity.

23. There is as yet no exhaustive, diachronic study of heresiology in the late antique world. There is a tendency among scholars either to focus on a particular heretic (such as Arius, Priscillian, Marcion) or heresiologist (Irenaeus, Hippolytus, Tertullian) rather than trace themes and styles across the centuries of the genre's development. Three recent treatments of heresiology—Geoffrey S. Smith, *Guilt by Association* (New York: Oxford University Press, 2014); Kendra Eshleman, *The Social World of Intellectuals in the Roman Empire: Sophists, Philosophers, and Christians* (New York: Cambridge University Press, 2012); and Royalty, *The Origin of Heresy*—focus only on the earliest heresiologists, Irenaeus, Hippolytus, and Justin (none discusses the works of Epiphanius, Filastrius, Augustine, or Theodoret). Eshelman's study puts heresiology in dialogue with the literature of the Second Sophistic in order to think about the social and intellectual formation of Christian identity (how belonging was negotiated, more or less). Smith sees the development of the heresy catalogue as tied explicitly to its polemical quality, locating its origins in the pseudo-Pauline corpus and the discourse of false teachers, whereas Royalty focuses on the discourse of orthodoxy and heresy in the New Testament (and, to a lesser extent, Second Temple Judaism).

24. Filastrius of Brescia (death ca. 397 C.E.), author of the *Book of Diverse Heresies*, does not feature prominently in this study, though where relevant I have made use of his text. For more on the heresiology of Filastrius, see the excellent dissertation of David Maldonado-Rivera, "Encyclopedic Trends and the Making of Heresy in Late Ancient Christianity" (Ph.D. dissertation, Indiana University, 2016).

heretics. Their texts, moreover, form what Bakhtin terms a chain of utterances, a communal discourse that "give[s] rise to particular genres" defined by compositional, stylistic, and thematic coherence and refined literary language.[25] Precisely because heresiology was a genre of aggregation and collection, the heresiologists continually refined their texts by drawing upon the knowledge and language of their contemporaries and predecessors. In Bakhtinian terms, this intertextual responsiveness, which is both implicit and explicit, functions as a chain of heresiological utterances: "Each utterance is filled with echoes and reverberations of other utterances to which it is related by the communality of the sphere of speech communication. Every utterance must be regarded primarily as a response to preceding utterances of the given sphere.... Each utterance refutes, affirms, supplements, and relies on the others, presupposes them to be known, and somehow takes them into account."[26] In this sense, the heresiologist's descriptions of the heretics act as utterances addressed both to a specific interlocutor and to the entire enterprise of heresiological cataloguing. The deliberate forging of an intellectual tradition of heresiology, what has been called a *traditio haereticorum*, exhibits how error was schematized and classified as well as how the genre itself evolved and adapted over centuries.[27] It is a telling fact that early modern heresiologies written in the seventeenth century by figures such as Thomas Edwards, James Cranford, Richard Vines, and Ephraim Pagitt not only bear an uncanny rhetorical and structural resemblance to their late antique predecessors but also explicitly cite them as models.[28]

The study of Christian plurality and divergence articulated the conditions and contents of a distinctly Christian world written in the language of Christian theology, history, and scripture. My interest is not in the truthfulness or historical accuracy of the heresiologists' descriptions of the heretics but rather in how these polemical texts articulate their understanding of Christian and human diversity both in macroscopic and in microscopic terms. I analyze how the heresiologists built a literary language that theorizes heresy as a whole—a developmental theory of heretical error—and specific heretics as parts within and yet apart from that whole. As they scrutinized their world, the heresiologists translated the microscopic, the minutiae of the habits and customs of particular Christian peoples, into

---

25. Mikhail Bakhtin, "The Problem of Speech Genres," in his *Speech Genres and Other Late Essays*, ed. Caryl Emerson and Michael Holquist, trans. Vern W. McGee (Austin: University of Texas Press, 1986), 60–102, 64, 65.

26. Ibid. 91.

27. Averil Cameron, "How to Read Heresiology," *JMEMS* 33.3 (2003): 471–92, at 477.

28. See, for example, Ann Hughes, "Thomas Edwards's *Gangraena* and Heresiological Traditions," in *Heresy, Literature, and Politics in Early Modern English Culture*, ed. David Loewenstein and John Marshall (New York: Cambridge University Press, 2009), 137–59; and her *Gangraena and the Struggle for the English Revolution* (New York: Oxford University Press, 2004), esp. 55–129.

the macroscopic, broader extrapolations about human nature, human diversity, and human behavior. To that end, I focus on the paradigms and techniques that the late antique Christian heresiologists used to array, historicize, and characterize Christian ethnographic knowledge. The heretics were invaluable yet highly unstable theoretical playthings through which Christian authors navigated and systematized the diversity of the entire human world. The heresiologists used the heretics not only to define the borders of Christianity but also to create the Christian conditions for understanding the contents and diversity of the world. As the Christian ethnographic gaze contemplated the differences of the peoples of the world, the Christian turn toward ethnography signaled not just ethnography *by* Christians but also ethnography *of* Christians.[29] In so doing, this ethnographic discourse, at once aspirational and polemical, constructed the boundaries of late antique Christianity itself.

The expansive gaze of Christian authors and travelers infused their writings with ethnographical and geographical maps of piety and impiety, religion and irreligion: to travel in the world in texts was to construct Christianity, to deny expressions of Christianity, and to envision the potential for Christianity everywhere.[30] The Christian narrative of sacred history encompassed the elaboration, both macroscopically and microscopically, of holy topographies and hallowed ethnographies. To watch the world become Christian—to see it materialize with respect to both place and people—was to watch the promise of scripture unfold. And to capture this transformation was to blend Christian missionary activity and ethnographic writing. Ethnography conveyed an ideology "employed by

29. To say the heresiologists are ethnographers is not dependent upon their use of the term *ethnos* to identify the heretics; ethnography and ethnicity are not one and the same. Ethnography is neither the study of ethnicities nor an effort to identify their fundamental criteria; it is the study of how population groups of religious, political, military, and ethnic orientation were written and categorized. Josephus's description of the Essenes in Book 2 of his *Jewish War* is ethnographic not because it concerns Jews (an *ethnos*) but because it treats the Essenes as a collectivity of people with particular customs, habits, rituals, doctrines, rules, etc. Ethnic groups are surely one type of people subject to ethnographic analysis, but if ethnography is a heuristic category—which I think it is—it encompasses much more than writing ethnicities. Ethnography represents the writing of customs, habits, and practices of groups (and even individuals) while its author ponders how these habits reflect broader theoretical and classificatory exigencies. Such writings often work to fashion coherence out of diffuse intellectual knowledge. In the very act of arraying knowledge by school of thought, doxographies, for instance, evoke a sense of intellectual groupism, however false or misleading. Descriptions of religious professionals, rituals, armies, symposia, travels, triumphs, gladiatorial games, etc., all contain ethnographic elements. *Pace* David M. Olster, "Classical Ethnography and Early Christianity," in *The Formulation of Christianity by Conflict through the Ages*, ed. Katherine B. Free (Lewiston, N.Y.: Edwin Mellen Press, 1995), 9–31; and Aaron P. Johnson, *Religion and Identity in Porphyry of Tyre: The Limits of Hellenism in Late Antiquity* (Cambridge: Cambridge University Press, 2013).

30. See Andrew S. Jacobs, *Remains of the Jews: The Holy Land Christian Empire in Late Antiquity* (Stanford: Stanford University Press, 2004), 103–38.

Christians to tell themselves a new story of religious Empire."[31] Heresiological literature is thus deeply embedded in larger corpora of varying genres. In writing about the world they inhabited, their relationship to it, and their interpretation of it, Christian writers infused various genres of writing, including letters, sermons, commentaries, travelogues, monastic handbooks, and hagiographies, with an awareness of macroscopic paradigms and microscopic description. This study is, then, not meant to be exhaustive but rather aims to focus in on a particular textual endeavor, heresiology, that is simultaneously rhetorical, theological, geographic, ethnographic, and epistemological.

As the heresiologists investigated the diversity of Christian sectarianism across the Mediterranean, they produced a textual world and worldview driven by the comparison of theologies and dispositions. To the extent that heresiological writers functioned as ethnographers, whether armchair or fieldworker, they did more than simply regurgitate stereotypes, provide moral warnings, and convey imperial propaganda. My focus is on heresiology as an illustration of Christian classification and organization of knowledge. I explore how Christian authors framed their texts ethnographically by amassing data, marshaling their discoveries, fashioning explanatory models, and theologizing and negotiating their own authorial abilities. The process of organizing knowledge by writing people constructed categorical and discursive binaries. Heresiologies identified the similarities and differences among Christians by creating a categorical framework, even if just discursive, within which to house them. Within the context of late antiquity, Jeremy Schott has rightly emphasized how theories of knowledge, classification, and their generic forms were written in conjunction with imperial ideologies:[32]

> Universal history, ethnography, and figurative reading strategies—the tools of philosophers and apologists alike—owed much of their shape to the specific political context in which they were practiced. The leverage of these universalizing discourses lay not in "pluralism" or "inclusivity," as sometimes has been suggested; rather, the political potency of universalism resided in its simultaneous demand for comprehensiveness and difference. The distinction between universality and particularity that grounded these intellectual discourses closely paralleled the asymmetrical relationship of courses of social privilege and social control. Ethnography and universal history sought a comprehension of diversity homologous to the imperial desire for control of diverse territories and peoples.

---

31. Jacobs, *Remains of the Jews*, 107. I share Keith Hopkins's understanding of ideology in his "Christian Number and Its Implications," *JECS* 6.2 (1998): 185–226, as "a system of ideas which seeks to justify the power and authority of a set of ethical prescriptions and metaphysical explanations, and also, of course, to justify the power and authority of a particular set of interpreters of these ideas" (217).

32. Jeremy M. Schott, *Christianity, Empire, and the Making of Religion in Late Antiquity* (Philadelphia: University of Pennsylvania Press, 2008), 166.

Even as Schott stresses that the classification of knowledge worked in tandem with a larger imperial discourse of control, he foregrounds the tensions embedded within ethnographic theorization: writers were compelled to emphasize coherence and difference simultaneously. Indeed, the heresiologists are remarkably ambivalent about their discourse as a mechanism of comprehensiveness and control. In thinking about heresiology as an expression of Christian ethnography, I want to ask how its authors negotiated the push and pull of coherence and difference; how they worked to distill and essentialize heretics as communities that were both macroscopically similar and yet microscopically different from each other; and how they thought about and went about translating peoples into words. Finally, I wish to investigate how the writing and the editing processes imposed not only a self-reflexivity but also an epistemological paradox upon the heresiologists, in which the capacity to make and know the world of Christianity and the architect of the world of Christianity became fleeting possibilities.

One of the central claims of this project is that even as heresiological ethnography built a discourse of control and expertise, that very same discourse communicated the constraints of the heresiologists' knowledge about their object of study. As Christopher Herbert has incisively shown within the context of Victorian ethnography, the discourses of ethnographic totalization and restraint were, in fact, bound together as epistemological and investigative contradictions.[33] The heresiologists' claims of totalizing knowledge were undercut by their open acknowledgment of the conceptual and practical fissures within their texts: the heresiologists could not know any one heresy fully or know all the heretics in their entirety. Augustine's explication of this conceptual fissure in the edifice of his heresiology signaled his perception of the restricted epistemological reach of the ethnographic gaze and the ethnographic word. Augustine acknowledged that the theological distance and cultural gap between heresiologist and heresy precluded his ability to understand the heretics fully. Not only were there limits to what the heresiologists could know, but there were conceptual limits to how knowledge could be meaningfully processed. In expressing the discourse of totalization as aspirational rather than realized, the heresiologists emphasized their labor as collectors over and above their ability to find and enumerate a comprehensive whole of heresy. I am not arguing that the heresiologists, by demonstrating their detailed knowledge of and ability to refute the heretics, amassed for themselves some vague notion of scholastic or ecclesiastical authority. Instead, I am claiming that the heresiologists' stated understanding of the heretics cut in precisely the opposite direction. Heresiologies were not texts of control and totalization but catalogues marked by vulnerability, hazard, and fissure. Even as polemically constructed caricatures, the heretics proved an enigmatic, elu-

---

33. Christopher Herbert, *Culture and Anomie: Ethnographic Imagination in the Nineteenth Century* (Chicago: University of Chicago Press, 1991).

sive, and altogether destructive object of inquiry. To think with and through ethnography is to invite a scrutiny not simply of another or even oneself but to contemplate openly about the representative capacity of writers, language, and their texts. Ethnography encapsulates the tension between totality and partiality, comprehension and ignorance, and the insurmountable gap between human nature and the natural world. Ethnographic data hold the potential to inspire as much as puzzle and to fracture as much as unify. As Irenaeus succinctly put it, "it is not possible to name the number of those who have fallen away from the truth in various ways."[34] The overarching aim of this study, then, is to trace how the ethnographic impulse, embedded within certain strands of early Christian discourse, informed theorizations of religious diversity and the classification of religious knowledge.

HOW TO READ HERESIOLOGY

Because the terms of early Christian devotion and tradition were developing and diverse, the history of formative Christianity evidences both the rhetorical and the institutional efforts by which boundaries between sects were constructed.[35] Heresiology was an effort by particular members of the still nascent Christian community to elaborate claims of tradition by specifying the terms of Christian principles, practices, and theology. As Christians spread themselves across the Mediterranean preaching the good news of Christ, and as peoples assumed the mantle of Christian identification in different ways and in different environments, theological and ecclesiastical diversity became increasingly endemic to Christian culture.[36] With the

---

34. Irenaeus, *Adv. haer.* 1.28 (SC 264:356–57). Throughout the chapters below, I have followed the translation for Books 1–3 of Irenaeus's *Adversus haereses*, of Dominic J. Unger et al., St. *Irenaeus of Lyons: Against the Heresies, Books 1–3*, 3 vols., ACW 55, 65, 64 (Mahwah, N.J.: Paulist Press, 1992–2012). For Books 4 and 5, I have followed, with substantial modification, the translation in ANF 1:462–567.

35. See, for example, David Brakke, *The Gnostics: Myth, Ritual, and Diversity in Early Christianity* (Cambridge, Mass.: Harvard University Press, 2010); Alain Le Boulluec, *La notion d'hérésie dans la littérature grecque, IIe–IIIe siècles*, 2 vols. (Paris: Études Augustiniennes, 1985); Daniel Boyarin, *Border Lines: The Partition of Judaeo-Christianity* (Philadelphia: University of Pennsylvania Press, 2004); Susanna Elm, Éric Rebillard, and Antonella Romano, eds. *Orthodoxie, christianisme, histoire* (Rome: École Française de Rome, 2000); Karen L. King, "Which Early Christianity?," in *The Oxford Handbook of Early Christian Studies*, ed. Susan Ashbrook Harvey and David G. Hunter (New York: Oxford University Press, 2008), 66–84; and her "Factions, Variety, Diversity Multiplicity: Representing Early Christian Differences for the 21st Century," *MTSR* 23 (2011): 216–37.

36. See Bart D. Ehrman, *The Orthodox Corruption of Scripture: The Effects of Early Christological Controversies on the Text of the New Testament* (New York: Oxford University Press, 1993); Elizabeth A. Clark, *The Origenist Controversy: The Cultural Construction of an Early Christian Debate* (Princeton: Princeton University Press, 1992); and Carlos R. Galvão-Sobrinho, *Doctrine and Power: Theological Controversy and Christian Leadership in the Later Roman Empire* (Berkeley and Los Angeles: University of California Press, 2013).

number of Christians multiplying across the Mediterranean,[37] disputes over the finer points of theological doctrine, ecclesiastical governance, exegesis, ritual observation, and canonical inclusion naturally followed. With each new church, the purported unanimity of the Christian movement was subjected to new threats of fissure and dissolution.[38] Paul himself, as his epistles clearly demonstrate, struggled to maintain order among the communities that he visited and to which he wrote. Communities forgot, disputed, or ignored his instructions about Christ's Gospel.[39] His First Letter to the Corinthians famously chastises them for their division and disunity:[40]

> Now I appeal to you, brothers and sisters, by the name of our Lord Jesus Christ that there be no divisions among you, but that you be united in the same mind and the same purpose. For it has been reported to me . . . that there are quarrels among you, my brothers and sisters. What I mean is that each of you says, "I belong to Paul," or "I belong to Apollos," or "I belong to Cephas," or "I belong to Christ." Has Christ been divided?

Early divisions among followers of Jesus were sown in overtly human terms: divisions were facilitated by allegiances to human leaders (a charge the heresiologists repeatedly made). While scripture had rightly forewarned its believers about division, dissension, and false prophets—"Indeed, there have to be factions among you, for only so will it become clear who among you are genuine"—it did not elaborate a plenary understanding of its origins, essence, and history.[41] While Simon Magus became the father of Christian heresy for the heresiologists, in the biblical narrative (Acts 8.9–24) he is not identified as such. He is a magician, first and foremost.

Just as early modern Christian ethnologists sought to fill in the gaps in the narrative of Genesis, early Christian heresiologists similarly worked to clarify in the Bible's broader warnings about sectarianism and disharmony. Nearly a century

---

37. For a creative, if speculative, analysis of Christian demographics, see Hopkins, "Christian Number and Its Implications."

38. On divisions within the earliest communities of followers of Jesus, see Wayne A. Meeks, *The First Urban Christians: The Social World of the Apostle Paul*, 2nd ed. (New Haven: Yale University Press, 2003), 51–73, 111–39; and James D. G. Dunn, *Unity and Diversity in the New Testament: An Inquiry into the Character of Earliest Christianity* (Philadelphia: Westminster Press, 1977).

39. Even a cursory reading of Paul's epistles to the Galatians, Corinthians, and Romans demonstrates the problems of obedience, truth, and communal coherence. See Royalty, *The Origin of Heresy*, 64–88.

40. 1 Cor. 1.10–13a. On the divisions at Corinth, see Margaret M. Mitchell, *Paul and the Rhetoric of Reconciliation: An Exegetical Investigation of the Language and Composition of 1 Corinthians* (Louisville: Westminster John Knox, 1992).

41. 1 Cor. 11.19. See also Matt. 7.15; 24.4, 11, 24; 2 Pet. 2.1; 1 John 4.11; 2 Cor. 11.4; Titus 3.10, among other verses that point to the problem of dissension and division.

and a half after the death of the apostle Paul, Irenaeus, bishop of Lyons, enumerated in the preface to his five-book refutation of heresies, *Adversus haereses*, the principal hazard of the heresy: it was unstable, erroneous, derivative, false, arrogant, and demonic. The heretics, Irenaeus warns, "believe differently about the same things as time passes and never have a stable doctrine, because they wish rather to be sophists of words than disciples of the truth."[42] Via their addenda and excisions, the heretics were said to mutilate the revealed truth of Christ. Rather than simply allow the truth to be, so Irenaeus claims, they massage it, augment it, recast it, and ultimately threaten its untrammeled facilitation through generations of Christians. Irenaeus's discourse about the heretics hinged upon a series of rhetorical and dispositional distinctions. Considering themselves exponents of (an alternative) system of truth, the heretics craftily "speak the same language" as (orthodox) Christians, though they "intend different meanings."[43] Their treachery, moreover, as Irenaeus diagnoses it, attests an underlying and more perilous condition: they persist and metastasize "under the pretense of knowledge."[44] Their so-called knowledge—while revealing detailed cosmologies, alternative scriptures, a multiplicity of deities, the impetus of creation, the divisions within the soul, the process of redemption, and the metaphysical principles of the universe—imported a grandiose claim of privileged authority into their schematization of a cosmic narrative. In supplanting the primacy of the God of the Bible and his Word, the creative and enlightening powers behind the creation of the universe and the human race, the heretics embarked upon a massive restructuring of revealed truth.[45] Reorienting the truths of the apostolic age not only complicated claims about the exclusive transmission of knowledge but also perpetuated an open and unfixed understanding of Christian tradition.

Scholars now regard Irenaeus's history of Christianity and Christian tradition, where truth always preceded falsity and heresy was conceptualized as an adulteration of a uniform, stable, continuous chain of tradition, as an ideological representation rather than a historical reality.[46] Since the pioneering work of Walter Bauer,

---

42. Irenaeus, *Adv. haer.* 3.24.2 (SC 211:474). On this point, see Karen L. King, "Social and Theological Effects of Heresiological Discourse," in *Heresy and Identity in Late Antiquity*, ed. Eduard Iricinschi and Holger M. Zellentin (Tübingen: Mohr Siebeck, 2008), 28–49.

43. Irenaeus, *Adv. haer.* 1 pr. 2.33–34 (SC 264:22).

44. Irenaeus, *Adv. haer.* 1 pr. 1.8–9 (SC 264:19). This is magnified by the fact that in the fourth-century Eusebius of Caesarea reported in his *Hist. eccl.* 5.7.1 a longer, more precise title for Irenaeus's work: "Exposé and Overthrow of What Is Falsely Called Knowledge."

45. See, for example, Irenaeus *Adv. haer.* 1.8.1–11.

46. For accounts of this scholarly shift, see Brakke, *The Gnostics*, 1–31; Royalty, *The Origin of Heresy*, 3–29; and Karen L. King, *What Is Gnosticism?* (Cambridge, Mass.: Belknap Press, 2003), though King's point is that even as scholars have worked to overcome the heresiologists' discourse of orthodoxy and heresy, they have nonetheless reinscribed this very same framework.

they have primarily treated the writings of the heresiologists as tendentious texts written to establish the narrative of a single, consistent orthodoxy over against derivative, corrupting heresy.[47] The history of early Christianity, scholars now emphasize, was never a history of singularity and uniformity; rather it was a history of diversity, discord, and disunity. To attend to this multiplicity of Christian voices, scholars developed what David Brakke identifies as the "variety of Christianities" model, which maps Christian diversity and disagreement. According to this narrative, the earliest centuries of the Common Era were a time of intense competition among various Christian groups—including the so-called proto-orthodoxy faction that would ultimately win out—all of which claimed to be the embodiment of true Christianity.[48] Brakke rightly criticizes the varieties model by emphasizing that it has tended to treat Christian diversity in rather static terms: it conceptualizes groups as discrete and bounded entities, perpetuating Irenaeus's idea that proto-orthodoxy was uniform and neatly delineated. In its place, Brakke argues for what he calls the "identity-formation" model. Building upon the work of Karen King, he emphasizes the scholarly shift that attends to "the strategies by which individuals and groups sought to define themselves. The historian does not take for granted the existence of defined groups, but instead interrogates how ancient peoples sought to create, transform, and challenge religious communities and practices."[49] And while many scholars have embraced the identity-formation model—exploring how heresy was constructed in relation to issues of law, gender, celibacy, and prophecy, among myriad other themes—the genre of heresiology and heresiological catalogues in particular have remained largely absent from this interpretive shift.[50]

In a provocative article entitled "How to Read Heresiology," the historian Averil Cameron raises a series of questions about the genre. She seeks to shift scholarly

---

47. See Walter Bauer, *Orthodoxy and Heresy in Earliest Christianity*, ed. Robert A. Kraft and Gerhard Kroedel, trans. Philadelphia Seminar on Christian Origins (Philadelphia: Fortress Press, 1971). The Bauer thesis has received much criticism since its publication both because many of its historical claims have been shown to be incorrect and because scholars argue that while it reframes the scholarly conversation about orthodoxy and heresy it did little to move beyond the binary itself. See, for example, Thomas A. Robinson, *The Bauer Thesis Examined: The Geography of Heresy in the Early Christian Church* (Lewiston, N.Y.: Edwin Mellen, 1988); Daniel J. Harrington, "The Reception of Walter Bauer's *Orthodoxy and Heresy in Earliest Christianity* during the Last Decade," *HTR* 73 (1980): 289–98; and Lewis Ayres, ed., *The Question of Orthodoxy* (special issue *JECS* 14.4 [2006]).

48. Brakke, *The Gnostics*, 7.

49. Ibid. 11.

50. See Caroline Humfress, *Orthodoxy and the Courts in Late Antiquity* (New York: Oxford University Press, 2007); Virginia Burrus, *The Making of a Heretic: Gender, Authority, and the Priscillianist Controversy* (Berkeley and Los Angeles: University of California Press, 1995); David G. Hunter, *Marriage, Celibacy, and Heresy in Ancient Christianity: The Jovinianist Controversy* (New York: Oxford University Press, 2007); and Laura Nasrallah, *An Ecstasy of Folly: Prophecy and Authority in Early Christianity* (Cambridge, Mass.: Harvard University Press, 2003).

attention away from thinking about heresiologies as sources of information and suggests that we should read them instead as "performative or functional texts."[51] Cameron contends that scholars have failed to comprehend the complexities within these texts, due in large part to the perception that Epiphanius's *Panarion*, in many ways the classic example of the genre, is an uninventive and hyperbolic text. Insofar as the *Panarion* reflected banal generalizations about the need to dispel error and articulate the topography of true Christianity, it was an uninspired, rote polemical dispute between two mutually exclusive yet dependent theological categories: orthodoxy and heresy. Heresiology, despite its encyclopedic aspirations, was mired as much by the simplicity of its own dichotomous worldview as by its perceived lack of "imaginative content."[52] Scholars routinely assert that the heresiologies are tired screeds, largely devoid of sophistication and nuance.[53] But according to Cameron, to dismiss "heresiology as sterile or boring, as mere scholastic exercises, therefore misses several points at the same time."[54] Such a position fails to delve deeply into the details of these admittedly lengthy but surprisingly complex literary compositions.

Cameron contends that heresiology, shaped by "a poetics of [its] own,"[55] harbored a web of interrelated rhetorical, theological, political, ecclesiastical, and scholastic agendas. With respect to the *Panarion*, she notes that, "a less hostile view might be willing to recognize a degree of literary skill in the ways in which Epiphanius modelled the *Panarion* both on Song of Songs and on scientific treatises on snake bites and poisons."[56] With its persistent use of the rhetoric of entomology, herpetology, and medicine, the *Panarion* presents itself as a work shaped by precision and the rhetoric of science. To that end, it explicitly engages with classical models, referencing at its outset Nicander's *Theriaka*—a poem enumerating venomous animals—and also contests classical literary tropes: "For the Greek authors, poets and chroniclers would invoke a Muse when they undertook some work of mythology.... I, however, am calling upon the holy Lord of all to come to the aid of my poverty."[57] Cameron is especially emphatic that heresiological literature

51. Cameron, "How to Read Heresiology," 474.
52. Ibid. 473.
53. See Brent D. Shaw, "Who Were the Circumcellions?," in *Vandals, Romans and Berbers*, ed. A. H. Merrills (Burlington, Vt.: Ashgate, 2004), 227–58; Frances M. Young, "Did Epiphanius Know What He Meant by 'Heresy'?," *StPatr* 17 (1982): 199–205; and Clemens Scholten, "Die Funktion der Häresienabwehr in der alten Kirche," *VC* 66 (2012): 229–68.
54. Cameron, "How to Read Heresiology," 484.
55. Ibid. 472.
56. Ibid. 476. On the relationship between heresy and poisonous beasts in the *Panarion*, see Joseph Verheyden, "Epiphanius of Salamis on Beasts and Heretics: Some Introductory Comments," *Journal of Eastern Christian Studies* 60 (2008): 143–73.
57. Epiphanius, *Pan*. pro. 2.1.3–4 (GCS, n.F., 10:169). On Nicander, see A. S. Gow and A. F. Scholfield, eds., *Nicander: The Poems and Poetical Fragments* (London: Bristol Classical Press, 1997), 28–93.

should be read as part of a broader effort on the part of Christian elite to establish their own sociology of knowledge. Inasmuch as the *Panarion* "enshrines certain fundamentals about heresiological literature," it produced a broader heresiological discourse that bound together techniques of naming, differentiating, classifying, prescribing, refuting, and hierarchizing. It is worth considering why Augustine enumerated eighty-eight heretics, Filastrius one hundred fifty-six, Epiphanius eighty, Theodoret sixty-one, Irenaeus nineteen, and Hippolytus thirty-six, not only in relation to the shifting landscape of heresy—however real or imagined that landscape may have been—but also as reflections of editorial, structural, and ethnographic practices.[58] Indeed, heresiology, as a generic chain of utterances, offered "a structured system of explanation" about the heretics that placed them at the center of theories and arguments about human difference, epistemology, scholasticism, hermeneutics, and pedagogy.[59]

Taking up Cameron's various suggestions, my reading of heresiology does not explicitly focus on questions related to orthodox identity-formation or historical information about the heretics. Instead, it interprets heresiology as a genre that produced a culture and discourse of Christian knowledge—how it constructed Christianity as the repository of this knowledge and tradition—through the act of naming and describing people as heretics. Heresiology is a major literary site "in the formation of a Christian intellectual system."[60] In elaborating even the most minute of heretical customs and doctrines—from baptismal rituals and intricate cosmologies to dietary habits and alternative scriptural interpretations—the heresiologists confront how the procession, production, and ordering of knowledge underscored and altered the very foundations of Christianity and the Christian world. The interplay between form and content requires particular attention precisely because the heresiologists presented their texts as updated, synchronous (with the times) accounts of the ever-changing state of the heretical world. By styling knowledge of the heretics as handbooks, universal histories, genealogies, dialogues, curatives, and so on, the heresiologists utilized various literary forms to articulate and adjust their theological ambitions and their theorization of heretical profusion. Heresiologies were not static, inert, uninventive screeds. Rather, I will argue that they were creative, if polemical, meditations on the dangers, values, and limits of knowledge.

---

58. Counting the number of heretics in heresiologies can be an exceedingly difficult task. Within any given entry, there are often multiple names (of leaders and groups): Do a father and son duo represent two heresies, or one? Likewise it is also not always clear when an author is describing diversity within a group or a related but distinct group. There are also instances when a writer acknowledges the existence of more heresies but fails to name them. Indeed, among the nineteen heresies I ascribe to Irenaeus is a group he does not name but does describe at the end of *Adv. haer.* 1.28. Although my calculations may differ from the totals of others, I think they accurately reflect the general sense of the numerical differences among the heresiologists.

59. Cameron, "How to Read Heresiology," 477.

60. Ibid. 482.

The heresiologists specifically and repeatedly parsed the value of social and intellectual discourse, the very lifeblood of ethnography. They worried that cross-cultural contact unsettled their claims to exclusive truth. Discovering, let alone seeking, knowledge was not unproblematic. Christian inquiry and heresiological inquiry had their limits. But, as Edward Peters has emphasized, Christians were hardly the first to debate the merits of knowledge acquisition: "The debates concerning the validity of knowledge gained by travel and observation began in the ancient world with Homer and continued through Platonic and Stoic ethics and epistemology, the work of ethnographers and historians, Augustan political propagandists, and the romances of Alexander the Great."[61] Curiosity, "the unseemly interest in acquiring knowledge," had enormous disruptive potential; it was an indication of an unbalanced self.[62] The curious person was defined by uninhibited passions and desires. And he became, in Christian parlance, the epitome of heresy. To inquire about the wrong things and in the wrong way was the very core of the heretical disposition. For the heresiologists, however, there was a complementary and more dangerous fear. If the heretics were defined by epistemological hubris, a form of knowledge that subverted the singular authority of God, the act of investigating the heretics carried with it the fear that to know them was somehow to acquire the taint of heresy oneself.[63] Guilt by association—the paradox of ethnographic intimacy—was both a rhetorical tactic that the heresiologists used to create chains of error and a problem that they confronted themselves in the very act of writing their texts. Their fear was that the need to missionize against heresies by writing about them would become the heresiologists' own undoing.[64] The heresiologists worried not only that knowledge of the heretics would ultimately weaken their own orthodoxy but also that even in attempting to identify and describe the heretics they actually legitimated their existence.[65] Despite the fact that the heresiologists studied the heretics in order to destroy them, they nonetheless

61. Edward Peters, "The Desire to Know the Secrets of the World," *JHI* 62.4 (2001): 593–610, at 596.

62. Ibid. 597. On ethnological curiosity and the forging of the study of religion, see Stroumsa, *A New Science*, 22–32, 41–42, 66–72.

63. See Kendra Eshleman, "Becoming Heretical: Affection and Ideology in Recruitment to Early Christianities," *HTR* 104.2 (2011): 191–216.

64. Christians were not the only or the earliest ancient writers to invoke the fear of knowing as the fear of becoming. Isaac, *The Invention of Racism*, 225–47, has elaborated numerous examples of Roman authors expressing fear of foreigners. The fear was expressed as one of cultural contamination and corruption, though it was not primarily articulated, in Isaac's telling, at the level of the individual ethnographer who feared exploration per se (though there are plenty of fearful travel accounts). Within the Christian intellectual system, the correlation between knowing and becoming perpetuates the development by Christians of a dichotomy between truth and falsity, religion and superstition, orthodoxy and heresy.

65. Tertullian makes this point expressly in his *Rule against the Heretics (De praescriptione haereticorum)* 17–19. Epiphanius, too, throughout his *Panarion*, navigates the treachery of heresy with rhetorical hesitation and ambivalence. See, for example, his entry on the Gnostics (*Pan.* 26).

expressed anxiety about acquiring and preserving this knowledge. The heresiologists devised and ordered a Christian epistemological system that thrust two competing realities into contention: knowledge of the heretical world and the rejection of that knowledge. The entire heresiological apparatus ensnared its authors in the throes of a paradoxical project: "How can a Christian [heresiologist] justify laboring to preserve in minute detail the memory of a satanically inspired system of degradation and evil?"[66]

MAPPING CHRISTIANITY: HERESIOLOGY, HISTORY, AND SECTARIANISM

In Tomoko Masuzawa's narrative of *The Invention of World Religions,* Victorian anthropologists were one of two primary investigators and collectors of the customs of various non-Christian religions scattered beyond Europe.[67] Masuzawa lists a few of their myriad ethnographic interests: natural religion, myths, rituals, cosmologies, metaphysical systems, and doctrines. They sought, in turn, to translate these habits and rituals, religious particulars, into coherent religious systems governed by transhistorical principles, religious universals. Anthropologists and Orientalists, the other primary investigators of non-Western religions, became the academics most devoted to the study of non-European, nonmodern peoples, especially their religions or superstitions, or both, as a direct result of shifting European attitudes toward the notion of religious society.[68] As European society presented itself as guided by logic and rationalism, it perceived the rest of the world to be in the grip of supernatural forces. The social sciences—political science, economics, and sociology—had emerged in the early nineteenth century as the academic-scientific site for the study of the human and social structures of modern European society.[69] Making sense of the rest of the world beyond Europe would be

---

66. Herbert, *Culture and Anomie,* 168. I have replaced Herbert's "missionary" with "heresiologist."

67. The pioneering figures include Max Müller, William Robertson Smith, James Frazer, Émile Durkheim, Edward Burnett Tylor, James Hunt, Thomas Huxley, and James Cowles Prichard. For an overview of Victorian anthropology, see Stocking, *Victorian Anthropology,* and his *Race, Culture, and Evolution: Essays in the History of Anthropology* (Chicago: University of Chicago Press, 1982); see also James Buzard and Joseph Childers, eds., *Victorian Ethnographies* (Bloomington: Indiana University Press, 1998): special issue, *Victorian Studies* 41.3 (1998): 354–494; and Sadiah Qureshi, *Peoples on Parade: Exhibitions, Empire, and Anthropology in Nineteenth-Century Britain* (Chicago: University of Chicago Press, 2011).

68. Masuzawa, *The Invention of World Religions,* 17–21.

69. At the end of the eighteenth century, the academy was divided between the natural sciences on the one hand and arts and letters on the other. In the nineteenth century, however, a series of disciplines arose that existed between these two fonts of knowledge. History, the great ideographic discipline, as Masuzawa calls it, adopted the language of the natural sciences even as it turned to "matters human and social, rather than natural phenomena" (ibid. 14–15). And as history

the task of Orientalism and anthropology.[70] While these armchair anthropologists conceptualized tribal religions as "expressions of some basic and natural human propensities and behaviors in the face of the mysterious and the superhuman," orientalists eschewed claims of a generic religious essence and instead identified oriental religion as possessing "a vast and powerful metaphysical system deeply ingrained in the social fabric of a particular nation, and in the psychical predilections of its individual citizens and subjects."[71] The scholarly theorizations of both anthropologists and orientalists contributed to the nineteenth-century scholarly discourse that gave birth to our contemporary category of world religions.

As this taxonomic scheme took shape over the course of the nineteenth century, the hallmarks of religion—even with the rise of the *Religionswissenschaft* in the second half of the nineteenth century—were invariably parsed through the language and principles of Christianity.[72] Inasmuch as Christianity was, in the words of the Rev. Robert Flint (1838–1910), "the only religion from which, and in relation to which, all other religions may be viewed in an impartial and truthful manner," its comparative value lay in its theological supremacy.[73] For the academics that perpetuated this discourse, Christianity was the sine qua non of religiosity. The other religions of the world—the beliefs and practices attested by the rest— were not only expressed through the discourse of Christianity. They also reinforced, through their deviations, oddities, archaisms, and so forth, that Christianity remained atop the hierarchy of universal religions.[74] The British physician James Cowles Prichard (1786–1848), the pioneer of nineteenth-century ethnology, the science of human races, adhered to a strict biblical anthropology, which treated Christianity as the governing principle of human history:[75]

---

became increasingly dominated by scientific language and claims, three additional nomothetic disciplines emerged: political science, economics, and sociology. These were fields devoted to the social and human structures of modern European society. At the same time, however, two other disciplines emerged in which the object of study was nonmodern and non-European: anthropology and Orientalism.

70. As Stocking, *Victorian Anthropology*, puts it: "Ethnology may be viewed as a science of leftovers or residues" (48). On the development of various types of anthropology, see also, Frederik Barth et al., *One Discipline, Four Ways: British, German, French, and American Anthropology* (Chicago: University of Chicago Press, 2005).

71. Masuzawa, *The Invention of World Religions*, 17, 18.

72. For a clear description of this development, see King, *Orientalism and Religion*, 35–41.

73. Robert Flint, "Christianity in Relation to Other Religions," in *The Faiths of the World: A Concise History of the Great Religious Systems of the World* (London: William Blackwood and Sons, 1882), 335–64, at 336.

74. Masuzawa, *The Invention of World Religions*, 2–3, 47–49, 77, 212.

75. "In Britain in the 1850s, 'ethnology,' was in fact the most general scientific framework for the study of the linguistic, physical, and cultural characteristics of dark-skinned, non-European, 'uncivilized' peoples. As such, it is the most relevant focus for inquiry into the proximate origins of evolutionary anthropology, and the more distant origins of the anthropology of the twentieth century"

Prichard believed that just as in the beginning all men were one, so had God in the beginning revealed to all men the one true religion.... His concern with civilization was not to trace its origins but to defend its foundations, and in defending both primitive revelation and human unity he was in fact defending the principle that all mankind had once been and were rightfully subject to a single ethical dispensation.

It was the comparative theologians and armchair anthropologists of the nineteenth century who asserted in volume after volume that the world was filled not with properly transcendent and transnational religions but instead with local, pseudo, or incomplete religions.[76] Writers such as Prichard tried valiantly to ensure that the study of the world's other religions—compiled by travelers, missionaries, colonial administrators, and, in rare cases, scholars—not only served the interests of Christianity but also were compatible with Christian dogma and scripture. The title of Rev. Thomas Smyth's 1851 treatise, *The Unity of the Human Races Proved to Be the Doctrine of Scripture, Reason and Science*, proudly proclaims the theological perspective of Victorian ethnology.[77] And yet biblical anthropology, the study of diversity within a single, unified species, was both supported and undermined through the collection of the customs, habits, and traditions of primitive peoples. The data of travelers, missionaries, and ethnographers seemed to overwhelm the biblical narrative. And projects designed to fill in the ethnological gaps in the biblical account often created a disunity of cultures, races, and religions even as they insisted upon the fundamental unity of humankind. That very effort, as Isaac La Peyrère discovered, could easily lead to accusations of heresy.

For ethnologists and ethnographers, the irony of hurling accusations of heresy was that heresy itself served as an invaluable tool in the elaboration of a scripturally based Christian account of human unity as religious unity. Heresy was, after all, a choice.[78] While that choice may have been old and long since forgotten by the people who made it, the heresiologists, as the mouthpieces of a Christian

---

(Stocking, *Victorian Anthropology*, 47). The block quotation is from Stocking, ibid. 49. The unity of humankind did not, however, prevent anthropologists from constructing cultural and racial hierarchies.

76. The most notable texts advocating this distinction are Frederick Denison Maurice, *The Religions of the World and Their Relations to Christianity, Considered in Eight Lectures Founded by the Right Hon. Robert Boyle* (London: John W. Parker, 1847); Charles Hardwick, *Christ and Other Masters: An Historical Inquiry into Some of the Chief Parallelisms and Contrasts between Christianity and the Religious Systems of the Ancient World*, 2 vols., 2nd ed. (Cambridge: Macmillan, 1863); Joseph E. Riddle, *The Natural History of Infidelity and Superstition in Contrast with Christian Faith* (London: J. W. Parker, 1852); and C. P. Tiele, *Outlines of the History of Religion to the Spread of Universal Religions*, trans. J. Estlin Carpenter, 7th ed. (London: Kegan Paul, Trench, Trübner, 1905).

77. Thomas Smyth, *The Unity of the Human Races* (New York: Putnam, 1850).

78. On the semantic transformation of the word *hairesis* from the neutral term meaning "choice" and thus "school of thought" to the pejorative *heresy* as deviation and error, see Marcel Simon, "From Greek Hairesis to Christian Heresy," in *Early Christian Literature and the Classical Intellectual Tradition*, ed. William R. Schoedel and Robert L. Wilken (Paris: Éditions Beauchesne, 1979), 101–16.

orthodoxy, identified and railed against this process—this contentious choice—of religious degeneration. Heresy could also be easily mapped on to (and out of) other expressions of behavioral and habitual difference. Epiphanius used the heretics to explain the rise of all religious and cultural differences by making nations, cult, and culture manifestations of heresy.[79] Polemical investigations by the heresiologists authorized and even empowered subsequent generations to study all manner of religious and national difference, no matter how repulsive and dangerous. In the first quarter of the seventeenth century, Samuel Purchas, the traveler and Anglican cleric, published three massive volumes—known collectively as *Purchas His Pilgrimage; or, Relations of the World and the Religions Observed in All Ages and Places Discovered from the Creation unto This Present*—in which he reconciled the experience of his travels and the biblical worldview of Christian truth.[80] In one particularly famous passage, he justified his decision to describe various irreligious people—whose "absence of religion was an absence of Christian Truth"[81]—by appealing both to biblical precedent and to the writings of the heresiologists:[82]

> Now if any man thinke, that it were better these rotten bones of the passed, and stinking bodies of the present Superstitions were buried, then thus raked out of their graves besides that which has been said I answere, That I have sufficient example in the Scriptures, *which were written for our learning to the ends of the World,* and yet depaint unto us the ugly face of Idolatry in so many Countries of the Heathens, with the Apostasies, Sects, and Heresies of the Jewes, as in our first and second booke is shewed: and the Ancient Fathers also, *Justin, Tertullian, Clemens, Irenaeus, Origen,* and more fully, *Eusebius, Epiphanius, and Augustine* have gone before us in their large Catalogues of Heresies and false Opinions.

Here, as both Masuzawa and Schott have emphasized, Purchas situates himself as an empowered collector precisely because he writes from the position of Christian truth.[83] In that regard, both he and the heresiologists shared a theological ambition: to catalogue the world in the vernacular of Christian and biblical orthodoxy.

---

79. See Jeremy Schott, "Heresiology as Universal History in Epiphanius' *Panarion*," ZAC 10.3 (2006): 546–63.

80. Samuel Purchas, *Purchas His Pilgrimage; or, Relations of the World and the Religions Observed in All Ages and Places Discovered, from the Creation unto This Present* (London: William Stansby, 1617). On Purchas, see Timothy Fitzgerald, *Discourse on Civility and Barbarity: A Critical History of Religion and Related Categories* (New York: Oxford University Press, 2007), 193–230.

81. Ibid. 203.

82. The passage is from the preface, "To the Reader," of the 1617 edition.

83. Masuzawa, *The Invention of World Religions*, 51–52; Schott, *Christianity, Empire, and the Making of Religion*, 174–75. For Purchas, as Masuzawa explains, "plurality in religion is necessarily a matter of divergence from the unity and singularity of God, whether it is the plurality of gods among the idolaters, the plurality of religions in the present state of the world, or the sectarian plurality within Christianity itself. The problem of heresy, too, could be recognized as an aspect of this last type of plurality" (52).

The heresiologists, like the comparative theologians and missionaries of later centuries, described customs and habits through the contrast between orthodox center and heretical periphery, even when the two were located in the same exact space. In short, they elaborated an ethnographic foundation for the comparative Christian worldview. Heresiologists took great pains to define the heretics in the most effective terms for their own polemical purposes. It was their prerogative to define true Christianity from a place of knowledge about false Christianity, a knowledge they sought to control through their very descriptions of it.

Because, as Daniel Boyarin has put it, the "heresiologists are the inspectors of religious customs," they operated as the collectors and, indeed, inventors of Christian diversity.[84] The aim of the heresiologists was to create representations—self-serving and polemical representations—of what the heretics did and said. Heresiological ethnography puts into practice the famous maxim of Franz Boas that "to the ethnologist, the most trifling features of social life are important."[85] It is about the microscopic, which sets in motion the production of bigger and broader systems of living. But microscopic analysis, whether through fieldwork or armchair aggregation, "does not occur spontaneously in an intentional vacuum or as the consequence of mere 'curiosity,' but is inherently a motivated and leveraged activity, a positive rhetoric loaded from the first with ideological and emotional, as well as practical, implications."[86] Anthropologists go into the field and study peoples "because of what has been implanted in them."[87] Like Pausanias, who guided his readers through the topography of Greece, and Diogenes Laertius, who guided his readers through the philosophical schools, heresiology offers its readers an intellectual map of the sectarian world.[88] Heresiologists surveyed theologically and polemically the *oikoumenē* (οἰκουμένη, the known or inhabited world) that was Christian, while also striving to *make* the *oikoumenē* Christian. They positioned themselves as courageous and necessary—if not hesitant—experts about the evolving contours of the Christian world. Their texts supplied reasons for seemingly inexplicable differences between Jews, Christians, heretics, and pagans. The science of heresy theorized not only the genesis of heresy but also its impact across all of human history.

---

84. Daniel Boyarin, "Apartheid Comparative Religion in the Second Century: Some Theory and a Case Study," *JMEMS* 36.1 (2006): 3–34, at 3.

85. Franz Boas, *Race, Language, and Culture* (Chicago: University of Chicago Press, 1940), 632.

86. Herbert, *Culture and Anomie*, 227.

87. Burridge, *Encountering Aborigines*, 5.

88. See Susan E. Alcock, John F. Cherry, and Jaś Elsner, eds. *Pausanias: Travel and Memory in Roman Greece* (New York: Oxford University Press, 2001); and Allen Brent, "Diogenes Laertius and the Apostolic Succession," *JEH* 44.3 (1993): 367–89.

OUTLINING THE PROJECT

This is a book about both ancient ethnography and ancient heresiology. In my reading, the two are inextricably linked. The ensuing chapters are organized thematically, rather than chronologically, precisely to demonstrate this point. This thematic structure better captures my interest in the stabilizing and destabilizing qualities—the discursive fits and starts, fissures and connections—of ethnographic knowledge and theories of classification within the context of late antique heresiology. Instead of tracing a diachronic style or genre, which might erroneously suggest a single genealogy or systematic process of thought, I have configured this book to illustrate how ethnography *functioned* within heresiological literature as a tool for organizing or disorganizing sects. My aim is to understand how the production of Christian ethnography engulfed the heresiologists in a series of conceptual, structural, and literary paradoxes and to show how these textual problems shaped centuries of Christian discourse about religion, irreligion, and the writing of people. Readers will notice that certain scholars—Christopher Herbert, Jeremy Schott, David Chidester, Clifford Geertz, James Clifford, and Averil Cameron, among others—receive outsized attention over the course of this book. The reason is simple: I have found the works of these authors immeasurably useful in thinking about late antique heresiology specifically and the history of Christian ethnography more broadly. They have clarified, challenged, and refined my own ideas—and, to that end, I have chosen to be explicit about my influences. My references to Victorian ethnography and contemporary ethnographic theory are a conscious effort to think beyond the confines of late antiquity: to gesture at, however preliminarily and fragmentarily, the effects and implications of the production of Christianity, Christian theology, and the discourse of heresy for the history of writing peoples and their religions (and lack of religion).[89] The point of these comparisons, moreover, is to highlight the enduring challenges of writing people through a discourse that presents itself as absolute and comprehensive yet is, at the same time, unsettled and constrained. They serve to reinforce the paradoxical qualities of ethnographic investigation, which, I suggest, were further complicated by the Christian discourse of heresy.

Chapter 1 begins with contextualization. I survey the forms and functions of ethnography in antiquity to provide the analytical foundation for my discussion of

---

89. As Burridge, *Encountering Aborigines*, has incisively argued: "The point is not simply that anthropology, until recently, and particularly in the nineteenth century, has relied on and used the materials provided by missionaries, traders, travelers, administrators, explorers and others, but that anthropologists, especially the field anthropologists of this century, like all others involved in the expansion of the European cultural heritage, have been and are imbued with missionary purpose. In part, this purpose consists and has consisted in a determination to bring to others, less fortunate, a better, wider, more civilized, more satisfying way of life" (17–18).

Christian heresiology as a mode of ethnographic writing. Through analysis of the works of Herodotus, Pliny, Josephus, Tacitus, Diodorus Siculus, and others, I identify the methodological, theoretical, and descriptive contours of classical ethnography. Precisely because ethnography was not a formal genre, I advocate the idea of an *ethnographic disposition*. The ethnographic disposition encapsulates the process and effects of writing people and defining cultural systems. If we conceive of ethnography as a multifaceted process in which information about a particular people is collected and then theorized, the ethnographic disposition encompasses the suppositions behind these methodological and theoretical decisions. I pose two interrelated questions about the ethnographic method. What were the sources and methods with which ethnography was written? And how was the collected information applied? The answer reveals the bipartite scope of ethnographic writing about the ancient world: (1) microscopic ethnography, descriptions of the customs and habits of peoples, and (2) macroscopic ethnography, the use of grand paradigms such as genealogy, typology, and astrology to explain habits, customs, phenotypes, and behaviors. By identifying the vast array of microcosmic habits, practices, and beliefs across the world, and theorizing human diversity via such macroscopic analysis, ethnographers balanced efforts to describe peoples against the desire to routinize this process.

Chapter 2 describes the ethnographic microcosms of the heretics as recounted in the heresiologists' polemical writings. I analyze the heresiologists' description of heretical customs and habits, including dietary practices, dress, rituals, and textual traditions, in order to parse the relationship between heresy, theology, and praxis. In tracing how ethnography was written "Christianly" (how Christians developed their own ethnographic vernacular), I emphasize—through a close reading of Epiphanius's description of the ascetical Messalians—how the study of the heretics both upended and reinforced ethnographic tropes and aspirations. While the microscopic facets of Christian ethnography often parallel classical ethnographic descriptions, they reorient those descriptive tendencies with theological language. The heresiologists used the opinions and practices of the heretics to produce sectarian communities and to identify heretical dispositions. In that way, the heresiologists constructed a culture of heresy in order to dismantle it.

In chapter 3, I analyze how the heresiologists contested heretical models of human and Christian diversification. While disputes between the heresiologists and the heretics revolved around matters of ecclesiology, prophecy, scripture, and dogma, they also encompassed vehement disagreement over attempts to explain human behavior and customs in the context of sacred history. Insofar as the heresiologists were aware that the heretics had their own macroscopic paradigms of ethnography, they attacked these elaborate theories. With specific attention to Hippolytus of Rome and his *Refutation of All the Heresies*, I describe the attempt to delegitimize the heretics' astrological theories and cosmological-mythological narratives of human diversification.

Hippolytus's prolonged and intricate engagement with these heretical models—imported, he charges, from pagan traditions and myths—illustrates the ethnographic terms in which heresiological inquiry and polemic were framed. Hippolytus assailed these alternative models precisely because he aspired to lay down his own truly Christian explanation of human and heretical difference. It is the very appearance of such disputes that signals their implications for understanding the Christianization of ethnographic writing. The terms and trajectories of these disputes point toward heresiology's fundamentally ethnographic logic.

Chapter 4 explores the rhetorical and ethnographic strategies utilized by Epiphanius of Salamis and Theodoret of Cyrrhus to organize the diverse world of Christian heresy. Though contextually and stylistically distinct, Epiphanius's *Panarion* and Theodoret's *Compendium of Heretical Fables* evidence their authors' parallel efforts to delineate their roles as ethnographers of the Christian tradition. Epiphanius deploys a universal genealogy of knowledge to organize his ethnographic data, whereas Theodoret proposes a schematic typology—built around the actions of demonic forces—to array his knowledge of the heretics. Epiphanius further suggests in his *Panarion* that his model of heresy and heretical expansion explains the *totality* of human history as well as all cultural, national, and religious difference. For him, the rise of sectarianism reflects the structure of all human difference: to map heresy is to map the entirety of the known world. But in the context of various Greco-Roman precedents of macroscopic ethnography, Christian ethnography functioned not only to explain human origins and diversity but also to elaborate an underlying human unity. Theodoret and Epiphanius are quite careful to express the Christian longing for a reunited human race, a pre–Genesis 11 world of a singular symbolic Christian language. Heresiology articulated the nature and possibility of a fundamental human unity.

Chapter 5 analyzes heresiological theorizations of social discourse and exchange, the lifeblood of ethnography. Tertullian's *Rule against the Heretics* adamantly insists on the theological futility of investigating heresy. His exegesis of Matthew 7.7— "Search, and you shall find"—attests the soteriological fulfillment of Christ, whose presence precludes any further need for inquiry. Tertullian cautions against study and inquiry born of curiosity—where heresy serves as the epitome of curiosity— because they lead the mind astray. Heresiology thus becomes a meditation on the nature and limitations of Christian knowledge. The heresiologists' fear—that they will delve too deeply into the abyss of heresy—ran up against their self-described effort to serve the greater Christian world as its doctrinal cartographers and polemical ethnographers. The danger of dialoguing with heretics signaled the paradoxical nature of Christian ethnographic inquiry: the danger that the necessity of pastoral care and education—exposing heresy—would contaminate and hereticize the inquirer. To counteract the pollution of the heretics, the heresiologists deployed a rhetoric of antiethnographic ethnography. They expressed their disdain for engaging with and collecting knowledge about the heretics just as they heralded their triumph over these blasphemous peoples.

I argue in chapters 6 and 7, about Epiphanius and Augustine, respectively, that the Christianization of ethnography and ethnographic paradigms accentuates the dangers of heresiological inquiry and the limits of so-called heresiological authority. As they try to order and number the totality of the heretical world, Epiphanius and Augustine reflect on the impossibility of their task. They cogitate about their inability to understand foreign customs, to translate peoples into texts, to manage, in essence, an impossibly large and ever-expanding repository of knowledge, a repository that they themselves helped to create. The heresiologists are all too aware that the world, despite the rise of Christianity, is beyond systematization and plenary understanding. Heresiology exposes the aporetic core of ethnographic writing; it is a task at once beyond the scope of the written word and of the human mind. In chapter 6, I discuss the ethnographic and epistemological limitations of Epiphanius's *Panarion*. Surveying and organizing the heretical world forces the heresiologists, like various classical ethnographers before them, to reflect upon their ability to comprehend the totality of Christian world around them. Epiphanius further acknowledged that heresy knew no geographical or territorial boundaries: it was a counterworld residing in his orthodox world. I demonstrate that Epiphanius not only admits this loss of control but also in a sense embraces it. There is no attempt to hide the fissures within his knowledge; they reflect his humanity and humility. Although Epiphanius persistently devised rhetorical and structural schemes to combat the ever-changing contours of the heretical world, he was consciously aware of his shortcomings, fears, and failures.

In chapter 7, I turn to Augustine's understudied *De haeresibus* to consider how he confronts not only the textual possibilities and limitations of epistemological representation but also the theoretical capacity to comprehend his heretical environs. Through intertextual reading, tireless research, and personal experience, Augustine edited the work of his antecedents and contemporaries into a slender heresiological handbook. By explicitly adding and subtracting heretics, Augustine presented his text as a polemical palimpsest of ethnographic knowledge. But although Augustine insisted on his expansive knowledge of the heretics, he readily admitted to falling short. His text is totalizing in aspiration, perhaps, but not in practice or even in theory. Instead it attests a stark conversation about the capacity of texts to represent and circumscribe ethnographic phenomena. What is especially revealing about Augustine and his text is the precise manner in which he framed his limitations not simply as a collector of abstract knowledge but as a living, practicing, flesh-and-blood heresiologist. Augustine was self-consciously aware of his inability to move from observer to observed, from heresiologist to heretic. For Augustine, the limitations of heresiology were insurmountable because they were fundamentally ethnographic.

1

Heresiology as Ethnography
The Ethnographic Disposition

Let us go on again to another to expose once more the obscure, savage, poisonous teachings of the members of the remaining sects who, to the world's harm, have gotten cracked by the bogus inspiration of the devil. After exposing the opinion of such people who yearn for the worst . . . and crushing it by God's power because of its harmfulness, let us call on God for aid, sons of Christ, as we set our minds to the investigation of the others.

—EPIPHANIUS OF SALAMIS

I handed out half-sticks of tobacco, then watched a few dances; then took pictures—but results very poor. Not enough light for snapshots; and they would not pose long enough for time exposures. —At moments, I was furious at them, particularly because after I gave them their portions of tobacco they all went away. On the whole my feelings toward the natives are decidedly tending to "Exterminate the brutes."

—BRONISLAW MALINOWSKI

This book seeks to enumerate the ways in which Christians articulated their ethnographic knowledge of the heretics—how they categorized it, described it, and constructed it.[1] It also explores the theological categories and intellectual motivations that underlie heresiological ethnography. "Categories," as the sociologist Rogers Brubaker notes, "structure and order the world for us. We use categories to parse the flow of experience into discriminable and interpretable objects, attributes, and events. . . . They thereby make the natural and social worlds intelligible, interpretable, communicable, and transformable."[2] For the heresiologists, heresy was a

---

1. The two epigraphs to this chapter are cited from Epiphanius, *Pan.* 38.8.6–7 (GCS 31:71), and Bronislaw Malinowksi, *A Diary in the Strict Sense of the Term* (Stanford: Stanford University Press, 1989), 69.

2. Rogers Brubaker, *Ethnicity without Groups* (Cambridge, Mass.: Harvard University Press, 2004), 71.

way of imagining and categorizing the world in overtly theological terms: to understand how the world necessitated knowledge of heretical their own, how the heretics behaved, thought, and defined themselves and their own universality, how those behavioral and theological differences came to be. And because heresiological ethnography was an instrument of classification, it set the parameters not only for what constituted heresy but also for how to study it. As Brubaker explains:[3]

> When we make sense of our experience by seeing objects, persons, actions, or situations as instances of categories, this always involves more than mere sorting. It always carries with it expectations and "knowledge" ... about how members of those categories characteristically behave. Such beliefs and expectations are embodied in persons, encoded in myths, memories, narratives, and discourse, and embedded in institutions and organizational routines.

Heresiological literature did not simply describe and polemicize the customs, doctrines, and origins of the heretics; it also provided authoritative interpretations of their practices and theology. The heresiologists understood the truth of heresy in ways the heretics did not. They constructed and conveyed this knowledge to their readers as didactic ethnography.

In this chapter I wish to elaborate the contours of my usage of ancient and modern ethnographic evidence to illuminate the genre and practice of heresiology. I have necessarily been selective in my choice of ancient and modern examples with which to compare the Christian heresiologists. This is both an accession to the realities of limited space and an acknowledgment of the wide range of forms and styles that constitute both ethnographic writing and the analytical practice of comparison. Ethnography is neither singular nor systematic in either its ancient or its modern form. Rather, it comprises a variety of methods, discourses, interests, techniques, forms, and rhetorical tools. Comparison, as David Frankfurter rightly insists, "is the very foundation of *generalization*.... Our use of 'religion,' 'science,' 'magic,' 'amulet,' 'canon' ... is not a simple 'emic' translation of some unambiguous Greek or Latin or Hebrew word but a second-order, heuristic category of classification that implies applicability to a particular spectrum of like data."[4] I have juxtaposed Christian and non-Christian sources not to suggest dependency of the former upon the latter but rather to highlight the continuities and discontinuities between the two. I am not claiming that the ethnographic patterns that I identify in this book "exist apart from their *heuristic* function in making sense of religion in context or that they grasp in any way the

---

3. Ibid. 72.
4. David Frankfurter, "Comparison in the Study of Religions of Late Antiquity," in *Comparer en histoire des religions antiques: Controverses et propositions*, ed. Claude Calame and Bruce Lincoln (Liège: Presses Universitaires de Liège, 2012), 83–98, at 85.

totality of content or experience."⁵ Instead, I hope that comparing Christian and non-Christian sources enables us to make better sense of heresiology as a genre that produces, organizes, and even destroys ethnographic knowledge. My aim is to emphasize how Christians used techniques of writing peoples in ways both similar to and different from Greek, Roman, and Jewish writers. I am interested in how the heresiologists contemplated and modified well-attested ethnographic problems to elaborate their own perspectives and understanding of the world in Christian terms.

I begin this chapter with a discussion of ethnography in the ancient world—as both a heuristic category and a literary process—in order to lay the foundation for my discussion of how early Christian writers theologized the writing of peoples. With specific attention to the writings of Josephus, Herodotus, Diodorus Siculus, Plutarch, Tacitus, and others, I enumerate not only various ethnographic styles and contexts but also some of the fundamental interests and methods that informed the study of human diversity and difference in the ancient world. Comparison was always lurking over ethnographic writing to establish hierarchies of peoples both within and outside a given society, to create genealogical bonds, to defend traditions, and to justify slavery and conquest, among myriad other reasons. In that regard, Herodotus was quite right: "Custom is king of all" (νόμον πάντων βασιλέα εἶναι).⁶ Peoples were invariably presented as equivalent to their customs, behaviors, and traditions. The ethnographers of the ancient world compiled an astonishing amount of detail about the dietary practices, cultic rituals, dress, governments, economies, topographies, pedagogies, and so forth, of different categories of peoples. Ethnographic writing was often dominated by the comparative effort to create a disjuncture between a cultural center and a periphery organized around diverging habits and customs, behaviors and mentalities, and political structures and policies (among other factors). This binary, however, was part of a much larger ethnographic discourse that informed the study and classification of societies and their people, on the one hand, and the world and its peoples, on the other. Ethnographic mapping provided the intellectual space in which to theorize the causes and sources of human differences and similarities.⁷ And by blurring the distinction between individuals and the culture or nation to which they belonged, ethnographers denied a sense of individualism and independence of thought and behavior. Models of human difference depicted people as members of groups with readily identifiable and fixed dispositions.

5. Ibid. 88.
6. Translation altered from Herodotus, *Hist.* 3.38, trans. A. D. Godley, LCL 118 (Cambridge, Mass.: Harvard University Press, 1921), 50–51.
7. On similarities and connections between ancient peoples, in particular, see Erich S. Gruen, *Rethinking the Other in Antiquity* (Princeton: Princeton University Press, 2011), 223–351.

ETHNOGRAPHY IN ANTIQUITY: GENRE, TRADITION, AND HISTORY

In the most rudimentary or, indeed, purely etymological sense, ethnography is the writing of peoples (ἔθνος, if we take it as a designation of peoplehood, community, or ethnicity).[8] It names the literary activity by which peoples are rendered into the written word. While the idea of ethnography, facilitated by a certain curiosity, was a manifestly real preoccupation in the Greco-Roman world, the term "ethnography" as designating an academic discipline dates to the nineteenth century.[9] As Tomoko Masuzawa has shown, anthropology was one of two disciplines—the other was Orientalism—formed in the nineteenth century to study non-European peoples, what she calls "the rest."[10] Anthropologists were specifically interested in the tribes and supposed primitives of the world, those peoples and places not covered by economics, political science, sociology, and Orientalism.[11] It is with the work of the classicist and philologist Felix Jacoby that discussions of ethnography as an ancient genre or category truly began.[12] Writing in the early twentieth century, Jacoby undertook anew the task of collecting, arranging, editing, and commenting upon the abundant fragments from ancient prose works that were lost or incomplete.[13] In contrast to Carl Müller's chronologically arranged *Fragmenta His-*

---

8. For a useful discussion of the term *ethnos*, see C. P. Jones, "῎Εθνος and Γένος in Herodotus," *CQ* 46.2 (1996): 315–20. See also the work of Jonathan M. Hall, *Ethnic Identity in Greek Antiquity* (New York: Cambridge University Press, 1997) and *Hellenicity: Between Ethnicity and Culture* (Chicago: University of Chicago Press, 2002). As he explains in the former, while "the English words 'ethnic' and 'ethnicity' are derived from the Greek *ethnos* (plural, *ethne*), even the most cursory survey of the ancient sources is sufficient to demonstrate that *ethnos* could embrace a wider variety of meanings than simply 'ethnic group.' While it certainly can describe groups of people, its use does not appear to be strictly circumscribed in any defined sociological sense" (33). It can refer to descriptions of all sorts of people who share a common identification, including philosophers, soldiers, foreigners, sects, and religious leaders.

9. It is true, of course, that ethnography as a practice and anthropology as a discipline have long and quite complex histories. On this point, see the work of Dell Hymes, ed., *Reinventing Anthropology* (New York: Vintage, 1974); John J. Honigmann, *The Development of Anthropological Ideas* (New York: Dorsey, 1976); Henrika Kuklick, *The Savage Within: The Social History of British Anthropology, 1885–1945* (New York: Cambridge University Press, 1991); and Thomas C. Patterson, *A Social History of Anthropology in the United States* (New York: Berg, 2001).

10. Tomoko Masuzawa, *The Invention of World Religions; or, How European Universalism Was Preserved in the Language of Pluralism* (Chicago: University of Chicago Press, 2005), 15.

11. Ibid. 15.

12. Carl Müller, ed., *Fragmenta Historicorum Graecorum*, 5 vols. (Paris: Firmin Didot, 1841–70); and his *Geographi Graeci Minores*, 3 vols. (Paris: Firmin Didot, 1855–61). See also, Felix Jacoby, "Über die Entwicklung der griechischen Historiographie und den Plan einer neuen Sammlung der griechischen Historikerfragmente," *Klio* 9 (1909): 80–123.

13. Some fragments are simply references to the author, his birthplace, or the title or content of his work, or both. Other, more substantive fragments include actual citations and/or substantive discussion (and naturally disagreement) about the author's claims, project, conclusions, and argument.

toricorum Graecorum and *Geographici Graeci Minores*, Jacoby's project, *Die Fragmente der griechischen Historiker* (*FGrH*), proposed to organize ancient prose writers by literary style and genre.[14] To justify his arrangement, Jacoby elaborated an integrated theory of Greek prose writing in which genres emerged out of an ur-prose tradition. He contended that prose writing in its earliest stages was a composite endeavor, indistinguishable by genre. Genealogy, mythography, ethnography, and geography were all part and parcel of historiography. This model of historiography (vis-à-vis Müller's strict bifurcation of historical and geographical writing) posited historical writing as a capacious endeavor—which, Jacoby stressed, was the case throughout antiquity. Despite the differentiation and evolution of style and genre over time, Jacoby insisted that the various ancient genres remained essentially interdependent and forever interrelated.[15]

In the decades since the publication of Jacoby's work, numerous scholars have offered incisive criticisms and augmentations of his underlying thesis.[16] While it would be impossible to catalogue these abundant criticisms, it is nonetheless important to discuss how scholars have conceptualized ethnography as one of the "basic types of historical writing,"[17] a tradition of writing about foreign lands, and a hybridized form of various methodological and textual conventions.[18] Ethnography entailed surveying, categorizing, and theorizing this manifold diversity, and,

14. See Felix Jacoby, *Die Fragmente der griechischen Historiker* (*FGrH*), 3 vols. in 7 (Berlin, Weidmann, 1923–59).

15. Hecataeus of Miletus served as Jacoby's prime example of the origins of ethnography, genealogy, history, and geography, the latter two of which were united by Herodotus. For Jacoby, the various strands of historical writing began as indistinguishable endeavors and even as they slowly emerged as distinct genres (with Herodotus and Hecataeus), they were forever interrelated and, in essence, never really distinct. See Jacoby, "Über die Entwicklung der griechischen Historiographie." For a recapitulation of Jacoby in a more modern guise, see Oswyn Murray, "History," in *Greek Thought: A Guide to Classical Knowledge*, ed. Jacques Brunschwig and Geoffrey E. R. Lloyd, trans. Catherine Porter (Cambridge, Mass.: Belknap Press, 1996), 328–37. On Hecataeus, see Lucio Bertelli, "Hecataeus: From Genealogy to Historiography," in *The Historian's Craft in the Age of Herodotus*, ed. Nino Luraghi (New York: Oxford University Press, 2001), 67–95; and Katherine Clarke, *Between Geography and History: Hellenistic Constructions of the Roman World* (New York: Oxford University Press, 1999), 56–66.

16. See G. Schepens, "Jacoby's *FGrHist*: Problems, Methods, Prospects," in *Collecting Fragments/ Fragmente sammeln*, ed. Glenn W. Most (Göttingen: Vandenhoeck & Ruprecht, 1997), 144–72; Joseph E. Skinner, *The Invention of Greek Ethnography: From Homer to Herodotus* (New York: Oxford University Press, 2012), 30–58; Clarke, *Between Geography and History*, 59–76; Charles Fornara, *The Nature of History in Ancient Greece and Rome* (Berkeley and Los Angeles: University of California Press, 1998); Emma Dench, *Romulus' Asylum: Roman Identities from the Age of Alexander to the Age of Hadrian* (New York: Oxford University Press, 2005), 41–46; and Eram Almagor and Joseph Skinner, eds., *Ancient Ethnography: New Approaches* (New York: Bloomsbury, 2013), esp. 1–22.

17. Fornara, *Nature of History*, 1.

18. On the idea of an ethnographic tradition, see Richard F. Thomas, *Lands and Peoples in Roman Poetry: The Ethnographical Tradition* (Cambridge: Cambridge Philological Society, 1982).

in turn, articulating a relational position to and even apart from it. Emma Dench, refining the work of Jacoby, situates ethnography in relation to history, as "a feature of ancient historical discourse," and frames the totality of ethnography as relating to matters both minute and grandiose:[19]

> When ancient historians engage in traditions of delineating the lands and customs of "other people," they are drawn into rhetoric and practices that came to be regarded in antiquity as quintessentially historical. These include the assertion of the authority of the writer and his text, claims of veracity and the superiority of the account to that of predecessors. They also include interest in historical change, causation, and explanation (not least of imperial rule), patterns of the rise and fall of individuals and powers, and broadly didactic concerns such as the provision of vicarious experience and case studies of exemplary behavior.

Underlying much ethnographic writing in antiquity was an expansive and reflective disposition, what Dench calls the "ethnographic gaze": "the characterization of 'other peoples' particularly with reference to their customs, practices, and the behavior that typifies them and/or their lands."[20] The particularities of peoples not only vibrantly color historical narratives but also illustrate how minutiae shape the course of history, cosmology, geography, and religious systems. Ethnography functioned as an intellectual-feedback loop in which the instantiation of ideology shaped interpretive strategies, the collection of data, and the consequent analysis, even as new data and its collection shaped ethnographic values and those same interpretive strategies. Ethnography did not simply describe the world as it was; it created an imagined sense of where the world had been, where it was now, and where it would be through the language of custom, habit, origins, discovery, and exchange.[21] Ethnography's capacity to explain the differences within the world, to foreshadow history, and to justify conquest and expansion was an immensely powerful ideological and textual tool.[22] In other words, ethnography depicted various types of peoples with dispositions that created cultural, social,

---

19. Emma Dench, "Ethnography and History," in *A Companion to Greek and Roman Historiography*, ed. John Marincola (Malden, Mass.: Blackwell, 2007), 493–503, at 493.

20. Ibid. 496.

21. On ethnography and representation in antiquity, see François Hartog, *The Mirror of Herodotus: The Representation of the Other in the Writing of History*, trans. Janet Lloyd (Berkeley and Los Angeles: University of California Press, 1988), 310–70. On discovery and exchange, see Jerry H. Bentley, *Old World Encounters: Cross-Cultural Contacts and Exchanges in Pre-Modern Times* (New York: Oxford University Press, 1993); and Greg Woolf, *Tales of the Barbarians: Ethnography and Empire in the Roman West* (Malden, Mass.: Wiley-Blackwell, 2011), 8–31.

22. See Claude Nicolet, *Space, Geography, and Politics in the Early Roman Empire*, trans. Hélène Leclerc (Ann Arbor: University of Michigan Press, 1991); Elizabeth Rawson, "Geography and Ethnography," in her *Intellectual Life in the Late Roman Republic* (London: Duckworth, 1985), 250–66; and C. R. Whittaker, *Rome and Its Frontiers: The Dynamics of Empire* (New York: Routledge, 2004), 63–87.

and intellectual hierarchies defining the proper parameters for interaction and exchange.[23]

Following in the lineage of ancient historians who have disputed and altered Jacoby's historiographic thesis, James Rives outlines an ethnographic tradition through a discussion of the interplay between literary form and descriptive content.[24] In the introduction to his translation and commentary on Tacitus's *Germania*, Rives contends that the ethnographic tradition originated with Hecataeus of Miletus's now lost *Periēgēsis* or *Periodos Gēs* ("a leading around the world"), which presented the peoples and places of the Mediterranean world through the prism of an extended journey.[25] Rives's demarcation of tradition does not, however, posit an explicitly evolutionary progression (i.e., stages) of the ethnographic tradition. It offers instead a descriptive account of the broad forms of classical ethnography. Ethnography was, in some instances, reflective of the practical needs of sea captains and explorers, aiming "to publish, at the least, a basic record of the ports along seas or river routes,"[26] whereas in other cases it served historiographical needs. As the historian Charles Fornara has noted: "Ethnographic tracts appear as digressions from the exposition of *res gestae*."[27] The historical narrative "treat[ed] ethnography as an excursus within a longer historical composition."[28] Herodotus's *Histories* discusses the Egyptians, Scythians, Libyans, and Persians at length;[29] Caesar's *Gallic*

---

23. Benjamin Isaac, *The Invention of Racism in Classical Antiquity* (Princeton: Princeton University Press, 2004), 170–94.

24. James B. Rives, "Introduction," in Tacitus, *Germania: Translated with Introduction and Commentary*, ed. and trans. James B. Rives (Oxford: Clarendon Press, 1999), 11–21.

25. Ibid. 12–15. The first book of Hecataeus's text covered Europe, and a second considered Asia, Libya, and Egypt.

26. This is what Rives calls the "periegetic tradition," which encompassed two related generic forms: the more technical *periplous* narrative ("sailing around") and the less formal, more expansive *periēgēsis* ("leading around"). Notable works include the anonymous *Periplous of the Erythraian Sea*, Arrian of Nicomedia's *Periplous of the Euxine Sea*, pseudo-Skylax's *Periplous*, and the fragmentary *periplous* of Pytheas of Massalia. On the details, see Scott Fitzgerald Johnson, "Travel, Cartography, and Cosmology," in *The Oxford Handbook of Late Antiquity*, ed. Scott Fitzgerald Johnson (New York: Oxford University Press, 2012), 562–94.

27. Fornara, *Nature of History*, 14. See also, Wiebke Vergin, *Das Imperium Romanum und seine Gegenwelten: Die geographisch-ethnographischen Exkurse in den "Res Gestae" des Ammianus Marcellinus* (Berlin: de Gruyter, 2013).

28. Rives, "Introduction," 14.

29. Herodotus's *Histories* discusses the peoples and customs of Egypt (2.2–182), Scythia (4.5–82), Libya (4.168–99), and Persia (his comments on Persian customs and habits are interspersed throughout the text, though Book 7 contains the most ethnographic information). See Rosaria Vignolo Munson, *Telling Wonders: Ethnographic and Political Discourse in the Work of Herodotus* (Ann Arbor: University of Michigan Press, 2001); and Rosaria Vignolo Munson, ed., *Herodotus*, vol. 1, *Herodotus and the Narrative of the Past*, and *Herodotus*, vol. 2, *Herodotus and the World* (New York: Oxford University Press, 2013).

War describes the Gauls and Germani;[30] Diodorus Siculus's *Library of History* discusses Arabia, Greece, Egypt, India, Scythia, Ethiopia, and Mesopotamia;[31] and Sallust's *Jugurtha* incorporates ethnographic details about the Numidians. In each case, these histories display and demonstrate the utility and the allure of ethnographic detail in service of the particularities of universal, political, military, and geographical historical narrative.[32]

Precisely because most ethnographic material was routinely subsumed within larger narratives and textual forms, many scholars have been reluctant to identify a formally structured genre or independent tradition of ethnography in the ancient world. Even so-called ethnographic monographs—Hellanicus of Lesbos's *Aigyptiaka* and *Persika*, Xanthus the Lydian's *Lydiaka*, Manetho's *Aigyptiaka*, Berossus's *Babyloniaka*, and the lost texts described by Jacoby—were brimming with historical and geographical details. As Rives explains,[33]

> This tradition gained considerable momentum from the conquests of Alexander the Great, which brought Greeks into direct and regular contact with a huge range of peoples. As a result, there was a steady stream of ethnographic writers from the Ionian Megasthenes, who in the early third century BC composed a celebrated account of India (*FGrH* 715), down to the indefatigable Cornelius Alexander "Polyhistor", "the very learned", who in Rome during the last century BC composed works on Bithynia, Egypt, Libya, and India, among others (*FGrH* 273).

And whereas Rives concedes that the "larger historical component" of these texts "may even have overshadowed the ethnographic framework,"[34] I remain sympathetic to the general position that ethnographic writing was a *real* interest and preoccupation of ancient authors. Scholars will surely continue to disagree about how to describe the ancient impulse for writing peoples, but they would no doubt agree that it remained a pervasive interest across radically different textual

---

30. See Andrew M. Riggsby, *Caesar in Gaul and Rome: War in Words* (Austin: University of Texas Press, 2006), 47–72.

31. For more on Diodorus Siculus's *Library of History*, see Iris Sulimani, *Diodorus' Mythistory and the Pagan Mission: Historiography and Culture-Heroes in the First Pentad of the "Bibliotheke"* (Leiden: Brill, 2011); and Kenneth S. Sacks, *Diodorus Siculus and the First Century* (Princeton: Princeton University Press, 1990).

32. On the relationship between universal history and ethnography, see Walter Ameling, "Ethnography and Universal History in Agatharchides," in *East & West: Papers in Ancient History Presented to Glen W. Bowersock*, ed. T. Corey Brennan and Harriet I. Flower (Cambridge, Mass.: Harvard University Press, 2008), 13–59.

33. Rives, "Introduction," 13. If, as Rives hypothesizes, treatises of independent ethnography may have seemed historical to their readers, the notion of an independent ethnographic tradition remains muddied and problematic. But the diffusion of ethnography across genres need not preclude an effort to trace its discursive, methodological, and rhetorical emphases.

34. Ibid.

genres.³⁵ But however much the detail, form, and structure varied, these texts captured the seemingly endless depths of the world's diverse configurations of peoples and places. From historiographical and historical narratives to philosophical treatises, to accounts of war, to travelogues, to astrological texts, to dramas, to geographies, to national or religious histories, the diverse array of texts from the ancient world that display an ethnographic impulse demonstrates the difficulty of isolating an ethnographic tradition. The diversity of techniques that inform the writing of peoples signifies that ethnography was and remains a constellation of preoccupations, born of ancient and modern moments, respectively.

It is easier, perhaps, to identify ethnographic curiosity than it is to speak of an ancient genre, a fixed tradition, or a formal style embedded within historiographical and geographical texts.³⁶ Consider, for example, Tacitus's description of the Jews in his *Histories*.³⁷ Although his explicit concern is the Jewish War and the military campaign of Titus, he pauses his narrative to offer a brief history of Jerusalem, which, in fact, is an ethnographic excursus about the Jews and their history, temple, land, rituals, death rites, and meals.³⁸ He notes, too, their general disposition toward one another and toward the rest of humanity: "The Jews are extremely loyal toward one another and always ready to show compassion, but toward every other people they feel only hate and enmity ... and although as a race they are prone to lust, they abstain from intercourse with foreign women; yet among

---

35. See, for instance, Anthony Kaldellis, *Ethnography after Antiquity: Foreign Lands and Peoples in Byzantine Literature* (Philadelphia: University of Pennsylvania Press, 2013). While Kaldellis's emphasis on the capacity of ethnography to induce internal self-reflection is immensely important, his focus on historiographical writing is but one illustration of a much larger ethnographic project in antiquity and beyond.

36. See, for example, Lucian of Samosata's *A True Story* (*Vera hist.*), trans. A. M. Harmon, LCL 14 (Cambridge, Mass.: Harvard University Press, 1913). A parody of an ethnographic journey, *A True Story* mocked the tradition of "poets, historians and philosophers ... who have written much that smacks of miracles and fables, ... imaginary travels and journeys of theirs, telling of huge beasts, cruel men and strange ways of living" (*Vera hist.* 1.2–3 [LCL 14:248–51]). What unfolds in Lucian's text is the ethnographic imagination gone wild. He writes of a journey to the moon and a great battle between the Moonites and Sunites, a foray inside the stomach of a whale, a short stay at an island made of cheese, an extended respite on the Isle of the Blessed, as well as encounters with vulture dragoons, grass-plume riders, millet shooters, garlic fighters, flea archers, sparrowcorns, crane dragoons, mergoats, clan crawfish, corkfeet, Calypso, etc. Parody works, of course, only by operating from a place of established tradition or sense of truth—in this case, a sense of the trajectory of ethnographic writing.

37. For an incisive and exhaustive discussion of this passage as ethnographic analysis, see René Bloch, *Antike Vorstellungen vom Judentum: Der Judenexkurs des Tacitus im Rahmen der griechisch-römischen Ethnographie* (Stuttgart: Steiner, 2002), esp. 68–97.

38. For a detailed analysis of Tacitus's writings about the Jews, see Gruen, *Rethinking the Other in Antiquity*, 179–96; and Louis H. Feldman, *Jew and Gentile in the Ancient World* (Princeton: Princeton University Press, 1993), 45–50, 94–98, 183–96, 299–304, 430–36.

themselves nothing is unlawful."[39] The point is not that Tacitus offered an honest or balanced account of the Jews but precisely that he provided a generalizing description, built on the reification of an entire community into a particular disposition and way of life defined by *outré* practices and obstinate attitudes. The Jews were a provincial group who not only abstained from interaction and intercourse with foreigners but readily adopted a specific bodily practice—namely circumcision—to stand apart: "They adopted circumcision to distinguish themselves from other peoples by this difference."[40] Louis Feldman is quite right that Tacitus and other Roman writers who generalized about the Jews "may have based their comments more on ethnographic tradition than on actual—and flawed—observation."[41] Insofar as ethnography "reveals the character and psychology of a people, and is a descriptive and aetiological key to their actions, and thus historical explanations," it operates as an essentializing discourse.[42] It is a discourse that casually links the history, practices, and beliefs of a people to a core mentality.

THE ETHNOGRAPHIC DISPOSITION

By corralling works together under the rubric or title "ethnography," it becomes easier to observe how works that display the textual flavor of ethnography—considerations of territory, climate, topography, wonder, agriculture, religious customs, dress, eating habits, origins, governmental structure, and so forth—present, organize, and interpret their findings. The diversity of ways in which peoples were written pushes us toward a more capacious understanding of ethnography and ethnographic writing. The scope of writing peoples compels us to observe the multiplicity of authorial objectives encapsulated in the textual construction. I suggest that we ought to treat ethnography as a *dispositional orientation* that intersects with and shapes writings about history, geography, theology, and literature even as these thematic interests mold the very techniques of ethnographic writing. I follow the work of Emma Dench, Greg Woolf, and James Rives, among others, which has demonstrated that ethnographic writing in the ancient world, and even ethno-

---

39. Tacitus, *Hist.* 5.5.1, trans. Clifford H. Moore, LCL 249 (Cambridge, Mass.: Harvard University Press, 1931), 180–83. The same sentiment appears in Josephus, *C. Ap.* 2.258, trans. H. St. J. Thackery, LCL 186 (Cambridge, Mass.: Harvard University Press, 1926), 396–97, where he paraphrases Apollonius Molon: "Of these facts Apollonius Molon took no account when he condemned us for refusing admission to persons with other preconceived ideas about God, and for declining to associate with those who have chosen to adopt a different mode of life."

40. Tacitus, *Hist.* 5.5.1 (LCL 249:182–83).

41. Feldman, *Jew and Gentile in the Ancient World*, 50.

42. I. G. Kidd, *Posidonius*, vol. 3, *The Translation of the Fragments* (New York: Cambridge University Press, 2004), 56.

graphic stereotyping, entailed a web of negotiations in the effort to comprehend the complexity of the surrounding world. Like them, in using ethnography as a textual marker I am intentionally implicating a wide array of ethnographic typologies and functions. What I call an "ethnographic disposition"—similar to Dench's notion of an ethnographic gaze—encapsulates the literary process and effects of writing peoples and defining cultural systems.[43] Ethnography was a discursive activity in which peoples were reified into textual units, assigned essential dispositions and distinctive practices and beliefs. It reflected an impulse for classifying peoples on the basis of how they behaved, where they came from, and how they came into existence. I am less intent than the historians of antiquity upon narrowly defining its perimeters—I reject the idea, for instance, that only a group described as an ἔθνος can be written ethnographically—or to align it with a distinctly historical project. Rather, in discussing ethnography within the context of the making of late antique Christianity, I am interested in looking at the how Christians developed their own ethnographic vernacular and thus forged a Christian ethnographic discourse through their obsessive writings about the heretics. Heresiology is, in this reading, an exercise not only in appropriating certain ethnographic tropes, themes, aspirations, and fears but also in reimagining them through the principles of Christian theology and theological interpretation. The heretics people the Christian world in ways that make them the natural, however disdained, objects of ethnographic inquiry.

If ethnography is a multifaceted process in which information about a particular people is collected and then theorized, the ethnographic disposition represents the underlying rationale for such methodological and theoretical decisions. In analyzing the process of textual construction, I am posing two interrelated questions about this authorial method: What were the sources with which ethnography was written? And how was the information contained therein gathered? When an author explicitly states the methods and sources of his ethnographic inquiry (and in many cases we are left merely to infer), it tends to follow one of three lines: autopsy, witnesses (from testimony and conversation), or the recycling or reinterpretation of textual precedents. Writers as diverse as Lucian, Pausanias, Josephus, Ammianus, Tacitus, and Herodotus underscore their personal travels and involvement in the events, places, and peoples they identify and describe.[44]

---

43. See also James Romm, *The Edges of the Earth in Ancient Thought: Geography, Exploration, and Fiction* (Princeton: Princeton University Press, 1992), who emphasizes the narrative, literary quality of investigations into the peoples and places at the farthest ends of the earth.

44. On autopsy, see O. Kimball Armayor, *Herodotus' Autopsy of the Fayoum: Lake Moeris and the Labyrinth of Egypt* (Amsterdam: Gieben, 1985); Rosalind Thomas, *Herodotus in Context: Ethnography, Science and the Art of Persuasion* (New York: Cambridge University Press, 2000), 168–248; John Marincola, *Authority and Tradition in Ancient Historiography* (New York: Cambridge University Press, 1997), 63–85, 276–79; and Hartog, *Mirror of Herodotus*, 260–370.

Historiographers, ethnographers, and geographers alike wrap themselves in the credibility—what Stephen Greenblatt has called the "discursive choice"—of autopsy: I have been; I have seen; I know.[45] Josephus's avowedly historiographical method, like Herodotus's preferred process of assembling information, emphasizes his firsthand knowledge of events of the Jewish War, though not to the exclusion of alternative modes of inquiry. In contrast to the Greeks, who had written histories without visiting the pertinent sites and, furthermore, had "put together a few things from hearsay reports" (ἐκ παρακουσμάτων ὀλίγα συνθέντες), Josephus was an eyewitness to history: "I, on the contrary, have written a veracious account, at once comprehensive and detailed, of the war, having been present in person at all the events. I was in command of those whom we call Galilaeans, so long as resistance was possible."[46]

In other cases, writers draw on the testimony of witnesses to bolster their narratives. In briefly recounting the history of Lydia, for example, Herodotus describes a protracted war between the Lydians, then ruled by King Alyattes, and the Milesians. During the course of battle, the Lydians inadvertently set fire to the temple of Athene at Assesos (they had intended merely to burn crops), which, Herodotus notes, was thought to have inflicted upon Alyattes a protracted and incurable illness. Seeking a remedy, the Lydians ventured to the oracle at Delphi, but "when the messengers came to Delphi the Pythian priestess would not reply to them before they should restore the temple of Athene at Assesos."[47] The details and context of the story need not concern us. What I wish to emphasize is Herodotus's immediate point of clarification: "I know the truth, for the Delphians told me; the Milesians, however, add to the story."[48] Unspecified testimony, from unknown witnesses or simply "what I have heard," to quote Pausanias, similarly guides authors writing about events, peoples, and places.[49] Diodorus Siculus's introduction to his discussion of the Ethiopians in his *Library of History* illustrates the piecemeal nature of writing ethnographically in a work of history:[50]

---

45. Stephen Greenblatt, *Marvelous Possessions: The Wonder of the New World* (Chicago: University of Chicago Press, 1991), 123.

46. Josephus, *C. Ap.* 1.9 (LCL 186:180–83).

47. Herodotus, *Hist.* 1.19, trans. A. D. Godley, LCL 117 (Cambridge, Mass.: Harvard University Press, 1981), 22–23.

48. Herodotus, *Hist.* 1.20 (LCL 117:22). Translation modified. He continues at 1.20, "The Milesians add to the story, that Periander son of Cypselus, being a close friend of Thrasybulus who then was sovereign of Miletus, learnt what reply the oracle had given to Alyattes and sent him a dispatch to tell Thrasybulus, so that thereby his friend should be forewarned and make his plans accordingly" (LCL 117:22).

49. Pausanias, *Descr.* 3.7.1, trans. W. H. S. Jones and H. A. Ormerod, LCL 188 (Cambridge, Mass.: Harvard University Press, 1926), 38–39.

50. Diodorus Siculus, *Library of History* 3.11, trans. C. H. Oldfather, LCL 303 (Cambridge, Mass.: Harvard University Press, 1979), 112–14.

Concerning the historians (τῶν συγγραφέων), we must distinguish among them, to the effect that many have composed works on both Egypt and Ethiopia, of whom some have given credence to false report and others have invented many tales out of their own minds for the delectation of their readers, and so may justly be distrusted. For example, Agatharchides of Cnidus in the second Book of his work on Asia, and the compiler of geographies, Artemidorus of Ephesus, in his eighth Book, and certain others whose homes were in Egypt, have recounted most of what I have set forth above and are, on the whole, accurate in all they have written. For, to bear witness ourselves, during the time of our visit to Egypt, we associated with many of its priests and conversed with not a few ambassadors from Ethiopia as well who were then in Egypt; and after inquiring carefully of them about each matter and testing the stories of the historians, we have composed our accounts so as to accord with the opinions on which they most fully agree.

Ethnographers such as Diodorus scrutinized textual precedents and drew upon them freely.[51] Like historiographers and geographers, the ethnographers made textual choices and judgments in relation to an existing body of knowledge. They offered new interpretations, which had their own afterlives. The ancient tendency toward armchair ethnography—the interpretation of peoples via textual rather than experiential knowledge—displays how the ethnographic disposition relied upon a process of intertextual reading. Ethnographic analysis was, in many instances, doubly interpretive: ethnographers had to reinterpret the findings of previous authors who had already situated their data within their own narratives.

Ethnography in antiquity encompasses not only the collection of data but also its theorization, which attempts to explain the puzzles of the natural world and the people within it. Reflections on the practices, habits, and phenotypes of peoples— the facets of microscopic or particularistic investigation—engendered theorization and disquisition on the causes, conditions, and factors of human diversity (the macroscopic explanations of these microscopic data). The transformation of minutiae into grander historiographical arguments served not only to illuminate the observable differences among the people of the world but to regularize those differences in accordance with natural and supernatural phenomena. Such taxonomic or ideological ordering depended upon a chain of ethnographic knowledge.

---

51. Because there is no evidence that writing people required an especially rigorous program of travel and observation, though this was true in certain cases (see Caesar, Pausanias, Herodotus, and Pytheas of Massalia, among others), reliance upon earlier sources was a routine component of ethnographic writing. Unlike contemporary ethnographers who venture into the field to observe their subjects firsthand—this has not always been the case, of course: think Durkheim, Frazer, and Benedict— ancient writers wrote freely of peoples with whom they seemingly had no personal contact at all. On the use of libraries to produce ethnography, see Woolf, *Tales of the Barbarians*, 66–79. Because much ethnography was written with second-order data, it seems apposite to think of our ancient authors as armchair or uncritical anthropologists.

To organize and arrange ethnographic knowledge meant to posit the causes and effects of human diversity. Interpretive paradigms were utilized alongside data pools not only to try to explicate the causes and forces of the diversity of human behavior and habits but also to categorize the peoples of the observable world.

In his *On Isis and Osiris* (*De Iside et Osiride*), the biographer, historian, and middle Platonist Plutarch (ca. 46–120 C.E.), for instance, used the Egyptian myth and cult of Isis to expound his theory of the "structure and genesis of the cosmos."[52] Daniel Richter has persuasively argued that Plutarch dwelt on the myth of Isis and Osiris to solidify a cultural hierarchy between Greece and Egypt. To that end, Plutarch used allegory to argue "that the Egyptian cult of Isis, left uninterpreted by Greek philosophy, is barbaric in the sense that it leads the soul to a superstitious and false apprehension of the divine."[53] The Egyptians did not possess an accurate knowledge about the meaning of their own traditions and culture. The interpretive maneuvers of Greek and Roman authors brought coherence and order to competing notions of culture and knowledge. It was the Greek or Roman—and eventually Christian—ethnographer, who "employing his expert training in the linked practices of observation and theorizing, could generate ethnographic knowledge."[54] It was the ethnographer alone who knew how to arrange, analyze, and interpret these data "into convincing wholes."[55] He provided ordered ideas of culture and cultural difference. As interpreters of knowledge, ethnographers articulated their understanding of the world around them and the cultures that inhabited it.[56]

In his discussion of ethnography in the ancient world, Greg Woolf identifies two of its dominant explanatory paradigms: genealogy and geography (the latter including subtypes such as climatology, cosmology, and astrology).[57] The ordering of ethnographic knowledge, whereby a people was either situated with respect to

---

52. Daniel S. Richter, "Plutarch on Isis and Osiris: Text, Cult, and Cultural Appropriation," *TAPA* 131 (2001): 191–216, at 191–92.

53. Ibid. 209.

54. Woolf, *Tales of the Barbarians*, 42–43.

55. Ibid. 43.

56. See also the excellent discussion of Ellen O'Gorman, "No Place Like Rome: Identity and Difference in the *Germania* of Tacitus," *Ramus* 22.2 (1993): 135–54.

57. Woolf, *Tales of the Barbarians*, 32–58. For geography, see 44–51; climatology, 44–48; astrology, 48–51. As Woolf explains, "genealogy and geography each offered general explanatory frameworks or paradigms within which ethnographic data might be made to make sense.... Paradigms also contribute to the structuring of knowledge when it is encoded in text. Ethnography, after all, literally means 'writing people.' As a discipline of recording it always involves the translation of people into texts. Paradigms operate in some ways like master narratives, and in others rather like sets of generic conventions" (36). On ethnography as conditioned by its allegorical possibilities (i.e., ethnography as a genre and practice of multiple meanings and multiple readings), see James Clifford, "On Ethnographic Allegory," in *Writing Culture: The Poetics and Politics of Ethnography*, ed. James Clifford and George E. Marcus (Berkeley and Los Angeles: University of California Press, 1986), 98–121.

location (within a larger cosmological framework) or identified via a genealogical tree, offers a model through which to explain human diversity and "to map ethnic groups."[58] Whereas the quest to locate origins (either spatially or genetically) and thus to explain the cultural, religious, and geographical heterogeneity of the world represents but one dimension of the larger project of arraying ethnographic data, the preoccupation with validating ancestral lineage guides much of the ethnographic tradition. Genealogy served as a tangible measure of cultural and ethnic priority (and, in certain instances, superiority).[59] Drawing upon the traditional appeal to genealogies, dating back to Homer, Woolf posits that it was possible to organize a line of descendants around a lone figure's individual eponym if it was "located sufficiently far back in mythic times."[60] Another of the genealogical functions of ethnographic writing, specifically what Woolf identifies as the process of "situating particular individuals or families at the centre of an ethnic history,"[61] holds the potential to distinguish specific population groups as well as to create associative bonds among them. Genealogies established proximity as much as they recorded separation: ties of fictive kinship proved functional tools by which communities were drawn together.[62] Here, again, texts represented ideas that, in all likelihood, lacked historicity. But, as our authors knew, just as representation became a weapon by which alliances could be forged or hostility explained, it likewise brought to bear unintended or unforeseen problems of philosophical import. The collection of evidence of peoples' ways of life, both by autopsy and with the aid of textual precedents, engendered problematic questions and realizations about the causes of human difference, the impossibility of cultural translation, the falsity of authorial objectivity, and the scope of ethnographic knowledge. There were certain methodological, philosophical, and textual assumptions that informed the process of ethnographic writing; others that became implicated *in* the writing process; and still more that emerged only from the process of writing peoples. As much as inquiry required ethnographic exempla, ethnographic writing demanded further inquiry and produced its own explanatory models.

---

58. Woolf, *Tales of the Barbarians*, 40.
59. See Elias Bickerman, "Origines gentium," *CP* 47.2 (1952): 65–81; T. P. Wiseman, "Legendary Genealogies in Late-Republican Rome," *GR* 21.1 (1974): 153–64; Hall, *Ethnic Identity in Greek Antiquity*, 40–51, 77–89, and *Hellenicity*, 15–29; Robert L. Fowler, "Genealogical Thinking, Hesiod's *Catalogue*, and the Creation of the Hellenes," *Proceedings of the Cambridge Philological Society* 44 (1998): 1–19; and Isaac, *Invention of Racism*, 109–48.
60. Woolf, *Tales of the Barbarians*, 41.
61. Ibid.
62. See Gruen, *Rethinking the Other in Antiquity*, 253–307; and Christopher P. Jones, *Kinship Diplomacy in the Ancient World* (Cambridge, Mass.: Harvard University Press, 1999).

HERESIOLOGY AS ETHNOGRAPHY

In an oft-cited remark, Clifford Geertz observed that "doing ethnography is like trying to read (in the sense of 'construct a reading of') a manuscript."[63] "Foreign, faded, full of ellipses, incoherencies, suspicious emendations, and tendentious commentaries," a manuscript, like an ethnography, is defined by its layers of content and its polyvalent structure: it is a literary palimpsest.[64] In much the same way that the manuscript presents itself as a textual relic with strata of meaning, my reading of heresiology as a Christianized mode of ethnography posits a similar effort to interpret the layers of heresy's meaning in the history of Christianity. By using the work of their predecessors, the heresiologists of the later Roman Empire, most notably Theodoret, Augustine, Filastrius, and Epiphanius, strove to organize the heretical world in a system of knowledge and to construct it in terms favorable to their orthodoxy. At the outset of the second proem of the *Panarion*, Epiphanius reports concisely, if vaguely, on the sources he has consulted and the techniques he has employed in writing his text. Just as for Diodorus Siculus, who heralds "that enthusiasm for the work which enables every man to bring to completion the task which seems impossible," for Epiphanius "a fondness for study" (φιλομαθίας) undergirds his exposition.[65] Epiphanius's articulation of a scholarly urge is a fitting rejoinder to the request "of beauty-loving men (ἐξ ἀνδρῶν φιλοκάλων) who urged my weakness on at various times and in various ways, and practically forced me to get at it."[66] The request from the presbyters Acacius and Paul, who asked Epiphanius to share his knowledge of the heretics, serves both to test the bishop's intellectual skill and to validate his expertise.[67]

Although Hippolytus's lost *Syntagma* and Irenaeus's *Adversus haereseon* were the principal sources for the *Panarion*, there is evidence to suggest that Epiphanius consulted a number of other works, including Eusebius of Caesarea's *Ecclesiastical History*, *Chronicle*, and *Praeparatio evangelica*, an unspecified work of Clement of Alexandria, the *Apostolic Constitutions*, Filastrius of Brescia's *Diversarum haereseon liber*, and the spurious chapter 30 of Tertullian's *Praescriptio haereticorum*, known as the work of pseudo-Tertullian.[68] The earlier heresiologies by Irenaeus and

---

63. Clifford Geertz, "Thick Description: Toward an Interpretive Theory of Culture," in his *The Interpretation of Cultures: Selected Essays by Clifford Geertz* (New York: Perseus, 1973), 3-30, at 10.
64. Ibid. 10.
65. Diodorus Siculus, *Library of History* 1.4.2 (LCL 279:19).
66. Epiphanius, *Pan.* pro. 2.2.4, 2.2.5 (GCS, n. F., 10:170).
67. For the *Letter of Acacius and Paul*, see Epiphanius, *Pan.* 1.1–13 (GCS, n. F., 10:153–54).
68. Richard Adelbert Lipsius, *Zur Quellengeschichte des Epiphanios* (Vienna: Braumüller, 1865), offers the most systematic review of Epiphanius's sources. Aline Pourkier, *L'hérésiologie chez Épiphane de Salamine* (Paris: Beauchesne, 1992), 53–75, surveys the literature more briefly (though she juxtaposes the knowledge of the various sources throughout her work). It remains inconclusive whether Epiphanius knew any of Justin's work or the *Elenchos* of Hippolytus. Pourkier, 93–117, offers a systematic

Hippolytus offered evidence for Epiphanius's historical-geographical-genealogical master narrative. A variety of texts—some heresiological, others not—provided details about the various sectarian groups that Epiphanius named and described.[69] Composed over layers of heresiological tradition, Epiphanius subsumed the works of his forebears and contemporaries to suit his own theological, stylistic, and rhetorical needs. The *Panarion,* in short, assimilated data to project its omniscience and expertise. Hearsay and the occasional firsthand observation—"I happened on some with my own ears and eyes"—likewise complemented his self-professed bookishness.[70] He writes, for example, of his knowledge of the Sethians: "I think I may have met with this sect in Egypt too—I do not precisely recall the country in which I met them. And I found out some things about it by inquiry in an actual encounter but have learned other things from treatises."[71]

Epiphanius balanced his need for evidentiary corroboration—his text's dependence on its predecessors—against his own claims of authorial control. His text was no mere compilation or catalogue: it was a highly ordered ethnography, at once macroscopically theorized and microscopically constructed. His text thus segued from its overarching master narrative into the details of lived heresy. What Epiphanius actually produced was a polemical dialogue—or rather, a series of dialogues—between Christianity's unity and its diversity, which was modulated "with the help of other people's words, created and distributed specifically as the words of others."[72] The *Panarion*'s polyvocality, the marshaling of orthodox sources alongside the presentation of quotations from the heretics themselves—was

---

comparison between the works of Hippolytus and Epiphanius. On Justin's reference to his lost work, *Against All the Schools of Thought That Have Arisen (The Syntagma),* see Alain Le Boulluec, *La notion d'hérésie dans la littérature grecque, IIe-IIIe siècles,* vol. 1 (Paris: Études Augustiniennes, 1985), 36–91; and now Geoffrey S. Smith, *Guilt by Association: Heresy Catalogues in Early Christianity* (New York: Oxford University Press, 2014), 49–86.

69. See the brief remarks of Frank Williams, trans. *The* Panarion *of Epiphanius of Salamis: Book I, Sects 1–46,* 2nd ed. (Boston: Brill, 2009), xxv–xxvii.

70. Epiphanius, *Pan.* pro. 2.2.4 (GCS, n. F., 10:170). The rarity with which eyewitness testimony is invoked—by the heresiologist himself or by a source—is hardly dispositive insofar as ancient ethnography was primarily a venture undertaken with written sources. Much emphasis, especially with respect to Augustine's *De haeresibus,* is placed on the collection of relevant material. Theodoret also trumpets his usage of sources and signals his genre's dependence upon his intellectual antecedents and contemporaries. See the diagram of heresiological interdependence in Gérard Vallée, *A Study in Anti-Gnostic Polemic: Irenaeus, Hippolytus, and Epiphanius* (Waterloo, Ont.: Wilfrid Laurier University Press, 1981), 6. Glenn Melvin Cope, "An Analysis of the Heresiological Method of Theodoret of Cyrus in the 'Haereticarum fabularum compendium'" (Ph.D. dissertation, Catholic University of America, 1990), ventures into a fairly detailed discussion of Theodoret's sources—contesting, for example, Vallée's claim that Theodoret was unaware of the *Panarion.*

71. Epiphanius, *Pan.* 39.1.2 (GCS 31:72).

72. Mikhail Bakhtin, *Problems of Dostoevsky's Poetics,* ed. and trans. Caryl Emerson (Minneapolis: University of Minnesota Press, 1984), 188.

harmonized via Epiphanius's biblical prooftexts and ethnographic model. His universalizing genealogy, the subject of chapter 4 below, was corroborated and realized through the words both of his fellow Christians and of his heretical foes. By incorporating the writings of the heretics, the *Panarion* juxtaposed theological and intellectual opinions on Epiphanius's terms. But the dialogic nature of his text is an illusion. In letting the heretics, on occasion, speak for themselves, Epiphanius used the heretics' own words to refute them.

Epiphanius's usage of extended quotations from the heretics not only valorizes his own investigative efforts—"to show all studious persons who are in search of truths of faith that I do not accuse people without reason but do my best to base what I say on reliable evidence"—it also enables him to insist on the radical disjuncture between his own voice and those of his opponents.[73] With passages from Ptolemy, Marcion, Origen (from his commentary on the first Psalm), Arius, Marcellus, Basil of Ancyra, George of Laodicea, Acacius, Melitius, Aetius, the Gnostic texts *Ascents of James* and the *Travels of Peter*, a *Gospel according to the Hebrews*, and the *Book of Elkasai*, Epiphanius, more than any other late antique heresiologist, turns the heretics' own writings against them.[74] He takes Irenaeus's maxim that "the very manifestation of their doctrine is a victory against them" to its textual extreme.[75] The heresiologists saw themselves as the rightful interpreters of other peoples' traditions, practices, and habits. Thus Epiphanius explained the true nature of the heretics not simply to those who asked for his expertise—both Epiphanius and Augustine received appeals to produce their heresiologies—but also to the heretics themselves.[76] The *Panarion*, most emphatically, reads as a dialogue both with and against heretical groups: the locution "you see"—as in "Don't you see?" or "Isn't it obvious?"—pervades the text.[77] The motif of seeing was used both in conversation with the heretics—"and you see, Origen, that your novel

---

73. Epiphanius, *Pan.* 73.23.1 (GCS 37:296).

74. Epiphanius, *Pan.* 31.5.1–6.10; 32.4.4–5.6; 33.3.1–7.10; 42.1–78; 64.6.1–7.4, 64.12.1–16.7; 66.6.1–6.11, 66.25.3–31.8; 69.7.2–8.5; 72.2.1–3.5; 73.2.1–22.8; 76.11.1–12.37. In acknowledging his *Panarion*'s literary dependence upon the writings of Irenaeus, Hippolytus, Clement, and other earlier Christian writers, Epiphanius underscores the continuity and tension within the textual tradition of heretical refutation. Heresiology, in its later iterations, bore the mark of a genre in tension with itself. Authors not only edited their texts numerically; they considered the structural mechanisms by which the undertaking could be limited, including scriptural strictures and efforts to define in precise terms the meaning of heresy.

75. Irenaeus, *Adv. haer.* 1.31.3 (SC 264:388).

76. Augustine was asked by the deacon of Carthage Quodvultdeus for a brief heresiological handbook. See Augustine, *Epistles* 221–24 in CCSL 46:273–81. See my discussion of this exchange and Augustine's text in chapter 7 below.

77. While the motif of seeing (ὁρᾷς) is found in nearly every entry of the *Panarion*, certain examples illustrate the point especially well: 31.28.1; 37.8.11; 48.3.6, 48.7.10; 51.10.3, 51.33.8; 57.5.2; 62.6.3; 65.5.7; 66.54.3; 69.62.8; 70.4.1; 73.36.4; 76.8.12, 76.38.2; 79.6.5.

nonsense is worthless"[78]—and with orthodox Christians, as a plea of avoidance: "And do you see how much there is of this charlatan's silly nonsense and drunken forgetfulness?"[79] The goal of heresiology was not just to deter Christians from becoming or associating with the heretics but also to reorient the heretics toward orthodoxy.[80] Epiphanius's text thus operated as an act of ethnographic illumination: it revealed the true nature and the teachings of the heretics not simply to ostracize them but, in fact, to bring them into the fold.

Tomoko Masuzawa and Christopher Herbert have likewise shown how Victorian ethnographers and philologists offered authoritative interpretations of the traditions and practices of foreign peoples. These Victorian writers located the original form of cultures and religions, uncovering the meanings that eluded the very people who lived them.[81] Buddhism, for instance, came to be regarded as a world religion only when Western academics (in the nineteenth century) began to study its texts in earnest. Precisely because, as Masuzawa notes, "there were no native adherents to be found in contemporary India, the land of Buddhism's origin . . . the very essence of this newly recognized religion was in the hands of European learned society. With the proper critical skills, those highly trained, monumentally devoted scholars would be in the best position, if not to say exclusive position, to grasp Buddhism's essential character."[82] There arose, then, a distinction between true or original Buddhism, which was the proper domain of Western philologists, and Buddhism on the ground, which belonged to missionaries, travelers, and casual observers. Similarly, Victorian ethnographers used their "intimate acquaintance" with primitive peoples "to make rational sense of them."[83] The task of the Victorian ethnographers of Polynesia, as Herbert deftly explains, was to find an answer to the "interpretive riddle" that defined primitive peoples' seemingly contradictory ways of life: to identify a way to represent the incoherencies of primitive peoples with an essential unity.[84] As Herbert, quoting Malinowski, avers: "'The natives obey the forces and commands of the tribal code, but they do not comprehend it'; almost by definition, only the learned European ethnographer can do that."[85] From Plutarch to the apologists and the heresiologists through the early comparative philologists and Victorian anthropologists, the discourse of

78. Epiphanius, *Pan.* 64.65.28 (GCS 31:508).
79. Epiphanius, *Pan.* 66.50.1 (GCS 37:87).
80. See Caroline Humfress, *Orthodoxy and the Courts in Late Antiquity* (New York: Oxford University Press, 2007), 235–37.
81. Masuzawa, *The Invention of World Religions;* and Christopher Herbert, *Culture and Anomie: The Ethnographic Imagination in the Nineteenth Century* (Chicago: University of Chicago Press, 1991).
82. Masuzawa, *The Invention of World Religions*, 126.
83. Herbert, *Culture and Anomie*, 198.
84. Ibid.
85. Ibid. 43.

ethnographic inquiry was fashioned via claims of interpretive expertise. The heresiologists, with their insistence on a radical distinction between truth and falsity, offered their own hermeneutical expertise as writers of other Christian peoples. They discovered, elaborated, and classified the very nature of the heretics and heresy. The heresiologists were ethnographic interpreters: they found original forms and essences, forms unknown to the heretics themselves.

If Christianity can be said to have developed a discourse for itself in various manifestations and to various ends, heresiology serves very much as the science (in the Foucauldian sense) of heresy. To follow the analysis that Foucault offers in his *Archaeology of Knowledge*, heresiology perpetuates and produces a structural form (the catalogue) that encompasses a field and discourse of knowledge.[86] When "a group of statements" and its attendant claims, norms, and coherence exercise "a dominant function (as a model, a critique, or a verification) over knowledge," a discursive formation emerges as a body of knowledge (it reaches what Foucault calls "a threshold of epistemologization").[87] As Foucault goes on to explain:[88]

> At this level, scientificity does not serve as a norm: in this archaeological history, what one is trying to uncover are discursive practices in so far as they give rise to a corpus of knowledge, in so far as they assume the status and role of a science. To undertake a history of the sciences at this level is not to describe discursive formations without regard to epistemological structures; it is to show how the establishment of a science, and perhaps its transition to formalization, have come about in a discursive formation, and in modifications to its positivity.... The analysis of discursive formations, of positivities, and knowledge in their relations with epistemological figures and with the sciences is what has been called, to distinguish it from other possible forms of the history of the sciences, the analysis of the *episteme*. This episteme may be suspected of being something like a world-view, a slice of history common to all branches of knowledge, which imposes on each one the same norms and postulates, a general stage of reason, a certain structure of thought that the men of a particular period cannot escape—a great body of legislation written once and for all by some anonymous hand.

Christian heresiologists simultaneously peeled back and erected layers of meaning, symbols, and language to explicate their understanding of the known world and elaborate a Christian discourse of history through the notion of heresy. They constructed a regime of knowledge, a worldview oriented by heresy. As an episteme, heresy functions as "the total set of relations that unite, at a given period, the discursive practices that give rise to epistemological figures, sciences, and possibly

---

86. Michel Foucault, *Archaeology of Knowledge*, trans. A. M. Sheridan Smith (New York: Pantheon, 1972), 184.
87. Ibid. 186–87.
88. Ibid. 190–91.

formalized systems."[89] Though the task of the heresiologist was explicitly polemical, it nonetheless signaled a classificatory impulse built upon the development of discourse of theologically oriented ethnography. Heresiological literature functioned as an expression of a Christian ethnographic disposition, which, above all else, negotiated the immensely difficult task of representing abominable yet alluring—and, indeed, theologically necessary—peoples in textual form.

Ethnography provided an especially useful lens through which to explore the contradictory logic of late antique Christian techniques of classification. Governed by theological principles and the discourse of truth and falsity, Christian ethnographic writing pitted the desire for comprehensive knowledge of the peoples and practices of the world against the repulsion of errant and devious traditions. Discovery of the heretics was a double-edged sword: it announced and textualized their falsity even as it sought to erase them completely. The Christian pursuit of knowledge of foreign peoples and practices was invariably corrective; it was designed to provide peoples with a new way of life. The heretics held enormous explanatory potential for the message of Christian orthodoxy; their theological purpose was to provide a contrast with truth by exemplifying error. But that very purpose created a dangerous dependency whereby orthodoxy required the constant meddling of heresy. Orthodox writers created, used, and theorized the object of their own demise. Therein lay one of the fundamental paradoxes of heresiological inquiry: the structures for classifying knowledge themselves broke down to reveal the impossibility of the heresiologists' endeavor itself. For, as Foucault notes, an episteme "opens up an inexhaustible field and can never be closed."[90] In that sense, heresiology was governed by an ethos of fear of contamination and an anxiety of permanence, as Michel-Yves Perrin has argued persuasively.[91] I submit that the anxiety Perrin ascribes to the heresiologists is built upon an ethnographic logic of cultural exchange. It is not just a fear of abstract doctrine but one of lived and continuous contact with the heretics: "In all the instructions delivered to both the catechumens and the faithful to 'run away from heretics' rings out distinctly: not only is this a merely intellectual rejection of opinions, ideas or beliefs considered to be wrong, but true believers must protect themselves from any physical contact with the people who champion them."[92] To that end, the heresiological project was a manifestation of ethnographic expertise. It provided expert knowledge to lay people in order to prevent contact and exchange. Thus it was as *ethnography* that heresiology prevented individual encounters with the heretics.[93]

89. Ibid. 191.
90. Ibid.
91. Michel-Yves Perrin, "The Limits of the Heresiological Ethos in Late Antiquity," in *Religious Diversity in Late Antiquity*, ed. David M. Gwynn and Susanne Bangert (Leiden: Brill, 2010), 201–27.
92. Ibid. 204.
93. The great historian of the later Roman Empire A. H. M Jones famously asked in an article from 1959, "Were the Ancient Heresies National or Social Movements in Disguise?," *JTS* 10.2 (1959): 280–98.

Christian ethnographers wrote about and thus constructed Christianity as if it were a world, an expansive theological topography in need of exploration, classification, and investigation, that fed a loop of ethnographic discourse and exchange. Like the Scythians of Herodotus and the Germans of Tacitus as well as the philosophical schools of Diogenes Laertius's *Lives of the Eminent Philosophers* and the Jewish sects of Josephus's *Jewish War* and *Jewish Antiquities*, the heretics were emblematic of certain erroneous traditions of knowledge, custom, and culture.[94] But unlike the Sadducees or Platonists, who existed among Jews and pagans as legitimate schools of thought, the heretics were defined by a disposition of hubris and transgression, which was central to Christian narratives of sacred history and theological theorizations of human diversity. Indeed, like the nations of Greek and Roman texts, which exemplified the diversity of the known world and galvanized efforts to understand it, the heretics became tools through which Christians told their own ethnographic history of diversity and difference as a history of error. In writing about and explaining their own internal differences, the heresiologists deployed, and in some cases simply invented, ancient paradigms of ethnography in order to classify and ultimately defeat the Christian plurality around them. Concurrently, Christian writers framed the plurality of opinions and groups endemic to their own Christian world as the underlying explanation for the manifest diversity within the known world. Christian self-investigation conceptualized the internal diversity of the church as a larger disquisition on the nature and causes of all human diversity. Christian authors engulfed the church and its intellectual traditions within a polemical project of ethnography: to write the peoples of Christianity in order to contest and, it was hoped, to control them.[95] Heresiology posed the relationship between human diversity and Christian diversity quite directly; the differences and variety within the world of Christianity and the world

---

Although Jones answered firmly in the negative, it is nonetheless clear from the extant evidence that the heresiologists explicitly invoked the language of ethnic reasoning in their delineation of the nature, origin, and identity of the heretics. Moreover, the facets of ethnographic writing incorporate more, much more, than a rote delineation of the qualities or criteria of nationhood. The ethnographic mark of heresiology turns as much on its descriptions of peoples as it does on the author's gaze upon the structure and capacity of his text to contain and define a field of knowledge.

94. On Diogenes Laertius, see Jørgen Mejer, "Diogenes Laertius and the Transmission of Greek Philosophy," *ANRW* 2.36.5 (1992): 3556–602. The latter part of 36.5 (3556–792) contains several essays on doxography, Diogenes, and Hippolytus of Rome, while the entirety of 36.6 pursues these themes. The best study of ancient Jewish sectarianism remains Albert I. Baumgarten's *The Flourishing of Jewish Sects in the Maccabean Era: An Interpretation* (Leiden: Brill, 1997). See also Shaye J. D. Cohen, *From the Maccabees to the Mishnah*, 2nd ed. (Louisville: Westminster John Knox, 2006), 110–66; and now Jonathan Klawans, *Josephus and the Theologies of Ancient Judaism* (New York: Oxford University Press, 2013).

95. On orthodox control of heresy, see Daniel Boyarin, "Apartheid Comparative Religion in the Second Century: Some Theory and a Case Study," *JMEMS* 36.1 (2006): 3–34.

writ large were recast as interdependent phenomena. The history of human difference paralleled and even became the history of sectarianism. The heretics, like the nations and the cultures that they represented, were treated as creatures of custom, susceptible to the piercing eye of Christian ethnographers. In exploring how Christians *wrote* their indigenous peoples, the heretics, I am explicitly casting heresiology as a textual endeavor that sought to rationalize the topography, customs, and wonders of its Christian and non-Christian environments.

In this light, Irenaeus's description of the Marcosians, a Gallic offshoot of the Valentinians, in his *Against the Heresies* serves as an apt illustration of Christian heresiology as ethnography.[96] He dwells at great length upon their cosmic mythology, interest in numbers and letters, misinterpretation of scripture, use of apocryphal writings, and so on, but he commences his ethnographic description with the figure of Marcus himself. Irenaeus begins by telling his readers that Marcus boasted of "correcting his teacher [Valentinus]";[97] that he was skilled in the magical arts; that he "deceived many men and not a few women";[98] and "was a forerunner of the Antichrist."[99] In Irenaeus's telling, Marcus views himself as the "matrix and receptacle of Silence (according to the teaching of Colorbasus)," as the font of the divine Monad.[100] Irenaeus enumerates in detail certain ritual illusions that Marcus performed, most notably a faux eucharistic rite that worked to ensnare the minds of weak women.[101] He explains: "As he feigns to give thanks over the cup mixed with wine, and draws out at great length the prayer of invocation, he makes the cup appear to be purple or red so that it seems that Grace, who is from the regions that are above all things, dropped her own blood into the cup because of his invocation."[102] Those who observe this wondrous ritual long for Grace to "rain upon them."[103] Women who have rejected his magic and returned to the church accuse Marcus of using love potions and charms in order to defile them sexually.[104] In his description of this rejection, Irenaeus insists that these women "withdrew from such company" (ἐχωρίσθησαν τοῦ τοιούτου θιάσου).[105] The Greek θίασος connotes more than just a company of persons; rather, it serves to identify a cultic retinue, a

---

96. Irenaeus, *Adv. haer.* 1.13–20. On the Marcosians and their death rite, in particular, see Nicola Denzey Lewis, "*Apolytrosis* as Ritual and Sacrament: Determining a Ritual Context for Death in Second-Century Marcosian Valentinianism," *JECS* 17.4 (2009): 525–61.
97. Irenaeus, *Adv. haer.* 1.13.1 (SC 264:188).
98. Irenaeus, *Adv. haer.* 1.13.1 (SC 264:188).
99. Irenaeus, *Adv. haer.* 1.13.1 (SC 264:190).
100. Irenaeus, *Adv. haer.* 1.14.1 (SC 264:206).
101. Irenaeus, *Adv. haer.* 1.13.2–5.
102. Irenaeus, *Adv. haer.* 1.13.2 (SC 264:190). Translation modified.
103. Irenaeus, *Adv. haer.* 1.13.2 (SC 264:192).
104. Irenaeus, *Adv. haer.* 1.13.5.
105. Irenaeus, *Adv. haer.* 1.13.4 (SC 264:198).

frenzied devotion, usually to Dionysus. It has the sense of a cult society. In this case, true Christian women knew to flee this devious social group.[106]

Insofar as Marcus positioned himself at the center of a complex cosmic system—oriented around numbers, letters, symbols, and the generation of cosmic beings—he garnered his authority from the possession of secret knowledge given to him by "the most exalted Tetrad."[107] Marcus transferred that knowledge to his disciples, who, as Irenaeus reports, insisted on their perfection vis-à-vis other Christians:[108]

> Some of his disciples, too, who wandered about among them, deceived many silly women and defiled them. They boasted of being so perfect that no one was able to come up to the greatness of that knowledge, not even were one to mention Peter or Paul, or any other of the apostles, and that they knew more than all others and alone imbibed the greatness of the knowledge and the unspeakable Power; and so they are free to do all things without fear of anyone in regard to anything.

Irenaeus insisted that the so-called perfect knowledge of the Marcosians was the direct cause of their libertine approach to life. Like Christ's apostles, Marcus's disciples preached a gospel, only theirs was a gospel of arrogance and hubris. For my purposes what is especially intriguing is how Irenaeus's description of Marcus and the Marcosians oscillates between the singular "he" of Marcus and the plural "they" of his disciples. In some cases, Irenaeus's comments about Marcus's disciples portrayed them as extensions of Marcus himself. Chapter 14 of Book 1, for instance, is concerned with Marcus alone, whereas chapter 15 adopts the language of both Marcus and Marcosians. The remaining chapters—16 through 20—all use pluralized language: "they" adulterate scripture with apocryphal writings; "they" distort and misinterpret the Pentateuch; "they" propound an incorrect theory of creation; and "they" practice various rites of redemption.[109] As Ismo Dunderberg notably remarks: "Irenaeus did not call the Marcosians a school, like other Valentinians, but a cult society (*thiasos*)."[110]

But Irenaeus's lengthy discussion of Marcosian rites suggests that there were occasions on which they not only separated themselves from the larger Christian

---

106. On women and the cult of Dionysus, see Ross S. Kraemer, "Ecstasy and Possession: The Attraction of Women to the Cult of Dionysus," *HTR* 72.1–2 (1979): 55–80.
107. Irenaeus, *Adv. haer.* 1.14.1 (SC 264:206).
108. Irenaeus, *Adv. haer.* 1.13.6 (SC 264:200–202).
109. On their use of spurious writings, see *Adv. haer.* 1.20. On their errant cosmic and scriptural interpretations, see *Adv. haer.* 1.16 and 1.18, respectively. On creation, *Adv. haer.* 1.17. On death rites, *Adv. haer.* 1.21.
110. Ismo O. Dunderberg, "The School of Valentinus," in *A Companion to Second-Century "Christian Heretics,"* ed. Antti Marjanen and Petri Luomanen (Boston: Brill, 2008), 83. For more on the idea of *thiasos*, see Walter Burkert, *Ancient Mystery Cults* (Cambridge, Mass.: Harvard University Press, 1987), 31–34, 38, 41–45.

congregation but also from each other.[111] The Marcosians were not a monolithic group; they were a movement, rife with inconsistency and incoherence. For instance, "they hand down [redemption] in such a varied and discordant manner."[112] Irenaeus lists, by my count, seven different redemptive practices, or perspectives, or both. (1) "Some prepare a bridal chamber," complete with mystical invocations, which produces a spiritual marriage "after the likeness of the conjugal unions on high."[113] (2) Others are baptized in water with an invocation to "the unknown Father of the universe, into Truth, the Mother of all, into him who descended upon Jesus."[114] (3) "Still others pronounce Hebrew names over those who are being initiated in order to bewilder them still more,"[115] while (4) "others" invoke a different redemptive formula.[116] (5) A fifth position advocates that "it is useless to lead the people to the water. So they mix oil and water together."[117] (6) Certain Marcosians rejected this overtly visible—that is, material—consecration; instead, they insisted that "redemption too must be spiritual; for the inner spiritual man is redeemed by knowledge."[118] (7) The final position pertains to redemptive procedures at death, when the individual is anointed with water and oil while invocations are made.[119] All these ritual variations operated out of the shared belief that the death rite represented the culmination of the Marcosians' secret knowledge about the cosmos and its creator. The performance of the rite enabled followers of Marcus to shed their material beings and ascend without interference, as eternal beings, into the upper reaches of the cosmic real. As Irenaeus explains: "The purpose of this is that these [dying] may become incomprehensible and invisible to the Principalities and Powers, and that their inner person may ascend above the invisible things."[120]

In his description of the father of all Christian heresy, Simon Magus, Epiphanius similarly stressed the habits of the Simonians. He reports that Simon compelled his followers to make offerings consisting of a mixture of dirt, semen, and menstrual emissions. In the eyes of the Simonians, "these are mysteries of life and

---

111. David Brakke, *The Gnostics: Myth, Ritual, and Diversity in Early Christianity* (Cambridge, Mass.: Harvard University Press, 2010), suggests that the Valentinians (and likely the Marcosians as well) "[did] not separate themselves from other Christians; rather, many of them [were] members of the same congregations as followers of Irenaeus and his allies" (36).

112. Irenaeus, *Adv. haer.* 1.21.2 (SC 264:298).

113. Irenaeus, *Adv. haer.* 1.21.3 (SC 264:298).

114. Irenaeus, *Adv. haer.* 1.21.3 (SC 264:298).

115. Irenaeus, *Adv. haer.* 1.21.3 (SC 264:298).

116. "The name which has been hidden from every Deity, Dominion, and Truth, with which Jesus the Nazarene clothed himself within the regions of the light of Christ—of Christ who lives by the Holy Spirit for the angelic redemption" (*Adv. haer.* 1.21.3 [SC 264:300]).

117. Irenaeus, *Adv. haer.* 1.21.4 (SC 264:302).

118. Irenaeus, *Adv. haer.* 1.21.4 (SC 264:302).

119. Irenaeus, *Adv. haer.* 1.21.5.

120. Irenaeus, *Adv. haer.* 1.21.5 (SC 264:304). Translation modified.

the fullest knowledge" (γνώσεώς τε τῆς τελειοτάτης).¹²¹ "But for anyone," immediately corrects the bishop, "to whom God has given understanding, knowledge is above all else a matter of regarding these things as abomination instead, and death rather than life."¹²² The heretical preoccupation with fantastical "principalities and authorities" within "various heavens" condemns this higher cosmological ordering to the exuberance of the human mind.¹²³ Decried both because they supplant the singularity of the Godhead and because they elevate the human mind beyond its means, these opinions denature, in Epiphanius's reasoning, the truth of scripture, the life-giving force of the Lord, and the transcendent divinity itself.¹²⁴ "How," he asks, "can unnatural acts be life-giving, unless perhaps it is the will of demons?"¹²⁵ Because the customs of the heretics are the products of human arrogance—themselves the product of demonic temptation—they emerge as emblems of theological reasoning gone awry. And reasoning is not without tangible, observable consequences: *how* the heretics think and *what* they think about orients the totality of their error-filled way of life.

In the aggregate, the heresiologists' descriptions of the customs and habits of the heretics reveal their underlying disposition to be not only arrogant and deceitful but also savage and insane. The *Theodosian Code*, redacted in the first half of the fifth century, made repeated reference to the madness and insanity of the heretics, most famously in a law delivered on May 30, 428, by the emperors Theodosius II and Valentinian III:¹²⁶ "The madness of the heretics must be so suppressed that they shall know beyond doubt, before all else, that the churches which they have taken from the orthodox ... shall immediately be surrendered to the catholic church, since it cannot be tolerated that those who ought not to have churches of their own should continue to detain those possessed or founded by the orthodox."¹²⁷ Here, the operative principle is the radical disjuncture between heresy and orthodoxy, the need for a literal as well as theological wall between the two. As such, they can share neither customs nor buildings in common. An earlier law,

121. Epiphanius, *Pan.* 21.4.2 (GCS, n. F., 10:243).
122. Epiphanius, *Pan.* 21.4.2 (GCS, n. F., 10:243).
123. Epiphanius, *Pan.* 21.4.3 (GCS, n. F., 10:243).
124. Epiphanius, *Pan.* 21.4.3–4, 5.5–6 (GCS, n. F., 10:243, 244).
125. Epiphanius, *Pan.* 21.5.7 (GCS, n. F., 10:244).
126. On the history and compilation of the *Code*, see John F. Matthews, *Laying Down the Law: A Study of the Theodosian Code* (New Haven: Yale University Press, 2000).
127. *CTh* 16.5.65 (*Theodosiani libri XVI cum Constitutionibus Sirmondianis*, ed. Theodor Mommsen and Paul M. Meyer [Berlin: Weidmann, 1905], 878). Translation from Clyde Pharr, *The Theodosian Code and Novels and the Sirmondian Constitutions* (Union, N.J.: Lawbook Exchange, 2001), 462. On the *Theodosian Code* and the motif of insanity, see Richard Flower, "'The Insanity of the Heretics Must Be Restrained': Heresiology in the *Theodosian Code*," in *Theodosius II: Rethinking the Roman Empire in Late Antiquity*, ed. Christopher Kelly (New York: Cambridge University Press, 2013), 172–94. See also, Humfress, *Orthodoxy and the Courts in Late Antiquity*, 233–68.

delivered in February 407, specified this point in purely ideological terms: "We have recently published our opinion in regard to the Donatists. Especially, however, do we prosecute with the most deserved severity the Manichaeans and the Phyrgians and the Priscillianists. Therefore, *this class of men shall have no customs and no laws in common with the rest of mankind.*"[128] The laws of the *Code* promoted a policy of classificatory segregation based on theological, ecclesiastical, and customary principles. Taken together, the two laws cited here (among others to be discussed in the next chapter) displayed an insistence that the heretics must be kept apart from all things associated not just with orthodox Christianity but with the entirety of the human race. The heretics were, as the discursive logic of the *Code* implies, a category unto themselves. The laws regarding the heretics were informed by the fear of a perceived parity between orthodox and heretical Christians—a sense that the heretics would gain legitimacy by appearing to be orthodox—on the physical landscape of the Roman Empire. Heretics could not be acknowledged to have sacred space, and they certainly could not be permitted to have churches.

But looming over this effort to construct the heretics in very precise ways was the reality that heresy, like all ethnographic objects, was beyond the reach of those who studied it. And the heresiologists were aware of these epistemological and translational dilemmas. Reports about the customs and habits of heretics, as representations of diverse ways of life, became meditations on the limited capacity of Christian authors to know, comprehend, and codify the history of sectarianism. In writing people, the ethnographer constructed microscopic or particular ways of life, behavior, and so forth, while also aligning these particularities with causes and effects or macroscopic theories and paradigms of ethnographic discourse. Indeed, the heresiologists did not simply deny their objects of study the name "Christian." More important, they theorized with the heretics about the relationship between human difference, knowledge (its acquisition, study, and contemplation), and the epistemological limits governing the textualization of an ever-diversifying world. Heresiological literature illustrated that the Christian *oikoumenē* was mired in division, strife, and contestation; to survey its contents was not simply to describe its inhabitants but to articulate its possibility, its potential to be whole. What lingers, to borrow Emma Dench's observation about ancient Roman ethnography, is that the spread of Christianity feeds a self-reflective ethnographic process. Christianity, through its writers and preachers, emerges as its own ethnographical subject, bringing the gaze inward to trace its own history and its own foreignness in order to bracket its defects and articulate its own essence.[129] In itemizing the nature of the heretics, having arranged them genealogically,

---

128. *CTh* 16.5.40 (Mommsen and Meyer, 867–68); emphasis added.
129. Dench, *Romulus' Asylum*, 61–69.

chronologically, or typologically, the heresiologists attempt to impose order on their heterodox objects via claims to an ethnographic expertise, a proper understanding of the nature and limits of Christian knowledge about the world.

CONCLUSION: THE PROBLEM OF ETHNOGRAPHIC KNOWLEDGE

"The making of ethnography is artisanal, tied to the worldly work of writing," writes James Clifford in his introduction to the essays that constitute *Writing Culture*.[130] He further identifies six ways in which "ethnographic writing is determined": contextually (by environment), rhetorically (by expressive conventions), institutionally (within and against traditions, powers), generically (the distinctiveness of the ethnographic genre), politically (who represents whom and how), and historically (the ever-changing conventions of ethnography).[131] The discursive, poetic, and performative qualities of ethnographic writing draw attention to how ethnography is produced. The conditions within which an ethnography is written determine its questions, form, subject, and method.[132] Likewise, the facets or contingencies that govern our own histories in our times determine the reception and the writing of ethnography in ways beyond our control. For Clifford, writing—and ethnographic writing in particular—is only partly the property of its authors. The production of ethnography entails more than interpretation, representation, and translation; it engenders a system of relationships between subject and object, informants and expert, and reader and author, which, in turn, cultivate phenomenological and epistemological consonance and dissimilitude. The performative spectacle of ethnography, the fantastical and the ordinary alike, is bound, authoritatively, to the phenomenological experience of autopsy, translated and transformed by the words of the ethnographic page.

In emphasizing the discursive components of ethnography (over and against visualist tendencies), Clifford thrusts expressive speech and the anthropologist's own voice to the fore of the ethnographic experience. The once-automatic authority ascribed to the anthropologist (with respect to his object of study) slowly frayed in the wake of the complex and ongoing critiques of representation itself. As the classic ethnographies of the early and mid-twentieth century distinguished between authorial subjectivity and textual objectivity,[133] the former was

---

130. James Clifford, "Introduction: Partial Truths," in Clifford and Marcus, *Writing Culture*, 1–26, at 6.

131. Ibid. 6.

132. Ibid.

133. For examples of so-called classical ethnography, which tends not to problematize the relationship between subject and object, see the works of Ruth Benedict, Raymond Firth, Margaret Mead, Paul Radin, and Franz Boas. See also Mary Louise Pratt, "Fieldwork in Common Places," and Renato

understood to be a stylistic flourish, not a determinative feature. The ethnographic text was the reportage by an author but not of the author. Clifford, however, insists upon a renewed focus on the means by which cultural texts are produced, not simply interpreted:[134]

> An interest in the discursive aspects of cultural representation draws attention not to the interpretation of cultural "texts" but to their relations of production. Divergent styles of writing are, with varying degrees of success, grappling with these new orders of complexity—different rules and possibilities within the horizon of a historical movement.... It is enough to mention here the general trend toward a *specification of discourses* in ethnography: who speaks? who writes? when and where? with or to whom? under what institutional and historical constraints?

The ethnographer's role in the ethnography itself, both having written it and having to some extent produced the data, exposes the dilemma of ethnographic description: writing peoples is always representative and interpretive. It is never free from the inclinations and preconceptions of its author. In serving the interests of its author, ethnography necessarily translates peoples into the vernacular of its author and his or her culture.

In his *Works and Lives: The Anthropologist as Author*, Clifford Geertz analyzes the complexities undergirding the production of ethnographic texts. He describes the problem in terms of signature (how the author or author-function is "made manifest in the text") and in terms of discourse (what is it that the author authors?).[135] Signature has cast a long shadow over ethnographic writing precisely because it has framed the problem not in terms of narrative but in terms of epistemology, namely "how to prevent subjective views from coloring objective facts."[136] Geertz continues: "The clash between the expository conventions of author-saturated texts and those of author-evacuated ones that grows out of the particular nature of the ethnographic enterprise is imagined to be a clash between seeing things as one would have them and seeing things as they really are."[137] Though he finds the subjective anxieties of authorization to be overstated, anthropologists, he laments, have too often conceived the problem of ethnographic description in terms of "the mechanics of knowledge" surrounding fieldwork.[138] The self/other dilemma of fieldwork was

---

Rosaldo, "From the Door of His Tent: The Fieldworker and the Inquisitor," in Clifford and Marcus, *Writing Culture*, 27–50 and 77–97; Patricia A. Adler and Peter Adler, "Of Rhetoric and Representation: The Four Faces of Ethnography," *The Sociological Quarterly* 49 (2008): 1–30; and John Van Maanen, *Tales of the Field: On Writing Ethnography*. 2nd ed. (Chicago: University of Chicago Press, 2011).

134. Clifford, "Introduction: Partial Truths," 13.
135. Clifford Geertz, *Works and Lives: The Anthropologist as Author* (Stanford: Stanford University Press, 1988), 8.
136. Ibid. 9.
137. Ibid.
138. Ibid.

prioritized over those of self/text process (the former somehow conceived as naturally solving the latter). Geertz diagnoses the problem of anthropological authorship through a discussion of Foucault's "What Is an Author?," which asserts a difference between producers of texts and founders of discursivity, and Roland Barthes's "From Work to Text," which hones a distinction between authors who produce works and writers who produce texts.[139] For Geertz, the anthropologist is both the Barthesian author and writer, "caught between wanting to create a bewitching verbal structure . . . and wanting to communicate facts and ideas."[140] And although the distinction between writing and authoring may lack, for Geertz, intrinsic value,[141] it nonetheless signals the tension between the practicalities of textual representation in the service of information (the text as a physical object with knowledge) and consciousness about the vernacular of knowledge production. Process and product are linked together as inseparable facets of ethnographic writing.

Anthropology, in Geertz's estimation, is trapped "mule-like" between its scientific aspirations and its literary explication.[142] Framed in terms of signature and discourse, the problem becomes a negotiation of uncertainty: "The uncertainty that appears in signature terms as how far, and how, to invade one's text appears in discourse terms as how far, and how, imaginatively to compose it."[143] Although heresiology is an extreme example of tendentious textual representation, the genre represents a prolonged engagement with the struggle to capture people in the written word, even when such words are divorced from objectivity, fact, and accuracy. Writing peoples without regard for accuracy involves its own sense of perils, exasperations, and impossibilities. In that sense, the ensuing chapters take seriously the various rhetorical maneuvers of the heresiologists by which they signal their fears, hopes, and dilemmas in writing about the heretics. Though organizationally, contextually, and stylistically distinct, the heresiological works of Irenaeus, Hippolytus, Tertullian, Epiphanius, Augustine, and Theodoret all reflect the authors' efforts to delineate their own roles as ethnographers and caretakers of the Christian tradition. Although the ideological rigidity of Christian discourse—the imposition of a discourse of truth—resists certain ethnographic needs, the danger of knowledge in a radically changing world is framed not just as an institutional problem but as a conceptual one: What can be known?

The pervasive rhetoric of travel, discovery, and peoplehood connotes an imaginative sense of ethnographic exposition.[144] In conjunction with its overtly polemical

139. Ibid. 17–20.
140. Ibid. 20.
141. Ibid. 19–20.
142. Ibid. 20.
143. Ibid.
144. On the relationship between empire, imaginative ethnography, and Christian expansion, see Harry O. Maier, "Dominion from Sea to Sea: Eusebius of Caesarea, Constantine the Great, and the

tone and character, my reading of heresiology as ethnography demonstrates that while writing heretics was configured within the rhetoric of an emerging orthodox Christianity, analogous to the moralizing or civilizing discourse in Greco-Roman ethnography, the ethnographic process was equally perilous because of its inevitable finitude and limits. The genre of heresiology interrogates the value of social discourse, attempts to define and parse the limits of Christian knowledge, and organizes the world of heresy, all while reflecting on the very nature of writing itself. In searching for information about the heresies while trying to understand and even justify their place within a world governed by the Christian God, heresiology often became a grander disquisition on the processes by which the world itself, and its divine architect, could and can be comprehended and systematized. Understanding heresy was an endeavor to explicate the expansiveness and limits of human comprehension of both natural and divine phenomena. The particularities of heretical habits were the microcosms of a larger macroscopic vision and history of the Christian world, and this polemical ethnography encapsulates the tension between knowing, knowing too much, and the very capacity to know at all. But there remains an unpredictable, even elusive quality to heresiologies, which indicates their literary complexity. While the stated justification for these massive compilations of evidence and commentary is altogether obvious, their findings and the implications of those findings impose a series of uncalculated conceptual and theoretical hazards. Despite its superficial protestations, heresiology is an epistemological vortex, impossible both in its conceit and in its execution.

Exegesis of Empire," and Karla Pollmann, "Unending Sway: The Ideology of Empire in Early Christian Latin Thought," in *The Calling of the Nations: Exegesis, Ethnography, and Empire in a Biblical-Historic Present*, ed. Mark Vessey et al. (Toronto: University of Toronto Press, 2011), 149–75 and 176–99.

2

Comparing Theologies and Comparing Peoples

The Customs, Doctrines, and Dispositions of the Heretics

> *When modern historians adopt the strategies as well as the content of the polemicists' construction of heresy to define Gnosticism, they are not just reproducing the heresy of the polemicists; they are themselves propagating the politics of orthodoxy and heresy. We should therefore not be surprised to observe twentieth-century historians employing the category of Gnosticism to establish the bounds of normative Christianity—whether in Protestant anti-Catholic polemic, intra-Protestant debate, or the colonial politics of Orientalism.*
>
> —KAREN KING

Like Karen King's suggestion that the modern discourse of orthodoxy and heresy mimics the ancient heresiologists' constructed binary,[1] I posit that a similar phenomenon—a lingering correspondence between ancient and modern discourses—characterizes the historical interplay between theology, religion, and ethnography. Toward non-Christian peoples, early ethnographers and armchair anthropologists explicitly perpetuated ancient Christian attitudes in which notions of Christian heresy became barometers of broader ethnographic investigations of religion and religious peoples.[2] For both ancients and (early) moderns, Christian theological

---

1. This chapter's epigraph is quoted from Karen King, *What is Gnosticism?* (Cambridge, Mass.: Belknap Press, 2005), 54. On this point, see also ibid. 20–21 and 110–48.

2. One sees this on display most clearly in the work of Tomoko Masuzawa, *The Invention of World Religions; or, How European Universalism Was Preserved in the Language of Pluralism* (Chicago: University of Chicago Press, 2005), who notes that Vincent Milner, for example, explicitly marshals the discourse of sectarianism in the study of world religions (47). His 1860 treatise is titled *Religious Denominations of the World: Comprising a General View of the Origin, History and Condition of the Various Sects of Christians, the Jews, and Mahometans, as Well as the Pagan Forms of Religion Existing*

principles structured not only the internal diversity of Christianity but also the peoples *without* Christianity. The union of comparing peoples and comparing theologies was a natural outgrowth of biblical anthropology, which posited a divine-human unity; the Bible was the framework within which the heresiologists wrote their texts. Genesis 11 explained the diversity of peoples across the world, and Christians used this broad schematization to elaborate their own ideas about physical, mental, and cultural differences. But heretics, like primitives, produced an ethnological problem: heresy was both a part of and apart from the history of Christianity. The heresiologists mediated this paradox through theological comparison; they sought to identify the theological causes that had produced heresy. Theology became the overarching prism through which the customs, habits, and mentalities of peoples within the Christian world or the worldview of the Christian heresiologists (or both) were articulated.[3] As Keith Hopkins has aptly phrased it: "The centrality of correct dogma, as a defining characteristic of Christian praxis, was a religious innovation."[4]

What distinguishes Christian ethnography, then, from earlier Greek and Roman examples is the centrality of theology as an ethnographic sorting device. It is a distinction of degree of difference. Theology becomes a way to classify the internal diversity of a rapidly growing religious movement. As Daniel Boyarin has argued: "One important strand of early Christianity, beginning with Ignatius and Justin Martyr, decided to see *Christianismos* as an entirely novel form of identity. Christianity was a new thing, a community defined by adherence to a certain canon of doctrine and practice."[5] In this telling of the formative centuries of Christian history, Christian identity was shaped by theological interests; or to be more precise, it was constructed in relationship to Judaism and heresy in distinctly theological terms.[6] Constructing this theological discourse becomes the dominant preoccupation of Christian authors in late antiquity. It should come as no surprise, then, that descriptions of Christians both good and bad, Jews, and pagans are all sorted through a theological lens. The comparative theology of heresiology *func-*

---

in the Different Countries of the Earth (Philadelphia: Bradley, Garreston, 1860). For the history of the relationship between the science of religion (*Religionwissenschaft*), anthropology, and theology, see Masuzawa 14–71.

3. See Michael Maas, "'Delivered from Their Ancient Customs': Christianity and the Question of Cultural Change in Early Byzantine Ethnography," in *Conversion in Late Antiquity*, ed. Anthony Grafton and Kenneth Mills (Princeton: Princeton University Press, 2009), 152–88.

4. Keith Hopkins, "Christian Number and Its Implications," *JECS* 6.2 (1998): 185–226, at 218.

5. Daniel Boyarin, "Apartheid Comparative Religion in the Second Century: Some Theory and a Case Study," *JMEMS* 36.1 (2006): 3–24, at 9.

6. Jonathan Klawans has argued in a recent article, "Heresy without Orthodoxy: Josephus and the Rabbis on the Dangers of Illegitimate Jewish Beliefs," *JJMJS* 1 (2014): 99–126, that Josephus articulated an incipient heresiology, analogous in content though not in form, to early Christian heresiology.

tions in the same literary manner as the comparative ethnographies of the classical world. Comparative theology *is* Christian ethnography. Christian ethnography constitutes a method for describing the internal diversity of the Christian tradition. I am not suggesting that Christians invented the notion of comparative ethnography or comparative theology; rather, I am arguing that in the world of Christian late antiquity, the distinction between ethnography and theology was altogether blurred. The two become one and the same precisely because theology more often than not determined the discourse of Christian cultic practices as well as of everyday practice.

The heresiologists positioned theology as a fundamentally ethnographic category in order to render peoples as theological groups. They used theologically inflected groupism—the imagining of communal coherence—as a way of categorizing and analyzing human and Christian diversity. Heresiology functioned as a literary articulation of the Christian desire not only to explain the diversity of Christian peoples but also to cast the diversity of the world as a historical process governed by Christian theological principles. To explain human diversity the heresiologists developed a Christian logic that served as an enduring model for centuries of Christian ethnography and ethnology. In juxtaposing the heresiologists with the writings of colonial missionaries and Victorian anthropologists, the ethnographic impact of the Christian conceptualization of heresy and religiosity become increasingly clear. As Tomoko Masuzawa notes: "There was a general tendency among these early modern authors to regard all matters of religious diversity and plurality of opinions in the vocabulary of 'denominations' and 'sects,' regardless of how securely within or how far beyond the pale of 'the correct religion' they might lie."[7] I am not proposing that there is a neat linear genealogy from late antiquity to Victorian and ultimately contemporary anthropology; rather, I am trying to consider the historical and discursive antecedents that put into place the mixture and then the separation of theology and ethnography. The long history and influence of Christian theological perspectives on the world and the customs and habits of its residents begins as Christianity cements its position as the religion of the expansive Roman Empire. The Christian ethnographic gaze, with its enduring, complex grip over medieval, early modern, and modern writers, is but the natural outgrowth of the fusion of classical culture and a Christian ideology of singular truth.[8] And as we shall see, that melding has cast a profound and enduring shadow over scholarly discourse about religion and the religions of the world.

In this chapter, I focus on how the heresiologists produced their ethnographies in microscopic terms; what John Marincola defines, in the context of ancient

---

7. Masuzawa, *The Invention of World Religions*, 57–58.

8. Benjamin Isaac, *The Invention of Racism in Classical Antiquity* (Princeton: Princeton University Press, 2004).

historiography, as "the study of a people's customs and way of life."[9] The heresiologists, through their polemical explorations, take a keen interest in how the heretics live and behave as Christians: what the heretics do, what they believe, and how they comport themselves in relation to the heresiologists' understanding of the Christian tradition. The ethnographic language of the *Panarion* is both explicit and pervasive. Epiphanius dwells on customs and habits of the heretics in nearly every entry: from the sexual perversions of the Gnostics to the castration of the Valesians and the sacramental rites of the Collyridians.[10] I begin with a discussion of the relationship between the categories *religio* and *superstitio* in order to situate heresiology as a magnification of the ancient discourse dedicated to regulating religious customs and habits. From there, I consider the philosophic notion of the way of life as a particularly appropriate measure of Christian ethnographic idealism; that is, how the heresiologists construe their treatises as part of a larger discussion about the proper manner in which a Christian should live and exist in the world. I then turn to the heresies themselves, as imagined and described in the writings of the heresiologists. I investigate how Christian heresiologists wrote peoples in the most obvious and basic sense: through descriptions of their customs, habits, and beliefs. Through such description, the heresiologists pursued two related ethnographic interests: to present the heretics as geographical, social, and intellectual groups with discernible habits and to identify an underlying heretical disposition. In each case, the heresiologists enacted this agenda through their own theological emphases. In writing about heretical customs, the heresiologists enumerate how the heretics' behavior and doctrines reveal their underlying dispositions.

COMPARATIVE RELIGION, COMPARATIVE THEOLOGY, COMPARATIVE ETHNOGRAPHY

Ethnographic writing has always taken an interest in the so-called religious customs of peoples, both those living in close proximity to the writer and those residing at the farthest ends of the earth. Peoples were defined or, better yet, imagined as communities with regard to a variety of traits and practices: food, warfare, marriage, gender norms, dietary tendencies, and worship. One need take only a cursory glance at Diodorus Siculus's *Library of History,* Pliny's *Natural History,* Iamblichus's *On the Mysteries,* or Josephus's *Jewish Antiquities* to see the correlation between peoplehood and piety. The emphasis placed on notions of priesthood, worship, and ritual all serve as barometers of the classical, pre-Christian conception of community. Even before the onset of Christianity, discussions of the

---

9. John Marincola, *Authority and Tradition in Ancient Historiography* (New York: Cambridge University Press, 1997), 2.
10. Epiphanius, *Pan.* 26.3.3–5.6, 26.11.1–11; 58.1.1–4.17; 79.4.6–9.3.

worship of the gods were commonplace features of cultural exploration. The classicists John North, Mary Beard, and Simon Price explain that the Roman discourse of *religio* and *superstitio* was not a distinction between true and false gods but rather a discussion of "different *forms* of human relations with the gods."[11] The danger of *superstitio*, defined as either "excessive forms of behavior, that is 'irregular' religious practices ('not following the customs of the state')" or "excessive commitment, an excessive commitment to the gods," was not that it was false but rather that it "could be seen as an extremely powerful and dangerous practice which might threaten the stability of *religio* and the state."[12] Although the term *superstitio* originally referred to the improper action of the individual, it slowly came to demarcate, over the course of the late republic and early empire, the practices of groups. By the early second century C.E. it also denoted "the religious practices of particular foreign peoples."[13] Jews, Egyptians, and eventually Christians were all exemplars of *superstitio* before Christianity itself appropriated the term and imbued it with a new theological meaning.[14]

The Christian connotation of *religio*, as Jeremy Schott has persuasively shown, emerges most clearly in the writings of Lactantius, the Latin Christian rhetorician at the court of Diocletian.[15] For Lactantius, Christianity was the only true *religio*. The world was composed not of various religions but rather of superstitions, or peoples "who took unto themselves new rites, so that they honored, in place of the gods, the dead who they thought were taken from among men into heaven."[16] *Superstitio* had been fundamentally reconceptualized: it connoted no longer the falsity of how one worshipped but instead the falsity of what one worshipped and why.[17] Schott captures the monumentality of this newfound perception of *religio* and *superstitio*:[18]

---

11. Mary Beard, John North, and Simon Price, *Religions of Rome*, 2 vols. (New York: Cambridge University Press, 1998), 1:216.

12. Ibid. 1:217. For a clear example, see Livy, *History of Rome* 39.8.

13. Beard, North, and Price, *Religions of Rome*, 1:221.

14. For Christian identification of Judaism and paganism as *superstitio*, see Daniel Boyarin, *Border Lines: The Partition of Judaeo-Christianity* (Philadelphia: University of Pennsylvania Press, 2004), 214–20. For a history of *superstitio* in the ancient world, see Dale B. Martin, *Inventing Superstition: From the Hippocratics to the Christians* (Cambridge, Mass.: Harvard University Press, 2004), 1–9, 140–86, 207–25.

15. Jeremy Schott, *Christianity, Empire, and the Making of Religion* (Philadelphia: University of Pennsylvania Press, 2008), 96–106. On Lactantius and *religio*, see Wilfred Cantwell Smith, *The Meaning and End of Religion* (reprint, Minneapolis: Fortress Press, 1991), 27–28, 224; and Richard King, *Orientalism and Religion: Postcolonial Theory, India and 'The Mystic East'* (New York: Routledge, 1999), 36–38.

16. Lactantius, *Inst.* 4.28 (*PL* 6:538).

17. As Lactantius frames it: "And it makes a difference, really, why you worship, not how you worship, or what you pray for" (*Inst.* 4.28 [*PL* 6:537]).

18. Schott, *Christianity, Empire, and the Making of Religion*, 106.

Lactantius's redefinition of *religio* marks an important moment in the emergence of "religion" as a distinct category in the Western intellectual tradition. With its characterization of *religio* as an act of cultural memory, Cicero's etymology reflects a thought-world in which cultic practices, texts, and mythologies were not distinguished from other cultural forms. Lactantius, in contrast, defines true *religio* as a set of *theological* propositions ... that are authentic precisely because they transcend culture.

In this account, the intellectual contours of heresiology were shaped by the necessities of theological confession, disputation, and refutation. As Talal Asad succinctly puts it: "It is preeminently the Christian church that has occupied itself with identifying, cultivating, and testing belief as a verbalizable inner condition of true religion."[19] The discourse of true religion, *vera religio*, was in fact a distinctly Christian creation, and the dichotomy between orthodoxy and heresy was its most obvious manifestation.[20] For Christian writers of late antiquity, truth and falsity were not simply the metrics of religiosity but the very foundations of its semantic universe. The importance of this binary metric is that it functions to identify the propriety of customs and habits as well as beliefs and doctrines. But this semantic emphasis did not displace the prominence of ethnic criteria as part of the discourse of late antique religion.[21] The Christian emphasis on a system of truth that comes to reside in the discourse of *religio* was very much a product of ethnic argumentation. The Christian reinterpretation of *religio* was a narrative of ethnogenic corruption. Or, as Schott aptly puts it: "To write a history of religions is simultaneously to conduct an ethnographic survey."[22]

The comparative theology of the heresiologists—the contrasts drawn by Christians between themselves and Jews, Greeks, Romans, and heretics—was interwoven with comparative ethnography in two senses. First, I suggest that comparative theology has ethnographic effects: because Christians read and defined the world theologically, the peoples within it were identified in theological terms. For Christians, heretics occupied the same theological space as foreigners did for Romans. Christians imagined this foreignness through the strictures of theology. Second, in a more straightforward sense, theological ideas accompany

---

19. Talal Asad, "The Construction of Religion as an Anthropological Category," in his *Genealogies of Religion: Discipline and Reasons of Power in Christianity and Islam* (Baltimore: The Johns Hopkins University Press, 1993), 27–54, at 48.

20. On this point, see Gedaliahu (Guy) G. Stroumsa, "Religious Contacts in Byzantine Palestine," *Numen* 36.1 (1989): 16–42; and Boyarin, *Border Lines*, 1–73, which posits a direct correlation between the true/false dichotomy and the categories of orthodoxy and heresy.

21. See Denise Kimber Buell, *Why This New Race: Ethnic Reasoning in Early Christianity* (New York: Columbia University Press, 2005); and Aaron P. Johnson, *Ethnicity and Argument in Eusebius' Praeparatio Evangelica* (New York: Oxford University Press, 2006).

22. Schott, *Christianity, Empire, and the Making of Religion*, 97.

ethnographic details: heretics are described both by what they believe (or fail to believe) and by what they do. And as we shall see, there is a direct correlation between the heretics' ethos—their way of life—and their worldview or their theological metaphysics. I am arguing that the interplay between these two facets of Christian ethnography—theology as ethnography on the one hand and theology with ethnography on the other—orients and informs the heresiologists' descriptions and refutations of the heretics. Moreover, as Richard King observes, this emphasis of Christian religiosity carries over into medieval, early modern, and even modern discourse: "Modern discussion of the meaning and denotation of the term *religio* tend to follow Lactantius's etymology, thereby constructing a Christianized model of religion that strongly emphasizes *theistic belief*."[23] Indeed,[24]

> with a shift towards doctrine as constitutive of the essence of religion, the Christian appropriation of *religio* also represented a new emphasis upon the importance of the written word and its correct interpretation. Religion becomes primarily concerned with doctrine; 'true religion' becomes a matter of orthodoxy; and religion becomes a tradition precisely in so far as it can justify itself in terms of these ancient truths.

For the heresiologists, theology was a structure through which orthodox and heretical culture diverged. The heretics proposed various cosmological, mythographical, and hermeneutical doctrines that set in motion not only a chain of beliefs but also particular practices. In the heresiologists' descriptions of the death rites of the Marcosians, a second-century Gallic offshoot of the Valentinians, theological determinism takes center stage. According to both Irenaeus and Hippolytus, the Marcosians' understanding of the cosmos' structure produced a ritualized response. They performed a baptismal rite at death, which provided an individual with secret theological knowledge about the cosmos and the Godhead.[25] The function of the ritual unction at death, as Nicola Denzey Lewis explains, was twofold:[26]

> First, deathbed *apolytrosis* was a necessary service, since the Marcosians believed that it equipped the dying individual with the information and protection necessary to navigate the hypercosmic realms successfully without becoming trapped in the Middle. Second, since all the "perfected" had to gather in the Pleroma together before the cosmos could be "rectified" at the Eschaton, it was crucial to perform those sacraments on earth that would assure that the Marcosian would indeed be perfect; without sacramental transformation, the ascending spirits could get trapped in the Middle so that, presumably, the number of the Perfect in the Pleroma would never be completed.

---

23. King, *Orientalism and Religion*, 37.
24. Ibid. 38.
25. See Irenaeus, *Adv. haer.* 1.21; and Hippolytus *Ref.* 6.41.
26. Nicola Denzey Lewis, "Apolytrosis as Ritual and Sacrament: Determining a Ritual Context for Death in Second-Century Marcosian Valentinianism," *JECS* 17.4 (2009): 525–61, at 557.

Cosmology does more than merely explain Marcosian praxis; it demands a set of actions in return. Theology not only orients the Marcosians' general way of life; it actually governs its particulars. As Karen King rightly notes of the heresiologists: "They tended to focus explicitly on doctrinal matters, although, given that they considered immoral practices and schism to be the direct consequence of poor theology, the rhetoric ranged more widely. As a result of this association, heresy could be determined either by doctrinal deviation or by social deviation."[27] Theology and practice in tandem solidify the human position within a cosmology of spheres, layers, and aeons. That is, theology explains the human condition, and the corresponding practice—in this case redemption—recapitulates that theological position with actions. The Marcosian redemption rite was the ritual enactment of a theological worldview.

Comparative theology functions for Christians as the essential expression for writing peoples in the ancient world. Once Christianity emerged onto the Mediterranean stage, it became of paramount importance to organize the world in relationship to Christian norms and principles, even as those principles were themselves being formulated. It is telling, indeed, that as Epiphanius begins his *Panarion*, he expresses a deep fear about his heresiological treatise: "The very necessity for the words of the controversy is putting me in such a sweat, on account of the readers' dissuasion and to show that these persons' practices, rites, and doctrines are the furthest thing from my mind and thus prove my independence of them with the words and the bitterness of my opposition."[28] Setting aside the sincerity and rhetorical posturing of Epiphanius's anxiety, I am concerned here with *what* it is he claims to fear, for it reveals the broad components of his heresiological ethnography. His treatise, he explains, breaks down along three lines of investigation: customs, religious rites, and teachings. His discussion of practices will include issues of diet, sex, care of the body, marriage, among others, while his examination of the heretics' rites consists mainly of baptismal, sacrificial, and eucharistic practices. Matters of doctrine, more literally "teachings," encompass an expansive list: cosmology, Christology, soteriology, and so on. The inclusion of doctrinal matters as an equivalent source of fear reflects the centrality of theology within the heresiologists' ethnographic project. For Epiphanius, theology, as much as philosophy, geography, and astrology, shaped the way the world was to be defined, delimited, and represented in texts.

Building on Greek, Roman, and Jewish philosophical traditions and ethnographic texts, Christians conceptualized a way of life as both lived and thought. It is a matter both of doctrine and of practice. But the transformative legacy of Christian ethnographic reasoning was the magnification of theological thought as a

---

27. King, *What is Gnosticism?*, 33.
28. Epiphanius, *Pan.* pro. 1.2.4 (GCS, n. F., 10:156).

category of comparative analysis both for heretical and orthodox Christians.[29] Indeed, Athanasius of Alexandria reminds his readers at the very start of his *Orations against the Arians*, "that the *thought* of the heretics [the Arians] was never, nor is it now, with us."[30] The heresiologists were preoccupied with using theological thinking as a tool of classification. For them, theology served as an interpretive lens through which to associate and dissociate peoples. And erroneous thinking signaled a deeper heretical disposition. The heretics' beliefs and practices illuminated their anti-Christian dispensation. The heresiologists not only tried to identify the fundamental character of heresy but also to identify the ways in which that character could be overcome.

DISPUTING WAYS OF LIFE

In his *Rule against the Heretics*, Tertullian announces an abrupt transition toward the end of his text. Having spent a great many words treating the heretics as more or less a common genus, he concedes that he should engage them more specifically: "I must not leave out a description of the heretics' way of life: futile, earthly, all too human, lacking in gravity, in authority, in discipline, as suits their faith."[31] While Tertullian used the discourse of "way of life" to evince the association between the heretics and the philosophers—a fundamental part of his broader argument that the heretics were a perverse admixture of philosophy and Christianity—his remark simultaneously communicated his ethnographic disposition: his interest in the customs, habits, and behavior—the way of life—of the heretics.[32] For, as John M. Cooper has shown in his *Pursuits of Wisdom*, philosophy in the ancient world was not just a speculative pursuit; rather it was described as a comprehensive approach to living that included diet, dress, pedagogy, bodily discipline, moral outlook, epistemology, contemplation, and ritual.[33] And although Cooper too easily separates philosophical and religious ways of life,[34] his overarching point is that systematic modes of thinking, whether guided by reason and

---

29. See Kenelm Burridge, *Encountering Aborigines, A Case Study: Anthropology and the Australian Aboriginal* (Elmsford, N.Y.: Pergamon Press, 1973), 8–23, 38–42.

30. Athanasius, *C. Ar.* 1.1.1, ed. William Bright (Oxford: Clarendon Press, 1870), 1: ὅτι τῶν τοιούτων οὔτε ἦν, οὔτε νῦν ἐστι 'μεθ' ἡμῶν' τὸ φρόνημα; emphasis added.

31. Tertullian, *Praescr.* 41.1 (SC 46:146). I have followed (with my own alterations) S.L. Greenslade's translation of *The Prescriptions against the Heretics* in *Early Latin Theology: Selections from Tertullian, Cyprian, Ambrose, and Jerome* (Louisville: Westminster John Knox Press, 1956), 25–64.

32. The uniqueness of this association is severely undercut by the contemporaneous Christian discourse among the apologists that presented Christianity as a philosophy in its own right. See Pierre Hadot, *What Is Ancient Philosophy?*, trans. Michael Chase (Cambridge, Mass.: Belknap Press, 2004), 253–58.

33. John M. Cooper, *Pursuits of Wisdom: Six Ways of Life in Ancient Philosophy from Socrates to Plotinus* (Princeton: Princeton University Press, 2012), 1–23.

34. Ibid. 9–11.

rational insight or by the dicta of scripture (philosophical or religious worldviews), did not simply orient human behavior but steered the totality of one's life. Philosophical and later Christian texts supplied a sort of aspirational ethnography: they prescribed the way an individual (or member of a philosophical school) should orient himself or herself. They wrote peoples generically and didactically. As Pierre Hadot writes of the Hellenistic and Roman eras: "Philosophy was a mode of existing-in-the-world, which had to be practiced at each instant, and the goal of which was to transform the whole of the individual's life."[35] Though these approaches to the ideal life differed—just as the heretics' conceptualizations of the Trinity or the canon of scripture differed—they shared a desire to articulate the relationship between thought and action.

With his segue into the way of life of the heretics, Tertullian offers brief remarks about the heretics' attitude toward baptism, catechumens, theology, women, ordination, proselytization, and ecclesiastical organization. As he describes the heretics with broad strokes—still evaluating them as a single entity of sorts—the underlying logic of his description is comparative: the customs and habits of the heretics are in opposition to the normative practice of true Christians. I quote Tertullian at length:[36]

> To begin with, one cannot tell who is a catechumen and who is baptized. They come in together, listen together, pray together. Even if any of the heathen arrive, they are quite willing to cast that which is holy to the dogs and their pearls before swine. The destruction of discipline is to them simplicity, and our attention to it they call affectation. They are in communion with everyone everywhere. Differences of theology are of no concern to them as long as they are all agreed in attacking the truth. They are all puffed up, they all promise knowledge. Their catechumens are perfect before they are instructed. As for the women of the heretics, how forward they are! They have the impudence to teach, to argue, to perform exorcisms, to promise cures, perhaps even to baptize. Their ordinations are hasty, irresponsible and unstable. Sometimes they appoint novices, sometimes men tied to secular office, sometimes renegades from us, hoping to bind them by ambition as they cannot bind them by truth. Nowhere can you get quicker promotion than in the camp of the rebels, where your mere presence is a merit. So one man is bishop today, another tomorrow. The deacon of today is tomorrow's reader, the priest of today is tomorrow a layman. For they impose priestly functions even upon laymen.

We see here in Tertullian's description a few of the common threads of heresiological ethnography, all of which are tied to an overarching heretical mentality: the arrogance of the heretical way of life informs their entire vision of Christianity.

---

35. Pierre Hadot, *Philosophy as Way of Life: Spiritual Exercises from Socrates to Foucault*, ed. Arnold I. Davidson, trans. Michael Chase (Malden, Mass.: Blackwell, 1995), 265.
36. Tertullian, *Praescr.* 41.2–8 (SC 46:146–48).

The heretics jeopardize the sanctity of baptism and the status of the baptized; they lack discipline (ritually, bodily, dispositionally, etc.); they empower women to act with authority within the congregation; they are indifferent to the particularities of theological doctrine; they tarnish the procedures of ordination; they disrupt notions of ecclesiastical hierarchy; and they trivialize priestly training. The heretics, through their various teachings and traditions, offer an alternative way of living Christianly that is oriented around, in Tertullian's telling, a hubristic disposition. They display a disregard for theological doctrine and impugn the ecclesiastical establishment.

Epiphanius's *Panarion* and Augustine's *De haeresibus* radically expand Tertullian's list of the heretics' customs and habits. Epiphanius explicitly associates sectarianism with ways of living. He notes, for instance, that Adam, the progenitor of the human race, lived in a time of univocity: there were no names for differences of opinions, beliefs, "or a distinctive way of life."[37] In the *Recapitulations*, pseudo-Epiphanius identifies the "superior way of life" of the Pharisees with a series of practices. They practice continence for a time and are celibate; they fast, clean vessels, tithe, pray constantly, and dress in shawls and robes.[38] When Epiphanius reaches the heresy of Marcion, he incorporates into his *Panarion* a separate tripartite treatise he tells us he had previously written against Marcion. The treatise begins by enumerating the contents of Marcion's canon in order to provide "a training ground . . . for the refutation of the strange doctrines of his invention."[39] The treatise culminates in a stylized dialectic comprised of Marcion's *scholia* (opinions) and Epiphanius's *elenchi* (refutations). In a dispute over the correct interpretation of Luke 11.5–13—especially Jesus's dictum about the distribution of loaves, fishes, and eggs—Epiphanius describes Marcion's fallacious interpretation as attesting a broader and equally fallacious way of life. He writes:[40]

> The willfulness of the swindler's way of life is exposed by this text. The way of life he practices is not for continence' sake, or for the good reward and hope of the contest, but for impiety and the badness of a wrong opinion. For he teaches that one must not eat meat, and claims that those who eat flesh are liable to the judgment, as they would be for eating souls. But this is altogether foolish. The flesh is not the soul; the soul is in the flesh.

Marcion argues, as do Valentinus, Colorbasus, the Gnostics, and the Manichaeans, that the "reincarnation of souls as well as transmigrations of the souls of ignorant persons" is "reembodied in each of the animals until it comes to awareness, and so,

---

37. Epiphanius, *Pan.* 1.1 (GCS, n. F., 10:169). In the pseudo-Epiphanian *Recapitulations* 1.3.1, the age of Hellenism is identified as one "of a more civilized way of life" (GCS, n. F., 10:163).
38. Pseudo-Epiphanius, *Rec.* 1.15.1 (GCS, n. F., 10:167).
39. Epiphanius, *Pan.* 42.11.2 (GCS 31:107).
40. Epiphanius, *Pan.* 42.11.15 *refut.* 24a–b (GCS 31:133).

cleansed and set free, departs to heaven."[41] Marcion's insistence on the radical disjuncture between soul and body ("that the body is a prison") tarnishes the Lord's equal emphasis on "our sojourn here in the flesh, and the coming resurrection of flesh and soul."[42] Epiphanius's digression on the soul, however, only intensifies his ire toward this argument about abstention from meat, which necessitates that he return to the subject: "I am going to speak once more of your bogus way of life, since you say eating meat is wicked and unlawful."[43] Fish and eggs, Epiphanius insists, are described as good gifts; they are divinely sanctioned. Heresiology, we might say, is not just a repository of polemical ethnography but also an active site of negotiation and contestation. In this instance, Epiphanius communicates his heresiology as a disquisition on contours of proper Christian conduct and dogma.[44] For Epiphanius, then, heresiological ethnography is descriptive, proscriptive, and prescriptive all at the same time.

With its pared-down rhetoric and straightforward structure (what I would call a list) Augustine's *De haeresibus* provides brief but quintessential descriptions of eighty-eight heresies. He begins his text by quoting back the specific requests of Quodvultdeus, the deacon of Carthage, who had pleaded with him for a handbook of heretics. Augustine notes that he had specified his desire to know what the heretics held with respect to:[45]

> "the faith, the Trinity, baptism, penance, Christ as man, Christ as God, the resurrection, the Old and New Testaments.... And absolutely every point on which they disagree with truth." Then you added, "those heresies which have Baptism and those which do not, and those after which the church baptizes, though she does not rebaptize; how she receives those who come to her, and what response she makes to teach of them in terms of law, authority, and reason."

Taking his cue from Quodvultdeus, Augustine emphasizes many of the particulars the deacon had inquired after while also giving prominent place to other pressing matters associated with the heretics, including diet, cosmology, worship rites, marriage, theodicy, communalism, Mariology, psychology (in the ancient sense), eschatology, anthropology, and other eclectic and *outré* habits. Augustine, at Quodvultdeus's request, essentialized the heretics into terse literary units.

---

41. Epiphanius, *Pan.* 42.11.15 *refut.* 24d (GCS 31:133).
42. Epiphanius, *Pan.* 42.11.15 *refut.* 24f (GCS 31:134).
43. Epiphanius, *Pan.* 42.11.15 *refut.* 24i (GCS 31:134).
44. See Jon Dechow, *Dogma and Mysticism in Early Christianity: Epiphanius of Cyprus and the Legacy of Origen* (Macon, Ga.: Mercer University Press, 1988).
45. Augustine, *Haer.* praef. 3.37–46 (CCSL 46:287). Capitalization modified. The prominence of baptism and rebaptism almost certainly derives from the contentious ecclesiastical rifts with the Donatists in North Africa. See Augustine, *De baptismo contra Donatistas*; and Geoffrey G. Willis, *Saint Augustine and the Donatist Controversy* (London: SPCK, 1950), 38–43, 52–68, 79–104, 119–25, 146–67.

Consider the heresy of the Adamians, named after Adam because "they imitate the naked state which was his before the sin."[46] More tellingly, Augustine reports, they oppose marriage, because Adam and Eve did not have sex before the fall. Men and women seek to embody through mimesis the prefallen state of humanity. And so "men and women assemble naked; they listen to the readings naked; they celebrate the sacraments naked. And for this reason they think their church is paradise."[47] The Adamians propose a model of Christian living that aspires to a biblical ideal. And in his three longer entries, most especially on the Manichaeans, Augustine expends great energy to identify the contours of their way of life. And so he tells us about Mani's idea of a radical dualism, between good and evil, eternal and coeternal, light and darkness.[48] He goes on to explain the Manichaeans' effort to return to God by way of purification—on ships made out of the substance of God—and how the consumption of food both inhibits and enables this process of return.[49] Throughout this brief tour of the world of the Manichaeans, he observes their abstention from meat, eggs, milk, and wine, their belief that agriculture is murder, their disdain for marriage and baptism, their association of Christ with the serpent of Genesis, their worship of the sun and moon, and their denial of free will.[50]

There is, however, an overarching logic to what Augustine labels Mani's "insane teaching (*insana doctrina*)."[51] As he explains, the Manichaeans "think that the substance of God is purified in their Elect by a kind of life the Manichaean Elect live, as though they live more holily and excellently than their Hearers. For they wanted their church to be composed of these two ranks, that is, the Elect and the Hearers."[52] Augustine's description ascribes to the Manichees a particular mode of life, born out of a dualistic ideological system. The implications of this system as a thoroughgoing way of life are fleshed out more fully in Augustine's famous debate with the Manichaean bishop Faustus.[53] The resulting text, *Against Faustus, a Manichee*, manufactured a debate between two learned ecclesiastical leaders, each of whom attacked his opponent as he defended his own version of the Christian

---

46. Augustine, *Haer.* 31 (CCSL 46:304).
47. Augustine, *Haer.* 31 (CCSL 46:304–5).
48. Augustine, *Haer.* 46.2–5.
49. Augustine, *Haer.* 46.6–8.
50. Augustine, *Haer.* 46.11–13, 46.15, 46.17–19.
51. Augustine, *Haer.* 46.1.2 (CCSL 46:312).
52. Augustine, *Haer.* 46.5.25–30 (CCSL 46:313).
53. See also Augustine's *De moribus Ecclesiae Catholicae* (*On The Catholic Ways of Life/Customs*) and *De moribus Manichaeorum* (*On Manichaean Ways of Life/Customs*), which, though often treated as one work, are technically two separate treatises. In the first case, Augustine describes—one may say idealizes—the catholic attitudes toward God, man, morality, and the world. In the second treatise, Augustine both describes and refutes the positions of the Manichaeans.

tradition.[54] In chapter 20, Faustus attempted to distinguish between a schism and a sect. The former is a group that "holds the same opinions and worships with the same ritual as others but wants only a division of the congregation," whereas a sect holds different opinions and worships God far differently.[55] Faustus rejected the assertion that Manichaeans were a schism either of pagans or of Jews.[56] In both cases, Manichaeans were simply too different from either group to be considered a schismatic relation; for "a schism ought to change either nothing or only a little from its origins."[57] The Manichaeans failed this test in relation to both Jews and pagans. They rejected the God of the Hebrew Bible (as well as the text itself) and vigorously contested pagan ritual practices. By contrast, Faustus mused, catholics ought to consider themselves a schismatic people:[58]

> In splitting off from the gentiles you took with you first of all the idea of monarchy, that is, the belief that all things come from God. But you transformed their sacrifices into agapes [communal meals] and their idols into martyrs whom you worship with similar prayers. You placate the shades of the dead with wine and meals; you celebrate the solemn feast days of the nations, such as the calends and the solstices, along with them. *From their life* [i.e., way of life] you have in fact changed nothing. You are indeed a schism from your parent group, having nothing different except your place of assembly.

Faustus tied catholic Christianity to the pagans, from whom he argued they were marginally distinct. To make that connection explicit, he argued that catholics embraced an *incorrect* way of living. They had foolishly taken on the practices and traditions of the gentiles. For Faustus, the catholics' way of life was not, in fact, sufficiently different from the gentiles' to merit the designation "Christian."[59] The point is that the charge of fallacious modes of living went both ways: orthodox and heretical writers both accused one another of false living. For both sides, the notion of way of life presented an opportunity to construct an ethnographic polemic.[60]

---

54. See Paula Fredriksen's *Augustine and the Jews: A Christian Defense of Jews and Judaism* (New York: Doubleday, 2008), 213–352; and François Decret, *Aspects du manichéisme dans l'Afrique romaine: Les controverses de Fortunatus, Faustus et Felix avec saint Augustin* (Paris: Études Augustiniennes, 1970), 51–70.

55. Augustine, *Faust.* 20.3 (*PL* 42:369). Translations from *Answer to Faustus, a Manichean*, ed. Boniface Ramsey, trans. Roland J. Teske, vol. 1, part 20 of *The Works of St. Augustine: A Translation for the 21st Century* (Hyde Park: New City, 2007), 262.

56. Augustine, *Faust.* 20.4.

57. Augustine, *Faust.* 20.4 (*PL* 42:370). On the relationship between schism and heresy, see Maureen A. Tilley, "When Schism Becomes Heresy in Late Antiquity: Developing Doctrinal Deviance in the Wounded Body of Christ," *JECS* 15.1 (2007): 1–21.

58. Augustine, *Faust.* 20.4 (*PL* 42:370); emphasis added.

59. Augustine, *Faust.* 20.4.

60. The remainder of chapter 20 is Augustine's twofold response to Faustus: He continues his assault on the theology, practices, and rites of the Manichaeans (i.e., their way of life); and he defends the catholic way of life from the charge that it derives from paganism.

The various examples collected here display competing modes of expressing the nature, practices, and spirituality of the Christian way of life. The disputes between Epiphanius and Marcion or Augustine and Faustus revolved around an understanding of what the Christian way of life entailed. The heresiologists insisted on a particular mode of living Christianly, whereas the heretics presented another. Hadot usefully describes how Christians represented their worldview as a way to live by appropriating the discourse of Greek and Roman philosophy:[61]

> Like Greek philosophy, Christian philosophy presented itself both as a discourse and as a way of life. In the first and second centuries, the time of the birth of Christianity, philosophical discourse in each school consisted mainly of explicating texts by the school's founders. . . . The discourse of Christian philosophy was also, quite naturally, exegetic, and the exegetical schools of the Old and the New Testament, like those opened in Alexandria by Clement of Alexandria's teacher, or by Origen himself, offered a kind of teaching which was completely analogous to that of contemporary philosophical schools.

Hadot goes on to trace a philosophical lineage in which Christianity created spiritual exercises to actualize spiritual progress.[62] The ideals of self-mastery and self-control, embodied most pronouncedly in monastic movements of the fourth and fifth century, were spiritual practices meant to provide a therapeutic concourse for the soul's progress. Even if monasticism was, in Hadot's word, the "perfection" of the Christian way of life, it did not emerge in an historical vacuum.[63] Rather, scholars rightly emphasize the ways in which Christian asceticism was formed as both a practice and a discourse in dialogue with sacred texts, theological debates, philosophical speculation, and ecclesiastical discontent.[64] As an expression of a Christian lifestyle, monasticism provided an answer to the question of how an individual should behave, both by living and by believing, as a Christian. But the resolution to this question was not singularly the domain of monastic writers and practitioners.[65] It was instead, I suggest, equally the concern of the heresiologists. Indeed, Augustine reports, via Filastrius, that an unnamed heresy (number 72 in *De haeresibus*) broadly champions the way of life of all heretics both in terms of practice and belief: "[Filastrius] says that from Rhetorius there arose a heresy of amazing stupidity which claims that all heretics live correctly and spoke the

---

61. Hadot, *What is Ancient Philosophy?*, 239.
62. Ibid. 242–48.
63. Ibid. 242, 247.
64. See William J. Harmless, *Desert Christians: An Introduction of the Literature of Early Monasticism* (New York: Oxford University Press, 2004).
65. Tellingly, however, Epiphanius insists in *De fide* 21.3 that monks and nuns in their status as virgins represent the apex of the catholic church.

truth."⁶⁶ For the heresiologists, to posit the proper expression of Christian living required an investigation into the depths and details of alternative modes of living Christianly. Heresiological ethnography thus served as the dialectical conjunction of proscriptive description and aspirational prescription. It was in heresiology that the ethnographic disposition turned most emphatically and sharply inward, in order to assess the experiential potential and propriety of the diverse and diversifying Christian world.

THE MESSALIANS: IMAGINING HERETICAL GROUPS

Entry 57 in Augustine's *De haeresibus*, the last for which Augustine explicitly credits Epiphanius as his source, is the heresy of the Messalians.⁶⁷ Their name, Augustine reports, is "derived from the Syrian language," though in "Greek they are called the Εὐχῖται; thus they get their name from praying."⁶⁸ He further notes that these People Who Pray are associated with the sects called the Euphemites, Martyrians, and Satanists (though Epiphanius had specified that these were pagan sects).⁶⁹ The Messalians follow an extreme way of life—so extreme, in fact, that it renders them heretics: "These people pray to such an excess that people have judged that they should, on this account, be included among the heretics."⁷⁰ The Messalians, in short, are heretics as much for what they do as for how they do it. According to Augustine, the Messalians misinterpret the scriptural injunction, from Luke 18.1 and 1 Thess. 5.7, to pray unceasingly. He further insists that a "sound interpretation" of these verses means not that one must pray always and at all times but rather that one must "not omit certain times of prayer on any day."⁷¹ But lest the reader think that it is prayer alone that constitutes the heresy of the Messalians, Augustine adds two other details about their way of life. First, Augustine reports that some say "that they tell fantastic and ridiculous tales about the purification of souls, such as, that a sow along with piglets are seen to leave the

---

66. Augustine, *Haer.* 57 (CCSL 46:335).

67. Augustine, *Haer.* 57 (CCSL 46:325–26). There are several studies devoted the Messalians, though the discourse is overwhelmingly interested in accessing the true, historical Messalians (i.e., deducing their origins, doctrines, practices, etc.). See, for example, Klaus Fitschen, *Messalianismus und Antimessalianismus: Ein Beispiel ostkirchlicher Ketzergeschichte* (Göttingen: Vandenhoeck & Ruprecht, 1998); Columba Stewart, *"Working the Earth of the Heart": The Messalian Controversy in History, Texts, and Language to A.D. 431* (Oxford: Clarendon Press, 1991); and Daniel Caner, *Wandering, Begging Monks: Spiritual Authority and the Promotion of Monasticism in Late Antiquity* (Berkeley and Los Angeles: University of California Press, 2002).

68. Augustine, *Haer.* 57 (CCSL 46:326).

69. Augustine, *Haer.* 57 (CCSL 46:326); Epiphanius, *Pan.* 80.1.3–4, 80.3.1–3.

70. Augustine, *Haer.* 57 (CCSL 46:326).

71. Augustine, *Haer.* 57 (CCSL 46:326).

mouth of a man when he is purified."[72] Although no other heresiologist reports on this particular detail, the other matter Augustine mentions about the Messalians is well attested among the later heresiologists.[73] "The Euchites," Augustine notes, "are said to believe that monks may not do any work to support themselves and thus profess to be monks so that they may be completely free from work."[74] The ostensible point of the Messalians' abstention from labor is to eliminate distractions from a life of continuous prayer.[75] The point of Augustine's brief remarks is rather simple: the Messalians misconceive their Christian piety. Prayer must be part of living Christianly but not to such an extent that it forecloses other scriptural obligations or fosters a particularly divisive Christian mentality. It is a question of interpretive balance and harmony. The Messalians, like those who practiced *superstitio* before them, err in their extremism; they err in the manner in which they conduct their lives.[76]

For Augustine, the Messalians were etymologically defined by what they did, even though they did more than what their name indicated. When Augustine's summary is juxtaposed with Epiphanius's protracted discussion of the Messalians, the ethnographic disposition comes into especially sharp relief, for no Christian text better illustrates the heresiologists' interest in collecting and arranging ethnographic knowledge than the *Panarion*. Indeed, the Messalians of the *Panarion* emerge as a discrete people defined by particular customs, habits, and doctrines. This ethnographic fashioning, the reification of essences, worked not only to create similarity across the heretics' diversity—to identify generalizable dispositions—but also to fashion communal dispositions or dispositional kinship.[77] By investigating how theological ethnography worked to describe, essentialize, and refute the heretics all at the same time, we can see at the microscopic level how a heresiologist, in this case Epiphanius, constructs a portrait of a heretical sect, blending history, biography, exegesis, and polemic to create an ethnographic caricature. That caricature, however, works not only to excise specific doctrines and customs from the church but also to create a comparative theological framework in which the heretics come to embody certain types of behaviors and interpretations.

---

72. Augustine, *Haer.* 57 (CCSL 46:326).
73. See Epiphanius, *Pan.* 80; and Theodoret, *Haer.* 4.11.
74. Augustine, *Haer.* 57 (CCSL 46:326).
75. This correlation is explicit in Theodoret, *Haer.* 4.11, though not in Augustine's *Haer.* 57. Epiphanius makes the connection implicit; see below.
76. On extremism and excess in Epiphanius, see *Pan.* 7.1.1; 13.1.4; 24.2.1; 26.3.4, 26.19.2; 27.2.9; 31.21.3, 31.24.1; 32.3.8; 34.22.4; 37.2.3, 37.8.3; 42.1.5; 48.4.6; 57.2.9, 57.10.1; 63.5.8; 64.3.4; 66.2.3–5; 67.1.3; 68.3.3; 76.20.3, 76.36.7; 79.1.4–5, 79.4.7; 80.4.1, 80.5.6.
77. For the language of kinship among the Gnostics, see David Brakke, *The Gnostics: Myth, Ritual, and Diversity in Early Christianity* (Cambridge, Mass.: Harvard University Press, 2010), 71–75.

In painting a particular portrait of the Messalians, Epiphanius fashions them into an irreducible core, which is revealed to be largely dispositional. The emphasis Epiphanius places on their contentious disposition is a way to ascribe to them a common personality, to classify them as a type of un-Christian people. He also uses this discussion of the Messalians, his final entry of the *Panarion*, to reflect more broadly about the theological justifications behind extreme modes of piety, especially the competing obligations and freedoms associated with the ascetical way of life. The renunciatory impulse—the idea of discipline and its limits—emerges as both a problematic and desirable mode of living throughout the *Panarion*.[78] In the case of the Messalians, Epiphanius contrasts proper and improper theologies of labor while simultaneously denouncing one expression of monastic piety and valorizing another. His account of the Messalians illustrates how the discourse of heresy is mediated through differing interpretations of the proper parameters of ascetical living. Epiphanius imagines the ideal ascetic—and later comes to celebrate ascetics as the epitome of the church—in contrast to not only the Messalians but also the monks upon whom the Messalians model their behavior. As Daniel Caner has observed about the People Who Pray: "We are dealing with a post-Constantinian ecclesiastical process of defining, consolidating, homogenizing, or rejecting forms of Christian life and expression that now came under the direction of a largely Mediterranean-based, Greco-Roman hierarchy with its own institutional perspective and concerns."[79] But the Messalians not only subscribe to a shared way of life; they also share a common disposition. And although much of the language of the Messalians' commonality is imaginary, following Benedict Anderson's famous analysis of the ways in which nations produce a shared culture, ideology, and tradition—with the heresiologists imagining heretical and orthodox culture despite its variation and diffusion—it also points toward the ethnographization of Christianity from the inside.[80] Doctrine and behavior, taken together, make up the backbone of the ethnographic analysis of Christianity's own internal diversity. The emphasis on doctrinally informed behavior signals a key concern of the *Panarion*: the presentation of the Messalians not just as an abstract intellectual movement but as a *lived and living* group of people. Christian writers made theological and doxographic disputes into ethnographic ones not only by blending them but also by consistently marshaling the language of peoples, groups, behavior, and disposition. That is, the heresiologists made the heretics into groups with discernible personalities that gave them the appearance of social and theological cohesion.

78. On the association between the heretics and various forms of renunciation (including food, marriage, sex, and possessions), see *Pan.* 30.17.3; 61.1.1–11; 75.3.1–3, 75.3.9. On heresy and attitudes toward asceticism, see *Pan.* 13.1.1; 16.1.2; 23.2.5; 26.13.1; 40.1.4, 40.2.4; 46.1.3; 58.4.5; 63.1.6–7; 66.58.1; 67.1.5–1.6, 67.2.9, 67.3.6, 67.7.8; 70.14.5–6; 75.1.5–6; *De fide* 13.2.

79. Caner, *Wandering, Begging Monks*, 84.

80. Benedict Anderson, *Imagined Communities: Reflections on the Origin and Spread of Nationalism*, rev. ed. (New York: Verso, 2006).

Epiphanius begins his discussion of the Messalians with a generalized excoriation of heresy as an act defined by an unquenchable shamelessness and foolishness. It is a ruinous phenomenon, destroying "the seed of Adam and Noah by bringing their chastity to an end by any number of methods, implanting whorishness in its victims by a variety of methods."[81] He quickly pivots to the Messalians themselves, who are "a foolish, entirely stupid [sect], wholly ridiculous, *inconsistent* in its doctrines and composed of deluded men and women."[82] He stresses at the outset not only their inconsistency—a point to which I shall return—but also the nature of their composition as a sect. As his description unfolds, it becomes clear that Epiphanius treats the Messalians not just as an abstract or diffuse ideology but also as a community of men and women who follow in the tradition of the pagan Messalians, who themselves "built certain houses for themselves, or flat places like forums, and called these prayer houses."[83] The emphasis on domiciles or prayer houses serves to identify these pagan men and women as a community or group of worshippers.[84] These pagan Messalians established sites of prayer both inside and outside cities, some of which were built like churches, synagogues, and oratories.[85] As a community of prayer, "they would gather in the evening and at dawn with much lighting of lamps and torches and offer God lengthy hymns by their sages and certain blessings, if you please, in the fond belief that they can appease God . . . with hymns and blessings."[86]

When Epiphanius finally arrives at the Christian Messalians proper, he sets them in direct relation with the pagan Messalians via their shared customs. And even though "they do the same things in open air, and spend their time in prayer and hymns," the Christian Messalians are described in strikingly different terms:[87]

81. Epiphanius, *Pan.* 80.1.1 (GCS 37:484–85).
82. Epiphanius, *Pan.* 80.1.2 (GCS 37:485); emphasis added.
83. Epiphanius, *Pan.* 80.1.4 (GCS 37:485).
84. For a wide-ranging discussion of the notion of community in the ancient world, see now Daniel S. Richter, *Cosmopolis: Imagining Community in Late Classical Athens and the Early Roman Empire* (New York: Oxford University Press, 2011). On the problems with and implications of notions of community among early Christians, see Stanley Stowers, "The Concept of 'Community' and the History of Early Christianity," *MTSR* 23 (2011): 238–56.
85. Epiphanius, *Pan.* 80.2.1 (GCS 37:486).
86. Epiphanius, *Pan.* 80.2.1–2 (GCS 37:486). Two other pagan sects, the Martyrians and the Satanists, evolved out of the pagan Messalians, though each was distinguished by a particular habit apart from excessive praying. The former blessed the bones of pagan Messalians who were put to death for "pagan lawlessness" (*Pan.* 80.2.3 [GCS 37:486]), whereas the latter represented themselves as servants of Satan. In each case, however, Epiphanius has aggregated these groups together "because, in their departure from the truth, they do the same things in the open air, and spend their time in prayer and hymns" (*Pan.* 80.3.2 [GCS 37:487]). The association between these three pagan sects gestures at a more capacious understanding of the Messalians; even as they are all associated together, they are not singularly defined by an obsession with prayer.
87. Epiphanius, *Pan.* 80.3.3 (GCS 37:487).

"Today, however, these people who are now called Messalians have adopted their customs. But they have no beginning or end, no top or bottom; they are unstable in every way, without principles, and victims of delusion. They are entirely without the foundation of a name, a law, a position, or legislation."[88] The apparent incoherence, illogic, and inconsistency of the Messalians did not preclude Epiphanius from producing a stereotyped and reductionist description of the sect. Indeed, his description created the sect's coherence through the aggregative effects of naming. Writing of the utility of the name Arius as a polemical tool throughout late antiquity, Lewis Ayres notes: "Such heresiological labels enabled early theologians and ecclesiastical historians to portray theologians to whom they were opposed as distinct and coherent groups and they enabled writers to tar enemies with the name of a figure already in disrepute."[89] I would emend Ayres's remark slightly. It is not simply the source of the naming that holds significance—whether based upon behavior, geography, doctrine, or leaders—but the act of naming itself. As the historian Eric R. Wolf has put it: "By turning names into things we create false models of reality."[90] By virtue of their name and the *Panarion*'s narrative about them, the Christian Messalians were given an associative identity and prehistory. And while Epiphanius's description emphasizes that they were "unstable in every way"—they lacked principles or even a name—he himself gave them these things. By supplying them with a name, he translated behavior and its attendant history into a form of communal cohesion. As the sociologist Rogers Brubaker incisively observes:[91]

> By *invoking* groups, they seek to *evoke* them, summon them, call them into being. Their categories are *for doing*—designed to stir, summon, justify, mobilize, kindle, and energize. By reifying groups, by treating them as substantial things-in-the-world, ethnopolitical entrepreneurs can, as Bourdieu notes, "contribute to producing what they apparently describe or designate."

The very fact that scholars continue to argue about whether, in historical terms, the Messalians were a distinct movement "with specific 'leaders' who propagated a coherent set of ideas and an antiecclesiastical outlook" demonstrates the importance

---

88. Epiphanius, *Pan.* 80.3.3 (GCS 37:487).

89. Lewis Ayres, *Nicaea and Its Legacy: An Approach to Fourth-Century Trinitarian Theology* (New York: Oxford University Press, 2004), 2. It should be noted that later in his discussion, Epiphanius does explicitly what Ayres describes. He associates a particular group of monks with the arch-heresiarch Mani: "Some of these brethren [refrain from all mundane labor]—as though they had learned this from the Persian immigrant, Mani, if I may say so" (*Pan.* 80.4.3 [GCS 37:489]).

90. Eric R. Wolf, *Europe and the People without History*, 2nd ed. (Berkeley and Los Angeles: University of California Press, 2010), 6.

91. Rogers Brubaker, *Ethnicity without Groups* (Cambridge, Mass.: Harvard University Press, 2004), 10. See also Heinrich von Staden, "Hairesis and Heresy: The Case of the *Haireseis Iatrikai*," in *Jewish and Christian Self-Definition*, vol. 3, *Self-Definition in the Greco-Roman World*, ed. Ben F. Meyer and E. P. Sanders (Philadelphia: Fortress Press, 1982), 76–100.

of Brubaker's observation.[92] Heretical peoples are written as intellectual, social, and cultural kin, led most often by a single teacher.[93] Throughout these polemical characterizations, then, the heresiologists describe the Christian sects as groups composed of real people.[94]

Although the heresiologist's perspective was obviously not, strictly speaking, historical, his agenda was to present it as such—to make its rhetoric *seem* like reality. It is a point that both Karen King and David Brakke have made abundantly clear: the scholarly discourse about heresy perpetuates heresiological binaries, tropes, and themes.[95] To that end, the descriptions of the heresiologists functioned as tools of reification; they worked to identify heresy as a category. The fact that among scholars the "predominant way of imagining the varieties of Christianity depicts them as discrete bounded groups" attests the enduring success of the heresiologists' portrayals of the heresies.[96] Thus "we can analyze the organizational and discursive careers of categories—the processes through which they become institutionalized and entrenched in administrative routines ... and embedded in culturally powerful and symbolically resonant myths, memories, and narratives."[97] The heresiologists arrayed cosmologies, ideologies, theologies, and practices into the category of heresy, which "aimed at transforming categories into groups or increasing levels of groupness."[98] As Daniel Caner has argued about Epiphanius's construction of the Messalians: "Epiphanius, having heard of such People Who Pray, simply used the Messalian label to bring together all the practices of disparate ascetic groups that caused him distress.... What disturbed Epiphanius was a complex of ascetic practices that could be found diffused in varying shades throughout much of Asia Minor and the neighboring East."[99] The *Panarion* imposed order and groupism where there was, in fact, ambiguity and diffusion. It is this invocation of heretical groupism—through naming, describing, and sorting the heretics—that the heresiologists deployed to construct their texts as a type

---

92. Caner, *Wandering, Begging Monks*, 84. See also Stowers, "The Concept of 'Community,'" who discusses the supposed connection between theology and notions of community as demonstrated by the Gospels (240–45).

93. On leadership, biography, and heresiology, see Young Richard Kim, "Reading the *Panarion* as Collective Biography: The Heresiarch as Unholy Man," *VC* 64 (2010): 382–413.

94. On the language of groups, see *Pan.* 8.8.6; 28.6.7; 32.3.1; 55.1.1; 59.1.1; 69.11.7; 70.15.1–6; 72.1.4; 73.23.3, 73.27.5–7; 80.1.4. On the language of peoples, see *Pan.* 21.1.1; 23.1.1; 24.6.1; 26.1.1–3, 26.10.13, 26.17.4; 27.4.1, 27.4.6, 27.7.1; 28.6.6; 29.1.2; 30.20.5, 30.25.14; 31.1.1; 32.4.1; 34.22.1; 35.2.3; 36.1.3; 38.1.1; 40.8.7; 41.1.3–4; 42.1.1; 43.1.3

95. The thesis is stated most concretely by Karen King, *What is Gnosticism?*, 20–21, 27, 52–54, 110–48, 166–69, 175–76, 202–5; and Brakke, *The Gnostics*, 1–28.

96. Ibid. 9.

97. Brubaker, *Ethnicity without Groups*, 13.

98. Ibid.

99. Caner, *Wandering, Begging Monks*, 100.

of ethnography. In fashioning the heretics into groups, the heresiologists, and Epiphanius most emphatically, were making heretics into ethnographic objects. They were forming them into groups, bounded, imagined, and diffuse, that were organized and oriented around shared customs, habits, doctrines, and dispositions.[100]

Although the *Panarion*'s polemical ethnography managed the heretics by making them into bounded entities, it simultaneously and tellingly worked to undercut any sense of empowerment that the language of groupism carried with it. The fear was that by describing them as an assemblage, however false the description, the heretics would be legitimated.[101] And so the *Panarion* worked to counteract that implication. By emphasizing the heretics' own incoherence, Epiphanius levied the double charge of illogic and illegitimacy against them. Like the frontier notion of "the religion of unbelievers," the Messalians were imagined to be a contradiction in terms: they were a coherent group of incoherence.[102] Their behavior and theology were marked by confusion, misunderstanding, and disorder. But it was not just through rhetorical obfuscation that the *Panarion* constructed and simultaneously polemicized the heretics. There was another and more universalizing facet of this project of uncritical, polemical ethnography. The Messalians could be evoked as a coherent group that was nonetheless dubbed incoherent because Epiphanius exposed not simply what they did and what they believed but, more important, the governing principles that defined their Christianity. The particularities of their lifestyle were but an expression of a more pernicious condition that identified the very incoherence of their being. In searching for a heretical disposition, Epiphanius built the Messalians into a confused unity. He had found their essence in a disposition that defined them as Messalians even as he described these people and their disposition as foolish, shameful, inconsistent, irremediable, and nonsensical. Their disposition made them both coherent and incoherent. It was the overarching supposition of his ethnographic investigation that enabled him to make both claims simultaneously. It was a tool that enabled the heresiologist to construct and dismantle an essentalized portrait of the heretics.

---

100. On this point, see Jean Gribomont "Le dossier des origines du Messalianisme," in *Epektasis: Mélanges patristiques offerts au Cardinal Jean Daniélou*, ed. Jacques Fontaine and Charles Kannengiesser (Paris: Beauchesne, 1972), 611–25, esp. 614–16. Caner, *Wandering, Begging Monks*, 96–104, argues strongly against the idea of describing the Messalians as a movement in historical terms.

101. For an analogous illustration of incoherent coherence in late antiquity, see my "The Double Bind of Christianity's Judaism: Law, Language, and the Incoherence of Late Antique Discourse," *JECS* 23.3 (2015): 445–80.

102. On the idea of "religion of the unbelievers," see David Chidester, *Savage Systems* (Charlottesville: University of Virginia Press, 1996), 73–115. For another useful example of heretical contradiction, see *Pan.* 46.3.1. Likewise, Epiphanius's entry on the Marcionites (*Pan.* 42) turns on the language of contradiction.

THE ASCETICAL DISPOSITION AS HERETICAL DISPOSITION: THE CONTENTIOUSNESS OF THE MESSALIANS

In his description of the *Panarion*'s eightieth and final heresy, Epiphanius stresses that the Messalians, like all proper heretics, are a people of estrangement. They are estranged from Epiphanius's notion of Christian truth insofar as they adhere to improper expressions of Christian behavior, interpretation, and reason. He tells us that the Christian Messalians gathered "[in mixed companies] of men and women, as though they had renounced the world and abandoned their homes."[103] They slept in public squares, again in mixed company, during the course of the summer. They led lives as beggars insofar as they "had no means of livelihood and no property."[104] And in that act of begging we see already one of their defining features: "They show no restraint."[105] Epiphanius further charges that the Messalians claimed multiple human and superhuman identities; they could be prophets, Christs, patriarchs, and angels. In a standard heresiological gesture, Epiphanius's response to this plurality of ontologies is simply to dismiss the Messalians as crazy: "But as to their calling themselves Christ, what sensible person can fail to see that the doctrine is crazy? Or [their] saying, 'I am a prophet!' . . . Why the errant nonsense? Why the idiotic doctrines?"[106] He next explains that "they have no notion of fasting" and that "they do anything without restraint, and eat and drink."[107] This pattern of behavior allows Epiphanius to develop a model for the Messalians, a way to reduce them to a mentality that encompasses the totality of their way of life. This disease of immoderacy, to use the *Panarion*'s preferred metaphor, explains how they live. This disposition so fundamentally orients their way of life that Epiphanius uses it to freely assume—without any knowledge—the degeneracy of other behaviors. He writes: "As to vice or sexual misconduct, I have no way of knowing. But they can have no lack of this either, especially with their custom of sleeping together in the same place, men and women."[108] Epiphanius extrapolated a mentality from behaviors and then read that mentality back into the Messalians to deduce unknown behavioral tendencies. Predictive or dispositional ethnography relied upon precisely this sort of circularity.

---

103. Epiphanius, *Pan.* 80.3.4 (GCS 37:487). On sexual promiscuity and primitive mentality, see John F. McLennan, *Primitive Marriage: An Inquiry into the Origin of the Form of Capture in Marriage Ceremonies,* ed. Peter Rivière (Chicago: Chicago University Press, 1970); and Herbert Spencer, *The Principles of Sociology,* 3 vols., 3rd ed. (London: Williams and Norgate, 1897–1906; reprint, Westport, Conn.: Greenwood, 1975): 1:632–35; 2:4.

104. Epiphanius, *Pan.* 80.3.4 (GCS 37:487).
105. Epiphanius, *Pan.* 80.3.4 (GCS 37:487).
106. Epiphanius, *Pan.* 80.9.6 (GCS 37:494).
107. Epiphanius, *Pan.* 80.3.6 (GCS 37:488).
108. Epiphanius, *Pan.* 80.3.7 (GCS 37:488).

Having already suggested the influence of the pagan Messalians on their Christian namesakes, Epiphanius, *in mediis rebus,* pauses to consider their Christian influences. He begins this stage of his entry by describing the Christian influence not in the language of behavior, strictly speaking, but through the language of opinion. He positions Christian Messalians as adherents to "a harmful doctrine or opinion," the source of which was the extreme simplicity of certain monks who, even though they were orthodox, "[did] not know the measure of citizenship in Christ."[109] The immoderation of these monks derived from their interpretation of the scriptural injunction "to labor for the food that endures for eternal life" (and not "for the food that perishes") as a demand to remain free from manual labor.[110] To challenge the falsity of this position, he fashions the profile for a paradigmatic ascetic lifestyle.[111] In so doing, he transforms the problem of idleness into a meditation on how to live life as a Christian ascetic in imitation of the scripture and the apostles.[112] In this imaginary ethnography, Epiphanius puts forward a model for Christian conduct. True Christian conduct, he insists, "tells us to renounce the world, abandon our possessions and property, sell what we have and give to the poor—but really to take up the cross and follow and not be idle and without occupation and eat at the wrong times, and not be like drones but 'to work with our own hands.'"[113] Epiphanius further enumerates the traits that defined fearful, God-inspired souls: such a disposition is "won by sacred doctrines, the study of holy scripture and the oracles of God, psalmody and solemn assemblies, holy fasts, purity and discipline, and voluntary manual work for righteousness's sake."[114] He explicitly appropriates even the motif of perpetual prayer to advance his romanticized portrait. Of these imagined ascetical figures, he writes: "And they recite nearly all sacred scripture and keep their frequent vigils without tiring or grudging, one in prayer, another in psalmody. They continually hold the assemblies that have been set by lawful custom and spend all their days in the offering of blameless prayers to God, with deep humility and woeful lamentation."[115] And they do so while also making time to perform manual labor. The true monks, as "the

---

109. Epiphanius, *Pan.* 80.4.1 (GCS 37:488).

110. John 6.27 at *Pan.* 80.4.4 (GCS 37:489). The analysis of the verse in the context of the Mesopotamian monks runs from *Pan.* 80.4.4–6.4.

111. On the relationship between heresy, orthodoxy, and ascetic behavior, see Teresa M. Shaw "Ascetic Practice and the Genealogy of Heresy: Problems in Modern Scholarship and Ancient Textual Representation," in *The Cultural Turn in Late Ancient Studies,* ed. Dale B. Martin and Patricia Cox Miller (Durham: Duke University Press, 2005), 213–36.

112. Gribomont, "Dossier," 611–25. The pursuits of genuine Christian lifestyles revolved around vastly different interpretations of the apostolic tradition and the relationship to the temporal world. On asceticism and the apostolic tradition, see Caner, *Wandering, Begging Monks,* 83–125.

113. Epiphanius, *Pan.* 80.4.1–2 (GCS 37:488), citing 1 Cor. 4.12. Translation modified.

114. Epiphanius, *Pan.* 80.6.4 (GCS 37:491).

115. Epiphanius, *Pan.* 80.4.6–7 (GCS 37:489).

servants of God who are truly founded on the solid rock of truth and build their house securely, perform their light tasks, each in his own trade, with their own hands."[116]

In addition, the honest toil of these unnamed ascetics affords them independence from "the defilement of those who are rich from unrighteousness," which makes their commitment to God all the more powerful and pious:[117] "Thus, along with the word and its preaching, they will have a clear conscience because they produce with their own hands, maintain themselves and, with an excellent disposition towards God and their neighbors, willingly share the alms that they have on hand, I mean [from] firstfruits, offerings and their own earnings, with the brethren and the needy."[118] In explicitly correlating a godly disposition with charity, Epiphanius demonstrates that just as a disposition could predict behavior, the details of behavior could likewise reinforce a disposition. Far from disrupting a pious mentality, manual labor, in fact, attested and solidified the ascetical disposition. Disposition, here as elsewhere, serves as the hermeneutical key to Epiphanius's heresiological investigation insofar as it provides an overarching framework through which to read behavior and doctrine. It provides the collective lens through which he can visualize his polemical ethnography. To that end, the elaboration of this model of ascetical habits and principles adds yet another layer of comparative ethnography to the *Panarion*. In contrasting the Mesopotamian monks with a fictitious ascetical group, Epiphanius illustrates how comparative theological analysis *functions as* comparative ethnography, in this case at the microscopic level. By transforming an interpretive disagreement into a much larger ethnographic disquisition, Epiphanius casts theology as the fundamental language of Christian ethnographic inquiry.

While the monks of Mesopotamia and the Messalians aspired to a life of piety, they erred both in their way of life and in their thinking. The monks' decision to wear "their hair long like a woman's" was in error because of the apostle's injunction that "'a man ought not to have long hair, inasmuch as he is the image of God.'"[119] Epiphanius also denounced them for wearing sackcloth since it "is out of place in the catholic church."[120] To make matters worse, he tells us that they "cut off their beards, the mark of manhood, while often letting the hair of their heads grow long."[121] In this regard, they explicitly contravene the *Didascalia apostolorum*'s command "not to cut the beard, and not to deck oneself with meretricious

---

116. Epiphanius, *Pan.* 80.4.6 (GCS 37:489).
117. Epiphanius, *Pan.* 80.4.8 (GCS 37:489).
118. Epiphanius, *Pan.* 80.6.2 (GCS 37:491).
119. Epiphanius, *Pan.* 80.6.5, 80.6.6 (GCS 37:492).
120. Epiphanius, *Pan.* 80.6.6 (GCS 37:492).
121. Epiphanius, *Pan.* 80.7.1 (GCS 37:492).

ornaments or have the approach of pride as a copy of righteousness."[122] Epiphanius is dabbling in Christian physiognomics, the discipline whereby an author "seeks to detect from individuals' external features their character, disposition, or destiny."[123] By insisting that the children of Christ should embody a mentality that did "not desire reward and credit from those who see them,"[124] Epiphanius links their appearance to behavior and ultimately to a deeper sense of pride. Their pride, however, was not their gravest error; rather, it was the disposition reflected in a particular behavioral choice. In something of a non sequitur, Epiphanius turns back to an earlier point to argue that it was the Messalians' excessively long hair that was their most troubling error. As he explains: "Long hair was proper only for the nazirites, because of the type. The ancient were guided by the type of him who was to come, and had long hair on their heads for prayer until the world's Prayer was to come and was answered."[125] But since "Christ . . . was obviously a head," and the Messalians "dishonor the head" by cutting their hair, they dishonor Christ.[126] Their habit was more than simply transgressive; it was positively anti-Christian: "The style is a contentious one, since the type of the Law is gone and the truth has come."[127] It was an act that fomented discord, cemented difference, and contested Christ. It was an act that revealed their way of thought: they possessed minds motivated by contentiousness and strife.

Epiphanius was clear that these monks had failed as inheritors and protectors of the apostolic tradition. They had, in fact, sown the very contentiousness that Paul had repudiated in his First Letter to the Corinthians: "But Paul says, 'if any seem to be contentious, we have no custom, neither the churches of God.' He rejected persons who had such customs and practices because, by the apostles' ordinance and in the eyes of God's church, they are contentious."[128] Epiphanius's digression about the ascetical orientation, with its own polemical and imaginative ethnographic emphases, identified a shared orientation between Messalians and their Mesopotamian antecedents. The "harmful doctrine" that the Messalians had learned from these monks leads him to a discussion of their shared idleness, which gives way in turn to a discussion of their shared contentiousness. This chain of commonality builds a genealogy of dispositions. Thus Epiphanius insisted that his discussion of the Mesopotamians and his imagined ethnography was no digression, but rather an obligation "since they have contracted the sickness of mind

---

122. Epiphanius, *Pan.* 80.7.1 (GCS 37:492). On the maintenance of beards, see *Didascalia apostolorum* 2.
123. Isaac, *Invention of Racism*, 165. For his broader discussion of physiognomics, see ibid. 149–68.
124. Epiphanius, *Pan.* 80.6.6 (GCS 37:492).
125. Epiphanius, *Pan.* 80.7.2 (GCS 37:492).
126. Epiphanius, *Pan.* 80.7.2 (GCS 37:492), citing 1 Cor. 11.4.
127. Epiphanius, *Pan.* 80.7.3 (GCS 37:492).
128. Epiphanius, *Pan.* 80.7.4 (GCS 37:492), citing 1 Cor. 11.16.

from the same source [i.e., contention], have truly come to grief from perversity of mind and have been made a sect with the horrid custom of idleness and the other evils."[129] And although Caner is right that Epiphanius "does not recognize any connection between their attitude toward work and their devotion to prayer"—the former of which was associated with their pagan predecessors, whereas the latter was derived from the Mesopotamian monks—the association, I believe, was in some sense obvious and implicit.[130] Moreover, Epiphanius made the association between idleness and perpetual prayer secondary to the establishment of a heretical disposition. He sought, through his comparative ethnographic analysis, to identify the essence that explained their entire approach to Christian living. Their behavior and its origins were wholly attributed to contentiousness, including their contravention of gender norms, their idleness, their calling themselves Christs, and their promiscuity. As expressions of a disposition, each of these habits was a particular illustration of a single, scripturally unsound essence.

But in coming full circle to uncover the Messalians' true essence, their contentiousness, Epiphanius produces a rather obvious tautology: they are heretics because they are contentious, and they are contentious because they are heretics. And so, when Epiphanius summarizes his description of the Messalians, he reiterates the point with which he began his discussion of them: "This is what I have heard about these people in their turn. They have become a joke in the eyes of the world and have spat up their vulgar thought and words, though they are incoherent and irremediable, and have abandoned God's building."[131] Like the Mesopotamian monks from whom they borrowed their idleness, they were immoderate yet simple, renunciatory yet licentious. In their behavior, they could be both excessive and abstemious. They simultaneously inhabited both ends of the heresiologists' ethical spectrum: asceticism and libertinism. This dichotomy, which Karen King discusses in the context of the Gnostics, rightly pointing out that it "relies heavily on the early Christian heresiological tradition," is yet another illustration of a relentlessly tendentious construction of the heretics.[132] The heresiologists who wrote about the Gnostics, and the Valentinians in particular, conceptualized their cosmological and epistemological attitudes as legitimating an ethics of extremes. The polemicists "described heretical behavior in terms of a false asceticism based on pride and impious hatred of the creator or a libertine immorality by which the Gnostics flaunted

---

129. Epiphanius, *Pan.* 80.7.5 (GCS 37:493).
130. Caner, *Wandering, Begging Monks*, 89. By "obvious and implicit," I mean that the Messalians embraced idleness in order to eliminate anything that would interfere with their constant praying. Epiphanius never explicitly links the two, but when he imagines his ideal monk (80.4.6–8), he points out that pious monks, dedicated to prayer, possess plenty of time for work. The two are not, in his view, mutually exclusive.
131. Epiphanius, *Pan.* 80.8.1 (GCS 37:493).
132. King, *What is Gnosticism?*, 202.

their superior spirituality and knowledge."[133] By rereading the relevant Nag Hammadi texts, King is interested in challenging this contradictory binary as a fallacious hermeneutical polemic, whereas I am interested in the implications and parameters of this charge as a *form* of polemic. To put it simply, I have been concerned with how this vacillating polemic serves the ethnographic logic of the *Panarion*. I wish not to correct the heresiologists' descriptions of the heretics—to find the real, historical Messalians—but rather to understand these descriptions as producing a manifestly Christian, highly polemical, doctrinal, and behavioral type of ethnography.

In the case of Epiphanius's Messalians, the dual charge of asceticism and excess does more than simply magnify their incoherent coherence. It also supplied Epiphanius with the polemical leverage to demystify this variance—to make sense of their nonsense, as it were. As Epiphanius's description came to focus on their contentiousness, he created a paradigmatic mentality that not only explained their contradictory behavior—their perpetual incoherence—but also overrode its particularities. Their contentiousness laid the foundation for his commentary about their incoherent coherence. It provided a means through which they could be both people who pray and people who are fundamentally combative and disputatious. Their coherence is their contentiousness even as that very contentiousness produces their variable behavior. In this way, Epiphanius did precisely what Enlightenment writers, colonial missionaries, and theologians would later do: construct an object of inquiry that could be reduced to a discrete, unchangeable essence, the effects of which were always correlative but not necessarily complementary.[134]

HERESIOLOGY AND CIVILITY: THE LEGACY OF THEOLOGICAL ETHNOGRAPHY

Epiphanius's emphasis on disposition worked to coalesce seemingly disparate heretical behavior and customary differences into a representation of a unified mentality. Through his polemical ethnography, he created a determinative essence for the Messalians. I read the *Panarion* as an effort to emphasize the universal over the particular, to create harmony out of dissonance. Epiphanius's system of heretical classification functioned in a manner strikingly similar to nineteenth-century

---

133. Ibid. This inauthentic ethic, as King describes it, extends well beyond the fraught category of the Gnostics. It encompasses not only the Messalians but a host of heretical parties, including the Pythagoreans, Dositheans, Carpocratians, Valentinians, Secundians, Ophites, Marcionites, Montanists, Noetians, Manicheans, Hieracites, Anomoeans. See Peter Anthony Mena, "Insatiable Appetites: Epiphanius of Salamis and the Making of the Heretical Villain," *StPatr* 67 (2011), 257–63, on the relationship between Epiphanius's use of medical imagery and the sexual excesses of the heretics.

134. On this point, see Walter H. Capps, "The Interpretation of New Religion and Religious Studies," in *Understanding the New Religions*, ed. Jacob Needleman and George Baker (New York: Seabury Press, 1978), 101–50.

theories of imperial or apartheid comparative religion, which, as the historian of religion David Chidester has incisively observed, organized human diversity "into rigid, static categories" for the purpose of "simplifying, and thereby achieving some cognitive control over, the bewildering complexity of a frontier zone."[135] Chidester explains further the techniques that scholars utilized to create these human groupings:[136]

> Theorists in Europe, especially during the last quarter of the nineteenth century, arranged disparate evidence from all over the world into a single, uniform temporal sequence, from primitive to civilized, that claimed to represent the universal history of humanity. . . . By the 1850s . . . the imperial science of comparative religion had completely obscured its entanglement in a global conquest. Not only divorcing itself from its own origins—the dependence of its very existence upon the violent reality of colonial frontiers—this imperial comparative religion erased all of the historical, geographical, and political contexts in which its data had been embedded. As a result, all that remained for analysis in the disembodied evidence . . . was a mentality, whether that mentality was designated as religious, magical, superstitious, or primitive.

Like Chidester's colonial comparativists, Epiphanius acknowledged distinctions between specific heretical groups even as he insisted on the unity of their un-Christian mentality. Although the *Panarion* did not completely take its objects of inquiry out of context, it did aggressively construct a monolithic conception of heresy as a generic category. Epiphanius placed sectarian opinion—heretical thinking and action born of that mental condition—at the center of his history of the world.[137] As Epiphanius explains to the readers of his *Panarion*: "We are dealing with . . . kinds of knowledge, with faith in God and unbelief, with sects, and with heretical human opinions that misguided persons have been sowing in the world from man's formation on earth till our own day."[138] And, in the very act of defining eighty heresies over against a single orthodoxy, Epiphanius reified sectarian diversity into its own unity. Heresiology was, as Karen King aptly phrases it, a process of "describing various texts and teachings, emphasizing their differences from one another, while at the same time and despite clear recognition of their manifold differences connecting them in a linear genealogy to a single essential character."[139]

The *Panarion*'s heresiological ethnography laid a conceptual and theological foundation for the fixation of ethnologists and early anthropologists on mentalities

---

135. Chidester, *Savage Systems*, 21–22.
136. Ibid. 3. This point is similarly made by Masuzawa, *The Invention of World Religions*, 16–19, 43–44, 79–86.
137. See *Pan.* 3.3.4, which I will discuss in more detail below in chapter 4.
138. Epiphanius, *Pan.* pro. 2.2.3 (GCS, n. F., 10:170).
139. Karen King, *What is Gnosticism?*, 32.

and dispositions. Uncritical ethnography was as much about theology and interiority, however implicit, as it was about customs and habits. The fact that, as Stephen A. Tyler notes, ethnographers have had to work so hard to distance themselves from missionaries and colonial administrators by "disclaim[ing] any self-interest connected with Christianity" attests the lingering connection.[140] Colonialism, Christianity, and anthropology went hand-in-hand-in-hand. The Eurocentric veneer of anthropological ethnography—the very legacy anthropologists were so eager to erase—was predicated on the history of Christian missionizing and colonialism and the discourse of belief and interiority. One need only consult Talal Asad's famous discussion of Clifford Geertz's anthropological definition of religion to see how ethnographers continue to construct religion with theological principles. Geertz "appears, inadvertently, to be taking up the standpoint of theology"[141] by insisting that religious symbols must "affirm something."[142] As Asad explains: "The requirement of affirmation is apparently innocent and logical, but through it the entire field of evangelism was historically opened up, in particular the work of European missionaries in Asia, Africa, and Latin America."[143]

Writing of Victorian ethnology as mediated through the pioneering figure of James Cowles Prichard (1786–1848), the father of English ethnology, George W. Stocking, Jr., describes the sources that early ethnologists and anthropologists used to study human diversity:[144]

> Although articles in early ethnological journals sometimes reflected personal experience overseas, Prichardian ethnology was essentially an activity of the study, not the field.... The material on which Prichard built his ethnology came largely from the printed pages of books. Many of these were very old ones: the ancient historian-geographers who described the peoples at the margins of the classical world; the chroniclers of barbarian invasions of the Roman Empire; and the early antiquarian accounts of the national histories of Europe—testimony to the continuity of Prichardian ethnology with deeply rooted traditions of speculation about human diversity. From the beginning, however, Prichard also drew on more contemporary travel accounts; and as the years and editions went by, his volumes became more and more compendia of the travel literature of nineteenth-century Europeans abroad.

---

140. Stephen A. Tyler, "Ethnography, Intertextuality and the End of Description," *American Journal of Semiotics* 3.4 (1985): 83–98, 90. On this point, see also Burridge, *Encountering Aborigines*, 1–42. Cf. Timothy Larsen, *The Slain God: Anthropologists and the Christian Faith* (New York: Oxford University Press, 2014).
141. Asad, "Construction of Religion," 43.
142. Clifford Geertz, "Religion as a Cultural System," in his *The Interpretation of Cultures: Selected Essays by Clifford Geertz* (New York: Basic Books, 1973), 87–112, at 98–99.
143. Asad, "Construction of Religion," 43.
144. George Stocking, Jr., *Victorian Anthropology* (New York: Free Press, 1991), 79.

Epiphanius, as I explained in the previous chapter, used the equivalent resources: the writings of heresiologists past, bishops and theologians present, and the heretics' very own texts.[145] He further claimed, in his entry on the Gnostics, for example, that he had met them in the flesh. He writes: "For I happened on this sect myself... and was actually taught these things in person, out of the mouths of the people who really undertook them."[146] And again, a few paragraphs later: "I indicated before that I have encountered some of the sects, though I know some from documentary sources, and some from the instruction of testimony of trustworthy men who were able to tell me the truth."[147] Although he leaves the details of his encounter unspecified, he includes this meeting for obvious reasons. Emphasizing his own personal experience with the Gnostics adds an element of legitimacy to his description of their sexual perversities, scriptures, dietary habits, and elaborate cosmologies. His encounter likewise adds an element of urgency to his account. If the Gnostics are actually engaged in such reprehensible conduct, which Epiphanius's truthful reporting indicates, the church and his readers have an obligation to combat the diseased, barbaric condition of the Gnostics. Put simply, they must civilize these heretical savages.[148]

Epiphanius explicitly used the discourse of barbarism and civility as he described the literature of the Carpocratians, an offshoot of the Gnostics. Their literature, he writes, "is such that the intelligent reader will be astounded and shocked, and doubt that human beings can do such things—not only civilized people like ourselves, but even those who [live with] wild beasts and bestial, brutish men, and all but venture to behave like dogs and swine."[149] There was an imperative to intervene against this depravity—the text, after all, is called the *Panarion*, which means *Medicine Chest*—to heal those who had contracted the disease of heresy. The heresiologists' duty to redeem the heretics from error—to correct their way of life—reflected an ethnographic disposition built upon comparative theology and the notion of *vera religio*. And this discursive project, the recasting of ethnography as a salvational enterprise, had profound and long-lasting historical consequences.[150] Civility,

---

145. While the *Panarion*'s entry on the Messalians does not include citational references, the text as a whole is a veritable cornucopia of heresiological reinscription. It is, far and away, the most citationally built of the late antique heresiologies. Epiphanius is the only heresiologist, so far as I can tell, who marshals his literary predecessors and opponents at such great length. There is no parallel within the heresiological corpus on the order of Epiphanius's appropriations from Irenaeus, Marcellus, George of Laodicea, Basil of Ancyra, Melitius, Proclus, Methodius, Origen, Marcion, Turbo, Athanasius, and Aetius.

146. Epiphanius, *Pan.* 26.17.4 (GCS, n. F., 10:297).

147. Epiphanius, *Pan.* 26.18.1 (GCS, n. F., 10:298).

148. For an analogous invocation of civilization and the attendant contradictions, see Patrick Brantlinger, *Taming Cannibals: Race and the Victorians* (Ithaca: Cornell University Press, 2011).

149. Epiphanius, *Pan.* 27.5.1 (GCS, n. F., 10:306).

150. Herbert, *Culture and Anomie*, 150–203.

missionizing, and theological truth had become inextricably linked. As Christopher Herbert explains in his *Culture and Anomie,* the Victorian missionaries and ethnographers of Polynesia William Ellis (1794–1872), John Williams (1796–1839), and James Calvert (1813–92)[151]

> saw themselves as saving souls, as working to lessen the sum of human suffering, and as engaging in direct personal combat with Satan. Very likely they were also guilty, as their critics charged, of longing for personal glory and of seeking to use their activities in foreign lands to enhance the influence of the Evangelical party in church politics. But they were impelled by a further motive which gave their enterprise a quasi-scientific character from the outset.... This was their need to portray the countries selected for evangelism as sites of almost unqualified moral depravity.... In order to justify their aggressive incursions into native societies, missionaries needed therefore to be able to appeal to a discourse which endowed them with incontestable moral authority over indigenous populations. So it was a principal function of this discourse, which they made it their business to produce, to people the South Seas with the very beings that had, for expediency's sake, to be found there: depraved, brutish savages. Intervention in the lives of such people was not only permissible, it was an urgent duty.

In the same way, the enterprise of heresiology found what its discourse promised and produced: the discourse of heresiology, in that sense, peopled the Mediterranean with heretics. Rhetoric had outstripped reality. It is, as Herbert suggests, an ethnographic tautology: the ethnographer finds what his discourse needs.[152] Epiphanius thus constructed his *Panarion* not only to create an opposition between heterodox and orthodox ways of living but also to trace an underlying dispositional distinction. He found, wherever he metaphorically looked, the excesses, extremes, hubris, and vulgarity of the heretics. They were pseudo-Christian savages, unrestrained by any sense of limitation or boundary.

Epiphanius and the Polynesianists were both firmly interested in developing oppositional mentalities, for the former between orthodox and heterodox and for the latter between civilized and primitive (where the latter was now undergirded by the theological dichotomy of the former). Each utilized tendentious evidence to construct heretical or primitive worldviews, ideologies, and ways of living. At the same time, the process of constructing a disposition from ethnographic knowledge very much reinscribes the evidentiary function of ethnography. The discourse of heresiology uses the notion of the disposition to further reify its ethnographic object. Insofar as the heretics have readily identifiable dispositions, they are not abstract or diffuse intellectual entities but instead tangible peoples defined by perverse qualities. With Epiphanius's introduction of the very first Christian

---

151. Ibid. 158.
152. Ibid. 157–59.

sect, the Simonians or those who followed Simon Magus, the interplay between practice, disposition, and peoplehood is made abundantly clear: "[The sect] is made up of people who do not rightly or lawfully [believe] in Christ's name, but perform their dreadful activities in keeping with the false corruption that is in them."[153] Because the heretics have an underlying disposition, they are no different than the various warmongering yet slothful tribes of Tacitus's *Germania*, the violent Gauls of Caesar's *Gallic War*, the hypercivilized Phaeacians of Homer's *Odyssey*, the masters and slaves of Aristotle's *Politics*, or the devious Iberians of Strabo's *Geography*.[154] The heretics are imagined with a sense of peoplehood even as the heresiologists work tirelessly to deny their humanity.[155] The ethnography of heresies "had in fact long stressed just this 'problem' of seemingly illogical combination of traits.... Analysis of this kind pointedly defines ethnography as an attempt to unriddle the symbolic interrelations of customs."[156] The heretics have customs and habits, rites and rituals, rules and regulations that make up their way of life—and, as a result, possess their own heretical culture—even as their hubristic, unrestrained mentality undercuts their claim to possess a legitimate Christian culture. They are, from the heresiologists' perspective, hostile to "the restraint which Christianity imposed upon them."[157] Epiphanius's attacks against the Messalians' coherence (and thus their culture) cleared the way for his own claim that the Christianity of the *Panarion* was the unifying and governing principle of the entire human race. The biblical anthropology advanced by his monogenic theory of human diversity—namely that all humanity was united by a pre-Christian and then explicitly Christian mentality—foresaw the eventual reunification of all peoples everywhere under the banner of Christianity.[158]

In his essay "The Forms of Wildness: Archaeology of an Idea," Hayden White argues that the discourse of wildness and savagery implicates both ethnographic and theological structures.[159] He explains that the motif of the savage

153. Epiphanius, *Pan.* 21.1.1 (GCS, n. F., 10:238).
154. Isaac, *Invention of Racism*, 163–68, 176–77. On mentalities and dispositions, see Homer, *Od.* 7–8; Tacitus, *Germ.* 15.1; 21.2; 30.2; 31.3; 35.2; 42.1; Caesar, *Bell. gall.* 3.19.6; Strabo, *Geogr.*, 3.4.5; Aristotle, *Pol.* 1254b 25–1255a 2 and 1255b20–22.
155. The sexual behavior of the Messalians, Epiphanius emphasizes in one telling quip, is the "intercourse of swine and cattle" (*Pan.* 80.8.3 [GCS 37:493]).
156. Herbert, *Culture and Anomie*, 197.
157. John Williams, *A Narrative of Missionary Enterprises in the South Sea Islands* (London: Snow, 1837), 129.
158. On monogenism, see Stocking, *Victorian Anthropology*, 44–50, 48–53, 66–68, 74–76, 245–46, 313–14; Colin Kidd, *The Forging of Races: Race and Scripture in the Protestant Atlantic World, 1600–2000* (New York: Cambridge University Press, 2006), 24–32, 62–167; and David N. Livingstone, *Adam's Ancestors: Race, Religion, and the Politics of Human Origins* (Baltimore.: The Johns Hopkins University Press, 2011).
159. Hayden White, "The Forms of Wildness: Archaeology of an Idea," in his *Tropics of Discourse: Essays in Cultural Criticism* (Baltimore: The Johns Hopkins University Press, 1979), 150–82.

operates to create not just binaries, but binaries with seemingly existential significance:[160]

> The notion of "wildness" (or, in its Latinate form, "savagery") belongs to a set of culturally self-authenticating devices which includes, among many others, the ideas of "madness" and "heresy" as well. These terms are used not merely to designate a specific condition or state of being but also to confirm the value of their dialectical antitheses "civilization," "sanity," and "orthodoxy," respectively. Thus, they do not so much refer to a specific thing, place, or condition as dictate a particular attitude governing a relationship between a lived reality and some area of problematical existence that cannot be accommodated easily to conventional conceptions of the normal or familiar.

Ethnographic writing encompassed a way of *seeing* the world, of negotiating and enumerating the cultural, social, political, and intellectual space occupied by a people and its traditions.[161] It is about articulating a perception, what White calls an "attitude," of the peoples and places of the world. But perceiving the world, mapping it discursively and literally, is an endeavor fraught with both real and imagined dangers. And theological ethnography—that is, ethnography driven by theological principles—is all the more dangerous, for it requires the ethnographer to investigate things that are not just repulsive but also destructive, unrestrained, insane, and even demonic.

The heretics thus represented an ethnographic paradox and opportunity. On the one hand, the existence of the heretics complicated the notion of a singular Christian truth and thus the possibility of a singular reunification of humanity. But on the other hand, the heretics were studied and written in order to be subdued and ultimately dismantled. And because their continued existence constituted a dangerous pollution—a metaphor that both heresiologists and Victorians used freely—they existed to be destroyed and reimagined as Christians.[162] Like the colonialists who slowly dismantled indigenous religious and political structures, Christians used, in the wake of Constantine, the power of the state to enforce their interpretation of Christian tradition. The intervention of the colonial apparatus against indigenous peoples finds correlation not only in sporadic acts of violence against heretics—like the burning of a Valentinian meeting place at Callinicum in 388—but also in the laws compiled in the *Theodosian Code*.[163] As Richard Flower and

---

160. Ibid. 151.
161. The subtitle of Kurt A. Raaflaub and Richard J. A. Talbert's anthology further drives home the sense of geography and ethnography as a way of seeing the world: *Geography and Ethnography: Perceptions of the World* (Malden, Mass.: Wiley-Blackwell, 2010).
162. See also Herbert, *Culture and Anomie*, 165–67, 178–81; and Chidester, *Savage Systems*, 43, 58, 87, 96–102, 101–9, 117, 127, 152, 160–65, 192, 219.
163. On the incident at Callinicum, see Neil B. McLynn, *Ambrose of Milan: Church and Court in a Christian Capital* (Berkeley and Los Angeles: University of California Press, 1994), 298–315.

Caroline Humfress have shown, the discourse of heresiology finds parallel expression in the laws preserved in the code.[164] The rhetoric of destruction marshaled against the heretics assumes legal consequences. There were, in theory, *material* consequences to the discourse of heresiological ethnography in late antiquity: "All members of diverse and perfidious sects ... shall not be allowed to have an assembly anywhere, to participate in discussions, to hold secret meetings, to erect impudently the altars of a nefarious treachery by the offices of an impious hand, and to present the false appearance of mysteries."[165] Not only could the state prohibit (and appropriate for itself) the gathering places of the heretics,[166] it could also confiscate their property,[167] annul their inheritances,[168] forbid them to enter the imperial service,[169] and prosecute them for crimes under various legal rubrics.[170] The laws of the *Theodosian Code*, like the heresiologies, use the rhetoric of madness, insanity, and uncontrollability to describe and denounce the heretics.[171] In this way, the laws function as material and ideological contributions to the development of a heretical mentality defined by contravention, perversity, and unrestraint.[172]

Indeed, writing their treatises on heretics and primitives, respectively, Epiphanius and Victorian anthropologists reduced cultural, religious, and theological complexities and behavioral nuances to generalities, dispositions, and stereotypes. They emphasized, most incessantly, the irrationality and illogic of their respective objects of inquiry. They were crazed, foolish, simple, and senseless. Recall the words that Epiphanius uses to open his account of the Messalians, which could as easily have been uttered by an uncritical Victorian anthropologist:[173]

---

164. Richard Flower, "'The Insanity of the Heretics Must Be Restrained': Heresiology in the *Theodosian Code*," in *Theodosius II: Rethinking the Roman Empire in Late Antiquity*, ed. Christopher Kelly (New York: Cambridge University Press, 2013), 172–94; and Caroline Humfress, *Orthodoxy and the Courts in Late Antiquity* (New York: Oxford University Press, 2007), 233–68.

165. *CTh* 16.5.15. See Laurette Barnard, "The Criminalisation of Heresy in the Later Roman Empire: A Sociopolitical Device?," *Journal of Legal History* 121 (1995): 121–46.

166. *CTh* 16.5.3, 16.5.4, 16.5.6.1–3, 16.5.8, 16.5.10, 16.5.11, 16.5.12, 16.5.15, 16.5.20.

167. *CTh* 16.5.17, 16.5.40.2.

168. *CTh* 16.5.7, 16.5.17, 16.5.40.3, 16.5.49, 16.5.58.4.

169. *CTh* 16.5.25, 16.5.29, 16.5.42, 16.5.48, 16.5.54.3, 16.5.58.7, 16.5.65.3.

170. On prosecution, see Humfress, *Orthodoxy and the Courts*, 181–82, 185–86, 217–19, 244, 251–52, 263.

171. For example, *CTh* 16.5.5, 16.5.6, 16.5.12, 16.5.15, 16.5.19, 16.5.24, 16.5.31, 16.5.32, 16.5.35, 16.5.38, 16.5.65.

172. It should be noted that the *Theodosian Code*, in its desire to clamp down on the heretics, imposed one particular penalty that was, in effect, antiethnographic and anticollection, insisting that the books of the heretics be burned (*CTh* 16.5.34.1). Like the colonizers, who collected knowledge and material objects from indigenous peoples just as they sought to reorient (i.e., destroy) their way of life, the heresiologists too are pushed and pulled in two contradictory directions: collect but destroy.

173. Epiphanius, *Pan.* 80.1.1 (GCS 37:484).

Shamelessness never gets enough, and foolishness is never satisfied. Rather, it has bared its mind and opened its mouth to everything, to ruin the seed of Adam and Noah by bringing their chastity to an end by any number of methods, implanting whorishness in its victims by a variety of methods. For another sect has actually arisen after these, a foolish, entirely stupid one, wholly ridiculous, inconsistent in its doctrines and composed of deluded men and women.

To that end, the colonial ethnographic perspective, both on the ground and in the libraries of European universities, mirrored the language, themes, and interests of Epiphanius's heresiological project. In their respective eras, each represented the epitome of uncritical Christian ethnography. In many ways, the former was the natural progeny of the latter. As Daniel Boyarin has incisively phrased it: "Heresiology is . . . a form of apartheid comparative religion, and apartheid comparative religion, in turn, a product of late antiquity."[174] In each case, the ethnographic imagination imposed a Christian structure and logic upon the diversity of the human race. In redefining the world through the language of Christianity, the heresiologists had imposed a new and distinctly Christian edifice upon the study of peoples and places of the natural world. The uncritical ethnographers of medieval, early modern, Enlightenment, and modern Europe were invariably perpetuators of that same language, whether consciously or not. As Herbert writes of the ethnographer William Ellis: "Christian missionaries are not social scientists in search of 'accurate information,' Ellis tells his readers . . . but rather are dedicated to counteracting 'delusive and sanguinary idolatries,' which are responsible for 'moral debasement and attendant misery.'"[175] The *Panarion*, despite its rhetoric of medicine and classification, was precisely the same sort of text. Epiphanius's text existed to counteract the delusive and sanguinary practices and doctrines of the sects that through their hubris and idolatry had corrupted the linear Christian progression of human history.[176] Epiphanius constructed his ethnographic objects to give the history of world a fundamental, if problematic, Christian appearance. The world was populated by and would continue to be populated by sects that required eradication both in texts and on the ground. As such, the world depended upon the revivifying promise of true Christianity to restore order.

---

174. Boyarin, "Apartheid Comparative Religion," 6.

175. Herbert, *Culture and Anomie*, 168. See also Anna Johnston, "The Strange Career of William Ellis," *Victorian Studies* 49.3 (2007): 491–501.

176. For the chain of degeneration set in motion by hubris and idolatry, see *Pan.* 3.3.4–10. For ancient explanations of degeneration, see Isaac, *Invention of Racism*, 89–91, 97, 108, 118–21, 126, 137–40. For early anthropological attitudes toward degeneration, see Margaret T. Hodgen, *Early Anthropology in the Sixteenth and Seventeenth Centuries* (Philadelphia: University of Pennsylvania Press, 1964), 254–71, 281–82, 378–82. For the Victorians on degeneration, see Herbert, *Culture and Anomie*, 35–41, 61–64, 215–22, 245–46.

CONCLUSION: HERETICAL CULTURE AND ORTHODOX WHOLENESS

Epiphanius's project, like that of his various heresiological colleagues, was to settle debates, by way of polemic, about modes of living Christianly. It was polemical ethnography, in the philosophical, Herodotean, and uncritical senses of the term. It was at once a way of thinking through the manner in which to transform the bodily existence into spiritual perfection—aspirational ethnography—and a way of cataloguing the actual customs that Christians practiced to align themselves more closely with God and represent the cosmos more perfectly. The heresiologists themselves were progenitors of a Christian therapy: their works provided structure for those wishing to live, behave, and believe as Christians. Having already expressed "the tenets of the faith of this only catholic church," Epiphanius pivots in his conclusion to the *Panarion* to a description of the "many ordinances as have actually been observed and are being observed in the church, some by commandment, others by voluntary acceptance."[177] Tellingly, his list begins with virginity and its various accommodations. And so "the foundation of the church is virginity which is practiced and observed by many, and held in honor," after which the church tolerates continence, widowhood, lawful wedlock, and second marriage.[178]

He goes on to describe the various orders of the church—which include priests, presbyters, deacons, subdeacons, virgins, deaconesses, exorcists, translators, and undertakers—and the procedures for celebrating the Sabbath. And while explaining the apostolic traditions that govern the celebration and worship of the Sabbath, Epiphanius again emphasizes the exceptional behavior (in both senses of the word) that orients the ascetics: "But the church's ascetics fast with a good will every day except the Lord's Day and Pentecost, and hold continual vigils."[179] The invocation of vigils leads him to a lengthier description of various liturgical practices and dietary abstinences, in which the monks, again, serve as an idealized counterpoint to the ordinary laity. He explicitly portrays the monks of the church in terms that recall and contrast with his early description of the Mesopotamians and the Messalians:[180]

> Many monks sleep on the ground, and others do not even wear shoes. Others wear sackcloth under their clothing—the ones who wear it properly, for virtue and repentance. It is inappropriate to appear publicly in sackcloth, as some do; and, as I said, it is also inappropriate to appear in public wearing collars, as some prefer to. But most monks abstain from bathing. And some monks have renounced their means of

---

177. Epiphanius, *De fide* 21.1 (GCS 37:521).
178. Epiphanius, *De fide* 21.3 (GCS 37:521).
179. Epiphanius, *De fide* 22.7 (GCS 37:523).
180. Epiphanius, *De fide* 23.6–8 (GCS 37:524–25).

livelihood, but devised light tasks for themselves which are not troublesome, so that they will not lead an idle life or eat at others' expense. Most are exercised in psalms and constant prayers, and in readings, and recitations by heart, of the holy scriptures.

And unlike the continual prayer of the Messalians, the orthodox practice of continual vigils and constant prayer further elaborates Epiphanius's earlier imaginative monastic ethnography. Here, without naming a particular monastic community or figure, without specifying geography, location, or type, Epiphanius briefly fashions a descriptive program of monastic customs and habits. But the orthodox monks are not simply a counterexample to the excessive Messalians and the heretical disposition writ large. Their function within the *Panarion* and *De fide* is to provide the basis for a positive, if idealized and not universally practical, articulation of a Christian way of living and thinking. For Epiphanius, they are the best the Christians have to offer. Hence they are the culmination and, indeed, the model for his entire ethnographic endeavor. Like the later Victorian ethnographers who did not hide their profound attachment to the superiority and normativity of their own culture, Epiphanius, as polemical ethnographer, celebrates the superiority of his own Christian culture.[181] And this celebration is explicitly conditioned by the preceding eighty entries. As Masuzawa aptly frames it: "The deviation and division within Christianity, too, are the results of the imperfection of the world, yet Christianity itself cannot be held responsible for this errant condition; nor does this sorry state of the world diminish the uniquely universal truth of Christian doctrine but on the contrary amplifies it."[182] There is no hiding Epiphanius's insistence on what constitutes the apex of Christian culture: it is all contained in *De fide*, which is the sine qua non of his heresiological endeavor. The church, he tells his readers, is "life, hope, and the assurance of immortality."[183] Orthodoxy is the metric through which he constructs the totality of his inquiry. It is his measure of civilization.

Throughout the *Panarion*, Epiphanius produces a notion of Christian culture as an institution of thought and praxis while describing and deconstructing competing models of heretical culture. And *De fide*, as his conclusion, functions as the formulation of a unified Christian culture wherein Epiphanius builds a theological entity, the holy city of God, determined by its creator and originator, and oriented around ordinances, doctrines, and practices. And in his attempt to dismantle the knowledge systems, traditions, and practices of the heretics, Epiphanius constructs a Christian culture of knowledge—a system of classification—through the language of comparative ethnography. "Culture as such," Christopher Herbert writes of the Victorians, "is not, therefore, a society's beliefs, customs, moral values, and

---

181. Epiphanius, *De fide* 20.3–25.5.
182. Masuzawa, *Invention of World Religions*, 55.
183. Epiphanius, *De fide* 19.1 (GCS 37:520). See also *De fide* 1.6–6.4, 14.1–14.7, 19.1, 22.1–2, 25.1–2.

so forth, added together: it is the wholeness that their coexistence somehow creates or makes manifest."[184] Epiphanius's *Panarion* strives toward a similar articulation of that wholeness. His treatise is a process of building cultural knowledge, of articulating the logic of Christianity, which unites its diverse array of members into a coherent whole. And as his concluding praise for the catholic church, *De fide*, makes clear, his understanding of the church is more than the sum of its individual parts and adherents. It is built upon a transcendent unification from the beginning of human history:[185]

> I shall make the case for truth, brief in its statement but sure in its teaching.... [I sing its praises] now, however, because it is the first, and ever since his incarnation has been united to Christ as his holy bride. It was created with Adam, proclaimed among the patriarchs before Abraham, believed with Abraham, revealed by Moses, and prophesied in Isaiah. But it was made manifest in Christ and exists with Christ.

Through his comparative methodology, Epiphanius formulates the contours of a unified Christian culture built upon faith and doctrine. He imagines the wider church as a community defined by practices, customs, character, and tradition. His ethnography of orthodoxy thus functions as a celebratory and didactic endeavor.

The orthodox have their own disposition, defined by customary values: "The custom of hospitality, kindness, and almsgiving to all has been prescribed for all members of this holy catholic and apostolic church."[186] Christian ethnography, like all ethnography, is a study in contrasts. As Epiphanius explains: "The church refrains from fellowship with any sect. It forbids fornication, adultery, licentiousness, idolatry, murder, all lawbreaking, magic, sorcery, astrology, palmistry, the observation of omens, charms, and amulets, the things called phylacteries. It forbids theatrical shows, hunting, horse [races], musicians and all evil-speaking and slander."[187] The church, by contrast, "continually enjoins prayer to God at the appointed hours."[188] The development of this orthodox culture—with its own rules, hermeneutics, signs, and symbols—is constructed not simply in oppositional terms but in oppositional *ethnographic* terms. His discussion of the customs and habits of true Christians speaks to a powerful reformulation of a way of life while his comparative theology attests a newfound way of thought. As the missionary anthropologist John Williams phrased it, only the gospel "can subdue the fierce passions of our nature."[189]

---

184. Herbert, *Culture and Anomie*, 5.
185. Epiphanius, *Pan.* 80.11.1–3 (GCS 37:495).
186. Epiphanius, *De fide* 24.1 (GCS 37:525).
187. Epiphanius, *De fide* 24.3–5 (GCS 37:525).
188. Epiphanius, *De fide* 24.6 (GCS 37:525).
189. Williams, *A Narrative of Missionary Enterprises*, 533.

The notion of living as a Christian and more specifically living as a Christian in the proper way—in coordination with apostolic values and interpretations—governs the *Panarion*'s comparative ethnographic conclusion. True Christians do not swear, abuse, curse, or lie. They fervently and humbly pray. They memorialize the dead, offer hymns at dawn and psalms at "lamp-lighting time."[190] "Most sell their goods and give to the poor."[191] All this ritualization and habituation, with respect to the monks, the priesthood, and the laity, comprises an overarching and resolute orthodox disposition, what Epiphanius calls "the character of the church":[192]

> Such is the character of this holy [mother of ours], together with her faith as we have described it; and these are the ordinances that obtain in her. For this is the *character of the church*, and by the will of the Father, the Son and the Holy Spirit it is drawn from the Law, the Prophets, the Apostles, and the Evangelists, like a good antidote compounded of many perfumes for the health of its users. These are the features of this chaste bride of Christ; this is her dowry, the covenant of her inheritance, and the will of her bridegroom and heavenly king, our Lord Jesus Christ.

Here is the ethic of *vera religio*, defined as much as by a character as by what it includes and excludes. Epiphanius describes a church that cultivates not only an epistemology but also a morality with respect to the natural and the supernatural world.[193] The *Panarion* is not only a clear articulation of a system of knowledge about the heretics. It is equally an elaboration of the church's character, its fundamental disposition. *De fide* is about identifying the delimiting the facets and limitations of Christian behavior and knowledge. It is about writing Christianity as a city of believers. It is an ethnography and topography of orthodoxy.

---

190. Epiphanius, *De fide* 23.1 (GCS 37:524).
191. Epiphanius, *De fide* 24.7 (GCS 37:525).
192. Epiphanius, *De fide* 25.1–2 (GCS 37:525–26); emphasis added.
193. On the notion of ethnography of morals in early Christianity, see Wayne A. Meeks, *The Origins of Christian Morality: The First Two Centuries* (New Haven: Yale University Press, 1993), 8–11.

3

Contesting Ethnography

Heretical Models of Human and Cosmic Plurality

> Unlike the travel text, however, which is, as such texts are by nature, one damn thing after another, the ethnographic text has a thesis, the thesis in fact that Lévi-Strauss has pursued for the quarter century or so since: namely, "the ensemble of a people's customs has always its particular style; they form in systems."
>
> —CLIFFORD GEERTZ

Like the classical ethnographers of the ancient Mediterranean, Christians wrote the peoples of their world selectively and self-interestedly.[1] Indeed, the heresiologists explicitly constructed images of sectarian parties by describing their customs, habits, and beliefs in relation to a genealogy of singular Christian truth. In describing and refuting the heretics, the heresiologists frequently stressed their opponents' appropriation of the opinions and practices of Greek philosophers, poets, and mythographers as well as those of the Celts, Assyrians, Egyptians, Babylonians, and Jews.[2] Heresiologies enumerated the heretics' devotion to alien and thus defiling philosophical doctrines and ethnographic paradigms or theories. The heretics, as hybridized Christians—part Christian, part Druidic philosopher; part Christian,

---

1. The chapter epigraph is cited from Clifford Geertz, *Works and Lives: The Anthropologist as Author* (Stanford: Stanford University Press, 1988), 37. Geertz is quoting Claude Lévi-Strauss, *Tristes tropiques*.

2. Hippolytus, for example, identifies the following arts, branches of knowledge, persons, and peoples that have found their way into the customs and beliefs of the Christian heretics: astrology, numerology, mystery cults, cosmogony, divination, Pythagoras, Epicurus, Thales, Empedocles, Heraclitus, Anaximander, Anaximenes, Anaxagoras, Archelaus, Parmenides, Leucippus, Democritus, Xenophanes, Ecphantus, Hippo, Socrates, Plato, Aristotle, Egyptians, Jews, Chaldeans, Brahmans, Druids, Pyrrhoneans, Arithmeticians, Stoics, and magicians. See, for example, Jared Secord, "Medicine and Sophistry in Hippolytus' *Refutatio*," *StPatr* 65 (2011): 217–24. On the doxographical record provided by Hippolytus, see Jaap Mansfeld, *Heresiography in Context: Hippolytus' Elenchos as a Source of Greek Philosophy* (New York: Brill, 1992).

part numerologist; part Christian, part diviner; and so on—were exemplars of corrupted intellectual pedigrees.³ As Kendra Eshleman has noted with respect to Hippolytus's heresiological project: "The real center of gravity of Hippolytus' history of error, and the source of its unity, is the thesis that Christian 'heresies' derive from pagan sources, especially Greek philosophy."⁴ Tertullian and Irenaeus likewise stressed the heretics' assimilation of the practices and doctrines of Greek and Roman intellectuals: "Notorious, too, are the dealings of heretics with very many magicians, charlatans, astrologers, and philosophers, devotees of speculation."⁵

Not only were the heretics rampant appropriators of pagan culture, but they also shared with pagans a core mentality about the world: both populations were driven by limitless curiosity. The heresiologists further argued that this curiosity illustrated the heretics' arrogance, fraudulence, and fundamental desire to transcend the limits of the human condition. As Tertullian sharply phrased it: such groups "say that God is not to be feared. So everything is free to them and unrestrained."⁶ Irenaeus reached a similarly cutting conclusion: the heretics "are discarding the truth and introducing deceitful 'myths and endless genealogies,' which, as the Apostle says, 'promote speculations rather than divine training that is the faith.'"⁷ Irenaeus's polemic, in fact, turns on the ethnographic implications of the heretics' curiosity: it is about genealogy and mythography as branches of knowledge that account for the world, its peoples, and its creator (or creators).

The ethnographic polemics of the Christian heresiologists extended beyond catalogues of praxis and doctrine to encompass debates about macroscopic theories—ethnographic paradigms such as genealogy and universal history—of human and Christian diversity and difference. Heresiological ethnography worked to establish Christian structures and categories that explained how Christians—and humans more broadly—came to behave and believe differently. And just as the heresiologists could describe a heretical sect by its corruption of scripture, sexually perverse proclivities, or dietary restrictions, they could likewise represent them as adherents of fallacious worldviews and ethnographic paradigms born of errant cosmological, astrological, and theological theories. The heretics devised not only "models for" the world (i.e., ways of life), as we saw in the last chapter, but also models of reality, "that is, symbolic conceptions of the general order of existence."⁸

---

3. On hybridity and heresy, see Daniel Boyarin, *Border Lines: The Partition of Judaeo-Christianity* (Philadelphia: University of Pennsylvania Press, 2004), 14–18, 208–20.

4. Kendra Eshleman, *The Social World of Intellectuals in the Roman Empire: Sophists, Philosophers, and Christians* (New York: Cambridge University Press, 2012), 231.

5. Tertullian, *Praescr.* 43.1 (SC 46:149).

6. Tertullian, *Praescr.* 43.3 (SC 46:150).

7. Irenaeus, *Adv. haer.* 1 pr. 1.1–4 (SC 264:18), citing 1 Tim. 1.4.

8. Kevin Schillbrack, "Religion, Models of, and Reality: Are We Through with Geertz?," *JAAR* 73.2 (2005): 429–52, at 429. As Geertz, "Ethos, World View, and the Analysis of Sacred Symbols," in his

For the heresiologists, it is the heretics' ideas of order—constructed by the heresiologists themselves—that demanded scrutiny and refutation precisely because they undermined the omnipotence of the Christian God. Heresiologists disputed the heretics' theories of religious difference but also of cultural particularity, human behavior, mental dispositions, and ethnogenesis. The comparison of ethnographic paradigms—both the way that heretics constructed their own understanding of the world and the sort of ethnographic polemic that heresiologists directed against these groups—facilitated debates not only about different theories of human and sectarian diversity but also about the parameters of Christian ideas of epistemology, cosmology, and theology. The heresiologists appropriated the ethnographic paradigms that pagans often used to construct and then subordinate subject peoples and cultural practices, while also ascribing to heretics such practices as would typically be associated with or revered by those very same pagan intellectuals. In so doing these writers invoked and strengthened the impression of a singular Christian reality, one that excluded both non-Christian intellectuals and the "Christians" who ostensibly resembled them. The intellectual genealogies developed by the heresiologists worked, then, to create enduring associations, at the level of both disposition and macroscopic theorization, between the pagans and the heretics.

While I shall dwell at some length on the orthodox Christian deployment of ethnographic models to explain sectarian proliferation later in this chapter (and for the entirety of the next), I wish to begin my discussion of the Christianization of macroscopic ethnography by elaborating the heresiologists' engagement with and refutation of competing sectarian theories of human difference. Various intellectual traditions and disciplines—astrology, divination, philosophy, numerology, and mythology—proffered theories of human diversity. These theories, determined by genealogical, climatological, or astrological patterns, attempted to explain the behavioral, dispositional, ritualistic, and phenotypical differences among the peoples (and Christians) of the known world.[9] According to the heresiologists, the heretics deployed the language of macroscopic ethnography to elaborate their own theological doctrines, religious practices, and cosmologies. As Greg Woolf has noted, ethnographic paradigms "provided a vital resource for those creating new ethnographic knowledge . . . and offered several routes for the invention of traditions."[10] The heretics, in short, strove to make sense of their world—to elaborate their own culture—through ethnographic analysis. And it was precisely

---

Interpretation of Cultures: Selected Essays by Clifford Geertz (New York: Perseus, 1973), explains, "[A people's] world view is a picture of the way things in sheer actuality are, their concept of nature, of self, of society. It contains their most comprehensive ideas of order" (126–41, at 127).

9. On paradigms of ethnographic analysis, see Greg Woolf, *Tales of the Barbarians: Ethnography and Empire in the Roman West* (Malden, Mass.: Wiley-Blackwell, 2011), 32–58.

10. Ibid. 57.

because the heretics used ethnography to construct their own (alternative) Christian tradition that the heresiologists devoted pages and pages of their texts to identify the weaknesses in the heretics' cosmological, philosophical, and mythographic systems.

By the late second and early third centuries, the tensions between competing models of human history, religion, and culture were entrenched within heresiological discourse. To that end, heresiological literature engaged with the enterprise of theorizing ethnographic difference in two essential ways. First, it was harnessed positively to advance an orthodox Christian interpretive model of the world. Second, the heresiologists embraced ethnographic reasoning in order to refute alternative theories of human and theological diversification while also privileging their own scheme. It is this twofold process—the protracted oscillation between co-option and rejection of ethnographic techniques—that I explore below. Both sides of this prolonged struggle advocated analytical trajectories that explained the nature, causes, and implications of human diversity.[11] In conceptualizing the contestation between orthodoxy and heresy as an ethnographic endeavor, I focus on their competing efforts to comprehend and construct their surroundings in distinctly Christian terms. To depict the world's underlying Christian structure, the heresiologists explicitly theologized preexisting ethnographic paradigms. Ethnography was a way for the heresiologists to naturalize the conditions that gave rise to sectarian diversity and to create the impression that there was a pure and given tradition of Christianity.

I begin my treatment of Christian macroscopic ethnography with a discussion of the heretics' deployment of two particular analytical paradigms: astrology (or astrological determinism) and cosmological mythography (or cosmological allegory).[12] In each case, I argue that the heretics applied ethnographic knowledge—falla-

---

11. For the perspective of the Nag Hammadi texts, see Denise Kimber Buell, *Why This New Race: Ethnic Reasoning in Early Christianity* (New York: Columbia University Press, 2005), 126–37; Philippa Lois Townsend, "Another Race? Ethnicity, Universalism, and the Emergence of Christianity" (Ph.D. dissertation, Princeton University, 2009); and Geoffrey Smith, *Guilt by Association: Heresy Catalogues in Early Christianity* (New York: Oxford University Press, 2014), 108–30.

12. The most systematic treatment of early Christian attitudes toward astrology is Tim Hegedus, *Early Christianity and Ancient Astrology* (New York: Peter Lang, 2007), which considers a massive amount of material, including writings from the New Testament, Augustine, Bardaisan, Hippolytus, Tertullian, pseudo-Clement, Origen, and Priscillian, among others. See also now Kathleen Gibbons, "Who Reads the Stars? Origen's Critique of Astrological Geography," in *The Routledge Handbook of Identity and the Environment in the Classical and Medieval Worlds*, ed. Rebecca Futo Kennedy and Molly Lewis-Jones (Abingdon, Oxon.: Routledge, 2015), 230–46. On astrology as esoteric tradition in antiquity, see Kocku von Stuckard, "Jewish and Christian Astrology in Late Antiquity: A New Approach," *Numen* 47 (2000): 1–40. Among Jews and Christians, astrological knowledge was not summarily rejected; rather it was a fundamental component of their discourses about cult theology, time, magic, determinism and volition, and religious and political legitimization.

ciously, in the eyes of the heresiologist—to map the contours of their cosmic worldview. At the macroscopic level, ethnographic classification was how Christians depicted themselves and their neighbors within the world. For both heretics and heresiologists, macroscopic paradigms functioned as an ideological prism through which writers imagined Christianity's capacity to categorize the totality of human knowledge about the world. Heresiology explicated how true Christianity—and *only* Christianity, not adulterated Christian heresy—could adduce the inner workings of the natural world, human diversity, and religious plurality. With both rewritten mythography and applied astrology, Hippolytus articulated his fear of the heretics as a fear of alternative theories that organized the universe and the people within it. The Christian conceptualization of the world, its macroscopic ordering and its microscopic materialization, remained firmly under attack by the hereticization of ethnographic knowledge. Christians and heretics were thus debating how to conceptualize, comprehend, and control the world they inhabited. The vehemence of heresiology's polemic reflects, I would suggest, the stakes of this ideological dispute.

REJECTING PARADIGMS: HIPPOLYTUS, ASTROLOGY, AND HERETICAL MASTER NARRATIVES

The ten-book *Refutation of the All the Heresies* (*Refutatio omnium haeresium* or Ὁ κατὰ πασῶν αἱρέσεων ἔλεγχος)[13] is frequently but somewhat controversially attributed to Hippolytus, an ecclesiastical figure in early third-century Rome, who engaged in theological and ecclesiastical controversies with the Roman bishops Zephyrinus (r. 199–217 C.E.) and Callistus (r. 217–22 C.E.).[14] In the *Refutatio*, Hippolytus explained the practices and opinions of the heretics, as he simultaneously used this profusion of ethnographic information to enumerate the intellectual trajectory of sectarianism. Although he discussed the many forces and factors that

---

13. The Greek edition I have used for Hippolytus is *Refutatio omnium haeresium*, ed. Miroslav Marcovich (Berlin: de Gruyter, 1986). I have followed (with alterations) the translation in ANF 5:9–153. For a good entry point into the text, see the Gabriella Aragione and Enrico Norelli, eds., *Des évêques, des écoles et des hérétiques: Actes du colloque international sur la "Réfutation de toutes les hérésies," Genève, 13–14 juin 2008* (Lausanne: Éditions du Zèbre, 2011).

14. The following offer detailed, if not always convincing, treatments of the various questions pertaining to the historical and authorial Hippolytus: Allen Brent, *Hippolytus and the Roman Church in the Third Century: Communities in Tension before the Emergence of a Monarch-Bishop* (New York: Brill, 1995); J. A. Cerrato, *Hippolytus between East and West: The Commentaries and the Provenance of the Corpus* (New York: Oxford, 2002); and Emanuele Castelli, "The Author of the *Refutatio omnium haeresium* and the Attribution of the *De universo* to Flavius Josephus," in Aragione and Norelli, *Des évêques, des écoles et des hérétiques,* 219–31. I will continue to refer to Hippolytus as the author of the text since the identity of the author is less important than the date of its composition in the early third century C.E.

had given rise to philosophical parties and Christian heresies, Hippolytus also exerted considerable energy to combat alternative models for organizing notions of human difference and creation. Undergirding his analysis of the heretics' origins and diversity was a narrative of true Christianity, which posited a continual tradition from Jesus through the apostles into his own day. In the case of both the unbroken chain of orthodoxy and the fragmented proliferation of heresies, his text propounded its vision of the makeup of the Christian world through the discourse of ethnography. Hippolytus utilized various facets of ethnographic writing— including classificatory language, genealogy, mentality, and genealogical analysis— to solidify the truth of his narrative and to frame his opponents' history, birth, and practice in the language of false ethnography. As he challenged certain theorizations of human difference, Hippolytus used his heresiology to elaborate his own theory of human diversity. His ethnographic disposition thus emerges both in contestation with and in relation to the heretics' own claims to read the world via astrology, numerology, and mythography. To illustrate the contested ethnographic ground of heresiology, I have chosen to discuss two examples of the heretics' own theorization of human diversity: the cases of astrological determinism—the relationship between the stars and human behavior, phenotypes, and orientation—and cosmological mythography, the relationship between myth, cosmology, and the human being. Hippolytus's description and disapprobation of these models was framed within a conceptual vernacular that sought to establish the *Christian* state of the world and the human position within it. Ethnography now served to color and explain the world of Christianity.

In Book 4 of his *Refutation*, Hippolytus cites and summarizes the far-reaching claims and procedures of the astrological arts as delineated by the second-century physician and Pyrrhonian skeptic Sextus Empiricus (ca. 160–210 C.E.) in his *Against the Astrologers*.[15] Alongside the numerical theorists who "suppose that they interpret life" (τὸ ζῆν διακρίνειν νομιζόντων) and the magicians who harnessed "the powers of secret knowledge" (ἀπορρήτων μαθημάτων ... τὰς δυνάμεις), the astrologers presented themselves as fonts of an exclusive knowledge of the future.[16] By deriving and fixing the horoscope—the act of identifying the stars at the

---

15. For the text, see Sextus Empiricus, *Math.* (Book 5) trans. R. G. Bury, LCL 382 (Cambridge, Mass.: Harvard University Press, 1949), 322–71. *Against the Professors* attacks six arts or disciplines on Pyrrhonian (skeptical) grounds: the grammarians, rhetoricians, geometricians, arithmeticians, astrologers, and musicians. For the outlines of Sextus Empiricus's biography and philosophical thinking, see Alan Bailey, *Sextus Empiricus and Pyrrhonean Scepticism* (New York: Oxford University Press, 2002), and Luciano Floridi, *Sextus Empiricus: The Transmission and Recovery of Pyrrhonism* (New York: Oxford University Press, 2002). For a precise concordance of Hippolytus's reliance on Sextus's *Against the Astrologers* (*Against the Professors*, Book 5), see Marcovich, *Hippolytus*, 18–31.

16. Hippolytus, *Ref.* 4.15.1, 34.1 (Marcovich 109, 122). For a survey of Hippolytus's discussion of astrology, see Hegedus, *Early Christianity and Ancient Astrology*, 279–305.

moment of birth—as well as mapping the sidereal influences over territories and nations (astrogeography or ethnographic astrology), the astrologers purported to understand the causes of human biological and dispositional diversity as well as the fated trajectories of human lives. For nearly thirty chapters of the *Refutatio*'s fourth book, Hippolytus describes the practices of the Chaldean astrologers via a recapitulation of Sextus's text. He outlines and refutes at length their claim to provide an accurate prognostication, through the analysis of the position of the stars, of the contours of a particular human life, the nature of a particular person's disposition, and his or her physiological features. Though he insists that the astrological art of the Chaldeans was unstable and untrustworthy in its own right, the falsity of their practice had been magnified by the fact that it now resided within Christian intellectual circles. He rails against the proximate ascendancy of the Peratic heretics, a Gnostic sect "who have cultivated the art, becoming disciples of the Chaldeans ... having changed the names [merely]," and "have from this source concocted their heresy."[17] They are astrologers, not Christians. Hippolytus's refutation, above all else, strove to expel astrology from the (still developing) Christian intellectual tradition as a legitimate or even complementary branch of knowledge: "We will prove that the astrological arts are incoherent, intending thereafter to invalidate also the Peratae as a branch growing out of an unstable root."[18] Astrology's infiltration into the lexicon of Christian dogma and cosmology tarnished the professed genealogical purity of Christian truth by undermining the claims of Christian knowledge about the world and God. The Peratae, Hippolytus maintained, "deriving their doctrine from astrologers, act despitefully toward Christ" by importing into the sphere of Christian doctrine an alternative narrative of human destiny and design.[19] Before exploring Hippolytus's discussion in detail, it is necessary to briefly consider the ethnographic dimensions and implications of ancient astrological discourse.

Tamsyn Barton and Greg Woolf both situate Greco-Roman astrological discourse and astrology at the nexus of cosmological, geographical, imperial, and ethnographic theorization.[20] It is from the works of Manilius, the first-century-C.E.

---

17. Hippolytus, *Ref.* 4.2.3 (Marcovich 93; my translation). For his full discussion of the system of the Peratae, see *Ref.* 5.12–18. On astrological determinism among the Gnostics, see Horace Jeffrey Hodges, "Gnostic Liberation from Astrological Determinism: Hipparchan 'Trepidation' and the Breaking of Fate," *VC* 51.4 (1997): 359–73; and Nicola Denzey Lewis, *Cosmology and Fate in Gnosticism and Graeco-Roman Antiquity: Under Pitiless Skies* (Boston: Brill, 2013), 165–80.

18. Hippolytus, *Ref.* 4.2.3 (Marcovich 93; altered from ANF). See Klaus Koschorke, *Hippolyt's Ketzerbekämpfung und Polemik gegen die Gnostiker: Eine tendenzkritische Untersuchung seiner "Refutatio omnium haeresium"* (Wiesbaden: Harrassowitz, 1975), esp. 25–55.

19. Hippolytus, *Ref.* 5.13.1 (Marcovich 174).

20. See Woolf, *Tales of the Barbarians*, 48–51; and Tamsyn Barton, *Ancient Astrology* (New York: Routledge, 1994), 157–207. On astrology and fatalism, see Katharina Volk, *Manilius and His Intellectual Background* (New York: Oxford University Press, 2009), 59–76.

astrological poet, and Ptolemy, the second-century-C.E. mathematician and astronomer, for whom scholars reconstruct principles and implications of ancient astrological discourse. Manilius's *Astronomica,* a poetic study of astrology and its effect upon microcosmic reality, described a system of cosmic-terrestrial interdependence such that the investigation of sidereal phenomena allowed humans to gather knowledge of the cosmos and apply it to various global and particular problems.[21] As the opening section of the poem proclaims, Manilius traversed the study of the heavens "to mark how it controls the birth of all living beings through its sign."[22] Manilius, as a "hard" astrologer, someone who ascribed causative (not merely associative) control to the stars, propounded a system that assigned the cosmos the all-encompassing power to determine the fate of humankind.[23] As an explanatory mechanism for the course of history, the governance of the home and the city, the paths of war, and filial relations, among other conditions, institutions, and historical phenomena, Manilius's treatise theorized, if ambiguously, the ethnographic impulse embedded within ancient astrological discourse. As Katharina Volk explains, "The ethnic and national differences among the peoples of the earth are due to the fact that different signs of the zodiac dominate different regions, crucially influencing the appearance and lifestyle of their inhabitants."[24]

Manilius was clearly following in the philosophical tradition (Presocratic, Platonic, Aristotelian, Stoic, etc.) of harnessing the explanatory capacity of cosmology to elucidate the observable phenomena of the natural world.[25] Moreover, because the universe itself was "formed by the diverse elements of nature—air and fire, earth and stretched-out sea," cosmological investigation conditioned the study of

---

21. For Manilius in general, see Volk, *Manilius and His Intellectual Background*; François Paschoud, "Deux études sur Manilius," in *Romanitas, Christianitas: Untersuchungen zur Geschichte und Literatur der römischen Kaiserzeit,* ed. Gerhard Wirth (Berlin: de Gruyter, 1982), 125–53; and now Steven J. Green, *Disclosure and Discretion in Roman Astrology: Manilius and His Augustan Contemporaries* (New York: Oxford University Press, 2014).

22. Manilius, *Astr.* 1.17, trans. G. P. Goold, LCL 469 (Cambridge, Mass.: Harvard University Press, 1977), 6.

23. Volk, *Manilius and His Intellectual Background,* 61.

24. Ibid. 102. On Volk's point, see Manilius, *Astr.* 4.696–806 (LCL 469:276–86). The most thorough treatment of Manilius's astrogeography (or ethnographic astrology) is found in Godefroid de Callataÿ, "La géographie zodiacale de Manilius (*Astr.* 4, 744–817), avec une note sur l'Énéide virgilienne," *Latomus* 60 (2001): 35–66. Manilius details the distinguishing features of the various peoples and lands of the known world. As Callataÿ observes, the poet is especially interested in charting the differences between nations via an elaboration of dissimilarities of skin color, vocal intonation, language, customs, agricultural practices, and animal husbandry.

25. On the intersection of cosmology, astrology, and philosophy, consult Barton, *Ancient Astrology,* 32–63; and David E. Hahm, *The Origins of Stoic Cosmology* (Columbus: Ohio State University Press, 1977).

geography, ethnography, and climatology.[26] Although the *Astronomica* is unsystematic on the point of detailed ethnographic causation, Manilius's concluding remarks do causally link the relationship between the structure of the heavens—what Volk terms "the macrocosm" of astrological discourse—and geographical and humanistic organization, two microcosmic effects.[27] This conceptual broadening of the cosmic horoscope had two primary implications: first, that "thus is the world for ever distributed among the twelve signs, and from the signs themselves must the laws prevailing among them be applied to the areas they govern," and second, that "every man [must] shun or seek a place to live in, so hope for loyalty or be forewarned of peril, according to the character which has come down to earth from high heaven."[28] As Volk explains, "on earth as it is in heaven, man is ruled by the stars, not only through his horoscope, but also in terms of his dwelling place and country of origin."[29] The order of the world of men followed the order of the stars.

At one particular juncture in his poem, having outlined the geographical distribution of the signs—each sign rules a particular region, "wherein the signs should claim their predominant influence"—Manilius linked the physiology of human differences with climatological and geographical forces:[30]

> The Ethiopians stain the world and depict a race of men steeped in darkness; less sun-burnt are the natives of India; the land of Egypt, flooded by the Nile, darkens bodies more mildly owing to the inundation of its fields: it is a country nearer to us and its moderate climate imparts a medium tone. The Sun-god dries up with dust the tribes of Africans amid their desert lands.

Shortly thereafter in the poem, this language (along with other naturalistic phenomena) was streamlined into a fairly straightforward theory: "The signs shine upon the special regions to which they have been allocated and imbue with their climate the peoples that lie beneath."[31] There was a correspondence, then, between astrological determinism and climatological determinism. And while Manilius had offered an explicit "assignation of zodiac signs to zones," which could implicate climatological

26. Manilius, *Astr.* 1.248–49 (LCL 469:22–24). See Volk, *Manilius and His Intellectual Background*, 61 n. 8: "Manilius appears to vacillate between considering the stars themselves to be independent agents and regarding them as the mere tools of such diverse superior powers as the universe, god, nature, and fate. However, this does not constitute a contradiction, since, in the poet's pantheistic cosmos, *mundus* ('universe'), *deus* ('god'), *natura* ('nature'), and *fatum* ('fate') to some extent function as synonyms, and the starry sky can likewise be referred to as *mundus* and thus be identified with the cosmos as a whole."
27. Ibid. 102–3, 212–15, 221–23.
28. Manilius, *Astr.* 4.4.815–17 (LCL 469:286–88).
29. Volk, *Manilius and His Intellectual Background*, 102–3.
30. Manilius, *Astr.* 4.700 (LCL 469:278); block quotation from *Astr.* 4.723–29 (LCL 469:280).
31. Manilius, *Astr.* 4.742–43 (LCL 469:278).

effects, the vast majority of his treatise explained the relationship between zodiacs and zones in mythological and historical terms. Astrology, for Manilius, was part of wider cultural matrix that bound together ideas about myth, history, nation, worship, disposition, and physiology.

Ptolemy's *Tetrabiblos* similarly elaborated a systematic theorization of the intersection of astrology, climatology, physiognomy, and ethnography.[32] Indeed, the entirety of Book 2 of his *Tetrabiblos* is an investigation of geographical or ethnographic astrology. The book begins by explaining the distinction between the two main parts (μέρη) or branches of astrology, the first of which governed territories, countries, or both (and would be the focus of his Book 2), and the second of which governed the individual (Book 3):[33]

> Since, then, prognostication by astronomical means is divided into two great and principal parts, and since the first and more universal (γενικωτέρου) is that which relates to whole races, countries, and cities (ὅλα ἔθνη καὶ χώρας καὶ πόλεις λαμβανομένου), which is called general, and the second and more specific is that which relates to individual men, which is called genethlialogical, we believe it fitting to treat first of the general division, because such matters are naturally swayed by greater and more powerful causes than are particular events.

The distinction between mundane and genethlialogical astrology—the former applies to corporate or national character, events, and effects, whereas the latter claims predictive determination over individual character through fixing the horoscope at birth—illustrated the bipartite dominion of the astrological arts. For Ptolemy, neither the nation nor the individual was beyond the reach of its explanatory and deterministic capacity.

Following in the footsteps of the second-century sophist Polemo of Laodicea, Ptolemy articulated a tripartite division of the world: "The demarcation of national/ethnic characteristics (ἐθνικῶν ἰδιωμάτων τὰ ... διαιρεῖσθαι) is established in part by entire parallels and angles, through their position relative to the ecliptic and the sun" and included the northern parallels, the southern parallels, and the central region.[34] Those who were "far removed from the zodiac" in the

---

32. Barton, *Ancient Astrology*, 182–83. See also her *Power and Knowledge: Astrology, Physiognomics, and Medicine under the Roman Empire* (Ann Arbor: University of Michigan Press, 2002), 84, 92–94, 120–22. For more on Ptolemy, astrology, and ethnography, see Benjamin Isaac, *The Invention of Racism in Classical Antiquity* (Princeton: Princeton University Press, 2004), 99–101. An especially useful resource is J. Lennart Berggren and Alexander Jones, *Ptolemy's Geography: An Annotated Translation of the Theoretical Chapters* (Princeton: Princeton University Press, 2000), 4–54. See also the very useful work of Germaine Aujac, *Claude Ptolémée, astronome, astrologue, géographe: Connaissance et représentation du monde habité* (Paris: Éditions du CTHS, 1993).

33. Ptolemy, *Tetrabiblos* 2.1, trans. F. E. Robbins, LCL 435 (Cambridge, Mass.: Harvard University Press, 1980), 116–18.

34. Ptolemy, *Tetrabiblos* 2.2 (LCL 435:120).

"more northern parallels" inhabited a cooler climate and were themselves cooled (white in complexion, for example).[35] Similarly, "the southernmost of them are in general more shrewd and inventive, and better versed in knowledge of things divine because their zenith is close to the zodiac and to the planets revolving about it."[36] Those who existed in the middle, between the extremes, "share in the equable temperature of the air, which varies, to be sure, but has not violent changes from heat to cold. They are therefore medium in coloring, of moderate stature, in nature equable, live close together, and are civilized in their habits" (καὶ τοῖς ἤθεσιν ἥμεροι τυγχάνουσι).[37] Ptolemy's text, however, moved beyond this tripartite schema and introduced a fourfold world, each quarter of which was ruled by a triad of zodiacal signs. The northwestern quadrant of the world, which was governed by Aries, Leo, and Sagittarius, consisted of the territories Britain, Galatia (Transalpine), Germany, Bastarnia, Gaul (Cisalpine), Apulia, Sicily, Tyrrhenia, Celtica, and Spain.[38] The nations of this quarter had a general similarity—they were "independent, liberty-loving, fond of arms, industrious, very warlike, ... cleanly, and magnanimous," and yet they were distinguished by their familiarity or proximity (or both) to one of the three zodiacal signs of the region.[39] Because, for instance, Britain was more familiar with Aries, they were "fiercer, more-headstrong, and bestial," whereas the Sicilians, following Leo, were "more masterful, benevolent, and co-operative."[40] In detailing ethnic mentalities, Ptolemy explicitly intruded into the domain of the ethnographers and the physiognomists; astrology, he contended, provided a systematic explanation of human diversity via analysis of climatological and cosmological principles. As a mode of geographical and cosmological ethnography, climatic determinism was, in fact, embedded within Ptolemy's work (as well as in the *Astronomica*'s descriptions).[41] Ptolemy conjoined ethnographic difference with climatological phenomena, which were, in turn, bound by cosmological principles.

Although Manilius and Ptolemy differ over details regarding the mechanistic elements of astrology, they both ascribed the ethnic stereotypes of various nations

---

35. Ptolemy, *Tetrabiblos* 2.2 (LCL 435:122).
36. Ptolemy, *Tetrabiblos* 2.2 (LCL 435:124).
37. Ptolemy, *Tetrabiblos* 2.2 (LCL 435:124).
38. Ptolemy, *Tetrabiblos* 2.3 (LCL 435:128).
39. Ptolemy, *Tetrabiblos* 2.3 (LCL 435:134).
40. Ptolemy, *Tetrabiblos* 2.3 (LCL 435:134).
41. On climatological and environmental determinism (the influence of nature on human difference and behavior) in ancient literature, see Jonathan M. Hall, *Hellenicity: Between Ethnicity and Culture* (Chicago: University of Chicago Press, 2002), 196–98; Isaac, *The Invention of Racism*, 55–109; and Rosalind Thomas, *Herodotus in Context: Ethnography, Science and the Art of Persuasion* (New York: Cambridge University Press, 2000), 75–101.

to astrological and broader cosmological patterns.[42] For both of them, "ethnographic difference is made meaningful by contextualizing it within the greater structure of the cosmos."[43] In creating a hierarchical dependence between the realm of the cosmos and the world of men, astrology postulated a system of governance over the entire universe and its human participants. Whether at the level of the individual or of the nation, astrology sought to organize the world by measurable, observable rules and regulations. The inhabitants of the universe, despite their seeming infinitude and diversity, could be ordered by the fixed and perpetual patterns of the stars. The state of the world was organized and comprehended at both the macroscopic and microscopic levels through an investigation of the heavens. Strabo, the late first-century-B.C.E./early first-century-C.E. geographer, distills the implications of geography and astronomy for the study of human difference:[44]

> All those who undertake to describe the distinguishing features of countries devote special attention to astronomy and geography. . . . Everything of this kind, since it is caused by the movement of the sun and the other stars as well, as by their tendency towards the center, compels us to look to the vault of heaven, and to observe the phenomena of the heavenly bodies peculiar to our individual positions; and in these phenomena we see very great variations in the positions of inhabited places. So, if one is about to treat of the differences between countries, how can he discuss his subject correctly and adequately if he has paid no attention, even superficially, to any of these matters?

To understand and organize the natural world, one must look to the cosmos. And to comprehend the cosmos, one must study the movement of the heavenly bodies. Ethnography, in this view, is but a reflection of supernatural forces.

HIPPOLYTUS: COMBATTING ASTROLOGICAL ETHNOGRAPHY

According to Hippolytus, the Elchasaite, Peratic, and Aratean heresies were all in the thrall of the promise and power of astrological knowledge.[45] But because these heretical groups shared an interest in astrology, they could be all refuted in one

---

42. Woolf, *Tales of the Barbarians*, 51.
43. Ibid.
44. Strabo, *Geogr.* 1.1.13-14, trans. Horace Leonard Jones, LCL 49 (Cambridge, Mass.: Harvard University Press, 1917), 25-27.
45. On the relationship between astrology and the Elchasaites, Peratae, and Arateans, respectively, see *Ref.* 9.16; 5.12-17; 4.46-50. For an analysis of Hippolytus's descriptions, see Hegedus, *Early Christianity and Ancient Astrology*, 279-305. On the identity and history of the Elchasaites more broadly, see Gerard P. Luttikhuizen, "Elchasaites and Their Books," in *A Companion to Second-Century 'Christian Heretics,'* ed. Antti Marjanen and Petri Luomanen (Boston: Brill, 2008), 335-64.

stroke: once astrology was exposed as a fraudulent mode of knowledge, the heretics' dependence upon this body of knowledge exposed their own fallacious teachings. It was error and refutation by association. Possessing the power of the horoscope, astrologers "could be seen as an independent means of discovering the future."[46] The astrological arts emphatically bound human fate to the power of the stars and seemed to produce a comprehensive framework for understanding what causes human history and behavior. Not only did the art of astrology challenge notions of human free will; it also denied the omnipotence of the Christian God, who became subservient to the position and power of the stars. This weakening of God's power was further accomplished through the heretics' appropriation of astrological theories about the particularities of human difference. The heretics embraced an organizational model of human diversity—a way of explaining both personal and communal characteristics throughout the world—that was untenable for Christian writers and for the Christian interpretation of scripture and sacred history.[47] To that end, Hippolytus laid out a sweeping, although entirely appropriated, response. By systematically engaging with the ethnographic theory of astrological determinism—the theory that the positions of the zodiac causally conditioned human phenotypes, personalities, and attitudes—Hippolytus fashioned a significant part of his heresiology as a debate over the terms of ethnographic and macroscopic theorization.

Hippolytus's plan of attack against the astrologers focused on the particulars of their *technē* (τέχνη)—what Sextus termed "a method of attack at close quarters"—rather than a general denial of the celestial impact upon the terrestrial or the impossibility of a singularly fatalistic or predetermined mode of existence.[48] To dispel the so-called prescience of the astrological art and knowledge, Hippolytus forswore the very possibility of fixing the horoscope. Put simply, he says, "it is impossible to fix the horoscope."[49] This ambiguity demolished the entire astrological enterprise: "For from this are derived the rest of the cardinal points."[50] Obtaining a horoscope required the astrologers' knowledge of the precise moment of an

---

46. Barton, *Ancient Astrology*, 72.

47. See Barton, *Power and Knowledge*, 62–69; and her *Ancient Astrology*, 71–85; Wolfgang Hübner, *Zodiacus Christianus: Jüdisch-christliche Adaptionen des Tierkreises von der Antike bis zur Gegenwart* (Königstein: Beiträge zur Klassischen Philologie, 1983); Alan Scott, *Origen and the Life of the Stars: A History of an Idea* (New York: Oxford University Press, 1991); and Thomas O'Loughlin, "The Development of Augustine the Bishop's Critique of Astrology," *AugStud* 30.1 (1999): 83–103. On the relationship between astrology and free will in Christian late antiquity, see Kyle Harper, *From Shame to Sin: The Christian Transformation of Sexual Morality in Late Antiquity* (Cambridge, Mass.: Harvard University Press, 2013), 122–30.

48. Hippolytus, *Ref.* 4.2.3 (Marcovich 93); Sextus, *Math.* 5.49 (LCL 382:342). See also Augustine, *Haer.* 70.1.13–21 (CCSL 46:334).

49. Hippolytus, *Ref.* 4.4.1 (Marcovich 95).

50. Hippolytus, *Ref.* 4.3.1 (Marcovich 93).

individual's generation, from the moment either of conception or of actual birth (the two possible points from which the horoscope can be dated).[51] Having dismissed the possibility of affixing the moment of conception, Hippolytus, quoting from Sextus verbatim, proceeded to frame the process of ascertaining the moment of birth as equally fraught. Aside from wondering what exactly constituted the moment of birth—"when the fetus begins to incline towards the orifice, or when it may project a little, or when it may be borne to the ground?"— Hippolytus defied any astrologer (via a midwife or attendant) to pinpoint the moment of birth.[52] But even if one granted the astrologers the ability to mark the moment of the child's existence from physical birth or conception, the second fallacious link of the horoscope's chain obviated the first. By the clanging of a metallic rim (or gong), what Sextus calls the "horologe," word of the child's birth was transmitted to the astrologer, who "from an elevated place is contemplating the stars."[53] But, as Hippolytus reminds his readers, just as there was a temporal lag between the descent of the axe and the tree's fall, so too did time elapse between the moment when the gong was struck and when the sound reached the astrologer. And in the interim, the position of the stars had changed. Finally, it was not at all easy, Hippolytus insisted, to read the constellations of the sky, least of all because the position of the rising star will agree with the horizontal position of the observer: "In one place its declination will be supposed to be the horoscope, and in another the ascension the horoscope."[54]

Each of the three steps in fixing the horoscope was described, scrutinized, and summarily dismissed. Having recounted and refuted the procedures undergirding the determination of the horoscope, Hippolytus next considered the astrologers' predictive claims. Sextus Empiricus had distinguished two methods the Chaldeans had deployed "in making their forecasts of the 'effects.'"[55] The first, which he terms the "simpler" effects, "are those which occur by reason of the Sign or the simple power of a star—as, for instance, that 'this particular star when it is in this particular Sign produces men of such and such a kind.'"[56] The causal paradigm correlated a single sidereal position with an individual's disposition or character. The second, "more exact" paradigm examined a series of sidereal arrangements (a star's position in the horoscope, the midheaven, and the anti-midheaven) to ascertain the precise anthropological effects. The difference lay in the degree of methodological sophistication, not in the effect's claims; both astrological modes claimed the same

---

51. Sextus, *Math.* 5.55–67.
52. Hippolytus, *Ref.* 4.4.1 (Marcovich 95).
53. Hippolytus, *Ref.* 4.4.4 (Marcovich 96).
54. Hippolytus, *Ref.* 4.5.1 (Marcovich 97). Hippolytus reads the tripartite process of affixing the horoscope not as a series of exigent possibilities but rather as a mess of impossibility.
55. Sextus, *Math.* 5.41 (LCL 382:340).
56. Sextus, *Math.* 5.41 (LCL 382:340).

findings. Since it bore no relevance to his central contention against the folly of astrological anthropology or ethnography, Hippolytus reported that they proffered "an account concerning the action of the zodiacal signs, to which they say that the things being generated (therein) are assimilated ... for instance, that one born in Leo will be brave."[57]

A few chapters later in the Book 4, he returns to a discussion of astrological determinism and the portentous "art of divination."[58] Though Hippolytus uses yet a second term to categorize all forms of Greek speculation (μεριμνητής, those with an anxious mind), the anxiety of the astrologers corresponds precisely to the Chaldean art:[59]

> There are some who ascribe to the stars figures that mold the ideas and dispositions of men, assigning the reason of this to births [that have taken place] under particular stars; they thus express themselves: those who are born under Aries will be of the following kind: long head, red hair, contracted eyebrows, pointed forehead, eyes grey and lively, drawn cheeks, long-nosed, expanded nostrils, thin lips, tapering chin, wide mouth. These, he says, will partake of the following nature: cautious, subtle, perspicuous, prudent, indulgent, gentle, over-anxious, persons of secret resolves, fitted for every undertaking.... They, in the majority of cases, end their days in a foreign land.

Hippolytus included descriptive biological and dispositional accounts for each of the twelve signs of the zodiac. The text of the *Refutation*, unfortunately, is corrupt at the point at which Hippolytus concludes his foray into the deterministic potential of the astrological signs. And while his consideration of the astrological art derived from its prevalence among certain Christian sects, Hippolytus was nonetheless adamant that the astrologers' account of human diversity itself was fundamentally flawed. The blind were leading the blind. Indeed, as he reminded his readers, the claims of "sidereal influences themselves" were easily refuted:[60]

> For those who have been born at the same time do not spend the same life, but some, for example, have been made kings, and others have grown old in fetters. There has been born none equal, at all events, to Alexander the Macedonian, though many were brought forth along with him throughout the earth; [and] none equal to the philosopher Plato. Wherefore the Chaldean, examining the time of the birth in any particular latitude, will not be able to say accurately, whether a person born at this time will be prosperous.

While Hippolytus never himself systematically or specifically described astrology as a causative factor in ethnographic reasoning, he explicitly invoked the impossible

---

57. Hippolytus, *Ref.* 4.6.1 (Marcovich 98; altered from ANF).
58. Hippolytus, *Ref.* 5.15.3 (Marcovich 110).
59. Hippolytus, *Ref.* 4.15.4 (Marcovich 110).
60. Hippolytus, *Ref.* 4.5.4 (Marcovich 97); block quotation from Hippolytus, *Ref.* 4.5.4 (Marcovich 97). Cf. Sextus, *Math.* 5.88 (LCL 382:360). The passages are nearly identical, save for some minor stylistic variations.

confluence of ethnography, geography, and astrology, again via quotation from Sextus. In other words, he went far beyond the position that Woolf attributed to Manilius, positing not just that astrology was insufficiently capable of mapping the known world but that this incapacity reflected its utter fraudulence.[61] While Hippolytus directed his ire against genethlialogical astrology—the fixity of individual identity and life by means of the horoscope—he was still contesting a model that attempted to rationalize human difference, both phenotypically and dispositionally.

But the Christian debate over astrology's diminution of God's power was as much about the relationship between fate and free will as it was about Christianity's explanatory capacity. How did Christians conceptualize the natural world and the cosmos, and how did they understand the human position between the two? The Peratae, for instance, marshaled the evidence of astrology to propound their model of Christian creation. Citing their cosmology from an unnamed book of theirs, said to be "praised among them," Hippolytus observed the power of "erratic stars, from which is derived perishable fate."[62] According to Hippolytus, the Peratae simply altered the names for traditional astrological terms, elements, and principles:[63] "the heresy of the Peratae is altered in name only from the art of the astrologers . . . and they maintain that all those stars together which are beheld in the firmament have been causes of the generation of this world."[64] Their doctrinal system is simply astrology allegorized. The power of the zodiac, too, came under assault insofar as astrologers proposed that the erratic world of the planets was governed by the immovable world of the fixed zodiacal signs.[65] What mattered to Hippolytus was the *association* between these two worlds as aspects of a singular cosmos. It was a question of "correspondence between the microcosm and the macrocosm," the idea that "the cosmos is seen as interconnected within one universal chain of action and reaction."[66] The Peratae claimed that they had access to a singularly powerful knowledge about the world, its creator (or creators), and the human position in it; they alone possessed the knowledge to free individuals from their cosmically ordered fate.[67]

---

61. See also Sextus, *Math.* 5.98.

62. Hippolytus, *Ref.* 5.14.1, 5.14.5 (Marcovich 177, 179).

63. On the list of names, see *Ref.* 5.16.1–10. They used the names Cronus, Prometheus, Osiris, Isis, Neptune, Attis, Medea, Helen, Aoai, Uo, Uoab, Ino, Soclan, Carphacasemeocheir, Euno, Misyr, Praxidica, among numerous others.

64. Hippolytus, *Ref.* 5.15.1–2 (Marcovich 181). According to Hippolytus, they further allegorize the astrologers' notion of the horoscope to match their own view of an emanated universe (*Ref.* 5.15.3–5).

65. "[The astrologers] lay down, that one world derives from the other world a certain power, and mutual participation [in that power], and that the subjacent obtain this participation from the superjacent portions" (*Ref.* 5.13.1–2 [Marcovich 174–75]).

66. Hegedus, *Early Christianity and Ancient Astrology*, 287, 1.

67. Hippolytus, *Ref.* 5.16.1.

Likewise, the heretics who devoted themselves to Aratus's astrological poem, the *Phaenomena* (written in the third century B.C.E.), combined it with the details and persons of scripture to produce a Christian allegorical understanding of the heavens.[68] They transposed various biblical figures and ideas—Adam, the devil, the Logos, the Law, among others—onto various constellations and thus generated a Christian cosmological system: "He asserts that Cepheus is Adam, Cassiopeia Eve, Andromeda the soul of both of these, Perseus the Logos," and so forth.[69] But, as Tim Hegedus notes, "those who formulated the Aratean system did not attempt a simple series of direct one-to-one correspondences. Instead, they allowed for a certain amount of repetition in their view of the constellations, such that the basic Christian story could be retold in various ways by means of different groupings of constellations."[70] Hippolytus, in fact, presented three Aratean interpretations of the constellations, each of which offered variations on certain common themes.[71] All these Aratean interpretations, while striving for "a system of religion" (τὴν θεοσέβειαν συνιστᾶν), embraced "dancing and silliness" rather than truth.[72] "For," as Hippolytus contends, "the stars do not yield these things, but men of their own accord, for the designation of certain stars, thus called them by names, in order that they might become to them easily distinguishable."[73] The devil was not in the largely incoherent details that Hippolytus presented: quite the opposite. It was the broad or generic association between the heretics and astrology that drove Hippolytus's argument. It was the classificatory implications of astrology as a coherent system of knowledge that so threatened a Christian understanding of the relationship between humans and their creator. Astrology, both for individual thinkers and for communities of thought and practice, adhered to a false narrative and reverenced false powers. The principle at issue was one of macroscopic theorization. Nicole Kelley articulates the stakes of Christian debates over astral determinism in the context of her analysis of pseudo-Clement's *Recognitions*:[74]

> Clement's speech in *Recognitions* 9.19-29 is, on the whole, designed to make one point obvious: that astral determinism simply cannot be real given the wealth of empirical evidence that argues against it. Here Clement cites a larger number of

---

68. On Aratus, see Douglas Kidd, *Aratus: Phaenomena* (New York: Cambridge University Press, 1997), 1–23.
69. Hippolytus, *Ref.* 4.49.1-2 (Marcovich 136–37). On these associations, see, for example, *Ref.* 5.47.2, 47.5; 48.2.
70. Hegedus, *Early Christianity and Ancient Astrology,* 281.
71. According to Hegedus, the first retelling runs from *Ref.* 4.47 to 4.48.6; the second, from 4.48.7 to 4.48.14; and the third, from 4.49.1 to 4.49.4
72. Hippolytus, *Ref.* 4.50.1; 4.46.5 (Marcovich 136, 131).
73. Hippolytus, *Ref.* 4.50.2 (Marcovich 136).
74. Nicole Kelley, "Astrology in the Pseudo-Clementine *Recognitions*," *JEH* 59.4 (2008): 607–29, at 617.

ethnographic examples, starting with the Seres, whose laws against murder and adultery are more powerful than the influence of Venus and Mars (*Rec.* 9.19.2–3), and concluding with the example of the Jews, who live all over the world yet retain customs different from those of their Gentile neighbors.

Embedded within the discourse of ancient astrological determinism is the proposition that the stars provide both cosmic and human order. The Christian discourse of heresy is thus dependent upon an understanding of *how* God has organized his creation, and how humans can render that creation explicable and, more important, predictable. It is the *ethnographic* suppositions of astral discourse that undergird Hippolytus's heresiology. Hippolytus was telling a story of Christianity's control over the contours of the world, its nature, its sectarianism, and the human condition. In order to elaborate his own genealogical narrative, he first had to do away with competing systems of ethnographic analysis and classification. Christian attacks against astrological thinking thus reflect a desire not only to unmoor any connection between determinism and cosmic order but also to deny that astrology was a legitimate branch or system of ethnographic knowledge.

Indeed, since the qualities of the individual born under Virgo were in no way related to the sign's name, the ethnographic determinism of the entire paradigm collapsed under scrutiny:[75]

> For, according to them, it is not possible for an Ethiopian to be born in Virgo; otherwise he would allow that such a one is white, with long straight hair and the rest. But I am rather of opinion, that the ancients imposed the names of received animals upon certain specified stars, for the purpose of knowing them better, not from any similarity of nature.

What is striking about Hippolytus's argument here is the terms on which it proceeds and its larger import for his text as a whole. The entirety of his *Refutatio* analogized the theorizations and practices of the Celtic Druids, Babylonian astrologers, Assyrian numerologists, Indian Brahmans, Jewish prophets, and Greek philosophers with the now-burgeoning world of Christian heresy. Not only did the heretics readily appropriate from these cultural elites and their intellectual practices; they also functioned as their intellectual kin. The heretics were the most recent illustration of diversity within the known world. By proposing a precise intellectual and conceptual correspondence between these two categories of knowledge practitioners, Hippolytus fashioned a world that was now marked by its Christian and, indeed, heretical character. At the same time, the substance of his argument turned upon an analysis of the macroscopic facets of ethnographic theorization. His refutation of a particular heretical appropriation—the

---

75. Hippolytus, *Ref.* 4.6.2–3 (Marcovich 98–99). For the same passage, see Sextus, *Math.*5.102.

incorporation of astrological knowledge into the Christian tradition—became a debate about the validity of certain paradigms for understanding the nature and causes of human diversity. And although Hippolytus eventually offered his own model for understanding human diversity, built upon biblical precedents, most notably Genesis 11, his text blurred the distinction between heretical etiologies and human, cultural, religious, and ethnic etiologies. In rejecting the work of the astrologers and astrologically inclined heretics, Hippolytus conceived his heresiology as a text that sought to identify and thus connect the root causes of philosophical, religious, and ethnic diversity of thought, practice, and custom. The task of explaining the rise of the heretics emerged as an outgrowth of Christian efforts to categorize the intellectual and cultural world around them. Even in dismissing certain principles of knowledge, we see clear evidence here of the textual mechanisms by which Christians appropriated and applied the logic, techniques, and paradigms of classical ethnographic discourse. In contesting heretical theories of human difference, Hippolytus was engaged in a dispute over macroscopic ethnography: he was disputing the viability of particular ethnographic models to map Christianity onto both the internal diversity of Christianity itself and the external diversity of all humanity.

ETIOLOGIES TRANSFORMED: HERETICIZING MYTHOLOGY, COSMOLOGY, AND HUMAN BEHAVIOR

Although the primary areas of the heretics' error were philosophical, astrological, and genealogical (both intellectually and biologically), Book 5 of the *Refutatio* posited another source of these doctrinal machinations. The book begins with a brief explanation of its contents: it seeks to enumerate the heresies of the Naasseni, the Peratae, the Sethians, and the tenets of a certain Justinus. And while the charge leveled against the Naasseni concerned their dependence on the philosophical systems of the Phrygians, Thracians, Assyrians, and Egyptians, the opinions offered by the heresiarch Justinus are of a curiously different kind, proceeding "from the marvelous tales of Herodotus the historiographer" (ἀλλ' ἐκ τῶν Ἡροδότου τοῦ ἱστοριογράφου τερατολογιῶν).[76] Justinus, having abandoned the holy books of Christianity, was accused of appropriating the "legendary accounts prevalent among the Greeks" and using them as models for his own doctrinal positions on "the generation of the universe" (εἰς τὴν τῶν ὅλων γέννησιν), angelology, and anthropology.[77] Hippolytus, expressing a familiarity with Justinus's now-lost book *Baruch*, explains that the heretic transposed the legendary account of Heracles'

---

76. Hippolytus, *Ref.* 5.5 (Marcovich 140).
77. Hippolytus, *Ref.* 5.23.1, 5.25.4 (Marcovich 198, 200).

sexual relations with the half-woman, half-serpent Echidna,[78] mother of Agathyrsus, Gelonus, and Scythes, into an allegory of cosmic creation and the role of Christ in that process. In the *Histories* itself, Heracles' sexual encounter with Echidna was one of three accounts that Herodotus included to identify the origins of the Scythian land and its inhabitants. Supposedly conveyed by the Greeks of Pontus, the legend posited that Scythes, the youngest child of Heracles' sexual encounter with Echidna, received the right to stay "in the country now called Scythia" because he alone possessed the skill to draw the bow of Heracles and don his father's vessel-tipped girdle.[79] And "from Scythes son of Heracles," reported Herodotus, "comes the whole line of the kings of Scythia."[80] Though Herodotus himself placed stock in the third of the three traditions of Scythia—that the Scythians fled Asia on account of their conflict with the Massagetae and displaced the Cimmerians from their ancestral land (which was then renamed Scythia)—and rejected the myth of Heracles and Echidna, Hippolytus explicitly glossed the story's latter half and its larger context. He excised its context as the foundation of the Scythians' ancestral line in order to frame his discussion of Justinus's heretical reinterpretation of the myth.[81]

Though Hippolytus bracketed Justinus's cosmological narrative with thoroughly dismissive rhetoric, he explained the details of the narrative itself in rather dispassionate prose. What Hippolytus enumerated is a complex and at times confounding sequence of events in which Justinus used the hierarchy of the creative agents of the universe to uncover the true condition of humanity and its creators. Justinus offered not only a history of the universe and its creation but also an explanation of the origins of Christianity and an etiology of sexual and marital practices, all of which he elucidated through his both literal and allegorical exegesis of the cosmological narrative. The universe, according to Justinus, was governed by three unbegotten principles: the Good One known as Priapus, the Father called Elohim, who lacked foresight and was invisible, and the female named Edem, who was of two minds and two bodies—the cosmological equivalent of the serpentine Echidna.[82] Ensnared by each other, Edem and Elohim copulated and

---

78. Though she is described without the proper name Echidna in both Hippolytus's summary and in Herodotus's *Histories*, both texts employ the adjective ἐχίδναν/ἐχίδνης to describe this hybrid creature.

79. Herodotus, *Hist.* 4.8 (LCL 118:206) On Herodotus's ethnographic analysis of the Scythians, see François Hartog, *The Mirror of Herodotus: The Representation of the Other in the Writing of History*, trans. Janet Lloyd (Berkeley and Los Angeles: University of California Press, 1988), 12–33.

80. Herodotus, *Hist.* 4.10 (LCL 118:208).

81. Herodotus, *Hist.* 4.11 (LCL 118:210). See Hippolytus, *Ref.* 5.25.4.

82. Hippolytus, *Ref.* 5.26.1.

produced twenty-four angels (twelve paternal and twelve maternal).[83] The angels in toto represented Paradise, which was the conjugal joy of Edom and Elohim, while each angel individually symbolized a tree of the garden in Paradise.[84] According to Justinus, the angels received "the most beautiful earth," which was, "from the parts [of Edem] above the groin of human form and from gentle parts" (ἀπὸ τῶν ὑπὲρ βουβῶνα ἀνθρωποειδῶν καὶ ἡμέρων χωρίων), out of which the angels fashioned mankind;[85] the lower parts of Echidna, those resembling a snake, generated the animal kingdom.[86] Having completed the creative process, Elohim ascended "to the elevated parts of heaven," where he discovered the Good One, who charged him to stay there in the highest reaches; Elohim promptly assigned Edem dominion over the earth in his place.[87] The angels, who managed the world with a satraplike authority as agents of Edem, released the evils of famine and disease upon the world in accordance with the will of Edem.[88] Heartbroken by her separation from Elohim, Edem further ordered the angel Babel (also known as Venus) "to cause adulteries and dissolutions of marriages among men," in order that humanity could experience her own marital pains.[89] Baruch, one of Elohim's angels, was sent to Paradise to insist that man ignore Naas (the malicious maternal angel). Baruch implored Adam and Eve to refrain from eating of the tree of knowledge of good and evil, which represented Naas himself.[90] While Naas repeatedly chastened humanity's spirit (and by fiat Elohim) with punishments and transgressions, Baruch insisted that humanity follow the remaining eleven (paternal) angels of Edem, "who possess passions, but are not guilty of transgression."[91] Naas, by contrast, had committed a grave act of sin: he had intercourse with both Adam and Eve, which gave rise to adultery and sodomy.

Justinus's morality play, wherein the rise of vices and virtues was attached to cosmic fighting, served as background to the process by which the Good One attempted to redirect the gaze of humanity toward Himself. Naas perpetually thwarted Baruch's efforts to convince generations of supposed divine adherents

83. The maternal angels were eventually divided into four principles, and each principle was represented as a river of the οἰκουμένη. See Hippolytus, *Ref.* 5.26.11.

84. For instance, Baruch, the third of the paternal angels, is the tree of life. Naas, the third of the maternal angels, is the tree of knowledge of good and evil.

85. Hippolytus, *Ref.* 5.26.7 (Marcovich 202).

86. In the process of creation, Edem bestowed a soul upon Adam and Eve, while Elohim gave them a spirit. Hippolytus, *Ref.* 5.26.9.

87. Hippolytus, *Ref.* 5.26.14 (Marcovich 204).

88. Hippolytus, *Ref.* 5.26.11.

89. Hippolytus, *Ref.* 5.26.20 (Marcovich 204–5). Naas is tasked with chastening "the spirit of Elohim which is in men, in order that Elohim, through the spirit, might be punished for having deserted his spouse, in violation of the agreements entered into between them" (*Ref.* 5.26.21 [Marcovich 205]).

90. Hippolytus, *Ref.* 5.26.7.

91. Hippolytus, *Ref.* 5.26.22 (Marcovich 205).

(Moses and the biblical prophets, most notably) to follow the precepts of Elohim and to return to the Good One. As this cyclical game of instruction and disruption persisted, Elohim chose Heracles, an uncircumcised prophet, to free the spirit of the Father from the wickedness imposed by its maternal angelic captives. The twelve labors of Heracles were allegorized as divinely sanctioned efforts to defeat the angels of the spirit's captivity. Having "divest[ed] him of his power," the maternal angels ultimately foiled Heracles' efforts to propel the commands of Baruch into the earthly world below.[92] It was only during the reign of Herod that Baruch found a prophet who could resist the enticements of the angels. Jesus, son of Joseph and Mary, obeyed Baruch and directed humanity to the exalted Father and Priapus. Naas, enraged at Jesus's faithfulness to the Father and his message, "caused him to be crucified."[93] Justinus further asserted, according to Hippolytus, that a number of Greek legends—Leda and the swan, Ganymede and the eagle, Danaë and gold—were allegorized tales of the cosmological events that he had just enumerated. Inasmuch as Hippolytus charged Justinus with borrowing from Herodotus, Justinus holds the opposite: he enlightens the truth of Greek myths.

Although Hippolytus's condensed version of Justinus's narrative lacks the ethnogenic details of Epiphanius's *Panarion*, it operated, as we shall see in the next chapter, similarly to Epiphanius's history of heresy. The account functioned as an allegorical mechanism by which Greek legends could be subsumed within and explained by a Christian cosmological superstructure. Hippolytus decried the systematic attempts of the pseudo-Gnostic Justinus to meld together heresy and legend as an interpretive paradigm that blurred the genealogical divisions he erected between revealed Christian opinion on the one hand and the philosophical, astrological, and mythological conjecture of the nations on the other.[94] The analytical and heresiological implications of Hippolytus's protracted discussion—an ethnographic digression in the classical sense—were threefold. First, the philosophers, as the theological representatives par excellence of the gentile nations (τὰ ἔθνη), had no standing in the genealogy of Christian knowledge. Second, as both a source to be used and (potentially) to be elucidated, the philosophical reflections of the Greeks, Romans, Babylonians, Druids, and Indians existed wholly apart from the traditions of the Christian *oikoumenē* (the known, inhabited world). Third, the theological pursuits of these nations fundamentally failed to accord with an Adamic (in the case of Epiphanius) or Noahide (in the case of Hippolytus) lineage of divine knowledge and devotion.[95] Like philosophy, Greek legends constituted disruptive and corrupting barriers to the stability and succession of the Christian epistemo-

---

92. Hippolytus, *Ref.* 5.26.28 (Marcovich 206–7).
93. Hippolytus, *Ref.* 5.26.31 (Marcovich 207).
94. Hippolytus, *Ref.* 5.28.1.
95. Epiphanius, *Pan.* 2.4–5; 18.1.3; Hippolytus, *Ref.* 5.31.1–6.

logical boundaries, insofar as Justinus's ability to find Christian truth within Greek legends posited a meaningful relationship between the two categories or kinds of knowledge. Knowledge and its proper transmission defined the genealogical distinction between Christians and the gentile nations, philosophers, astrologers, arithmeticians, mythologizers, and heretics.

The heretics, furnished with their derivative opinions—even if those opinions served to illuminate the true meaning of antecedent sources, tales, legends, and so forth—further unsettled the ordering of Christian knowledge by introducing their own books and founding their own pedagogical institutions.[96] To allay his fears of widespread adoption of heretical opinions and acceptance of an alternative history of Christian tradition, Hippolytus proposed that his readers ignore the heretics altogether. In making the case for blissful ignorance, he invoked the travails of Odysseus, who fended off the seductive and destructive voices of the Sirens by filling his companions' ears with wax and having himself bound to the mast of his ship. With an overtly Christian emendation, Hippolytus reimagined Odysseus's shrewdness and resolve to make his point about the limitations of knowledge and engagement: "And my counsel to my readers is to adopt a similar tactic . . . to smear their ears with wax and sail through the tenets of the heretics, not even listening to those [opinions,] easily capable of enticing (them) toward pleasure, like the sweet-toned song of the Sirens, or, by binding oneself to the Cross of Christ, obeying faithfully, not to be distracted."[97] The Greek legends, it seems, had a Christian use after all.

HIPPOLYTUS'S MASTER NARRATIVE: INTELLECTUAL GENEALOGY

Genealogy held a prominent position within heresiological literature. Writers used it paradigmatically to illustrate the deviation of the Christian heresies, the succession of orthodox Christianity, the antiquity and history of the church, and the proliferation of heterodox traditions.[98] For Hippolytus, genealogy was the tool

---

96. On Callistus's founding of a school, see Hippolytus, *Ref.* 9.12.20, 25. Irenaeus states that Valentinus founded a school and that Cerdon had one as well, *Adv. haer.* 1.27.2; 1.11.1. On schools in the *Panarion*, see Epiphanius 44.1.2; 46.2.4. On the heretics' own books, see Hippolytus, *Ref.* 5.14–15, 5.22–24, 5.27; 7.37; 8.19; 9.13–17. On the books of the heretics in Epiphanius see *Pan.* 26.8.1; 30.15.1; 38.2.4; 39.5.1; 40.2.1, 40.7.5; 45.4.1; 53.1.3; 62.2.4.

97. Hippolytus, *Ref.* 7.13.3 (Marcovich 280).

98. For more on the genealogical and procreative language of early Christian authors see Denise Kimber Buell, *Making Christians: Clement of Alexandria and the Rhetoric of Legitimacy* (Princeton: Princeton University Press, 1999), and *Why This New Race: Ethnic Reasoning in Early Christianity*, 63–93; and Caroline E. Johnson Hodge, *If Sons, Then Heirs: A Study of Kinship and Ethnicity in the Letters of Paul* (New York, Oxford University Press, 2007). On heresy and genealogy, see Susanna Elm,

by which he could narrate the Christian vision of the world in all its detail and division while also explaining the corrupting influence of the heresies. In his *Refutatio*, the rise of the gentile nations (and their genealogies) explicitly attested the antiquity of "a nation of worshippers [the pious] of God (τὸ τῶν θεοσεβῶν γένος) more ancient than all Chaldeans, Egyptians, [and] Greeks."[99] Christians, by becoming "friends of God," had already grafted themselves onto the lineage of this nation of worshippers, the antediluvian devotees of God.[100] The nation of worshippers (both before Noah and after Christ) was defined both positively and negatively: on the one hand by its piety and on the other by refraining from positing overly complicated cosmologies, investing in astrological symbols and arithmetic equations, and philosophizing incessantly about the nature of God. The gentile nations (τὰ ἔθνη), in contrast, who all trace their ancestry back to Javan son of Japheth,[101] not only remained affixed to a more recent pedigree, as descendants of rather than precursors to Noah; they were likewise related by their devotion "to questions of philosophy" (τὰ περὶ φιλοσοφίαν ἀπασχοληθέντα).[102]

Though Hippolytus never causally linked philosophy, astrology, idolatry, or magic with the emergence of the gentile nations as Epiphanius explicitly would in his *Panarion*, it is clear that he nonetheless defined and organized these nations by their shared interest in cosmological and philosophical speculation: they are, like their heretical offshoots, a unity of diversity. The "inability to find consensus concerning the deity" among the gentiles, which included the opinions of the natural, moral, and dialectical philosophers of Greece and the theological reflections of the Persian, Egyptian, Babylonian, and Indian sages and astrologers (among others), further illustrated the disorder of their epistemological relationship with God.[103] As with the Christian heretics, diversity of opinion attested divine alienation.[104] Because philosophy operated as a barrier to understanding the truths of divinity and creation, Hippolytus ventured to explain God's creative power in order "to

---

"The Polemical Use of Genealogies: Jerome's Classification of Pelagius and Evagrius Ponticus," *StPatr* 33 (1997): 311–18; Robert M. Royalty, Jr., *The Origin of Heresy: A History of Discourse in Second Temple Judaism and Early Christianity* (New York: Routledge, 2013), 3–118; and Richard Flower, "Genealogies of Unbelief: Epiphanius of Salamis and Heresiological Authority," in *Unclassical Traditions*, vol. 2, *Perspectives from East and West in Late Antiquity*, ed. Christopher Kelly, Richard Flower, and Michael Stuart Williams (Cambridge: Cambridge University Press, 2011), 70–87.

99. Hippolytus, *Ref.* 10.30.8 (Marcovich 407).
100. Hippolytus, *Ref.* 10.31.6 (Marcovich 408). Hippolytus explicitly circumvents his own call to explain the divine devotion of those who existed before Noah.
101. Hippolytus, *Ref.* 10.31.4–5 (Marcovich 408): "How would the worshippers of God not be of greater antiquity than all the Chaldeans, Egyptians, and Greeks, whose father was born from this Japeth [receiving] the name Javan, from whom [also came] the Greeks and Ionians?"
102. Hippolytus, *Ref.* 10.31.5–6 (Marcovich 409).
103. Hippolytus, *Ref.* 4.43.1 (Marcovich 127).
104. See Irenaeus, *Adv. haer.* 1.10; 3.1–4.

elucidate those causes [of creation], which the Greeks, failing to understand, supposed in boastful rhetoric to be the parts of creation, while being ignorant of the creator."[105] The Greeks' inability to grasp the truths of creation left them perpetually excluded from the lineage of the nation of worshippers.[106] To join this ancient γένος (race, nation, clan), then, required instruction in God's nature and creation, a task to which Hippolytus turns at the end of his treatise.[107] He appealed to the Greeks, barbarians, Chaldeans, Assyrians, Egyptians, Libyans, Indians, Ethiopians, Celts, and Latins as their advisor, a spiritual mentor of sorts, urging them to spurn the "fallacies of artificial discourse" and the "vain promises of plagiarizing heretics" and instead to embrace the truth and join the nation of worshippers of God.[108]

The heretics, according to Hippolytus, were in truth imitators of the Greek philosophers, not practitioners or participants in the tradition of Christian truth. Hippolytus dedicated a great deal energy and space to elucidating the philosophical doctrines of Plato, Pythagoras, Aristotle, Empedocles, and Thales, among others.[109] In Book 1 of his *Refutation*, for example, he surveyed Greek, Druidic, Indian, and Babylonian philosophical doctrines with relative care and dispassion, never polemicizing or even contesting their validity; he simply narrated their opinions programmatically.[110] And while these descriptions did include words of displeasure, bafflement, and outright disagreement and rejection, he reserved his harshest rhetoric almost exclusively for the heretics themselves. His investigation of philosophical opinions attended less to the specific invalidity of those philosophical systems and doctrines and instead served primarily to illustrate the theological and genealogical deviation of the heresiarchs. As the opening lines of his proem argued, investigating the details and varieties of philosophical opinion reflected the derangement and danger of the heretics: "For even [the philosophers'] incoherent tenets must be received as reliable, on account of the excessive madness of

---

105. Hippolytus, *Ref.* 10.32.5 (Marcovich 410).
106. See Hippolytus, *Ref.* 4.43; 10.6–8.
107. Hippolytus, *Ref.* 10.31.6.
108. Hippolytus, *Ref.* 10.34.2 (Marcovich 415–16).
109. While the proem of the work gestures explicitly at the errancy of the philosophers, it is contextualized and explained as an exercise of intellectual facilitation. There are instances in which Hippolytus challenges the philosophers directly—the riddles of Plato, for instance—but his ire is not directed toward the Greek philosophical tradition. He is content to push them aside, if only to focus his attention firmly on heterodox Christians.
110. In the introduction to his critical edition of the Greek text, Marcovich explains that Book 1—later referenced by Hippolytus himself as Τὰ φιλοσοφούμενα (*Ref.* 9.8.2 [Marcovich 343])—would come to exist independently as a *Synopsis of Greek Philosophy*. "It is not surprising," explains Marcovich, "that this succinct and handy *Synopsis of Greek Philosophy* had been early separated from the rest of the *Elenchos*, most probably to serve as a textbook in philosophy" (1).

the heretics" (ὑπερβάλλουσαν τῶν αἱρετικῶν μανίαν).[111] The theological ignorance, philosophical speculation, and astrological misguidance of the gentile nations were juxtaposed rather strikingly with the irrationality and contagion of the heretics. For Hippolytus, the philosophers garnered attention in their capacity as a resource for heretical leaders, who in turn duplicitously and secretively despoiled the teachings of Christ by altering the "evangelical and saving doctrine" of true Christianity.[112] The heretics not only altered apostolic teachings; they also appropriated and refashioned the opinions of the philosophers in the guise of Christian truth. At the same time, the substance of these opinions was in some sense immaterial to his argument. It was the very idea of introducing *anything* foreign into the realm of Christian truth that destroyed the tradition of the nation of worshippers. In fashioning themselves as teachers and purveyors of Christian truth, the heretics "act[ed] despitefully" toward the legacy and tradition of the disciples, which Hippolytus guarded as a successor of the apostles.[113]

In deriving their opinions from the philosophers, the heresiarchs attached themselves to a distinctly different theological and intellectual tradition. "Being parts of astrological discovery and the arithmetical arts of the Pythagoreans," the doctrines of the heresies were "invalid and far removed from the knowledge that is in accordance with religion" (ὄντα ἄκυρα καὶ μακρὰν τῆς κατὰ θεοσέβειαν γνώσεως).[114] Hippolytus began and ended his *Refutatio* with the same underlying proposition: the heretics grafted themselves onto the historically later (and theologically inadequate) opinions of the philosophers, astrologers, and arithmeticians, who belonged to an entirely different genealogy of knowledge. Hippolytus's capacious definition of philosophy similarly cordoned off the pedagogical contributions of the gentiles. Truth owed nothing to the "wisdom of the Greeks," the doctrinal tenets of the Egyptians, the incoherent fallacies and curiosities of the Chaldeans, nor either to the astonishment and demonism of the Babylonians.[115] The uncovering of the heretics' dependence upon the philosophers—Basilides upon Aristotle,[116] Marcus upon Pythagoras,[117] Marcion upon Empedocles,[118] the

---

111. Hippolytus, *Ref.* pro. 1 (Marcovich 54; altered from ANF). For more on the madness of the heretics, see Hippolytus, *Ref.* 9.12, 17. For the madness of the astrologers, to whom the heretics happily affix themselves, see *Ref.* 4.15.4.

112. Hippolytus, *Ref.* 7.19.9. The language is more vicious and direct in Tertullian's *Praescr.* 7.2–3, where he excoriates the philosophers for enabling the fanciful theorizations of the Christian heretics. On the same point, see Irenaeus, *Adv. haer.* 2.14.

113. Hippolytus, *Ref.* 7.31.8; pro. 6 (Marcovich 314, 55).

114. Hippolytus, *Ref.* 6.52.1 (Marcovich 272; altered from ANF).

115. Hippolytus, *Ref.* 10.5.1–2 (Marcovich 380).

116. Hippolytus, *Ref.* 7.14–21, 7.24.

117. Hippolytus, *Ref.* 6.52.

118. Hippolytus, *Ref.* 7.29–31.

Docetists upon the Sophists,[119] Monoïmus from Pythagoras,[120] Noetus from Heraclitus,[121]—upended the very idea of their being Christian. Precisely because the philosophical theories of Pythagoras and Plato, who "derived [their] tenets originally from the Egyptians, and introduced their novel opinions among the Greeks," were appropriated by the heretical leader Valentinus, Hippolytus charged that his heresy and its line of succession existed and operated outside the successive tradition of Christianity:[122] "And from this [system of Pythagoras and Plato], not from the gospels, Valentinus, as we have proved, has collected the [materials of] heresy—I mean his own [heresy]—and may therefore justly be reckoned a Pythagorean and Platonist, not a Christian."[123] Once the philosophical appropriations of the heretical leaders had been revealed, their disciples and devotees became nothing more than gentiles (ἐθνικοί), "whom Christ will in no way profit."[124] In binding together the heretics and pagan intellectual culture—the latter corrupting and being corrupted by the heretics—Hippolytus wove "heresy into a universal history of human knowledge."[125] It is telling, indeed, that Epiphanius seized on the insights of Hippolytus (and Irenaeus) to offer an even more systematic and structured analysis of the history and genealogy of sectarianism. In the process of amplifying and expanding Hippolytus's theory of heretical origins, Epiphanius explained that the diversification of heresy was the result of human hubris and the resulting communalization of people into discrete groups.

CONCLUSION: CONTESTING CONTOURS AND UNITING HUMANITY

Among the multiple ways in which Christians articulated their history and traditions, theories of human difference emerged as an especially fraught site of ethnographic contestation. Although the heresiologists chastised the heretics for any number of perceived transgressions, I have highlighted the macroscopic paradigms of astrology and cosmic mythography to illustrate the ethnographic logic of heresiological literature. Clearing away the brush of fallacious heretical opinion enabled the heresiologists to elaborate a unified theory of human history as a history of sectarianism in which human and sectarian diversity were conjoined phenomena. Heresiological texts, by disputing certain heretical theories and expounding other self-proclaimed orthodox schematizations, harnessed the power of the

---

119. Hippolytus, *Ref.* 8.11.
120. Hippolytus, *Ref.* 8.15.
121. Hippolytus, *Ref.* 9.7–10.
122. Hippolytus, *Ref.* 6.21.3 (Marcovich 229).
123. Hippolytus, *Ref.* 6.29.1 (Marcovich 237; altered from ANF).
124. Hippolytus, *Ref.* pro. 11; 7.19.9 (Marcovich 56, 286; altered from ANF).
125. Eshleman, *The Social World of Intellectuals*, 229.

ethnographic to rationalize the world in distinctly Christian terms. The corollary to the purported universalism of Christianity (or, in an earlier guise, Rome) is a supreme discomfort with the shared humanity of all the world's people. Paul Veyne explains the phenomenon:[126]

> The ancients knew that, in theory, humanity was one, but they did not want to know it. How long had they known it? How long had men thought that all humans belonged to one and the same species—Greeks and barbarians, free men and slaves? Classical philology has constructed an entire hagiographical novel on that question. It praises Cicero or Seneca for speaking of the "common society of the human race" (Cicero *De finibus* 3.19.62); it honors the Stoics for their so-called universalism; at times it affirms that, before those philosophers, the Greeks held the slave or the barbarian to be nonhuman; it sees in Terence's famous *"homo sum, humani nihil a me alienum puto"* ("I am a man, I count nothing human foreign to me") one of the great moments in history. Such is the tenacity of the idealistic—or rather the academic—illusion that confounds the reality of history with the image of that reality in the mirror of classical texts.

By insisting on the unity of humankind, Christianity articulated a shared human nature as it worked to normalize yet dismantle oppositional parties. Macroscopic ethnographic paradigms facilitated the development of a master narrative of human unity in which the stages of human evolution and devolution were explained through the language of heresy. And while the desire to situate heresy within an ethnographic narrative of human diversification signaled the potential for Christian reunification, it also asserted a textual control over the world at large. Christians reified their Jewish, heretical, and pagan opponents in texts by imposing their own analytical categories upon the world. If, as Kyle Harper stresses, the main drama of late antiquity was "the absorption of society by the church, the mainstreaming of religion," ethnographic theorization helped facilitate that project.[127] Ethnography served as a powerful tool through which writers could transpose the ideological suppositions and interests of their Christianity onto the Roman Empire and the broader world. And empire, as David Chidester has noted, "provided a frame of reference, a metaphoric horizon, for organizing knowledge about religion."[128] The heresiologists marshaled "material and symbolic resources to impose the categories, classificatory schemes, and modes of social accounting" into the discourses of theological inquiry and the political apparatus of the state.[129]

---

126. Paul Veyne, "*Humanitas*: Romans and Non-Romans," in *The Romans*, ed. Andrea Giardina, trans. Lydia G. Cochrane (Chicago: University of Chicago Press, 1989), 342–69, at 345–46.

127. Harper, *From Shame to Sin*, 135.

128. David Chidester, *Empire of Religion: Imperialism and Comparative Religion* (Chicago: University of Chicago Press, 2014), 85.

129. Rogers Brubaker, *Ethnicity without Groups* (Cambridge, Mass.: Harvard University Press, 2004), 43. On the relationship between the legal and theological discourses about heresy, see Caroline

In pointing toward the notion of the ethnographic thesis, the words of Geertz and Lévi-Strauss with which I began this chapter, emphasize the ethnographic endeavor to understand the symbolic import of customs and habits. But in the ancient world the appeal to organizational structures—the coalescing of human behavior into ordered symbolic systems—signaled a much greater ambition. Christians, like their Greek and Roman predecessors, designed thought systems not only to essentialize peoples via their customs and habits but also to organize the contents and contours of the totality of the world. Christian intellectuals— through heresiology—were engaged in a struggle to redescribe the world Christianly.[130] To explain heresy was to insist that humanity's fall and Christianity's rise were conjoined and determinative phenomena within human history. By classifying human diversity through ethnographic paradigms of cosmology, mythography, and genealogy, Christians transformed the history of the world into a history of Christianity, which now defined how events, both natural and supernatural, would unfold. Christian ethnographic inquiry thus sought to recast society in terms consonant with the history and mission of the church. Heresy was the centrifugal force out of which all history had been written and, indeed, Christianized. Heresiology functioned as an ethnographic map of heresy and humanity by blurring the distinction between the two. Heresiology was no mere repository of heretical knowledge: its seeming narrowness encompassed a much wider intellectual and cultural perspective. Hippolytus's concluding remarks encapsulate his role as heresy hunter, ethnographer, theologian, and missionary:[131]

> O men, Greeks and Barbarians, Chaldeans and Assyrians, Egyptians and Libyans, Indians and Ethiopians, Celts, and Latins, who conduct war, and everyone that inhabits Europe, Asia, and Libya. To whom I become an advisor, being a disciple of the benevolent Logos and humane [myself], in order that, hurrying, you may learn from us who the true God is and [what] is His well-ordered creation. Do not turn to the sophisms of artificial discourses, nor to the impious promises of plagiarizing heretics, but to the holy simplicity of modest truth.

By projecting an ordered, comprehensive system onto the history and heterogeneity of the known world, the heresiologists gave it an irrepressible Christian structure. Heresiologists composed a portrait of a decidedly Christian world, written in the language of heresy, in which ethnographic knowledge supplied the very conditions and terms for human reunification.

Humfress, *Orthodoxy and the Courts in Late Antiquity* (New York: Oxford University Press, 2007), 35–213, 234–68.

130. I am borrowing the notion of redescription as the effort to model from Jonathan Z. Smith's "Sacred Persistence: Toward a Redescription of Canon," in his *Imagining Religion: From Babylon to Jonestown* (Chicago: University of Chicago Press, 1982), 36–52.

131. Hippolytus, *Ref.* 10.34.1–2 (Marcovich 415; altered from ANF).

4

Christianized Ethnography
Paradigms of Heresiological Knowledge

> We need topographers to give us exact descriptions of the places where they have been. But because they have this advantage over us, that they have seen the Holy Land, they claim the additional privilege of telling us news about all the rest of the world. I would have everyone write about what he knows and no more than he knows, not only on this, but on all other subjects. One man may have some special knowledge at first-hand about the character of a river or a spring, who otherwise knows only what everyone else knows. Yet to give currency to this shred of information, he will undertake to write on the whole science of physics. From this fault many great troubles spring.
>
> —MICHEL DE MONTAIGNE

Michel de Montaigne frets, in his famous essay "On Cannibals," about the tendency of authors to look beyond their limited knowledge to extrapolate broader cultural similarities and differences.[1] For Montaigne the danger of writing places—just as with the danger of writing people—is to move from the particular to the general. Montaigne's insight is to identify the problem of writing and reifying culture through only the most minute information. To describe the foreign—whatever was external to oneself, with its distinct geography, religion, and culture—required awareness of the limits of cultural translation and the biases of the authorial position. Because uncritical ethnography was shaped by the didacticism of one's own culture, it reinforced a worldview that perceived that culture at the center of the world. Too often, Montaigne laments, surveys of the world's diverse contents endeavored to catalogue their vast differences in the hopes of ranking them and even erasing them altogether. In this chapter I trace the move Montaigne problematizes, from the particular to the general, in the writings of the late antique heresiologists. Just as the heresiologists contested philosophical and heretical

---

1. This chapter's epigraph is quoted from Michel de Montaigne, "On Cannibals," in his *Essays*, trans. J. M. Cohen (New York: Penguin, 1993), 105–19, at 108.

theories of cultural, religious, and ethnic difference, they also propounded their own schematizations of human diversity through an investigation of heretical difference. The heresiologists devised master narratives of heretical propagation through which they could organize the totality of heretical and human diversity. They fashioned a discourse of heresy that explained the particularities of heretical customs, habits, and doctrines through all-encompassing ethnographic models (i.e., macroscopic paradigms) of the heretics' origin, essence, evolution, and ultimate dissipation.

Even though the heretics were portrayed as deviations from a normative theological and apostolic tradition, they served a vital function in the narrative of Christian ascension.[2] The heretics were not only emblems of temptation and trial. They also became the conceptual scaffolding around which Christian ethnographic writing and theorization of the world's diversity were coordinated. Heresiology thus functioned as an intellectual mapping, much like uncritical ethnography of medieval and early modern Europe, wherein the particular habits and customs of the heretics and the causative mechanisms of this diversity were scrutinized.[3] To that end, this chapter explores the techniques that Christian authors used to write the laws of heresy as the laws of sacred history—to extrapolate the broad outlines of all human diversity—through ethnographic theorization. By situating the rise and spread of Christianity within a discourse of ethnographic investigation, in which the contents of the world were charted, Christian authors concurrently contemplated the very possibility of this endeavor as well as its merit. The problem of human and religious diversity was thus framed as both a theoretical question and a practical matter. First, how did the world become so diverse? And how did Christianity itself become so diverse, and what are the parallels between the two? Second, as a practical matter, the fact of diversity required an analysis of the heretics' customs, insofar as they were representations of a diversity of culture, religion, and ethnicity. The impulse to produce a seemingly exhaustive account of sects and heresies yielded ethnographies that bound the utility of heretical information to an array of loftier intellectual pursuits: the exposition of

---

2. See Eduard Iricinschi and Holger M. Zellentin, "Making Selves and Marking Others: Identity and Late Antique Heresiologies," in *Heresy and Identity in Late Antiquity*, ed. Eduard Iricinschi and Holger M. Zellentin (Tübingen: Mohr Siebeck, 2008), 1–27. The language of heresy and orthodoxy melded with a variety of Christian interests, so that they become embedded within debates and discussions about gender, law, ecclesiology, exegesis, etc.

3. One of the most intriguing implications for Christianized ethnography concerns its capacity to expand the scope of sacred history and missionary activity. See, for example, Scott G. Bruce, "Hagiography as Monstrous Ethnography: A Note on Ratramnus of Corbie's Letter concerning the Conversion of the Cynocephali," in *Insignis Sophiae Arcator: Medieval Latin Studies in Honor of Michael Herren on His 65th Birthday*, ed. Gernot R. Wieland, Carin Ruff, and Ross G. Arthur (Turnhout: Brepols, 2006), 45–56.

universal and ecclesiastical histories, the ordering of classes of knowledge, the defining of the parameters of Christian pedagogy, the production of Christian ethnographic language, among others.[4]

In this chapter, I am concerned with the Christian interpretation of macroscopic theories of ethnographic analysis as tools to aggregate knowledge: in other words, how Christian writers articulated the genesis and perpetuation of heresy in explicitly ethnographic terms. My argument is that the production of Christian ethnography functioned to theorize the Christianities within the world and to show that the world was predictably and irrevocably governed by Christian structures. To demonstrate this process of ordering heresy via ethnographic models or paradigms, I have chosen to discuss the heresiological works of Epiphanius of Salamis and Theodoret of Cyrrhus. Both Epiphanius and Theodoret articulated models of heretical origins and profusion that traced their entrenched position within Christian history. Epiphanius proposed a periodized history of sectarianism that situated the contemporary Christian dilemma of heretical profusion in a global genealogical history of ethnogenesis (the process or formation of ethnic groups, or nations, or both).[5] Beginning with Adam, he enumerated an elaborate pre-Christian history of sectarianism in which the problem of Christian heresy was only the most recent outgrowth of a far more ingrained historical phenomenon. Epiphanius ultimately collapsed, or simply analogized, the distinction between ethnic or cultural diversity on the one hand and religious diversity on the other. The history of Christianity *became* the history of the world and its manifold divisions. Theodoret, by contrast, eschewed any pre-Christian past. Instead, he offered a model that began with Simon Magus and followed a periodized typological structure: the devil produced ages of heresy that were organized around particular doctrinal cores. Heresy's ever-shifting disposition was thus a reflection of its demonic lineage, whereby the heresies were created anew after the forces of orthodoxy vanquished their predecessors. Though the trajectories of these two models are distinct, both theorize heresy as a process of progressive evolution and adaptation. Epiphanius and Theodoret both map the stages of heretical manifestation in the world. It is this heresiological periodization of ethnographic knowledge that I trace below.

---

4. On encyclopedism and heresiology, see Richard Flower, "Genealogies of Unbelief: Epiphanius of Salamis and Heresiological Authority" in *Unclassical Traditions*, vol. 2, *Perspectives from East and West in Late Antiquity,* ed. Christopher Kelly, Richard Flower and Michael Stuart Williams (Cambridge: Cambridge University Press, 2011), 70–87.

5. On ethnogenesis in the ancient and medieval world, see Charles E. Bowlus, "Ethnogenesis: The Tyranny of a Concept," in *On Barbarian Identity: Critical Approaches to Ethnicity in the Early Middle Ages,* ed. Andrew Gillet (Turnhout: Brepols, 2002), 241–56.

A PERIODIZED HISTORY OF HERESY: THE *PANARION*, GENEALOGY, AND GEOGRAPHY

In a missive requesting the advice of Epiphanius, the former Palestinian abbot and then bishop of Salamis in Cyprus, the superior abbots Acacius and Paul of Chalcis and Beroea relate the need for additional instruction about heretical Christians.[6] The monks explain that they are writing Epiphanius in hopes of expanding their minimal knowledge of the world of heresy into a full and more precise account: "We have heard names assigned to the sects (αἱρέσεσιν) by your Honor," and so "we are asking your Reverence to tell us explicitly the heresy (αἵρεσιν) held by each of these cults" (θρησκείας).[7] It is Epiphanius's fame (φήμη) and his righteousness as a pedagogical paragon that inspire the abbots to solicit the opinions of the bishop:[8] "For not we alone, but all who hear of you, confess that the Savior has raised you up in this generation as a new apostle and herald, a new John, to proclaim the things that ought to be observed by those who have undertaken this course."[9] Through this apostolic analogy, Epiphanius is described with a highly particularized expertise of tradition and valorized as the Christian voice of his era.

Epiphanius commences his project of organizing, describing, and refuting the heresies of the world with a brief reply to his monastic interlocutors. The pedagogical purpose of his text, emphasized by the call of the monks and the response of the bishop, sets the conceptual order for his curative ethnography.[10] His rejoinder, which is the first of two proems, begins with a succinct description of his overarching textual purpose: "I am going to tell you the names of the sects and *expose* their unlawful deeds like poisons and toxic substances."[11] He then segues into a table of contents wherein he explains the precise plan of his work: there are three volumes with seven sections into which the eighty sects have been arranged, twenty pre-Christian sects and sixty Christian sects.[12] In these prefatory remarks, most of the heresies are simply named (and in some cases Epiphanius lists multiple names for a single group), though a small number of sects are identified by specific

---

6. Epiphanius, *Pan.*, Letter of Acacius and Paul (GCS, n. F., 10:153–54). Translations of the *Panarion* throughout are from Frank Williams, *The Panarion of Epiphanius of Salamis*, 2 vols., NHS 35, 36 (Leiden: Brill, 1987, 1994).

7. Epiphanius, *Pan.*, Letter 1.9 (GCS, n. F., 10:154).

8. Epiphanius, *Pan.*, Letter 1.7 (GCS, n. F., 10:154).

9. Epiphanius, *Pan.*, Letter 1.6 (GCS, n. F., 10:154).

10. Epiphanius describes his text and its function in the language of therapy at *Pan.* pro. 1.1.2 and pro. 2.3.4–5.

11. Epiphanius, *Pan.* pro. 1.1.2 (GCS, n. F., 10:155);. emphasis added.

12. On the subject of ancient tables of contents, see Andrew M. Riggsby, "Guides to the Wor(l)d," in *Ordering Knowledge in the Roman Empire*, ed. Jason König and Tim Whitmarsh (New York: Cambridge University Press, 2007), 88–107.

characteristics.[13] The Alogi, the thirty-first Christian sect (or fifty-first overall), for example, are distinguished in Epiphanius's proem by their rejection of the Gospel and Revelation of John.[14] Having numbered, named, and arranged the sects once already in *Proem 1*, he offers this same enumeration yet again—"in this one of my summaries"—in order to direct his "scholarly readers" to the precise volume and section of each heretical entry.[15] He not only explains the precise division within his text—there are three volumes with seven sections—but he also lists and counts each of the sects within a given section of a volume: vol. 1, sec. 1: twenty sects; vol. 1, sec. 2: thirteen sects; vol. 1, sec. 3: thirteen sects; vol. 2, sec. 1: eighteen sects; vol. 2, sec. 2: five sects; vol. 3, sec. 1: seven sects; vol. 3, sec. 1: seven sects; vol. 3, sec. 2: four sects.[16] The table of contents of *Proem 1* mirrors both the form and the content of Epiphanius's prolonged heresiological discourse itself: it is a list that blossoms into a full-fledged polemicized ethnography of sectarianism. His text thus orders two types of content at once. It provides a meticulous account of heresy and its origins, and it orders the entirety of the world through an ethnography of heresy.

By situating heresy in a protracted and grand narratological sequence, Epiphanius's *Panarion* constitutes a significant departure from his heresiological predecessors. Irenaeus of Lyons began his *Adversus haereses* by describing and refuting the Valentinians before circling back to attribute the root of *all* heresy to the magician Simon Magus, whereas Hippolytus opened his *Refutation of All the Heresies* in classical Greece with the doctrines of the natural, moral, and dialectical philosophers.[17] Already in the skeletal ordering and numbering of the heresies in *Proem 1*, Epiphanius, by contrast, unveils his intention to tell an exhaustive tale of all the world's heresies, beginning with "their mothers."[18] In *Proem 2*, he amplifies his plan to offer an "account and discussion of faith and unbelief, of correct views and divergent views" by situating his narrative in the context of "the world's creation and what followed it."[19] Firmly rejecting the claim that heresy began only in the apostolic age or with the Greek philosophers, the *Panarion* orients its study of

13. On the multiplicity of names given to the heretics in different countries, see his remarks at *De fide* 6.4–5.

14. Epiphanius, *Pan.* pro. 1.4.5.

15. *Proem 1* repeats itself insofar as Epiphanius first lists each of the eighty heresies by name and number before he returns to explain the precise division of the volumes and sections and places each sect in its corresponding section and volume.

16. Epiphanius, *Pan.* pro. 1.5.2–5.9.

17. For a discussion of Epiphanius in the context of early Christian heresiology, see Aline Pourkier, *L'hérésiologie chez Épiphane de Salamine* (Paris: Beauchesne, 1992), 53–75. See now also the excellent treatment of Young Richard Kim, *Epiphanius of Cyprus: Imagining an Orthodox World* (Ann Arbor: University of Michigan Press, 2015).

18. Epiphanius, *Pan.* pro. 1.5.2 (GCS, n. F., 10:159).

19. Epiphanius, *Pan.* pro. 2.1.1 (GCS, n. F., 10:169).

sectarianism through a sweeping history of the world, proposing four successive generations (γενεαί) or ages of heresy.[20] Epiphanius articulates his vision of the world by creating a master narrative in which the history of the world and sectarian division become manifestations of a single intellectual genealogy of ethnogenic innovation. By beginning in the pre-Christian past (or the past that was not yet *manifestly* Christian), Epiphanius traces the history of heresy from Adam down into his own day with the Christian Messalians. In the process, he subsumes the history of the world under a history of religion and religious deviation.[21]

Epiphanius conceptualizes the present age as an effort to reclaim humanity's dormant Adamic past. As an experiential and theological template for the present, the past contextualizes and explains the underlying situation of the contemporary catholic church. The church's contests with her sectarian opponents belong to Epiphanius's decidedly Christian narrative of religious history, which he articulates as the uninterrupted history of heresy. The past, then, is not some long-forgotten relic but a continuously lived struggle between the truth of Christianity and the falsity of her protean opponents.[22] Epiphanius's account further imposes an order upon a disordered world by arraying its data in accordance with scriptural dicta. His text "expresses the omnipresent sign of divine providence" and infuses both ethnographic projects with a thoroughly Christian analytical apparatus.[23] He augments the baptismal formula of Colossians 3.11—"There is no longer Greek and Jew, circumcised and uncircumcised, barbarian, Scythian, slave and free"—to structure the pre-Christian history of his universal story.[24]

Following Colossians 3.11, which is an expansion of Galatians 3.28, Epiphanius correlates the Barbarian, Scythian, Hellene, and Jew of Paul's deutero-epistle with the four foundational or mother heresies: "From Adam until Noah, *Barbarism*. From Noah until the tower, and until Serug two generations after the tower, the *Scythian* superstition. After that, from the tower, Serug and [Terah] until Abraham, *Hellenism*. From Abraham on, the true religion which is associated with this same Abraham—*Judaism*, (named) for his lineal descendant Judah."[25] As ages of

---

20. Epiphanius, *Pan.* 8.3.1 (GCS, n. F., 10:188).

21. Epiphanius, *Pan.* 80.1.1–11.7.

22. For the historiographical impulse behind Christian heresiology see Hervé Inglebert, "L'histoire des hérésies chez les hérésiologues," in *L'historiographe de l'Église des premiers siècles*, ed. B. Pouderon and Y.-M. Duval (Paris: Beauchesne, 2001), 105–26.

23. Johannes Fabian, *Time and the Other: How Anthropology Makes Its Object* (New York: Columbia University Press, 2002), 4.

24. Song of Songs 6.8–9 is the other governing prooftext of the *Panarion*, which I will discuss below in chapter 6. For allusions to the verses, see *Pan.* pro. 1.1.3; *Pan.* 35.3.5–6; 80.10.3, 80.11.5.

25. Epiphanius, *Pan.* 8.3.2 (GCS, n. F., 10:188). On the sources, structure, and argument of Epiphanius's theorization of the nature of sectarianism, see William Adler, "The Origins of the Proto-Heresies: Fragments from a Chronicle in the First Book of Epiphanius' *Panarion*," *JTS* 41.2 (1990): 472–501.

human development, each of the four eras introduced and inscribed particular religious beliefs and conduct, which over time (after the age of Scythianism) ossified into cultural ethics and ethnic sensibilities. The first two ages, Barbarism and Scythianism, hew to the general framework of the biblical narrative of Genesis, with details from the apocryphal book of Jubilees added to refine the account's details.[26] Adam's disobedience sowed the initial seeds of human wickedness, which were further nurtured by Cain's act of fratricide.[27] In the lifetime of Jared, the great-grandson of Seth in the fifth generation after Adam, "came sorcery, witchcraft, licentiousness, adultery, and injustice."[28] The age of Hellenism (the third mother heresy) also bears responsibility for the introduction of sorcery and witchcraft, while the practices of astrology and magic are ascribed to Nimrod, who sits squarely on the edge of the Scythian and Hellenic ages.[29] It is worth noting that the comprehensive narrative of Epiphanius's pre-Christian history is neither wholly precise nor entirely consistent. There is an ambiguity of language and a repetition of cultural developments. His narrative assigns identical religious and cultural practices to different ages and various individuals. Wickedness, for example, is introduced among the human race on at least three occasions: with Adam, Cain, and Jared.[30] Though Epiphanius's account of the history of human error may be internally inconsistent, the general schema remains perfectly clear: each age produced certain anthropological, theological, and religious errors.

Epiphanius is explicit that among the earliest generations of Adam "there was no difference of opinion yet, no people that was at all different, no name for a sect, and no idolatry either."[31] Yet he likewise asserts that "everyone served as a law to

---

26. Jubilees 5.28; 7.1, 17; 10.15 at Epiphanius, *Pan.* 2.1. On the cosmic ethnography of Jubilees, see James M. Scott, "On Earth as in Heaven: The Apocalyptic Vision of World Geography from Urzeit to Endzeit according to the *Book of Jubilees*," in *Geography and Ethnography: Perceptions of the World in Pre-Modern Societies*, ed. Kurt Raaflaub and Richard J. A. Talbert (Malden, Mass.: Wiley-Blackwell, 2010), 182–96. Epiphanius has modified the narrative of Jubilees at *Pan.* 3.1–5, which may reflect his general familiarity with the text rather than exact knowledge. See also *Pan.* 39.6.1. On Epiphanius and Jubilees, see Annette Yoshiko Reed, "Retelling Biblical Retellings: Epiphanius, the Pseudo-Clementines, and the Reception-History of *Jubilees*," in *Tradition, Transmission, and Transformation from Second Temple Literature through Judaism and Christianity in Late Antiquity*, ed. Menahem Kister et al. (Leiden: Brill, 2015), 306–21.

27. See Epiphanius, *Pan.* 1.3.

28. Epiphanius, *Pan.* 1.3 (GCS, n. F., 10:172). The text, however, introduces an unresolved ambiguity with respect to the precise moment of each particular error's emergence: "But now in the time of Jared and afterward, [came] sorcery, witchcraft, licentiousness, adultery, and injustice" (νῦν δὲ ἐν χρόνοις τοῦ Ἰάρεδ καὶ ἐπέκεινα φαρμακεία καὶ μαγεία, μοιχεία τε καὶ ἀδικία, (Epiphanius, Pan. 1.3 [GCS, n.F., 10:172]). "But now" (νῦν δέ), the contemporary situation of Jared, stands alongside the vague pronouncement "and afterward" (καὶ ἐπέκεινα). At this point in his text, Epiphanius leaves the exact arrival of the religious errors unspecified.

29. Epiphanius, *Pan.* 3.11.

30. Epiphanius, *Pan.* 1.3.

31. Epiphanius, *Pan.* 1.9 (GCS, n. F., 10:173).

himself and conformed to his own opinion."³² This tension between uniformity and individuality, coherence of opinion and lawlessness, is resolved in his discussion of the age of Scythianism, where he claims that it was only prior to the destruction of the tower at Babylon that individuals lacked any signs of distinctive ethnic, religious, or cultural identity. Under the first two ages of humanity, the world was inhabited only by men of a single language and speech who comported themselves either with godliness or with ungodliness.³³ In affirming or rejecting natural law, the lone correlative of godliness, men did not foment sectarian divisions; they were simply behaving obediently or disobediently. During the age of humanity's division into seventy-two distinct peoples (and the allotment of land and bestowal of languages), Reu, of Noah's stock, bore Serug, who introduced idolatry into human consciousness with paintings and portraits.³⁴ Serug's grandson Terah went further still, making "images with clay and pottery."³⁵ The age of idolatry is marked by the bishop as the era of Hellenism—though in fact Hellenism had its roots with the Egyptians, Babylonians, and Phrygians.³⁶ The rites and mysteries of the Greeks, Epiphanius reports, "were brought [to them] by Cadmus, and by Inachus himself," which then became distinct heresies "during the lifetime of Epicurus, Zeno the Stoic, Pythagoras and Plato."³⁷

The transmission of errors occupies much of Epiphanius's attention in his discussion of the fourth and final of the mother heresies, Judaism. Originally known as Abramians, these ancestral worshippers of God were defined by the piety of their namesake. Their lineal descendants ultimately became the Jews (though they were not called Jews until the time of David) and were held by God's choice as "the true religion and circumcision."³⁸ The age of Judaism, however, as it moved further away from its Abrahamic ideal, was vitiated by the Jews' misinterpretation of divine legislation. The pedagogical import of biblical Law, though "giving its precepts physically," held a spiritual hope that the Jews had perilously failed to grasp.³⁹ For Christians the Lord Jesus Christ, the ultimate pedagogue, illuminated the truth of God's Law, replacing its types and symbols with spiritual truths.⁴⁰ The Jews' continued adherence to the legal obligation of circumcision upended their divinely sanctioned status.

This periodized narrative, framed in euhemeristic terms wherein mythological figures are accorded historical agency as human inventors of civilizing or barbarizing

32. Epiphanius, *Pan*. 1.9 (GCS, n. F., 10:173).
33. Epiphanius, *Pan*. 2.3.
34. Epiphanius, *Pan*. 3.4.
35. Epiphanius, *Pan*. 3.5 (GCS, n. F., 10:177).
36. Epiphanius, *Pan*. 3.11.
37. Epiphanius, *Pan*. 3.11; 4.2.6, 7 (GCS, n. F., 10:179, 182).
38. Epiphanius, *Pan*. 8.5.1 (GCS, n. F., 10:190).
39. Epiphanius, *Pan*. 8.5.4 (GCS, n. F., 10:190).
40. Epiphanius, *Pan*. 8.6.5–7.4.

tendencies, articulates the etiology of sectarianism as a history of culture.[41] Each mother heresy functioned, in Epiphanius's schema, as a cultural or devotional unit, which marked ethical, ethnic, and religious geneses, progressions, and deviations.[42] Barbarism and Scythianism, on the one hand, had precise beginnings and ends—they were historically closed—whereas Hellenism and Judaism, on the other, remained ambiguously open, as the Greek philosophical schools and the Jews endured into the era of Christianity. The former, while introducing certain base human errors, associated transgression with the disobedience of natural law, whereas the *divided* world of Hellenism and Judaism marked the introduction of an ethnic or, in Jeremy Schott's parlance, ethnogenic linkage between cultural development or decay and human religiosity.[43] There is a further distinction between the ages of Barbarism and Scythianism and Hellenism and Judaism. The former operated as ages of individuals, whereas the latter emerged in a world already divided by ethnocommunities. In the wake of the tower of Babel's fall, the world has become marked by its particularization and communalization.

Although both Judaism and Hellenism proliferated during the post-Babel reign of nations (the age of human difference), the former, defined by the practice of circumcision, oriented only the nation of Israel, whereas the latter broadly signified the practice of idolatry. In the case of Hellenism, moreover, Epiphanius intimates that the making of gods facilitated and reinforced the process of human division that made up the world after Babel. He argues:[44]

> And after [Scythianism] people made gods of wretched despots, or sorcerers who had deceived the world, by honoring their tombs. And much later they made Cronus, and Zeus, Rhea, Hera and the rest of them into gods, and then they made gods by worshipping Acinaces—and the Scythian Sauromatians made gods by worshipping

---

41. Jeremy Schott, "Heresiology as Universal History in Epiphanius' *Panarion*," ZAC 10.3 (2006): 546–63. See also Jonathan M. Hall, *Hellenicity: Between Ethnicity and Culture* (Chicago: University of Chicago Press, 2002), 125–71. On the enduring legacy of euhemerism, see Frank Lestringant, "The Euhemerist and the European Perception and Description of the American Indians," in *The Classical Tradition and the Americas*, vol. 1, part 1, *European Images of the Americas and the Classical Tradition*, ed. Wolfgang Haase and Meyer Reinhold (New York: de Gruyter, 1994), 173–88.

42. To the extent that Epiphanius feminizes the language of heresy insofar as the ages of heresy are described as mothers, by contrast men lead all the sectarian parties, save heresy 49, the Quintillianists or Priscillianists and heresy 79, the Collyridians. See Stephen J. Shoemaker, "Epiphanius of Salamis, the Kollyridians, and the Early Dormition Narratives: The Cult of the Virgin in the Fourth Century," JECS 16.3 (2008): 371–401. More broadly, orthodox writers routinely used feminized language to describe the heresies. On the relationship between heresy and the violation of gender norms, see Virginia Burrus, "The Heretical Woman as Symbol in Alexander, Athanasius, Epiphanius, and Jerome," HTR 84.3 (1991): 229–48: and her "Equipped for Victory: Ambrose and the Gendering of Orthodoxy," JECS 4.4 (1996): 461–75.

43. Schott, "Heresiology as Universal History," 555–62.

44. Epiphanius, *Pan.* 3.9–10 (GCS, n. F., 10:178).

Odrysus and the ancestor of the Thracians, from whom the Phrygian people are derived. This is why Thracians are named for the person called Thera, who was born during the building of the tower.

Tracking the genesis of heresy exposes the correlation between ancestral worship and the formation of communal identities, or peoplehood. Sectarianism arises from the production of individualized deviant opinions in the now-communalized world. As time passes, these opinions continually mutate and multiply. The nation, or the very construct of bounded community, now serves as the host within which individualized errors are transmitted. With the advent of the nation, individual opinion now possessed a foundation for its germination and immortalization. Thinkers of all varieties, from philosophers, astrologers, numerologists, prophets, and the like, harnessed the phenomena of community to advance their enlightened ideologies. And if communities were to dissipate for any reason, new iterations could easily form. Ancestral worship, then, was the logical outcome of a world marked by human division.

During his presentation of the age of Hellenism, Epiphanius ascribes the introduction of idolatry—the point at which sectarianism emerges—to the excessive freedom of human intellect:[45]

> Peleg was the father of Reu, and Reu was the father of Serug, which means "provocation"; and, as I have been taught, idolatry and Hellenism began among men with him. It was not with carved images yet or with reliefs in stone, wood or silver-plated substances, or made of gold or any other material, that the human reason invented evil for itself and, with its freedom, reason and intellect, invented transgression instead of goodness, but only with paintings and portraits.

Unbridled reason and intellectual speculation bred the very notion of evil and in so doing fomented alternative systems of worship. The introduction of idols not only signified an end to the exclusive relationship between humanity and the singular divinity but also marked the emergence of a sustained history of religious deviation with its soon-to-be manifold divisions. Whereas ungodliness had existed from the beginning among the peoples of Barbarianism and Scythianism, the idolatry of the Hellenistic era ruptured the religious history and lineage of humanity in an unprecedented manner. Humans did something far more dangerous than merely reject natural law: they indulged their excessive curiosity and rationality, and produced ethnogenic divisions with enormous sectarian consequences. Though Epiphanius's account of the rise of idolatry concerns only pre-Christian intellectual hubris (and the process by which reason precipitates humanity's separation from the goodness of natural law), the intellectual corruption of religious truth is the driving force of his world history—it rationalizes the Jewish sects, the Hellenistic schools of thought, and the Christian heresies as well.

---

45. Epiphanius, *Pan.* 3.4 (GCS, n. F., 10:177).

Indeed, it is the *transmission* of error in a world divided that propels this narrative of heresy's emergence, and Epiphanius aimed to expose its agents. Teaching spurred the production of deviant epistemological conceptualizations. It was the "historians and chroniclers" whose importation and dissemination of Egyptian imposture— heathen mythology—gave rise to the magical rites.[46] The philosophical schools, born of the Greeks' mysteries and rites, "devise[d] a concordant knowledge (ὁμόστοιχον γνῶσιν) of idolatry, impiety and godlessness."[47] Idolatry, having set in motion a progression of fallacies wherein the creation of false deities invited the theistic speculations of the philosophical schools, introduced new practices of devotion that further waylaid the godly. An exasperated Epiphanius challenges the Stoics' "promise of knowledge" with fate as the driving force within the universe.[48] "If it is fate," he reasoned, "that equips the educated and intelligent, no one should learn from a teacher."[49] And he further chastises the "poets, prose authors, historians, astronomers" and all the others who "made men's opinion giddy and confused" (ἐσκότωσαν καὶ ἐθόλωσαν) by planting fallacious arguments and introducing errant doctrines.[50] Even the Jews and Samaritans, who were keen to reject idolatry and affirm their desire "to know the one God," ultimately failed to distinguish themselves among the nations: they lacked "interest in more precise information" about God and the divine plan beyond the Law of Moses.[51] The presectarian religiosity of men, by contrast, was "not learned from teaching or writings" but operated by faith, apart from any institutional, national, philosophical, or pedagogical instruction.[52] The professionalism of knowledge not only stymied the unfolding of religious truth: it actively indoctrinated generations into systems of competing falsehoods. By creating a formal (i.e., legitimate) space and process in which erroneous opinions could be taught, the Greek philosophical tradition asserted and preserved its grip on the minds of men.

THE SECTS AS THE NEW NATIONS OF THE WORLD

In narrating the rise of Jewish and Samaritan sectarianism, Epiphanius fixates on the events of the Babylonian exile. After the Jews had been expelled from the land of Israel, the "elders approached Nebuchadnezzar in Babylon and begged that some of his own subjects be sent to Israel as settlers, to keep the country from becoming an uninhabited wasteland."[53] The king complied with the request and

---

46. Epiphanius, *Pan.* 3.11 (GCS, n. F., 10:179).
47. Epiphanius, *Pan.* 4.2.8 (GCS, n. F., 10:183).
48. Epiphanius, *Pan.* 5.2.4 (GCS, n. F., 10:184).
49. Epiphanius, *Pan.* 5.3.2 (GCS, n. F., 10:185).
50. Epiphanius, *Pan.* 8.2.1 (GCS, n. F., 10:187).
51. Epiphanius, *Pan.* 9.2.3 (GCS, n. F., 10:198).
52. Epiphanius, *Pan.* 2.3 (GCS, n. F., 10:174).
53. Epiphanius, *Pan.* 8.8.5 (GCS, n. F., 10:195).

sent "four groups of his own people (τῶν ἰδίων τέσσαρα γένη), called the Cuthaeans, Cudaeans, Sephharuraeans and Anagogavaeans [to Samaria] with their idols."[54] The land, however, was inhospitable to these new settlers; they were continuously ravaged by the attacks of wild beasts. While requesting aid from the king, the four nations maintained that "no nation could settle there unless it kept the law of God of heaven, given through Moses."[55] And so Nebuchadnezzar heeded their pleas and sent a copy of the Law and "Ezra, as a teacher of the Law, to teach the Law of Moses to the Assyrians who had settled in Samaria—the Cuthaeans and [the] others."[56] This is, put simply, the genesis of the Samaritans as a hybridized nation. Epiphanius further muses about the relationship between national identity and sectarianism: "It is an amazing coincidence that, to correspond with the four nations, four sects have also arisen in that very nation—I mean first, the sect of Essenes; second, of Gorothenes; third, of Sebuaeans; and fourth, of Dositheans."[57] When Epiphanius finally enumerates the underlying causes of sectarianism, having just explained the rise of divisive opinions within Israel during the exilic and postexilic periods, he embraces the metaphor of ethnogenesis:[58]

> Here I can begin my treatment of the subject of sectarianism (ἐντεῦθεν ἀρχή μοι γίνεται τῆς τοῦ ἐπαγγέλματος κατὰ αἱρέσεων πραγματείας), and I shall briefly explain how it arose. How else but in the same way in which tribes arose from the proliferation of the different languages, various nations emerged to correspond with each tribe and clan, every nation chose its own king to head it, and the result was the outbreak of wars, and conflicts between clashing nations.... So too at this time we have been discussing. Since there had been a change in Israel's one religion, and the scripture of the Law had been transferred to other nations—I mean to Assyrians, the ancestors of the colonist Samaritans—the division of Israel's opinion also resulted. And then error arose, and discord began to sow seed from the one true religion in many counterfeit beliefs, as *each individual thought best*, and thought that he was proficient in the letter [of scripture] and could expound it to suit himself.

Here all the pieces of Epiphanius's sectarian puzzle have come together, explicitly formulated: nations (i.e., communities) combined with individualized opinion yield sectarianism, a new means for error to proliferate. His aim in this historicized

---

54. Epiphanius, *Pan.* 8.8.6 (GCS, n. F., 10:195).
55. Epiphanius, *Pan.* 8.8.9 (GCS, n. F., 10:196).
56. Epiphanius, *Pan.* 8.8.10 (GCS, n. F., 10:196). On Samaritanism broadly, see *Pan.* 9.1–5.5. For his discussion of each of the emergent Samaritan sects: *Pan.* 10.1.1–5 for the Essenes; *Pan.* 11.1.1–3 for the Sebuaeans; *Pan.* 12.1.1–2 for the Gorothenes; and *Pan.* 13.1.1–2.1 for the Dositheans.
57. Epiphanius, *Pan.* 8.9.1 (GCS, n. F., 10:196).
58. Epiphanius, *Pan.* 8.9.1–9.4 (GCS, n. F., 10:196–97); emphasis added. Cf. Daniel Boyarin, *Border Lines: The Partition of Judaeo-Christianity* (Philadelphia: University of Pennsylvania Press, 2004), 206–8.

schema was to mark off ethical or religious deviation as ethnically or culturally particularist while asserting that the principles of Christianity existed apart from these errant preoccupations. But the history of sectarianism inculcates an ethnographic ordering not only of the world at large but of the Christian tradition itself. In the context of heresiology, the appeal to study heresy's roots and describe them in expressly generative terms not only reveals a kinship with the language of ethnography; it forms a persistent frame of reference for the totality of the undertaking. For Epiphanius, heresy is a natural human phenomenon insofar as it shapes and guides the contours of history. His text imposes a vision of sectarianism and religious genesis that forecasts the *longue-durée* proliferation of ethnographic and heretical division.

For Epiphanius, geographical, genealogical, and ethnogenic ordering are all affixed to the same narrative of sectarianism's birth and growth, which concludes that history is in fact dominated by the unceasing ascent of self-made (heterodox) innovation. Thus, even as he mimics his predecessors' genealogy of Christian heresy—it always begins with Simon Magus—and parrots their descriptions, he expands the genre's capacity to comprehend the world of religious opinion by constructing a religious history of the world alongside its historical twin, the birth of sectarianism. Christian heresies produce or sow the same ethnic particularities and epistemological errors as Hellenic and Jewish sects.[59] They are defined by deviant conduct and fallacious opinions that all hark back to the emergence of divisive opinions among nations, philosophers, Samaritans, and Jews. Although the history of the world, having just entered the era of manifest Christianity, has been recalibrated, the Christian heresies graft onto this previously articulated ethnogenic and ethnographic schematization. In short, contemporary sectarian proponents occupy the same historical and theological space as the heresies of the past. The process of error had not ceased, nor had its essential contents changed; the *Panarion* builds a successive chain of heterodoxy, beginning with the unstoppable force of Hellenic error. The ethnogenic mapping of the pre-Christian world has been supplanted by the rise of Christianity, wherein the Christian heresies function as the new nations of the world.[60]

---

59. On the use of ethnoracial language against the heretics, see Denise Kimber Buell, *Why This New Race: Ethnic Reasoning in Early Christianity* (New York: Columbia University Press, 2005), 116–37. On the charge of blackness with respect to the heretics, see Gay L. Byron, *Symbolic Blackness and Ethnic Difference in Early Christian Literature* (New York: Routledge, 2002), 9–10, 46, 105–8, 120–21.

60. Cf. A. H. M. Jones, "Were the Ancient Heresies National or Social Movements in Disguise?," *JTS* 10 (1959): 280–98; and W. H. C. Frend, "Heresy and Schism as Social and National Movements," in *Schism, Heresy and Religious Protest,* ed. Derek Baker (Cambridge: Cambridge University Press, 1972), 37–56.

For Epiphanius, the history of the world is an iterative cycle of orthodox and sectarian contestation.[61] The history of the world recounts the struggle to reclaim the untarnished Adamic legacy, to free humanity from the excesses of the idolaters, philosophers, Jews, and Christian heretics. The human creation of deities (idols) aptly foreshadows the tendency of the Christian heresies to reproduce; it also exposes how transgression produces a schematized narrative of both the past and the present. It is the task of the heresiologist to uncover and order this narrative. In combining the tradition of apostolic succession and the Hellenic and Jewish heresies with the genealogy of the nations in Genesis 10, Epiphanius organizes the entire history of the world as a history of religious exploits.[62] The generation of culturally specific idols and their corresponding deities, and the failure to comprehend the true meaning of divine (or even natural) law, disturb the linear, though periodized, progression of godliness evidenced by Adam, Abraham, and other biblical luminaries. The rise of heresy obscures the orthodox line of Christianity. The rise of Christian sectarianism follows a historical pattern, conditioned by the errors of human intellect. When Epiphanius characterizes the Melchizedekians as "inflated by a more excessive arrogance of thought" (περισσοτέρᾳ ἀλαζονείᾳ ἐννοίας ἀρθέντες), he has, in fact, encapsulated the heresiologists' most basic charge against the entirety of the sectarian world.[63] Those who depart from the knowledge inscribed by scripture and entrusted to the ecclesiastical hierarchy are stripped, via genealogical exclusion, of the designation "Christian."[64] In his attack on this same sectarian offshoot, Epiphanius explicitly appeals to the language of tradition and succession in defense of orthodoxy: "Apostolic traditions, holy scriptures and successions of teachers have made our boundaries and foundations for the upbuilding of our faith, and God's truth has been protected in every way."[65]

Since the catholic church is the lone offspring of its mother, an image culled from Song of Songs 6.9, it stands singularly apart from all the heretics, the "concubines" (παλλακαί) who came before and would come after the incarnation.[66] But the heretics, both Christian and pre-Christian, "have not been entire strangers to

---

61. Young Richard Kim, "Epiphanius of Cyprus and the Geography of Heresy," in *Violence in Late Antiquity: Perceptions and Practices*, ed. H. A. Drake (Burlington, Vt.: Ashgate, 2006), 235–52, studies the geographical distribution of the heresies of the *Panarion*. Like most of the scholarship on the geography of heresy, he treats the matter literally, locating each of the heresies within a fixed geographical location. See also Thomas Robinson, *The Bauer Thesis Examined: The Geography of Heresy in the Early Christian Church* (Lewiston, N.Y.: Edwin Mellen, 1988).

62. On apostolic succession, see Boyarin, *Border Lines*, 74–86; Allen Brent, "Diogenes Laertius and the Apostolic Succession," *JEH* 44.3 (1993): 367–89; and various essays in A. Hilhorst, ed., *The Apostolic Age in Patristic Thought* (Leiden: Brill, 2004).

63. Epiphanius, *Pan.* 55.9.1 (GCS 31:336).

64. For instance, *Pan.* 21.1.1, 21.2.1, 21.7.2; 27.3.3, 27.4.1; 29.1.2, 29.6.6, 29.7.1.

65. Epiphanius, *Pan.* 55.3.8 (GCS 31:329).

66. Epiphanius, *De fide* 5.6, 6.1 (GCS 37:501). See also, *De fide* 7.2 and *Pan.* 35.3.5–6.

the covenant and inheritance."⁶⁷ The very fact that "a faith which exhibited the character of Christianity and an unbelief which exhibited the character of ungodliness and transgression" persisted into the age of Scythianism suggests that participation in the genealogy of godliness (i.e., Christianity or the faith of Christianity) was an affirmative *choice* "until the time I have just mentioned."⁶⁸ Christianity was genealogical insofar as the generations of descendants were arranged by the piety of their leading devotees, even though a decision to disobey the law of nature (an act of ungodliness) excised one from the tree of faith. In the era of Christ, the same choice confronts those who are divorced from the pious lineage of Adam and Abraham. Epiphanius's typological reading of Abraham's children with Keturah and Hagar reveals that those born outside the true lineage nonetheless "received gifts," which "were a type of the good things to come, for the conversion of the gentiles to the faith and truth."⁶⁹ Abraham's children by Keturah received gifts of wealth (taken from raids in Damascus and Samaria), which would ultimately be returned to Christ ("to gain their share of the same hope"), since the magi were descendants of Keturah:⁷⁰

> And do you see how the truth has expressions and consequences? The sects too are concubines, and their children have received gifts, though the concubines have only received the name, and have only been called by Christ's name and received their few texts from the sacred scripture, so that, if they want, they can understand the truth by these. But if they do not wish to [understand] but return to Herod (for they are told not to return to Herod, but to go to their country by another way)—and if they do not do as they are told, the gifts are without purpose for them, just as their coming would have done the magi no good if they had returned to Herod. For these same sects debase the teachings of God's oracles in a way that resembles Herod's.

Genealogy often produces "a ranked order of relationships" (an expression of spatial and genetic difference).⁷¹ Epiphanius, on the other hand, while indebted to the procreative and hierarchized models of the Christian tradition, uses his *Panarion* to reunify humanity by tracing the sources of its disruption. Because the truth "was plainly revealed in the world at Christ's coming," access to the genealogy of true knowledge is no longer shrouded by the darkness of sectarian opinion.⁷² Epiphanius articulates a theory of monogenism—the idea of common human

---

67. Epiphanius, *De fide* 6.1 (GCS 37:501).
68. Epiphanius, *Pan.* 2.7 (GCS, n. F., 10:175). The ambiguous locution "until the time I have just mentioned" (ἕως τοῦ προδεδηλωμένου χρόνου) could mean either until the time of Abraham or of Noah; the text is vague on this point.
69. Epiphanius, *De fide* 7.3, 4 (GCS 37:503).
70. Epiphanius, *De fide* 8.4–5 (GCS 37:504).
71. Greg Woolf, *Tales of the Barbarians: Ethnography and Empire in the Roman West* (Malden, Mass.: Wiley-Blackwell, 2011), 41.
72. Epiphanius, *De fide* 6.8 (GCS 37:502).

descent—in terms that interpret human descent via Adam as Christian unity. Adam was not simply a prophet who knew God but, in fact, a proto-Christian: "What was [Adam], then, since he was neither circumcised nor an idolater—except that he exhibited the character of Christianity?"[73]

As I noted in chapter 1, ethnographic paradigms of genealogy unify as much as they separate.[74] Epiphanius's master narrative elaborates these twin organizational operations of ethnographic analysis. For him, orthodoxy is the counterpoint to the history of heresy even as it finds itself suffering from the very disease it seeks to destroy. The history of Genesis 11, expanded and augmented, had become a distinctly Christian history and, in the end, a history of heresy.[75] Epiphanius's periodized narrative of cultural and ethnic origins coupled with his main text's description and denunciation of heretical Christian beliefs and practices exist as a persistent, though surmountable, foil and disruption to the ancient succession of Christian generations. The presentation of a history of heresy, which is also a history of the world and of Christianity itself—as it existed from the very beginning of creation—unfolds as "a style of sociological writing that will describe whole cultures (knowable worlds) from a specific temporal distance and with a presumption of their transience."[76] Epiphanius presents a worldview that imposed an impending summation for humanity at large. "The world's time periods are no longer counted by lineages," he writes, since the genealogies of the present and the measure of time are ultimately "summed up in one unified whole," the "unshakable stay" of the church.[77] Truth and orthodoxy, for Epiphanius, remain totally bound to the language, both implicit and explicit, of genealogical argumentation. The process of excising heresies rests on an appeal to genealogical strictures, which align the heretics with the legacy of Jewish and Hellenistic error and against the inheritance of the church itself. The force of Epiphanius's genealogy of piety and divine knowledge, elaborated in his description of the pre-Christian sects, drives his theory that the history of the world is, in fact, a history of (orthodox) Christianity.

73. Epiphanius, *Pan.* 2.5 (GCS, n. F., 10:175).
74. This point is stressed both by Woolf, *Tales of the Barbarians,* and by Erich S. Gruen, *Rethinking the Other in Antiquity* (Princeton: Princeton University Press, 2011).
75. Genesis 11 retains its centrality in the history of Christian anthropology. See, for example, Margaret T. Hodgen, *Early Anthropology in the Sixteenth and Seventeenth Centuries* (Philadelphia: University of Pennsylvania Press, 1964), 207–51; Colin Kidd, *The Forging of the Races: Race and Scripture in the Protestant Atlantic World, 1600–2000* (New York: Cambridge University Press, 2006); and David N. Livingstone, *Adam's Ancestors: Race, Religion, and the Politics of Human Origins* (Baltimore: The Johns Hopkins University Press, 2011).
76. James Clifford, "On Ethnographic Allegory," in *Writing Culture: The Poetics and Politics of Ethnography,* ed. James Clifford and George E. Marcus (Berkeley and Los Angeles: University of California Press, 1986), 98–121, at 114.
77. Epiphanius, *De fide* 5.4 (GCS 37:501).

The ethnographic gaze—the wide and widening lens through which the world was reoriented and translated—became the vernacular of the ascendant catholic church. The tarnish of the age of Barbarism did not dispel Epiphanius's longing for a world free of sectarian opinion, a world he insists is immanently Christian and bound to the very experience of being human. For Epiphanius, the church, adhering to Nicene orthodoxy, recalls a distant past free from division and bound to the simplicity of faith in God and the laws of nature. To that end, the age of Barbarism symbolizes the potential of the age of Christianity to perfect the divine plan: to uproot the sectarian divisions of the Christian age through the revealed truth of Christ and to return to an antediluvian way of life. As Hayden White has put it, "insofar as a unified *humanity* is imaginable, it is conceived to be the possession of a single group."[78] The church succeeded in civilizing everything—in making humanity whole again—through its way of life. Existing heretical societies, "far from exhibiting the original state of mankind out of which 'civilized' society evolved, are in fact degraded vestiges of originally higher civilizations."[79] Epiphanius, having refined the inchoate ethnogenic and sectarian theorizations of Hippolytus, broadens the conceptual and epistemological scope of heresiological literature. The *Panarion* is not simply an attempt to organize the world of Christianity; it organizes the world as a whole by its latent Christianity. It is the *Panarion*'s master narrative—its macroscopic theorization—that sets the text apart from its predecessors. What was only hinted at in Hippolytus—the sectarian taint of philosophical schools and astrological speculation—has developed into a detailed exposition of the very nature of human religiosity. As Tomoko Masuzawa has put it, in a related context, "a display of the state of (religious) divisiveness could in fact enhance the unitary truth of Christianity."[80] The *Panarion*'s

---

78. Hayden White, "The Forms of Wildness: Archaeology of an Idea," in his *Tropics of Discourse: Essays in Cultural Criticism* (reprint, Baltimore: The Johns Hopkins University Press, 1986), 150–82, at 155.

79. Christopher Herbert, *Culture and Anomie: Ethnographic Imagination in the Nineteenth Century* (Chicago: University of Chicago Press, 1991), 61.

80. Tomoko Masuzawa, *The Invention of World Religions; or, How European Universalism Was Preserved in the Language of Pluralism* (Chicago: University of Chicago Press, 2005), 55. Epiphanius, as we have seen, proposed a theory of religious decay that tied together linked moments of impiety with human arrogance. There was a dispositional core to religious degeneration. Masuzawa observes a similar phenomenon in the context of nineteenth-century theological writing. Charles A. Goodrich (1790–1862), she writes, used the existence of religious diversity and division to bolster Christianity's superiority over all other religious traditions: "The very existence and the considerable prosperity of false religions—or what amounts to a vast reign of 'Satan's empire'—turns out to be proof of the absolute truth, necessity, and mercy of the Christian God. In short, in this formulaic calculation, the more numerous and powerful those benighted un-Christians are, the more is it certain that Christians have it right, for, ultimately, all the misfortunes of the world—including the current state of apparent powerlessness and failure of Christendom to reign universally—are attributable to original sin and the consequent universal perdition; and this truth about the human condition, it seems, Christians understand more profoundly than any other members of the human race" (56).

project is one of therapeutic ethnography: it is an effort to rectify and regulate a straying world. In Epiphanius's thinking, the church functions as the temporal and theological summation point precisely because it nullifies the counting of successive generations. Biblical monogenism is, in fact, Christian monogenism. In unifying all peoples under the genealogy of Christ, the line of Adam and Abraham, the catholic church thus offers all peoples, nations, and places the choice to resubmit themselves to the one true God.

All time, having been previously "divided into the sixty-two generations up until Christ," now exists in the single body of the church: "All things are completed in [the church], whether they are times and seasons, years and intervals of generations, and whether the age counts its dates by emperors, consuls, Olympiads or governorships."[81] The secession of lineages "will make it evident that the end of the age is separate from time, and will be over at the transition to the age to come."[82] For Epiphanius, the atemporal finality of Christ orients the progression of sacred time toward a decisive eschatological moment. Similar to apocalyptic temporality and its rigidly defined ages and kingdoms, which function as the theological counterweight to the eventual revelation of messianic deliverance, Epiphanius's history of the catholic church as told in his *De fide* counts the generations between Adam and Christ in order to plot what was only suggested in his universal history of sectarianism: an exegesis of the biblical precedent for the unerring lineage of Christianity. Although the heresies of Judaism and Hellenism endured, it was simply a matter of time—or the very undoing of time itself—before the epochs of sectarian opinion would be a remnant of an earthly past.

THEODORET OF CYRRHUS'S MASTER NARRATIVE: A TYPOLOGICAL ORDERING OF HERESY

In the middle of the fifth century—in the wake of the Council of Chalcedon, in 451—Theodoret, bishop of the Syrian city of Cyrrhus, composed four books, known as the *Compendium of Heretical Fables* (Αἱρετικῆς κακομυθίας ἐπιτομή or *Haereticarum fabularum compendium*), along with a fifth book, *The Compendium of Divine Doctrines* (Θείων δογμάτων ἐπιτομή or *Divinorum decretorum epitome*).[83] Taken together, the text is known as *The Discernment of Lies and Truth*

---

81. Epiphanius, *De fide* 5.5 (GCS 37:501).
82. Epiphanius, *De fide* 5.4 (GCS 37:501).
83. Theodoret, *Haereticarum fabularum compendium* praef. (PG 83:340B). I have generally followed the translation by G. M. Cope, "An Analysis of the Heresiological Method of Theodoret of Cyrus in the 'Haereticarium Fabularum Compendium'" (Ph.D. dissertation, Catholic University of America, 1990), 74–356, though I have modified inaccuracies and provided necessary clarifications.

(Ψεύδους καὶ ἀληθείας διάγνωσις or *Falsi verique distinctio*).[84] With descriptions of fifty-seven heresies and twenty-nine chapters on orthodox doctrine, this bipartite heresiological treatise organizes heresy not explicitly by genealogy but by the doctrinal consonances among the sectarian Christian parties. Theodoret subsumes the genealogical paradigm promoted by Hippolytus and Epiphanius under a typological (i.e., theological-doctrinal) genealogy.[85] His treatment of the heresies in Books 1 and 2 defines and organizes them in relation to doctrinal lineages. His master narrative imposes a typological ordering upon the heretical world that seeks to systematize the consistently evolving scope and substance of heretical inquiry. It is a model that strives to illuminate change among the heretics by way of a taxonomy drawn from the observation of various heretical parties. Book 1 arrays all those heresies that "invented another creator, . . . denied one beginning of the whole universe," and that say "that the Lord appeared among men by illusion."[86] Book 2 collects the heresies that hold the opposite, namely that the universe has a singular beginning, but "they address the Lord as a mere man."[87] "The core point of comparison between the two main heretical groups," as Helen Sillett has phrased it, "is Christology, and the errors made by the inadequate simultaneous expression of humanity and the divinity of Christ."[88] In Theodoret's telling, the heretics progressed in history by theological variation: each stage of heretical attack was organized around an overarching doctrinal type. As one stage failed, a new type would emerge.

While Theodoret inaugurates his discussion of the heresies with Simon Magus, in the *Compendium* Simon is not the sole heretical father of all the known heretics. Instead, he begets only the first of the two major Christological lineages: those who

---

84. Theodoret, *Haer. praef.* (*PG* 83:340B). On Theodoret generally, see Theresa Urbainczyk, *Theodoret of Cyrrhus: The Bishop and the Holy Man* (Ann Arbor: University of Michigan Press, 2002); István Pássztori-Kupán, *Theodoret of Cyrus* (New York: Routledge, 2006); and Adam Schor, *Theodoret's People: Social Networks and Religious Conflict in Late Roman Syria* (Berkeley and Los Angeles: University of California Press, 2011). Helen Sillett has treated the largely unstudied *Discernment of Lies and Truth* in her essay "Orthodoxy and Heresy in Theodoret of Cyrus' *Compendium of Heresies*," in *Orthodoxy, Christianity, History*, ed. Susanna Elm, Éric Rebillard, and Antonella Romano (Rome: École Française de Rome, 2000), 261–73. Much of what she writes about Theodoret is incisive, though I would alter her characterization of late antique heresiology. She asserts that by becoming "encyclopedic epitomes, cataloguing the history of heresy through brief descriptions and labels," heresiology, a once-vibrant genre, had become flat and unsophisticated (270). I would suggest just the opposite, in fact. It is as epitomes that heresiology reveals its sophistication and the heresiologists their skill as armchair ethnographers.

85. See Averil Cameron, "How to Read Heresiology," *JMEMS* 33.3 (2003), 471–92, at 478. For a related application of Theodoret's typological inclinations, see Derek Krueger, "Typological Figuration in Theodoret of Cyrrhus's *Religious History* and the Art of Postbiblical Narrative," *JECS* 5.3 (1997): 393–419.

86. Theodoret, *Haer. praef.* (*PG* 83:337C).

87. Theodoret, *Haer. praef.* (*PG* 83:337D).

88. Sillett, "Orthodoxy and Heresy," 269.

invent a divine hierarchy.⁸⁹ Simon is juxtaposed with Ebion, who in Book 2 is construed as the second foundational figure in shaping the contours of the history of heresy. In each case, their pedigrees would ultimately be supplanted by future heresies, which tried to eradicate orthodox Christianity precisely where previous generations of heretics had failed. At Book 3, the taxonomic typology relaxes its grip on the text, and instead we find a collection of heretical miscellany. Theodoret names six unrelated heresies, which emerged contemporaneously with the two Christological categories of Books 1 and 2, defined as "those who have sprouted between those former heresies [or more remote, temporally speaking] and these latter heretics [or nearer, temporally], who were the fathers of diverse doctrines" (τοὺς μεταξὺ τούτων κἀκείνων . . . βεβλαστηκότας, οἳ διαφόρων δογμάτων πατέρες ἐγένοντο).⁹⁰ The Nicolatians, Montanists, followers of Noetus of Smyrna, Quartodecimans, followers of Novatus, and those loyal to Nepos all exhibit an assortment of theological errors, ranging from polygamy to the misdating of Easter, unrelated to the overarching typologies of either Simon or Ebion. The six are allied by temporal chance in the midst of Theodoret's larger typological classification: "These teachings sprang up between those denying the humanity of our God and Savior and calling a mere man the one who is eternal God. And the majority of them languished as soon as they sprang forth, and remained dried up."⁹¹ The strict binary typology is broken as time passes, but it follows a pattern foretold by scripture. The parable of the tares (Matt. 7.15–20) forewarns of wolves in sheep's clothing (the heretics), which will be identified by their (bad) fruits (i.e., teachings): "These ill-blowing and all-abominable doctrines are sufficient to demonstrate their shared father."⁹² Like the heretics of Books 1 and 2, the six heretics of Book 3 have been defeated by the forces of orthodoxy and have fled from Christian strongholds. In Theodoret's telling, these theological temptations serve only to steady and strengthen the church's foundations.⁹³

In the first four books of the *Compendium*, genealogy operates as a tool by which Theodoret arranges the heretics within a broader typological framework. From Simon "sprang up" (ἀνεφύησαν) eight heretical offshoots: the Cleobians, Dosithians, Gortheni, Masbothei, Adrianistians, Eutychetians, and Cainites.⁹⁴ The

---

89. Augustine enumerates the Simonians first but does not describe Simon as the root of all heresy (though that may be his assumption). Hippolytus mentions Simon Magus in passing, noting that his successors took him as their beginning. But the explicit language of Simon as the root of all heresy is noticeably absent in Theodoret's treatise.

90. Theodoret, *Haer.* praef. (*PG* 83:337D; altered from Cope). See also *Haer.* 3 pro.

91. Theodoret, *Haer.* 3.6 (*PG* 83:408D–409A).

92. Theodoret, *Haer.* 3 pro. (*PG* 83:401A).

93. See Theodoret, *Haer.* 3 pro.

94. Theodoret, *Haer.* 1 pro. (*PG* 83:345B). The first four, as Cope, "An Analysis of the Heresiological Method of Theodoret of Cyrus," 86 n. 13, notes, are listed together by Hegesippus in his (mostly lost) *Hypomnēmata*. See Eusebius, *Hist. eccl.* 4.22.5.

language of succession (from διαδέχομαι, "take up [the word]" or "succeed") is deployed similarly to emphasize doctrinal heredity, not simply doctrinal parallelization or sequential ordering. Menander is described as the successor to Simon and then as the teacher of Saturnilus and Basilides. The heretic Prodicus is called the "successor" (διαδεξάμενος) to Carpocrates, whereas Valentinus is said not only to have received his "starting point" (ἀφορμάς) from Simon, Menander, Saturnilus, Basilides, Carpocrates, and Prodicus but in turn to have given rise to the heresy of Secundus.[95] At the turn of chapter 23, Theodoret refines his genealogical typology, declaring that the twenty-two heretics from Menander to Florinus in fact all "began from Simon [and] brought forth doctrines similar to one another: naming Aeons, and emanations of Aeons, and other emanations of emanations."[96]

Book 2 does not explicitly follow a genealogy of knowledge or chain of intellectual inheritance until chapter 5, where Theodotus is said to have "held these same [doctrinal] opinions with [Artemon but] led a different faction," which then germinated the Melchizedekians.[97] Although the consonance between Theodotus and Artemon is ambiguous (whether it is shared by coincidence or by inheritance), it is clear that Theodotus is the seed from which the Melchizedekians arise; they "are a division of these Theodotians."[98] The Elchasaites, moreover, "collected myths from various heresies," evidencing further intellectual dependence among the heretical factions.[99] And in Book 4, chapter 4 concerns the "Pasthyrians and others derived from the heresy of Arius."[100] Polemon is noted to have taken "his starting point from the writings" of Apollinaris.[101] In chapter 3, Theodoret describes the heresy of Aetius and his student Eunomius as an intensified offshoot of Arius: this sect "clearly increased the blasphemies of Arius."[102] Not only did they spread the essential theological message of Arius (thus carrying on his intellectual lineage), but also, like any living organism, they mutated and adapted to the challenges of orthodoxy. The *Compendium*, like heresiology more broadly, strives to establish doctrinal and temporal points of connection between and among the heretics of the world. The *Compendium* strives to find order amid the confusion it describes.

A heresiological system ordered by typology does not, as we see, necessarily dissolve genealogical relations; it can and does use them to illuminate the protean nature of the heresies while also prioritizing doctrinal similarity over against generative causation. The *Compendium* is not altogether dissimilar from the *Panarion*

95. Theodoret, *Haer.* 1.7 (PG 83:353B).
96. Theodoret, *Haer.* 1.23 (PG 83:372C–D).
97. Theodoret, *Haer.* 2.5 (PG 83:392A).
98. Theodoret, *Haer.* 2.6 (PG 83:392D).
99. Theodoret, *Haer.* 2.7 (PG 83:393A).
100. Theodoret, *Haer.* 4.4 (PG 83:421C).
101. Theodoret, *Haer.* 4.9 (PG 83:428A).
102. Theodoret, *Haer.* 4.3 (PG 83:417A).

in the way that both use generative-kinship connections between the heresies to complement their broader schematizations: a universal genealogy of heresy writ large for Epiphanius and a theological typology of heresy for Theodoret. Though shaped by their different emphases, Epiphanius and Theodoret both employ the same language of classification. Epiphanius describes most of the heresies as successors to their respective previous sects. The succession itself generally follows one of two patterns: a temporal succession (the ambiguous successor, in which chronology is the driving structure) or an actual genealogical (intellectual) descent.[103] As noted above, the language of succession, though not dominant for Theodoret, does organize almost the entirety of Book 1 as well as various heresies throughout Books 2, 3, and 4. To that end, many of the heresies in the *Compendium* progress along an organizational trajectory markedly similar to that of the *Panarion*. As the macroframeworks of the *Panarion* and the *Compendium* diverge in terms of organization, they conceptually gesture toward the same conclusion. In the cases of typology and genealogy both, the function is to schematize the disorder of the heretical world. Heresy is defined out of the tradition even as it is subsumed within the domain of Christian knowledge. In the *Panarion*, the universal genealogy conceptualizes the error of idolatry and human division by language and nation as the cause of all religious devolution.[104] Like Epiphanius's *De fide*, the *Compendium of Divine Doctrines* articulates the lineage of piety down into the catholic church. Theodoret tailors his treatise toward orthodoxy and, specifically, toward a refinement of its theological principles.

In the *Compendium* the emphasis on doctrine highlights the mutability and proximity of the heresies, framing the imperative for his Book 5, on orthodoxy:[105]

> Now I call upon those who are reading [this], to examine each of the heretical doctrines in comparison with the teaching of the truth. For on account of this, I wrote the fifth book. For it shall be seen, on the one hand, that the fifth book follows the sayings of the divine spirit, while the other books are the invention of all-depraved thought.

By fomenting ecclesiastical purges and synodic battles, the doctrinal history of heresy conversely maps Theodoret's discussions of orthodox doctrine. The *utility* of doctrinal heresy is precisely what propels Theodoret's typological model. It is

---

103. Epiphanius reports, for example, that Noetus "arose in his turn after Bardesanes, though not many years ago; it was about 130 years before our time" (*Pan.* 57.1.1 [GCS 31:343]). The Purists (*Pan.* 59) arose after the Valesians, but the Angelics (*Pan.* 60) are decoupled from the previous narrative. Succession, in these cases, is never explicitly described in the language of generative causation but merely as temporally connected or successive.

104. On degeneration and ethnography, see Herbert, *Culture and Anomie*, 215–22. On degeneration and biblical theology, see Colin Kidd, *Forging of the Races*, 71–85

105. Theodoret *Haer.* praef. (*PG* 83:340B; altered from Cope).

the formation of church doctrine via the interaction between heretical and orthodox theology that undergirds the typological paradigm, bringing into relief the necessity of coherent orthodox opinion:[106]

> Therefore, since we proved the shame of the lies and we stripped the heretical fables bare, their impiety became evident, and carry joylessness and incredulity to them, come let us compare them to the Gospel teaching. We made plain the difference between light and darkness, [between] the peak of health and the difficulty of sickness. For it is not [possible] to find a likeness that they agree with for the proposed comparison. For even the darkness, even if it also leaves behind the light, nevertheless produces the necessary utility for me. For the night brings about a respite for those who work during the day. And sickness has become profitable for many. For having recognized the Savior and Creator through this, and having proclaimed the expulsion of evils, they who obtained what they asked turned their attention to virtue.

The protreptic language here is overt. Theodoret's argument posits a cosmic struggle between two forces, those of light and darkness. The contestation between demonic and divine forces not only creates the seemingly chaotic history of Christianity; it also serves as the foundation around which Theodoret can systematically comprehend and seek to impose order upon the ebb and flow of Christianity's position throughout the world. His treatise expounds a theory of heresy that naturalizes the persistent and enduring threat of contrarian opinion by way of demonic intrusion. In essence, it grounds abstract notions of Christian temptation in a demonogenic narrative.

Theodoret argues that heresies arose from the work of the "wholly-evil demon, the destroyer of mankind," who, having lost "the roots . . . of polytheistic error, and himself being stripped bare of subjects, . . . invented different concepts of the insidious attacks."[107] In the preface to Book 2 of his *Compendium* (the typology conditioned by Ebion, which emphatically declares Christ's humanity), he explains the perpetuation of heresies as an unyielding effort by demonic forces to disrupt the ship of truth. The demon, unconstrained by principles of consistency, steadily works his way through a bounty of heresies, jettisoning what fails and refining what succeeds:[108]

> But these [heretics of Book 1] were only a few who would be easily counted, and these, dispersed in some of the cities, were surrounded by the thrusting opprobrium for Valentinus, Marcion, and followers of Mani, probably by refutation of those who are now entrusted to maintain the churches but are unable to convert the small remains of the impious heresies. And the demon, hostile to God, could not take

106. Theodoret, *Haer.* 5 pro. (*PG* 83:441A–B; altered from Cope).
107. Theodoret, *Haer.* 1 pro. (*PG* 83:341B; altered from Cope).
108. Theodoret, *Haer.* 2 pro. (*PG* 83:388B; altered from Cope).

satiety of war against the godly; but again he sends others to war against the truth, with teachings in complete opposition to the previously described heretical beliefs.

The heresies of the past, having failed to counteract the forces of light, belong to the annals of history. They have been summarily exposed, counted, and demolished. Theodoret did not invent the association between the demons and the heretics, but he did fashion an unprecedented heresiological master narrative that explained typological succession by means of demonic plotting.[109] In Theodoret's telling, demonic intercession is not, then, some haphazard or sporadic occurrence but a persistent and regulated effort to alter the contours of Christian history. Theodoret's heresiology thus marshals this cosmic struggle to explain the fluctuating conditions of the Christian world. Theodoret's heresiology theorizes Christian diversity by way of what the historian of religion David Chidester has called, in a different historical context, "Satanic structuralism."[110] The world began with one religion—the religion of Adam—but "through a long, gradual process of historical diffusion, a process determined . . . by Satanic influence, the one had become the many; the religions of the world had proliferated."[111]

Although Theodoret's outlook was narrower than Epiphanius's[112]—his was not a universal history of religion—his text deployed the logic and language of Satanic structuralism in unmistakably emphatic and adaptive terms.[113] Indeed, fourth- and fifth-century heresies—the enduring controversies generated by Arius, Nestorius, Eutyches, the Donatists, and Apollinaris, among others—reveal a worsening, adaptive demonic plot. Thwarted by God's apostles and future generations of orthodoxy, who have stamped out the infamous opinions of Simon and Ebion's legacy, the demonic power resumes its plan with new knowledge:[114]

---

109. See, for instance, David Brakke, *Demons and the Making of the Monk: Spiritual Combat in Early Christianity* (Cambridge, Mass.: Harvard University Press, 2006), 110–13, 165–66; and Elaine Pagels, *The Origins of Satan: How Christians Demonized Jews, Pagans, and Heretics* (New York: Vintage, 1995).

110. David Chidester, *Savage Systems: Colonialism and Comparative Religion in Southern Africa* (Charlottesville: University of Virginia Press, 1996), 242.

111. Ibid. 191.

112. Throughout the *Panarion* Epiphanius does, in fact, associate various heretics and heretical ideas and practices with Satan (the Evil One) and devils. See *Pan.* 23.2.5–6; 24.5.1; 25.1.3, 25.4.11; 26.2.5, 26.18.2; 27.3.3, 27.5.5; 32.2.9; 33.7.3; 34.2.15, 34.11.11, 34.19.1; 37.1.6; 38.3.6; 39.9.1; 40.5.1–5.5, 40.6.1–9; 42.1.1, 42.7.8, 42.14.2–3; 45.2.1; 47.1.4–2.1; 48.2.3; 51.1.5; 52.1.8; 59.4.12; 61.7.6; 63.3.1; 64.2.3; 65.1.1; 66.2.8, 66.16.1, 66.20.6; 68.3.1; 69.2.1; 75.2.1; 76.24.5; 77.1–3; 79.1.7; 80.3.1. Epiphanius does not prominently frame his theory of the rise of sectarianism, as elaborated in the earliest sections of the *Panarion*, through the logic of Satanic influence.

113. Chidester, *Savage Systems*, notes that "the explanation of religions as products of evil forces was popular with early Church forces, who often identified pagan gods as demons" (242). On the latter point, see the apologies of Tertullian and Justin Martyr.

114. Theodoret, *Haer.* 4 pro. (*PG* 83:412B).

But the Father of lies, whom the Lord reasonably called a murderer (for he always lays plots for the souls of men), contrived different devices of plots. For after understanding, as it seems, the things said concerning the God of the Universe on the part of the disciples of that one [i.e., Valentinus] to be wholly foul, so the message of their explanation did not hold plausibility. For some, on the one hand, said that the naked divinity appeared, and others, on the other hand, said that the human nature devoid of divinity performed the [divine] economy. He, the devil, mixed another impiety, devoid of the hyperbole of the former view.

Realizing the implausibility of its Valentinian creation, the Evil One marshals subtler, more nefarious ideas to challenge the pillars of truth. While heretical diversity had been used previously (by Irenaeus, Hippolytus, Tertullian, Epiphanius, and Augustine) to evidence the heresies' incompatibility with the singular apostolic succession or catholic truth, for Theodoret such diversity is an outward sign or remnant of previous, failed demonic attempts.

Even in the instances in which heresy possessed a demonogenic lineage, Theodoret ascribes heresy's longevity to the susceptibility of the human mind. Heresy's very livelihood hinges on the innate weakness of human existence.[115] As Theodoret declares while interpreting 2 Timothy, the apostle Paul (to whom Theodoret mistakenly attributes the epistle) "proves both the freedom of the will and the autonomy of the mind, which easily changes one's inclination to whatever one wants."[116] Heresy is a phenomenon bound up with human frailty. Similarly, during his refutation of the Sethians, Epiphanius supplements his periodized history of the heresy with a brief comment about culpability. After enumerating the various languages and peoples that arose in the aftermath of the tower's destruction, he ascribes the total content of his universal narrative to the handiwork of the devil:[117]

> Why is it, then, that these people have told their lies, interpolating their own mythology, imagining and dreaming of unreal things as though they were real, and banishing what is real from their own minds? But the whole thing is an idea of the devil which he has engendered in human souls. It is amazing to see how he deceived man into many offenses and dragged him down to transgression, to fornication, adultery and incontinence, to madness of idols and gluttony, and any number of such things—but never before Christ's coming ventured to say a blasphemous word against his own Master or mediate open rebellion.

As the instrumental realization of the demonic or divine plans, men and women emerge as the agents and markers of heresy in history.[118] Just as "the all-wise God of the universe entrusted the [Gospel's] cultivation of the barren world to a few

---

115. On this point, see the prologue to Book 2 of Theodoret's *Haer.*
116. Theodoret, *Haer.* 2 pro. (*PG* 83:385A).
117. Epiphanius, *Pan.* 39.9.1–3 (GCS 31:78–79).
118. See Theodoret *Haer.* 1 pro.; 2 pro.; 2.11; 3 pro.

men," the demon chose "men worthy of his own operation, . . . placing on them like a mask the title of Christians."[119] He sowed the seeds of wickedness ("planted the tares") before the gospel had been established—"immediately after those [apostles] began to cultivate and to scatter the seeds of piety"—"he presented the noxious drug of falsehood to humankind."[120] But heresy's persistence as a force at once natural and supernatural, caught between the world of men and the world of demons, exposes an important disjuncture within the rhetorical and theoretical edifice of heresiology. The rationalization of heresy as a necessary source of temptation *presupposes* the human ability to comprehend and triumph over it. Heresy's oscillation between natural and supernatural force exacerbates the epistemological limitations of the heresiologists as they struggle to solidify their evolving, yet always tenuous, knowledge of heresiological sources and tradition.

To account for Theodoret's typological arrangement Sillett has posited a plausible historical explanation, in which the *Compendium* is best understood as "a literary response to" the Nestorian controversies of 431 and 451.[121] Theodoret, having watched as Cyril and Nestorius waged synodal and doctrinal war against each other, interprets the vicissitudes of Christological contestation as an ever-encroaching, demonically generated force precisely "because heresy looked, to the bishops involved, a lot like orthodoxy."[122] The ever-shifting theological landscape thus necessitates a *discernment* of truths from lies. But Theodoret does not contest the heresies as he describes them; rather he (mostly) dispassionately identifies their distinguishing features as he works his way toward a systematic enumeration of orthodox praxis, doctrine, and belief. His typological ordering, hastened by the Christological controversies of the fifth century, reflects the fact that the demon fought his battle against the church from within: he worked to introduce heresy through the appearance of orthodoxy. Theodoret emphasizes that the demon used Nestorius as an "instrument, so to speak, continually undertaking his craft, in guise of orthodoxy."[123] Although the process by which the demon deploys his tricks in the name of God predates Nestorius—"for he undertook to attack everyone by the blasphemous fellowship of his name"—the current crises of the fifth century illustrate the demon's progression and evolution.[124] What was once easily discerned as outside the fold now requires far more exacting scrutiny and investigation. In

---

119. Theodoret, *Haer.* 1 pro. (*PG* 83:341B).
120. Theodoret, *Haer.* 1 pro. (*PG* 83:341C).
121. Sillett, "Orthodoxy and Heresy," 267.
122. Ibid. 271. On Nestorius, Cyril, Theodoret, and heretical discourse, see Susan Wessel, *Cyril of Alexandria and the Nestorian Controversy: The Making of a Saint and of a Heretic* (New York: Oxford University Press, 2004); and Silke-Petra Bergjan, *Theodoret von Cyrus und der Neunizänismus: Aspekte der altkirchlichen Trinitätslehre* (New York: de Gruyter, 1994).
123. Theodoret, *Haer.* 4.12 (*PG* 83:433A).
124. Theodoret, *Haer.* 2 pro. (*PG* 83:384 B).

each successive generation, the heresies become more entrenched, hew closer to the line of orthodoxy, and become more difficult to discern *as* heresies.

Theodoret's heresiological text directly confronts the problem of embedded heresy by augmenting heretical descriptions with orthodox instruction. In this manner, it follows Irenaeus, Hippolytus, and Epiphanius, all of whom articulate their respective visions of orthodoxy—or doctrinal truth—within their textual codas. Theodoret's treatise includes twenty-nine orthodox subjects, ranging from abstinence to judgment and giving his readers a systematic catalogue of orthodox teachings. Moreover, his text ventures beyond simple disputes over Christology and the proximate events of the fifth century's theological controversies: it includes theological delineations of cosmology, demonology, anthropology, creation, resurrection, and Parousia alongside practical considerations such as second marriage, repentance, virginity, and abstinence. Despite its typological framework, *The Discernment of Lies and Truth* remains styled and shaped by the language of its heresiological predecessors. And as the typological genealogies of Simon and Ebion recede, the text becomes an amalgam of heretical miscellanies ordered only by demonic machinations. Theodoret's text is an exemplar of the genre's structural capacity to adapt itself, to look backward and forward, as the persistence of heresy necessitates a consistent explanation even as heresies become increasingly diverse, versatile, and resilient.

CONCLUSION: CHRISTIAN CONTINUITY AND CURIOSITY

While the effects of erroneous opinions and practices are strikingly obvious in Epiphanius's condensed history of the world, his aspirations as a Christian writer are at once much grander and more subtle than those of his heresiological predecessors. Epiphanius's narrative of sectarianism reveals an acute transposition of the age of nations into the age of heresy. His use of an ethnographic model of heresy—a universal genealogy—not only explains the genesis of sectarianism but simultaneously recasts all human history as Christian history and all human difference as Christian difference. As Epiphanius and Theodoret thrust processes of ethnographic mapping to the forefront of their narratives of Christian dissension, they produce coherent, continuous, and even predictable patterns of Christian diversity. In elucidating the history and impact of cultural and religious progression and degeneration, and offering a typological theory of heretical diversification, heresiology binds its analysis of sectarianism to a worldview that aligns systematicity or macroscopic theorization with the production of heretical opinions. I have illustrated in this and in the previous chapter how the investigation of heresy's origins—and its ethnic and communal character—prefigures and ultimately structures taxonomies of Christian heresy. Having reached the epoch of Christianity, the negotiation of theological opinions now shapes the history of the world. The ethnography of heresy at once narrows the order of the world to its Christian aegis and yet defines the world by its Christian (theological) governance. The heresiologists' description of the heretics as the new nations of the world is part of a broader effort to impose a Christian logic on the study of the world's history, peoples, and places.

Heresiology, I have argued, functions as an unabashed illustration of this effort to make the world manifestly and exhaustively Christian by ordering its contents within repeating theological, genealogical, and taxonomic structures. As Irenaeus insisted, it was only through an understanding of the Christian whole that the parts of creation made sense: "The things made [in creation] are many and varied, and they are well fitted and consonant to the whole creation; however, looked at individually they are mutually contradictory and not in agreement."[125] Through an analysis of the disharmony within Christianity (and the world more broadly), the heresiological genre works backward, from dissonance to consonance, to extrapolate theories of human diversity. Heresiology became a natural history. As Foucault notes: "Natural history is a science, that is, a language, but a securely based and well-constructed one: its propositional unfolding is indisputably an articulation; the arrangement of its elements into a linear series patterns representation according to an evident and universal mode."[126]

Christians used their models to explain the conditions and contents, past and present, of the world at large. Because the express purpose of heresiology emerges out of a desire to impose a fixed order on the diversifying world, Christians devised systems and theories of knowledge production. To write Christian ethnography was to categorize the world through the lens of Christian knowledge. Macroscopic ethnography built the Christian "intellectual and imaginative universe" with order and rules amid seemingly uncontrollable chaos.[127] Indeed, this Christian sense of order, as Hayden White has observed, was informed by a particular sense of experiencing the world:[128]

> There is, therefore, an important difference between the form that the total humanity is imagined to have by Greek and Roman thinkers and that which it is imagined to have by Hebrew and Christian thinkers. To put it crudely, in the former, humanity is experienced as diversified in fact though unifiable in principle. In the latter, humanity is experienced as unifiable in principle though radically divided in fact. This

---

125. Irenaeus, *Adv. haer.* 2.25.2 (SC 294:252; my translation).
126. Michel Foucault, *The Order of Things: An Archaeology of the Human Sciences* (New York: Vintage, 1970), 136.
127. Averil Cameron, *Christianity and the Rhetoric of Empire: The Development of Christian Discourse* (Berkeley and Los Angeles: University of California Press, 1991), 21.
128. White, "The Forms of Wildness," 156.

means that perceived differences between men had less significance for Greeks and Romans than they had for Hebrews and Christians. For the former, differentness was perceived as physical and cultural; for the latter, as moral and metaphysical.

But, as Foucault insists in *The Order of Things,* classificatory language works only "if its descriptive exactitude makes every proposition into an invariable pattern of reality . . . and if the designation of each being indicates clearly the place it occupies in the general arrangement."[129] In other words, classification assumes not only the continuity of the system under discussion (in our case, sectarianism) but also the curiosity to discover in order to construct "a totality of representations."[130] As we shall see in the remaining chapters, these twin propositions—curiosity and continuity—emerge as deeply problematic and troubling principles for the heresiologists.

129. Foucault, *The Order of Things,* 159.
130. Ibid. 158.

5

Knowledge Fair and Foul

The Rhetoric of Heresiological Inquiry

And I applied my mind to know wisdom and to know madness and folly. I perceived that this also is but a chasing after wind. For in much wisdom is much vexation, and those who increase knowledge increase sorrow.

—QOHELETH 1.17–18

In the ancient world, critiques of curiosity were an outgrowth of protracted discussions about the value and purpose of right inquiry and the betterment of the self.[1] Plutarch, in his *De curiositate* (*On Being a Busybody*) lists curiosity (πολυπραγμοσύνη) first among the "unhealthy and injurious states of mind."[2] To inquire excessively was to be diseased by malice and envy and to turn away from the self.[3] In point of fact, he explains, the "busybody [literally, "the curious one"] is also more useful to his enemies than to himself, for he rebukes and drags out their faults and demonstrates to them what they should avoid or correct."[4] In Plutarch's imagining, the overeager inquirer becomes a vessel of the undesirable, base, and altogether reprehensible. In craving danger, he turns to other people and things in order to avoid turning his gaze upon himself. Though inquiry was described as an inescapably natural phenomenon, it was not a neutral endeavor. For ancient writers, it held the power to baffle as much as edify. To know was not always *to be* or *become* better, even if, as Aristotle had famously declared in his

---

1. On curiosity in antiquity, see P. G. Walsh, "The Rights and Wrongs of Curiosity (Plutarch to Augustine)," *GR* 35.1 (1988): 73–85; Andreas Kessler, Thomas Ricklin, and Gregor Wurst, eds., *Peregrina curiositas: Eine Reise durch den orbis antiquus zu Ehren von Dirk van Damme* (Göttingen: Vandenhoeck & Ruprecht, 1994); Maria Tasinato, *La curiosità: Apuleio e Agostino* (Milan: Luni, 2000); G. E. R. Lloyd, *The Ambitions of Curiosity: Understanding the World in Ancient Greece and China* (New York: Cambridge University Press, 2002); and Joseph N. Torchia, *Restless Mind: Curiositas and the Scope of Inquiry in St. Augustine's Theology* (Milwaukee, Wisc.: Marquette University Press, 2013), 27–91.
2. Plutarch, *Curios.* 515C, trans. W. C. Helmbold, LCL 337 (Cambridge, Mass.: Harvard University Press, 1939), 472–73.
3. Plutarch, *Curios.* 515D (LCL 337:474–75).
4. Plutarch, *Curios.* 516A (LCL 337:476–77).

Metaphysics, to want to know was to be human.[5] "If," as Peter Harrison has observed of ancient attitudes toward curiosity, "the natural state of the human being is to seek knowledge, its excess becomes the vice of curiosity."[6]

The Christian writers of the late antique amplified Plutarch's critique through the language of exclusive Christian truth, oriented around the simplicity and virtue of theological consensus.[7] Augustine argued that *curiositas* was a hubris born of Adam and Eve, a lustful pride traceable to the very core of the temporal human condition.[8] It was, put simply, "vain inquisitiveness dignified with the title of knowledge and science."[9] Curiosity, like pleasure, relied upon the senses to activate its latent potential. But unlike pleasure, its object was not the ideal of beauty; rather, the curious mind "pursues the contraries of these delights ... out of a lust for experimenting and knowing."[10] For Augustine, parroting 1 John 2.16, curiosity is the "lust of the eyes,"[11] the passion of the senses amplified and gone awry.[12] To temper the vice of curiosity, Plutarch had encouraged the busybody to turn his attention to sites of neutrality and betterment: "heavenly things and things on earth, in the air, in the sea."[13] But for many Christian writers, nature and the heavens were not unproblematic sites of innocent inquisition. Augustine argued that curiosity about the perplexities of the natural world was not, in itself, a rightful avenue of inquiry. The natural world alone could not provide a Christian with sufficient theological knowledge.[14] Moreover, the zeal for knowledge about the heavens could be a sign of vanity and godlike aspirations. The Gnostics, as we have seen in previous chapters, were chastised precisely for reaching deep into the cosmos, for aspiring to know, and thus—in the view of the heresiologists—to become divine.[15] As Irenaeus warned, the heretic "imagines that he has acquired

---

5. Aristotle, *Metaph.* 980a, trans. Hugh Tredennick, LCL 271 (Cambridge, Mass.: Harvard University Press, 1933), 2–3.

6. Peter Harrison, "Curiosity, Forbidden Knowledge, and the Reformation of Natural Philosophy in Early Modern England," *Isis* 92.2 (2001): 265–90, at 267.

7. On the importance of consensus in late antiquity as an outgrowth of the military, economic, and political crises of the third century, see Richard Lim, *Public Disputation, Power and Social Order in Late Antiquity* (Berkeley and Los Angeles: University of California Press, 1995), 24–30. See also Keith Hopkins, "Christian Number and Its Implications," *JECS* 6.2 (1998): 185–226, esp. 217–26.

8. On Augustine's creation of a genealogy of curiosity, see *De Genesi contra Manichaeos* 2.18.27–28. See also Torchia, *Restless Mind*, 96–264.

9. Augustine, *Conf.* 10.35.54 (CCSL 27:184). Translation from Henry Chadwick, *Saint Augustine: Confessions* (New York: Oxford University Press, 1998). See Hans Blumenberg, "Curiositas und Veritas: Zur Ideengeschichte von Augustin, Confessiones X 35," *StPatr* 6 (1962): 294–302.

10. Augustine, *Conf.* 10.35.55 (CCSL 27:184–85).

11. Augustine, *Conf.* 10.35.54 (CCSL 27: 184).

12. See Edward Peters, "The Desire to Know the Secrets of the World," *JHI* 62.4 (2001): 593–610.

13. Plutarch, *Curios.* 517C–D (LCL 337:484–85).

14. Augustine, *Conf.* 5.4.7.1–16.

15. See David Brakke, *The Gnostics: Myth, Ritual, and Diversity in Early Christianity* (Cambridge, Mass.: Harvard University Press, 2010), 29–89.

not a partial, but a universal knowledge of all that exists."[16] By contrast, critics of the Gnostics, and of heretics more broadly, insisted that the relationship between humans and God was governed by a certain degree of mystery and apophatic understanding.[17] There were limits to theological speculation, which not only restricted processes of knowledge acquisition but also defined the parameters of licit and comprehensible knowledge. As Harrison articulates it: "For the Fathers, human curiosity was distinguished both by its objects and by its underlying motivations. The curious mind aimed at that knowledge that surpassed human capacities or was forbidden, worldly, or useless. As to its motivations, curiosity was prompted by pride, vanity, or the desire to be like God."[18]

Heresiology, as I will demonstrate in this chapter, exacerbates the tension between pastoral duties and theological inquiry, between consensus and dissensus.[19] Detailed descriptions and classifications of heretics thus serve two functions: while they provide the reference point for heresiological refutation they also expose the details of illicit knowledge. In this chapter, I analyze the language and tropes that the heresiologists employed to describe their painstaking efforts to investigate heresy. Inasmuch as these writers illustrate what I have called the "ethnographic disposition"—an impulse for the collection, categorization, and theorization of knowledge—they openly worry about its potential to upset the coherence of their respective articulations of Christian doctrine, history, and practice. This fear, I will argue, indicates the nascent, slow, and increasingly prominent unraveling of heresiological expertise. By openly investigating what is to be shunned, heresiological ethnography strains the already blurred boundary between legitimate and illegitimate inquiry. Daniel Boyarin has rightly emphasized that while the Council of Nicaea was a turning point in the forging of a canonical orthodoxy, it did not, of course, put an end to debate and dissension. Instead, Boyarin suggests, Nicaea formalized an ideology that "debate was no longer considered appropriate for the determination of Christian truth."[20] The problem, however, as he immediately notes, is that "calls for such monovocality of truth and 'simplicity' without dialectic go back in Christian writing as far as Paul and are well represented in such

---

16. Irenaeus, *Adv. haer.* 2.28.9 (SC 294:290).

17. See, for example, Irenaeus, *Adv. haer.* 2.26, 2.28; Tertullian, *Praescr.* 7; 8; 34; Hippolytus, *Ref.* 7.32.3; Epiphanius, *Pan.* pro. 2.2.2–3; 27.2.9; 34.4.2, 34.24.1

18. Peter Harrison, "Curiosity," 267.

19. For the classical formulation of the tension through the language of academic and episcopal Christianity, see David Brakke, "Canon Formation and Social Conflict in Fourth-Century Egypt: Athanasius of Alexandria's Thirty-Ninth *Festal Letter*," HTR 87.4 (1994): 395–419. For criticisms of the binary between academic and episcopal Christianity and Brakke's response, see "A New Fragment of Athanasius's Thirty-Ninth *Festal Letter*: Heresy, Apocrypha, and the Canon," HTR 103.1 (2010): 47–66.

20. Daniel Boyarin, *Border Lines: The Partition of Judaeo-Christianity* (Philadelphia: University of Pennsylvania Press, 2004), 193.

Christian writers as Tertullian."[21] And, as Averil Cameron has stressed, the opposition to Christian dialectic did not go unchallenged.[22] Indeed, resistance to dialoguing with the heretics was not the only position taken by the heresiologists either in theory or in practice.

While "precise knowledge" (ἡ ἀκρίβεια: literally, "exactness"), as Epiphanius observed, "guides man, to protect him from error about either part of the truth," heresiological literature illustrates the tensions within textual efforts to expound *what* one must know and refrain from knowing to be a Christian.[23] Embedded within the ethnographic impulse of the early Christian authors—the impulse to describe, classify, and polemicize with systematic lists and etiologies of peoples, doctrines, belief systems, and the like—is a debate about the propriety of inquiry, social discourse, and investigatory fervor.[24] Theological, scriptural, and ethnographic inquiries were not neutral endeavors of pastoral protection. Even among the most learned ecclesiastics, inquiry was emblematic of the corrosive, restlessly inquisitive, heretical mentality. Inquiry encouraged exchange and openness, which created the space for individual choice. Heresy, by its very etymology, was an affirmative act of subversion. The word itself, as Tertullian explains, derives from the Greek for "choice" (αἵρεσις), which emblemizes the arrogance of a self-determined and appropriated rationality to augment the teachings of the gospel of Christ.[25] The heretic secures his own self-condemnation in the very *choice* to expand and thus adulterate the apostolic and scriptural traditions of Christianity. Heresy tested the distinction between pious and impious knowledge, as it highlighted the counterproductive effects of inquiry about both Christian heresy and orthodoxy. As they affirmed that social discourse and scholastic investigation were tied to an overarching concern about the dangers of collection and codification, the heresiologists knowingly pursued their ethnographic agendas on treacherous rhetorical, epistemological, and theological terrain.

HERETICAL DISCOURSE: PROBLEMATIZING DIALECTIC AND INQUIRY

If the binary between orthodoxy and heresy was a dispositional distinction between order, coherence, and constancy on the one hand and restlessness, volatility, and persistence on the other, the distinction was navigated in part through

---

21. Boyarin, *Border Lines*, 193.
22. See Averil Cameron, *Dialoguing in Late Antiquity* (Washington, D.C.: Center for Hellenic Studies, 2014).
23. Epiphanius, *Pan.* 62.7.7 (GCS 31:396). Against Aetius's ἀκριβολογία (strictness) and his μαθών τῆς διαλεκτικῆς (learning of dialectic) (*Pan.* 76.3.7, 76.2.1 [GCS 37:343, 341]).
24. On dialectic and religious orthodoxy see Boyarin, *Border Lines*, 151–201.
25. Tertullian, *Praescr.* 6.2 (SC 46:95).

discussions of the concept of inquiry. The heresiologists ruminate about their texts' participation in and perpetuation of a Christian discourse of uncertainty.[26] Although the heresiologists construed themselves as justified in describing and refuting the heretics, owing to their pastoral and ecclesiastical duties, the polemical vehemence with which the task was undertaken conceals the complexity of its scholastic, pedagogical, and ethnographic entanglements. The heresiologists are cognizant of the dangerous potential of their texts. This awareness reveals their fears about ethnographic inquiry as a means of erroneously sanctioning an unrestricted investigation of the world in all its mysterious diversity. I want to take seriously the heresiologists' rhetorical posturing—what Michel-Yves Perinn has called "the heresiological ethos"—and to claim that the fears, dangers, triumphs, methods, and redactions that they describe establish a certain heresiological mentality.[27] I contend that heresiology's overarching epistemological and scholastic framework transformed the polemical ethnographic project of mapping heresy into a referendum on the relevance and legitimacy of knowledge acquisition as both an investigative process and a tangible end result. If, as Carlo Ginzburg explains, "the essence of what we call anthropological attitude—that is, the permanent confrontation between different cultures—rests on a dialogic disposition," the heresiologists are antiethnographic ethnographers.[28] They fear and disdain the very act that their project necessitates. The process of elaborating an ethnographic model of heresy thus balances the destabilizing facets of heresiological knowledge against the stabilizing duties of ecclesiastical expertise.[29] The imperative to regulate the Christian way of life necessarily included an assessment of the value of study and learning. In other words, the heresiologists were, through their own

---

26. See, for instance, Gillian Clark, "Can We Talk? Augustine and the Possibility of Dialogue," in *The End of Dialogue in Antiquity*, ed. Simon Goldhill (New York: Cambridge University Press, 2008), 117–34; Averil Cameron, "Enforcing Orthodoxy in Byzantium," *SCH* 43 (2007): 1–24; H. A. Drake, *Constantine and the Bishops: The Politics of Intolerance* (Baltimore: The Johns Hopkins University Press, 2000); and Lim, *Public Disputation*, 70–148. Lim has carefully demonstrated and emphasized, however, "the porosity of boundaries that separated the so-called questioners from orthodox Christians" (178). The dialectical disjuncture between orthodoxy and heresy, like so much of the discourse, was an ideational construct.

27. See Michel-Yves Perrin's notion of the heresiological ethos in "The Limits of the Heresiological Ethos in Late Antiquity," in *Religious Diversity in Late Antiquity*, ed. David M. Gwynn and Susanne Bangert (Leiden: Brill, 2010), 201–27. Perrin outlines a heresiological ethos or the discourse of heretical discord and deception. Although the ethos is multifaceted, its core is simple: "True Christians should not mix with heretics" (202). Perrin's essay stresses that during times of doctrinal controversy tensions pulled the lives of the faithful in conflicting directions.

28. Carlo Ginzburg, "The Inquisitor as Anthropologist," in his *Clues, Myths, and the Historical Method*, trans. John Tedeschi and Anne C. Tedeschi (Baltimore: The Johns Hopkins Press, 1989), 156–64, at 159.

29. Claudia Rapp, *Holy Bishops in Late Antiquity: The Nature of Christian Leadership in an Age of Transition* (Berkeley and Los Angeles: University of California Press, 2005), 3–99.

self-reflective investigations, expounding upon the limits of yet another facet of Christianity's epistemology.

Tertullian, the prolific North African Christian author, pushed to demolish any genealogical consonance between the heretics and their Christian ethnographers.[30] To realize his objective, he explicitly forbade Christians to undertake the methods and conclusions of the dialogic philosophers, which the heretics had actively embraced.[31] There was simply no room for any perceived similarity between Christians and the truth of Christ and the unrestrained curiosity of the dialecticians.[32] The heresiologists consciously disassociated themselves from their heretical objects through a carefully tuned rhetoric of supplication and labor. By theorizing the legitimacy of inquiry and recounting, in turn, their own laborious scholasticism, they navigated the terrain of intellectual elitism by humbling themselves and their task. They tempered this desire for control over the known world by emphasizing their toil on behalf of their congregants. Richard Lim's remarks about Augustine's management of his authority, humility, and scholastic language pertain equally to the heresiologists' pursuits:[33]

> As a priest and later bishop, Augustine regarded his own pastoral care of his fellow Christians, who, in his view, could not be trusted to hold their own in discussions with heretics, as a primary concern. For this reason, among others, he was to write in ways that demonstrate more authority with a corresponding diminution in the amount of intellectual openness he was willing to grant himself in discussing matters of faith and belief.

As types of ethnographic theorists, the heresiologists asked *how* one knows, *when* one knows, when one knows *too much,* and when one must *cease* to know. Theorizing knowledge, both as an end in itself and as an investigative process, shaped the formation of a Christian intellectual tradition in which the limits of and utility for information were meticulously constructed. But there was a fine line between knowledge born of necessity and information born of curiosity. Heresiology was an instantiation of this protracted negotiation. The Christian struggle against the heretics was not only a referendum over proper belief and praxis. It also constituted a

---

30. On Tertullian generally, see Timothy David Barnes, *Tertullian: A Historical and Literary Study,* rev. ed. (Oxford: Clarendon Press, 1985); Geoffrey D. Dunn, *Tertullian* (New York: Routledge, 2004); and David E. Wilhite, *Tertullian the African: An Anthropological Reading of Tertullian's Context and Identities* (New York: de Gruyter, 2007).

31. On Tertullian's attitude toward philosophy, see Peter Iver Kaufman, "Tertullian on Heresy, History, and the Reappropriation of Revelation," *CH* 60.2 (1991): 167–79.

32. For a more complex account, see J. Rebecca Lyman, "2002 NAPS Presidential Address: Hellenism and Heresy," *JECS* 11.2 (2003): 209–22.

33. Richard Lim, "Christians, Dialogues and Patterns of Sociability in Late Antiquity," in Goldhill, *The End of Dialogue,* 149–81, at 161. See Rapp, *Holy Bishops in Late Antiquity,* 23–55, on pragmatic ecclesiastical authority.

much larger debate about the propriety of Christian efforts to understand and describe the world around them. How curious, in other words, were Christians permitted to be? And how did they regulate that urge to know and understand? How did heresiological knowledge define the ethnographic impulse of early Christian writers? The answers to these questions, I believe, reveal the beginnings of heresiology's unraveling.

In his *Rule against the Heretics* (*De praescriptione haereticorum*), Tertullian explicated the theological functions and repercussions of heresy within a broader discussion of the impulse toward inquiry.[34] Unlike the heresiological works of Irenaeus, Epiphanius, Theodoret, Augustine, and Hippolytus, Tertullian's text largely abstains from an analysis of particular heretical opinions and customs. Even Tertullian's claim late in the text to offer "a description of the heretics' way of life" (*conversationis haereticae descriptionem*) serves largely to meld various heresies into a single, generic mass of errors and temporal habits with which he contrasts the stability of the apostolic churches.[35] And although other works by Tertullian—most notably *Adversus Marcionem, Adversus Hermogenem, Adversus Praxean,* and *Adversus Valentinianos*—offer detailed descriptions of particular heretical figures, *De praescriptione* presents an abstract characterization of the essence of heresy.[36] Within this hybridized heretical disposition, Tertullian postulated an intellectual division between Christians and heretics by reifying their dispositions and tendencies through his analysis of the legitimacy of inquiry.

The treatise begins by dismissing those who express astonishment at the very existence of the heretics, since, Tertullian explains, the heresies were divinely foretold in scripture (Matt. 7.15; 24.4–24; 1 Cor. 11.19) as a phenomenological test: "For

---

34. *Praescriptio,* in its literal sense, refers to a precept, law, or rule; it does not, in fact, mean prescription. For the Latin of Tertullian's text, I have used SC 46. I have followed (with my own alterations) S. L. Greenslade's translation of *The Prescriptions against the Heretics* in *Early Latin Theology: Selections from Tertullian, Cyprian, Ambrose, and Jerome* (Louisville: Westminster John Knox Press, 1956), 25–64. The text is comprised of forty-four chapters, though one (spurious) manuscript contains an additional eight chapters (which Migne prints in his edition of the text) with a list of heresies (these addenda are ascribed to a figure known as pseudo-Tertullian).

35. Tertullian, *Praescr.* 41.1 (SC 46:146). The heretics are hasty with their ordinances, liberal in their acquisition of converts, and, most significant, corrupters of established truth. For a detailed analysis of the rhetorical structure of the text, see Charles Munier, "Analyse du traité de Tertullien De Praescriptione Haereticorum," *RevScRel* 59 (1985): 12–33.

36. In his five books *Against Marcion*, Tertullian disputes his dualism, rejection of the Hebrew Bible, and editing of the Gospels and the Letters of Paul. In *Adversus Hermogenem,* Tertullian contests Hermogenes' opinion that matter, coeternal with God, becomes the source of evil in the world (matter itself was not by nature evil). *Adversus Praxean* is mostly a theological dispute about the nature of the Trinity and the degree to which the Father and Son can be said to share the Incarnational experiences of the latter. *Adversus Valentinianos* is a refutation of the Valentinians and their claims to possess secret knowledge of God and the cosmos.

their purpose is that by holding a trial, faith would still possess approval."[37] The prevalence of heresy serves to uncover the specter of devotion, exposing those Christians—"a bishop or deacon, a widow, a virgin or a teacher, or even a martyr"—who lapse into heresy and forfeit their faithfulness.[38] For it is not faith, Tertullian insists, that is tested by persons, but persons by faith. Tertullian, like his heresiological predecessors and successors, is offering a scriptural and theological rationalization for the presence of heretics in the world. However much they are opposed to the teachings of God, the heretics ultimately serve the divine will. By contrast, the Christian tradition, represented by its theological principles, texts, rituals, practices, and apostolic succession, stands cordoned off from additions of any kind. The parallel that Tertullian draws between the heretics and the philosophers serves to demarcate the genealogy of Christian tradition and praxis and to posit a dispositional distinction between those Christians who are restless and those who are satisfied.[39] Aristotle's teachings on the value of relentless inquiry, the process by which knowledge is acquired, was harshly critiqued by Tertullian. In fact, he calls dialectical inquiry "fruitless questionings" (*quaestiones infructuosae*):[40] "Wretched Aristotle! He who establishes dialectic for these men, the art which destroys as much as it builds, crafty in its opinions, forced in its conjectures, stubborn in its arguments, maker of struggles, annoying even to itself, retracing everything, it will have treated nothing in its entirety."[41] In asking, famously, "What has Jerusalem to do with Athens, the church with the Academy, the Christian with the heretic?" Tertullian adamantly insisted upon the theological futility of protracted investigation of scripture, Christ, theodicy, divinity, and cosmology.[42] Insofar as the geographical locus of Christianity (Jerusalem, in Tertullian's question) attested further dichotomies of institution and loyalty, Tertullian enumerated a clash of worldviews through this tripartite schematization. He sought to recast the intellectual underpinnings of the Greco-Roman world

---

37. Tertullian, *Praescr.* 1.1 (SC 46:88).
38. Tertullian *Praescr.* 3.5 (SC 46:90).
39. The Gnostics, Epiphanius's twenty-sixth heresy (*Pan.* 26.1.1–19.6), exemplify the elasticity and precariousness of theological speculation and restless inquiry.
40. Tertullian, *Praescr.* 7.7 (SC 46:98). On Aristotle and dialectic in late antiquity, see Dirk Krausmüller, "Aristotelianism and the Disintegration of the Late Antique Theological Discourse," in *Interpreting the Bible and Aristotle in Late Antiquity: The Alexandrian Commentary Tradition between Rome and Baghdad*, ed. Josef Lössl and John W. Watt (Burlington: Ashgate, 2011), 137–50; and Leo J. Elders, "The Greek Christian Authors and Aristotle," in *Aristotle in Late Antiquity*, ed. Lawrence P. Schrenk (Washington, D.C.: Catholic University of America Press, 1996), 111–42.
41. Tertullian, *Praescr.* 7.6 (SC 46:97; altered from Greenslade). On Tertullian's pagan education, see Barnes, *Tertullian*, 187–210.
42. Tertullian, *Praescr.* 7.9 (SC 46:98). See, also, Justo L. González, "Athens and Jerusalem Revisited: Reason and Authority in Tertullian," *CH* 43 (1991): 17–25; and Wendy E. Helleman, "Tertullian on Athens and Jerusalem," in *Hellenization Revisited: Shaping a Christian Response within the Greco-Roman World*, ed. Wendy E. Helleman (Lanham Md.: University Press of America, 1994), 361–82.

through the language and strictures of Christian knowledge. Tertullian's recalibration of these three geographical, religious, and institutional symbols inaugurated the era of transformative Christianity: the terms of Academic culture were interpreted through the dogmatic ideology of Christianity. That culture, however, is itself engaged in the process of testing its own possibilities and limits as it simultaneously forbids protracted inquiry born of curiosity; for "'restless curiosity' and 'philosophy,' in fatal combination, were the parents of heresy."[43]

Tertullian enumerated a diktat incumbent upon all those who called themselves Christian: if the human experience within the world was to be understood, it must be guided by the principle that "Christ laid down one definite system of truth,"[44] which it then became necessary for all the nations to "believe without qualification."[45] Insofar as men and women possess an obligation to "seek in order that they may be able to believe," the corollary to that process of inquiry was an acknowledgment of epistemological finitude: for "there cannot be indefinite seeking of that which has been taught as the one and definitive thing."[46] The association Tertullian posits between philosophers and heretics presages the hazards of heresiological ethnography that were visibly negotiated in later examples of the genre. Unlike Augustine, whose dislike of the dialogic form reflected his conviction that it was ill suited for the ecclesiastical necessities of mass communication, Tertullian did not attack dialectic on account of its ecclesiastical futility.[47] Instead, he posited that dialogue was a symptom of a more troubling heretical disease: self-indulgent, hubristic inquiry. A principle that embraced investigation as scripturally mandated would transplant the disposition of the heretics—since the heretics are the emblems of unadulterated, limitless exploration—into Tertullian's vision of Christian tradition:[48]

> For if they are still seeking, they have still found nothing certain, and for that reason whatever they appear to hold in the interim, they expose their own doubts, as long as they are seeking. Therefore, you, who are seeking in the same manner, looking to

---

43. Peter Harrison, "Curiosity," 275. Epiphanius, *Pan.* 69.71.2, would similarly caution that dialectic apart from the gift of the Holy Spirit is the fundamental mark of heresy and the heretical disposition. See also *Pan.* 76.10.3, 76.10.3, 76.15.1, 76.36.3, 76.45.2, 76.54.23; 77.24.8.

44. Tertullian, *Praescr.* 9.3 (SC 46:102).

45. Tertullian, *Praescr.* 9.3 (SC 46:102).

46. Tertullian, *Praescr.* 9.3, 9.4 (SC 46:102; altered from Greenslade).

47. On late antique Christian appraisals and usage of dialogue, see Catherine Conybeare, *The Irrational Augustine* (New York: Oxford University Press, 2006), 1–60; Clark, "Can We Talk?," 117–34; Richard Miles, "'Let's (Not) Talk about It': Augustine and the Control of Epistolary," in Goldhill, *The End of Dialogue*, 135–48; Lim, "Christians, Dialogues and Patterns of Sociability in Late Antiquity," 117–34, 135–50, 151–72; and now Cameron, *Dialoguing in Late Antiquity*.

48. Tertullian, *Praescr.* 14.7–8 (SC 46:107–8; altered from Greenslade).

those who themselves also are seeking, the doubter to the doubters, the hesitator to the hesitators, blind, you must be led, by the blind into the ditch.

If it occurred under the conditions of *established* belief, to wander astray philosophically, exegetically, cosmologically, or ritualistically (the various manifestations of the call to seek) was to corrupt the tradition of Christianity and Christian truth.

The endeavor to expand one's epistemological horizon fallaciously operated as if knowledge was an end in itself. For Tertullian's Christianity, the search for knowledge was located in Christ, who made wisdom "freely accessible to all believers, irrespective of rank or birth."[49] As Richard Lim describes it, "Tertullian championed a paradoxical and radically inward-looking faith,"[50] which could be known through the precedents of scripture (and not via the dialectical pursuits of the Greek philosophers):[51]

> Our instruction is from the portico of Solomon, who himself had taught that the Lord must be sought in simplicity of heart. There is no use for those who had advanced a Stoic or a Platonic or a dialectic Christianity. After Jesus Christ there is no need for our curiosity, and after the Gospel no need of inquiry (*Nobis curiositate opus non est post Christum Iesum nec inquisitione post euangelium*). When we believe, we desire nothing beyond believing. For this we believe from the beginning, that there is nothing we ought to believe beyond [this].

His claim that Christ's Gospel halted the need for further inquiry about the nature of God among other things contested more than just the dialectical propensity of the Greek philosophers. Scripture itself could and did serve as the source for the compulsion among Christians, heterodox and orthodox alike, to discuss, exchange, study, and debate textual interpretation and theological doctrine. The sheer bounty of teachings available from the heretics, philosophers, and nations, a concerned Tertullian warns, engenders the possibility and likelihood of endless and worthless searching. For Tertullian, inasmuch as the heretics Marcion, Valentinus, Ebion, Simon, and Apelles universally appealed to Matthew 7.7, they inculcated an epistemological worldview in which spiritual fulfillment and stability were continually challenged and disrupted: "Therefore I shall be nowhere as I encounter 'seek and you shall find' everywhere" (*ero itaque nusquam dum ubique convenio 'quaerite et invenietis'*).[52] The heretics' appeal to the scriptural mantra "search, and you shall find" (*quaerite et inuenietis*, Matt. 7.7 and Luke 11.9) drove Tertullian to develop an exegetical strategy to limit the scope of Jesus's command. He insisted upon a

---

49. Lim, *Public Disputation*, 10.
50. Ibid.
51. Tertullian, *Praescr.* 7.10–13 (SC 46:98–99; altered from Greenslade).
52. Tertullian, *Praescr.* 10.9 (SC 46:104; altered from Greenslade).

literal interpretation of the verses as a way to moderate Christian inquiry.[53] A proper hermeneutic, with specific rules and procedures, served to limit both heretical interpretations and methods.[54]

De praescriptione accorded the misinterpretation of the scriptural injunction "to search persistently" to a combination of incorrect a-priori assumptions and to the neglect of the context of Jesus's injunction. In the first place, Tertullian explained, the dictum was promulgated *before* Jesus had revealed himself to be the Christ (and before Peter had proclaimed him to be the Son of God). "When thus far he had not been recognized, he still had to be sought," it was altogether appropriate to encourage curiosity and investigation, since the revelation of Christ was still unfolding.[55] In addition, the command to seek "applies only to the Jews" (*in Iudaeos competere*), for the Jews alone possessed the bounty of raw material (the Law and prophets) through which one could and should have found Christ.[56] Because the Jews dwelt in God's house and were given the promise by the God of Abraham, Isaac, and Jacob, they were implored by Jesus to search its contents anew.[57] "The nations, however, were never in God's house. They were ... always outside."[58] Because the apostles had not yet received the command "to go to the nations, who will be taught and baptized," the gentiles remained in a state of ignorance about the messianic claims of Jesus of Nazareth.[59] There was no knowledge base from which they could seek and find.[60]

Tertullian further contested Jesus's dangerously open-ended sanction of inquiry by proposing still more exegetical regulations to restrict its applicability. He claimed that exegesis was governed by the rules of reason, and such governance meant that exegesis had to attend to the specifics of matter, time, and limit: "As to

---

53. See the latter half of Geoffrey D. Dunn's "Tertullian's Scriptural Exegesis in *De praescriptione haereticorum,*" *JECS* 14.2 (2006): 141–55.

54. Geoffrey D. Dunn argues that the substantive issue at stake here is "the question of who had the right to interpret the Scriptures" (ibid. 145). Tertullian's argument, throughout the treatise, that scripture belongs only to true Christians, flowed into his articulation of the all-encompassing *regula fidei*.

55. Tertullian, *Praescr.* 8.4 (SC 46:99; altered from Greenslade).

56. Tertullian, *Praescr.* 8.7 (SC 46:100). See Dunn, "Tertullian's Scriptural Exegesis," 149. See also, Boyarin, *Border Lines*, 151–201.

57. Tertullian, *Praescr.* 8.4 (SC 46:99).

58. Tertullian, *Praescr.* 8.9 (SC 46:99; altered from Greenslade).

59. Tertullian, *Praescr.* 8.14 (SC 46:101; altered from Greenslade).

60. Tertullian's insistence, however, that "Search, and you shall find," belonged to a particularly Jewish context, which excluded the nations, seemingly obviated the universality of the Christian Gospel. Anticipating the objection, Tertullian conceded but qualified the implication of his argument: "Indeed, all the words of the Lord were ordained for everyone. They came to us through the ears of the Jews; and most were directed at (these) peoples; thus they establish not a property of admonition for us but an example" (*Praescr.* 8.16; [SC 46:101]).

matter, you are to consider what is to be sought; as to time, when; and as to limit, how far."⁶¹ Geoffrey Dunn has persuasively argued that Tertullian, though often viewed by scholars as the literalist exegete par excellence, varied his exegetical techniques to contrast with his opponents'. Thus, he "used whatever method his opposition did not use."⁶² Here, against the heretics, he is keen to perpetuate an adaptable exegetical system that cordons off heretical interpretation and, by extension, denies heretics the right to use—let alone consult—scripture. Tertullian thus binds the validity of investigation to the experience of spiritual fulfillment—born of reasonable methods of exegesis—so that "what you must seek is what Christ taught, [seeking] for such a time, assuredly, as you do not apprehend it, until, indeed, you do find it."⁶³ The principle was rather clear: belief in or knowledge of Christ nullified the necessity of further theological exploration. Tertullian's position proclaimed the pedagogical fulfillment of Christ: "Acceptance of the faith debars any prolongation of seeking and finding."⁶⁴

Tertullian's offensive against the inclination to seek additional instruction and to ask additional questions culminated in the elaboration of a rule of faith (*regula fidei*), the enumeration of just what it was that Christians qua Christians defended (*quid defendamus*).⁶⁵ The *regula* functioned as the repository for the inarguable tenets of Christianity. It was also the metric through which Tertullian's demarcation of valid avenues of theological and heresiological inquiry could be evaluated.⁶⁶ The rule expressed the singularity of God, who created the world through his Word (who is also called his Son), which the patriarchs and prophets attested. The Word "was brought down by the Spirit and Power of God the Father into the Virgin Mary . . . and lived as Jesus Christ; who thereafter proclaimed a new law and a new promise of the kingdom of heaven, worked miracles, was crucified, on the third day rose again, was caught up into heaven."⁶⁷ In Christ's place, the Holy Spirit guides believers who await final judgment. The contours of this rule of faith operated to circumscribe the invalidity of all questions—"This rule . . . raises no

61. Tertullian, *Praescr.* 10.1 (SC 46:103).
62. Dunn, "Tertullian's Scriptural Exegesis," 152. See also Clare K. Rothschild, "Christ the Foolish Judge in Tertullian's *On the Prescription of Heretics*," in *Tertullian and Paul*, ed. Todd D. Still and David Wilhite (New York: T & T Clark, 2013), 34–44.
63. Tertullian, *Praescr.* 10.2 (SC 46:103; altered from Greenslade).
64. Tertullian, *Praescr.* 10.4 (SC 46:103). On the problem of never-ending investigation and the Rule of Truth, see Irenaeus, *Adv. haer.* 2.27.1–2.
65. Tertullian, *Praescr.* 13.1 (SC 46:106).
66. See L. William Countryman, "Tertullian and the *Regula Fidei*," *SecCent* 2 (1982): 208–27; Eric F. Osborn, "Reason and the Rule of Faith in the Second Century AD," in *The Making of Orthodoxy: Essays in Honour of Henry Chadwick*, ed. Rowan Williams (New York: Cambridge University Press, 1989), 40–61; Everett Ferguson, "Tertullian, Scripture, Rule of Faith, and Paul," in Still and Wilhite, *Tertullian and Paul*, 22–33; and Dunn, "Tertullian's Scriptural Exegesis," 147–51.
67. Tertullian, *Praescr.* 13.3 (SC 46:106).

questions among us (*haec regula . . . nullas habet apud nos quaestiones*) except those which the heresies introduce and which make heretics."[68] The propriety of epistemological investigations hung on the supposition that "when the *forma* of the rule remains in its proper order, you may seek as much as you like."[69] Curiosity could be indulged, and areas of obscurity, darkness, and confusion could be illuminated, but only if they existed apart from or in total harmony with the uncontestable principles of Christian truth.[70] In demanding that theological inquiry be pursued in accord with the rule of faith (in terms of both content and obtainment), Tertullian's emphasis on epistemological humility and limits served to recalibrate the value of inquiry. The rule foreclosed unnecessary speculation, just as it demanded efforts to defend its inviolability. As Irenaeus insisted: "Keep order in your knowledge, [and] do not go beyond God himself; for no one can go beyond him. . . . It is, therefore, better and more useful that [true Christians] be unlettered and know very little and come near to God through love than that, thinking they know much and have much experience, they be found among the blasphemers of their Sovereign, by having fabricated another God the Father."[71]

After expressing his distaste for dialectic, Tertullian marshaled scripture yet again to broaden the scope of his earlier argument against debate by positing another reason for inquiry and dialogue to be forsworn. He adduced the precedent of Titus 3.10, which forbade extended contestation even for corrective purposes:[72]

> [Titus] forbids us to enter into investigations, to attach our ears to novel remarks, or to associate with a heretic "after one reproof," not after discussion. He forbade discussion, designating reproof as the reason to meet with a heretic, and only *one* correction because the heretic is not a Christian. He is to have no right to a second censure, like a Christian, before two or three witnesses, since he is to be censured for the very reason that forbids discussion with him.

Because the heretics reject books of the Bible, add to them, or adduce false exegesis (*adulter sensus*), the very groundwork for holding conversation evaporates into nothing. Tertullian insists that the heretics "are not to be admitted to any discussion of scripture at all" because they are not Christian.[73] Any engagement

---

68. Tertullian, *Praescr.* 13.6 (SC 46:106–7; altered from Greenslade).
69. Tertullian, *Praescr.* 14.1 (SC 46:107; altered from Greenslade).
70. Tertullian, *Praescr.* 14.1.
71. Irenaeus, *Adv. haer.* 2.25.4–26.1 (SC 294:254–56).
72. Tertullian, *Praescr.* 16.1–3 (SC 46:109–10; altered from Greenslade).

The text of Paul's Epistle to Titus refers to a first and a second correction: "After a first and second admonition, have nothing more to do with anyone who causes divisions, since you know that such a person is perverted and sinful, being self-condemned" (3.10). Tertullian's description of Titus omits reference to the second approbation.

73. Tertullian, *Praescr.* 15.3 (SC 46:109). On engaging with the heretics about scripture, see Kaufman, "Tertullian on Heresy."

with the heretics over scripture served to legitimate them *as Christians* by acknowledging that they possessed a claim "to call the Scriptures as an expert witness for their side."[74] Tertullian further reasons that participating in debates serves only to embolden the heretics, to legitimize their irrationality, and to induce those who waver in the faith to draw erroneous conclusions. An observer, watching such a dispute, "sees that you have accomplished nothing, the rival party being allowed equal rights of denial and affirmation and an equal status. As a result he will go away from the argument even more uncertain than before, not knowing which to count as heresy."[75] In giving the heretics equal standing, in Tertullian's view, Christians foundered even before they made their case. Insofar as dialogue posited a degree of symmetry between participants, it functioned as a space of legitimation. As Lim explains: "The very capacity to participate as an informed interlocutor in a literary or philosophical symposium was the preserve of a cultured man who has mastered the elaborate codes necessary for such a performance. . . . Conversely, the ideal dialogue could not operate if the interlocutors did not share this common outlook."[76] By participating in disputations and engagements with the heretics, Christians unknowingly sanctioned the heretics' connection to a tenuous (third-century) Christian intellectual and cultural space and in the very process bound themselves to the philosophical tradition of dialectic.[77]

Although the rejection of inquiry suited the project of an orthodox community of Christians determined to deny its philosophical pedigree, the task of refuting the heretics exposed the paradox of *paideia*.[78] If, as Tertullian famously quipped, the philosophers were "the patriarchs of the heretics" (*patriarchis haereticorum*), the rhetorical and philosophical training that empowered Christian authors to critique Greco-Roman culture and its heretical offspring nonetheless established an intellectual bond between them. The threat of a perceived cultural symmetry between these three classes of professional inquirers (philosophers, heretics, and heresiologists) threatened to collapse the carefully calibrated discourses of Christian pedagogy, expertise, and ministry.[79] Because the task of contesting the heretics fell to them—as members of an ecclesiastical or learned class—it threatened to endow the

---

74. Dunn, "Tertullian's Scriptural Exegesis," 145.

75. Tertullian, *Praescr.* 18.2 (SC 46:111).

76. Lim, "Christians, Dialogues and Patterns of Sociability," 163.

77. Lim, *Public Disputation*, demonstrates the dialectical reputations of Manichaeism (88–92) and the Anomoeans (119–30).

78. On Christian efforts both to own and to disown their claims to *paideia*, see Peter Brown, *Power and Persuasion in Late Antiquity: Towards a Christian Empire* (Madison: University of Wisconsin Press, 1992), 35–70; Lim, "Christians, Dialogues and Patterns of Sociability," 151–72; and Denise Kimber Buell, *Making Christians: Clement of Alexandria and the Rhetoric of Legitimacy* (Princeton: Princeton University Press, 1999), 50–78, 119–30.

79. See Tertullian, *An.* 3.1.

heresiologists with the specter of an elite or "set-apart status," which already carried the taint of heresy.[80] Because factionalization and erroneous exegesis belonged to a genealogy of a professionalized knowledge—"Where was Marcion then, the shipowner of Pontus, the student of Stoicism? Where was Valentinus then, the disciple of Plato?"—the creation of a protective class of inquirers, the heresiologists, necessitated rhetorical and pastoral bulwarks against the onslaught of inquiry.[81] However much heresy was rationalized as an inevitable facet of the history of Christianity, its continued presence posed a twofold dilemma for its opponents. On the one hand, the heretics, as Tertullian insisted in line after line of his treatise, *embodied* the desire to inquire assiduously. They were inquiry personified. And yet, on the other, their very existence demanded inquiry, research, and refutation. The existence of the heretics thwarted Tertullian's ability to articulate the limits of Christian inquiry. Widespread ignorance, despite Tertullian's best hopes, was neither a plausible nor a compelling strategic vision. Indeed, the refutation of the heretics necessarily subverted this denunciation against ceaseless inquiry. Heresiology inaugurated an ethnographic feedback loop of persistent and protracted discovery and discourse. As Augustine surmised two centuries later: "It is a big help for the heart of the believer to know what one should not believe, even if one cannot refute it with skillful argumentation."[82] How, then, did Christians manage these conflicting compulsions? How did they conceptualize and articulate their textual investigation, research, and discoveries?

THE RHETORICS OF HERESIOLOGY: MASTERY AND TRIUMPH

Near the start of his remarks on Mani and the Manichaeans, Epiphanius pauses briefly to justify his foray into the life of this arch-heresiarch. Emphasizing his willingness to retread familiar territory in the name of truth, Epiphanius tasks himself with introducing his subject "from the very beginning."[83] He declares that he has "been at pains to convey [the minutest facts of Mani's family, most especially the means by which his master accrued his wealth] in full detail for your information, so that those who care to read this will not go uninformed even of the remote causes of every affair."[84] The claim that the heresiologist can command complete knowledge of any one heretic and, indeed, survey the totality of the heretical

---

80. Lim, "Christians, Dialogues and Patterns of Sociability," 168.
81. Tertullian, *Praescr.* 30.1 (SC 46:126).
82. Augustine, *Haer. epil.* 3.51–53 (CCSL 46:344).
83. Epiphanius, *Pan.* 66.2.1 (GCS 37:17).
84. Epiphanius, *Pan.* 66.2.1 (GCS 37:17).

world—"to omit nothing about the divisions, splits, differences and schisms which have arisen in the world"—undergirds the rhetorical integrity of his *Panarion*.[85] The most salient articulation of the syllogistic structure of heresiological discourse comes in fact from the fourth-century monastic writer John Cassian rather than from the heresiologists themselves. Having expended considerable effort systematically describing the causes and effects of human vice, Cassian defends his protracted discussion with an appeal to comprehension. The resulting formulation is not only a succinct encapsulation of the diagnostic principles of theological anthropology; it is an apt summary of the substructures of heresiological inquiry. John writes: "Let this not strike anyone as superfluous or irksome. For unless the different kinds of wounds have been explained and the origins and causes of the diseases have been investigated, the appropriate medical remedy will not be able to be administered to the sick and the means of maintaining perfect health will not be able to be passed on to the well."[86] In the case of both heresiology and asceticism, the effectiveness of refutation and the struggle for self-mastery necessitate an exhaustive investigation of the causes, conditions, and sources of the adversarial passions and parties. Insofar as diagnosis comes before prescription and proscription, the successful administration of the heresiological curative is predicated on an examination of the conditions of the disease itself. The genre's utility turns on its conferral of an effective theological cure. And the success of this textual medicine is explicitly bound to the scope of its inquiry and the depths of its knowledge.

The language of each of Epiphanius's eighty sectarian sections not only emphasizes the annihilation of the poisonous heresies but also reiterates an expansive and unequivocal refutation. To accomplish his task, to "make these shocking disclosures for the readers' correction," Epiphanius stresses the exhaustiveness of his investigation. And the fruits of his investigation serve not only to instruct his readers but to emphasize the arduousness of his intellectual journey.[87] Having, for instance, defeated Ptolemy and his followers, he uses the triumphant occasion to announce his text's insatiable ambition to discover all the heresies of the world: "Since I have achieved your disgrace through the things I have said, I am going over the imposture of the others—calling on God as the aid of my meager ability, so that, in every people (παρ' ἑκάστῳ ἔθνει), I may discover the doctrine they have wickedly invented and make a spectacle of it."[88] Epiphanius uncovers the full spectrum of the peoples of the heretical world, presenting his object of study, tellingly,

---

85. Epiphanius, *Pan.* 70.15.6 (GCS 37:249). For parallel comments see also *Pan.* 8.7.4; 25.14.4–5; 25.17.1–3; 32.3.1; 48.15.1; 52.1.6; 60.2.1; 66.2.1–2; 69.42.1; 77.19.6; *De fide* 12.5.

86. John Cassian, *Institutes* 7.13 (CSEL 17:137); trans. Boniface Ramsey, *John Cassian: The Institutes* (Mahwah N.J.: Paulist Press, 2000), 175.

87. Epiphanius, *Pan.* 48.15.3 (GCS 31:240). Having incorporated the diverse though related musings of the heretics, the text equalizes their erroneous suppositions with disdain and mockery.

88. Epiphanius, *Pan.* 33.8.11 (GCS, n. F., 10:459).

in the language of ἔθνη (peoples/nations). This task is, I believe, functionally analogous to the geographical and ethnographic treatises of Pliny, Strabo, Diodorus Siculus, Herodotus, Tacitus, and Pomponius Mela, all of which searched the diversity of the known world and translated its significance through the language of cultural hierarchization, ideological dominance, and foreign exoticism.[89] Epiphanius's remarks about the Tascodrugians, also known as the Montanists or Phrygians, display the authorial compulsion that organizes his task: "I promised to withhold nothing about any sect I know, but to disclose what I have learned by word of mouth, and from treatises, documents, and persons who truly confirmed my notion. . . . I give all the facts, as I said, with accuracy, about each sect."[90] Richard Flower has, in fact, argued that the content and form of heresiological literature function jointly as an overwhelming display of knowledge, bolstering claims of ecclesiastical and scholastic authority.[91] Epiphanius, however, acquires knowledge of the heretical world in order to destroy it. He has no desire to appropriate knowledge from the heretics or to decry the decline of the catholic church; rather he collects knowledge, paradoxically, in order to erase it.

Epiphanius, in fact, does not simply question or berate the heretics about their opinions; instead, he actually uses his text to engage them in debate.[92] He constructs, at various junctures in the *Panarion*, dialogues between accuser and accused. The bishop articulates an opinion of a heretical group—often citing the words of its leader from a sermon, treatise, or letter—and then responds with his own refutation (if not mockery). In his description of Aetius and the Anomoean heresy, for example, Epiphanius announces: "Now then, not to waste my time investigating him, let me refute him from the things he said himself to certain

---

89. See, for instance, François Hartog's *The Mirror of Herodotus: The Representation of the Other in the Writing of History,* trans. Janet Lloyd (Berkeley and Los Angeles: University of California Press, 1988), 209–59, which calls attention to the rhetoric of otherness—inversion, comparison, analogy, translation, naming, classifying, describing, etc.—as the technical strategy of ethnographic analysis. On ethnographic discovery through talking and reading, see James Redfield, "Herodotus the Tourist," *CP* 80.2 (1985): 97–118; Paul Demont, "Figures of Inquiry in Herodotus's *Inquiries*," *Mnemosyne* 62 (2009): 179–205; C. R. Whittaker, "Ethnic Discourses on the Frontiers of Roman Africa," in *Ethnic Constructs in Antiquity: The Role of Power and Tradition*, ed. Ton Derks and Nico Roymans (Amsterdam: Amsterdam University Press, 2009), 189–206; and John E. Coleman and Clark A. Walz, eds., *Greeks and Barbarians: Essays on the Interactions between Greeks and Non-Greeks in Antiquity and the Consequences for Eurocentrism* (Bethesda Md.: CDL Press, 1997).

90. Epiphanius, *Pan.* 48.15.1–3 (GCS 31:240).

91. Richard Flower, "Genealogies of Unbelief: Epiphanius of Salamis and Heresiological Authority" in *Unclassical Traditions*, vol. 2, *Perspectives from East and West in Late Antiquity*, ed. Christopher Kelly, Richard Flower, and Michael Stuart Williams (Cambridge: Cambridge University Press, 2011), 70–87. On Epiphanius and authority, see also Boyarin, *Border Lines*, 206–14; and now Andrew S. Jacobs, "Epiphanius of Salamis and the Antiquarian's Bible," *JECS* 21.3 (2013): 437–64.

92. See his remarks at *Pan.* 76.54.30.

persons in a dialectical communication."⁹³ This reconstructed dialogue is no imposture; it is a researched, meticulous dispute over the terms of Christian theological truth. As Epiphanius explains: "I shall insert your propositions, one after another, and beside each statement and proposition put the answers to and refutations of your syllogistic arguments, so that God's servants and true champions, reading this and learning the whole of your absurdity, can laugh at it."⁹⁴ What follow are Epiphanius's thirty-six lengthy responses to Aetius's thirty-six propositions, which, of course, culminate in the triumph of orthodoxy. And although the bishop "stamped on the serpent . . . with the foot of orthodoxy," the two sides were never, in fact, engaged in the same method or legitimacy of argumentation.⁹⁵ Orthodoxy had pious reason and scripture at its disposal, whereas heresy relied upon trickery and nonsense. For "in the end, talking and hearing nonsense is a deception to the many, but a joke to the wise."⁹⁶ It seems that the very idea of genuinely dialoguing with heretics was a fiction.

Hippolytus and Irenaeus likewise tout their respective mastery over the heretical realm, accentuating not only the detail and precision of their refutations but also the effort with which they have applied themselves to amass their knowledge. Irenaeus uses the language of scripture to reinforce his text's investigatory polemic and its pedagogical aspirations. A lone citation from the Gospel of Matthew (10.26) serves as a heresiological maxim: "For nothing is covered that will not be revealed, and nothing hidden that will not be known."⁹⁷ Complete exposure—its acquisition and transmission—becomes the overarching theme of Irenaeus's tractate, as its full title conveys ("Exposé and Overthrow of What Is Falsely Called Knowledge," Ἐλέγχου καὶ ἀνατροπῆς τῆς ψευδωνύμου γνώσεως).⁹⁸ Irenaeus, in fact, pinpoints inexact comprehension of the heretics' doctrines—the remedy for which he is eager to supply—as the essential misstep of earlier efforts to counteract the theological divergences of the Valentinians:⁹⁹

> For it is not possible for anyone, who does not know the disease of those who are not well, to cure those who are sick. This was the reason that my predecessors—much superior men to myself, too—had been unable, however, to refute sufficiently (*satis potuerunt contradicere*) the Valentinians, because they were ignorant of these men's

---

93. Epiphanius, *Pan.* 76.10.3 (GCS 37:351).
94. Epiphanius, *Pan.* 76.17.1 (GCS 37:362).
95. Epiphanius, *Pan.* 76.54.38 (GCS 37:414). In his *Public Disputation*, 149–81, Lim emphasizes the relationship between curiosity and disputation in the late fourth and early fifth centuries. (His analysis pertains mostly to the work of the Cappadocian fathers and John Chrysostom.)
96. Epiphanius, *Pan.* 76.54.18 (GCS 37:411).
97. Irenaeus, *Adv. haer.* 1 pr. 2.53–55 (SC 264:24), citing Matt. 10.26.
98. Eusebius of Caesarea, *Hist. eccl.*, 5.7.1, trans. Kirsopp Lake, LCL 153 (Cambridge, Mass.: Harvard University Press, 1926), 450.
99. Irenaeus, *Adv. haer.* 4 pr. 2.11–25 (SC 100.2:382–84; altered from ANF).

rules; which we have with all diligence transmitted to you in the first book, in which we have also shown that their doctrine is a recapitulation of all the heretics. For which reason also, in the second, we have had, as in a mirror, a sight of their complete destruction. For they who oppose these men [the Valentinians] by the right method, do thereby oppose all who are of an evil mind; and they who overthrow them, do in fact overthrow every kind of heresy (*evertunt omnem haeresim*).

Indeed, the very structure of his text works to correct the errors of his predecessors. After he relates more or less descriptively the particularities of the heretics in Book 1—"to the best of our ability, we will give you a concise and clear report on the doctrine of these people"—Irenaeus turns in Book 2 to the task of refutation proper.[100] There he contests the implications of Gnostic cosmologies and the layers of divine workmanship as he also reaffirms the omnipotence of God as the lone creator and governing force of the universe.[101] When he adds the weight of scripture to his tractate in Book 3, he emphasizes that a commitment to the full expository cycle of heresiology—description, refutation, and scriptural ballast—ensures his treatise's effectiveness: "Therefore, recall what we said in the first two books; and if you add to the following, you will have from us a most complete refutation of all the heresies, and you will resist them confidently and more insistently."[102]

In framing his protracted work as an effort to "furnish you [the reader] with the complete work of the exposure and refutation of knowledge, falsely so called," Irenaeus expands the relationship between exposure and refutation.[103] He renders heresy a phenomenon that is situational and particularistic, yet governed by a universal nucleus of error.[104] Writing heresiology serves not only to denounce the errors of the heretics, whatever the specific nature of their fallacious opinions; it also devises an essential ontology and history of the heretics that it can encompass fully and irrefutably. As Epiphanius explained, at the conclusion of his discussion of the Audians (the seventieth heresy of his *Panarion*): "I think that is enough about this group in its turn. Once more, I shall pass them by and investigate the rest, so as to omit nothing about the divisions, splits, differences and schisms which have arisen in the world.

---

100. Irenaeus, *Adv. haer.* 1 pr. 2.42–43 (SC 264:22).
101. On the singularity of God's intellect and God's creative power in Irenaeus, see Eric F. Osborn, *Irenaeus of Lyons* (New York: Cambridge University Press, 2001), 27–73. Richard Norris, "The Transcendence and Freedom of God: Irenaeus, the Greek Tradition and Gnosticism," in *Early Christian Literature and the Classical Intellectual Tradition,* ed. William R. Schoedel and Robert L. Wilken (Paris: Éditions Beauchesne, 1979), 87–100, emphasizes how in Book 2 the "question of God" is the substantive ground of contestation (89).
102. Irenaeus, *Adv. haer.* pr. 3.20–23 (SC 211:18).
103. Irenaeus, *Adv. haer.* 4.41.4 (SC 100.2:994).
104. For a broader argument about "discursive unity" in early heresiological argumentation, see Karen L. King, "Social and Theological Effects of Heresiological Discourse," in *Heresy and Identity in Late Antiquity,* ed. Eduard Iricinschi and Holger M. Zellentin (Tübingen: Mohr Siebeck, 2008), 28–49.

For even though they are not that much changed in faith and [different] in behavior, if I can help it I am still not going to omit any separate group which has its own name."[105] Although heresies with distinct names were continuously emerging and spreading out in the world—names, it should be noted, that were often supplied by the heresiologists—they were all species of a single genus. The universal applicability and force of the heresiologists' refutation derives in large measure from their fabrication of a shared heretical disposition. For Irenaeus, the Valentinians, Simonians, Marcionites, Marcosians, Ebionites, Encratites, Barbeliotes, Ophites, Cainites, Nicolaitans, followers of Ptolemy, Colorbasus, Menander, Saturninus, Basilides, Carpocrates, Cerinthus, and Cerdo all share a self-determined sense of epistemological superiority and pride.[106] From the perspective of the heresiologist, heretics excise, supplement, deny, misinterpret, and augment scripture at will; they perform exotic and base rituals; and they opine fanciful doctrines, all of which derive from their belief that they are the exclusive possessors of an intimate knowledge of divine truth. "Truth," as Tertullian mocks heretical reasoning, "was waiting for some Marcionite or a Valentinian to set her free."[107]

It was the shared hubris of the heretics that caused them to adulterate the traditions of Jesus, and to be classified, however paradoxically, as a unity of diversity. Indeed, the rhetorical crux of heresiological literature was to represent the heretics' diversity as, in fact, uniform in purpose, effect, and origin. Irenaeus, as he articulates Christianity's rule of truth, announces the sweeping potentiality of his treatise:[108]

> Since, therefore, the exposé and refutation of all the heretical sects is different and multiform, and since we have resolved to give an answer to every one according to its own standards, we have deemed it necessary first of all to give an account of their source and root, in order that you may know their most sublime Profundity, and understand the tree from which such fruits come forth.

In divulging the theological and ritualistic particularities of various heretical parties, he identifies for his readers the analytical tools—what I have called "ethnographic paradigms"—by which the heresies could be arranged, organized, and situated for refutation.[109] As we saw above in chapters 3 and 4, the commonality he and other heresiologists imputed to the heretical world stems, in large part, from their perpetuation of a genealogical, typological, and universal historical narrative

---

105. Epiphanius, *Pan.* 70.15.6 (GCS 37:249)
106. Irenaeus, *Adv. haer.* 2.25–30, emphasizes the epistemological arrogance of the heretics.
107. Tertullian, *Praescr.* 29.2 (SC 46:125).
108. Irenaeus, *Adv. haer.* 1.22.32–38 (SC 264:310).
109. On Irenaeus's techniques of forging truth and healing the poison of the heretics, see Elaine Pagels, "Irenaeus, the 'Canon of Truth' and the 'Gospel of John': 'Making a Difference' through Hermeneutics and Rituals," *VC* 56.4 (2002): 339–71.

of successive heresies.[110] Irenaeus's knowledge of the Valentinians, like Hippolytus's study of the Naasseni, imposed and enacted a systematic refutation that was applicable to "every kind of heresy."[111] As Irenaeus himself succinctly puts it: "Since we have disproved the followers of Valentinus the entire crowd of heretics is refuted."[112] The world of heresy was elaborated and constructed by the earliest generation of heresiologists to facilitate quite simply and straightforwardly their complete mastery of it. But as we shall see, as the heretical plurality swelled both numerically and geographically, the techniques of creating heretical commonality slowly cracked under the pressure of the conceptual and practical demands of the genre's all-encompassing ethnographic outlook.

Hippolytus similarly commences his *Refutatio* with an unwavering commitment to a plenary investigation, exposition, and refutation of the heresies. He begins his analysis with a discussion of the heretics' intellectual forebears, the Greek philosophers. The relationship between these intellectual kin necessitates the breadth of his inquiry: "One must not dismiss any (οὐδένα) tale [speech, story, fable: μῦθον]" of these philosophers, since the madness of the heresies twists and contorts even the most banal of philosophical doctrines.[113] The failure of adumbration is doubly destructive, as it enables the heretics to escape scrutiny while attesting the investigative shortcomings of the learned protectors of true Christianity. Because ignorance imperils his readers and congregants, Hippolytus announces his desire to chronicle in full the heresies and their intellectual kinsmen: the philosophers, astrologers, diviners, arithmeticians, magicians, Brahmans, Druids, and Chaldeans.[114] Thus, the starting point of Hippolytus's investigation is its presentation of everything known of the world of philosophy, astrology, and foreign wisdom: "We have chosen to leave behind nothing of the doctrines belonging to the nations (προῃρήμεθα μηδὲν τῶν παρ' ἔθνεσι δογμάτων καταλιπεῖν) on account of the gossipy villainies of the heretics."[115] Indeed, Hippolytus explains the motivation for his divine commission as *the fear of omission*.

---

110. Hippolytus, *Ref.* 6.7.1; Irenaeus, *Adv. haer.* 1.23; Epiphanius, *Pan.* 21; Filastrius, *Diversarum haereseon* 29.1; Augustine, *Haer.* 1; Theodoret, *Haer.* 1.1. See also Alberto Ferreiro, *Simon Magus in Patristic, Medieval and Early Modern Traditions* (Leiden: Brill, 2005).

111. Irenaeus, *Adv. haer.* 4 pr. 2.24–25 (SC 100.2:384). On the unity and diversity of heresy, see also Hippolytus, *Ref.* 5.6.4.

112. Irenaeus, *Adv. haer.* 2.31.1–2 (SC 294:324).

113. Hippolytus, *Ref.* pro. 1.1 (Marcovich 54; altered from ANF).

114. For Hippolytus on the Greek philosophers, see *Ref.* pro. 1.23; for Brahmans, see *Ref.* 1.24; for Druids, see *Ref.* 1.25; for Chaldeans, see *Ref.* 4.1–8; for arithmeticians, see *Ref.* 4.14–15; for diviners, see *Ref.* 4.35–37; for magicians, see *Ref.* 4.28–34; for Persians and Babylonians, see *Ref.* 4.43; and for Egyptians, see *Ref.* 4.43–44.

115. Hippolytus, *Ref.* 4.7.4 (Marcovich 99; altered from ANF). The substance of this formulation is repeated at 9.31.2: πᾶσί τε ἀνθρώποις ἐφόδιον ἐν βίῳ <οὐ> μικρὸν καταλιπόντες (Marcovich 378). For the rhetoric of lack of omission (and the positively phrased totality of comprehension) see *Ref.* pro. 5; 4.5.6, 4.6.1, 4.42.2, 4.45.1, 4.51.1; 5.28.1; 6.6.1; 7.27.7, 7.31.8, 7.38.6; 9.6.1, 9.17.3, 9.31.1, 9.31.2.

Immersed in the world of philosophical and heretical opinions, Hippolytus embraces the labor of his work insofar as it ensures a full revelation of the secrets of the heretics:[116]

> Since, however, reason compels us to enter into the vast depth of narrative, we did not consider being silent, but in exposing the doctrines of all these [groups] in detail, we shall keep nothing hidden. Now it seems necessary, even if the inquiry will become longer, not to resist labor; for we shall not leave behind a small cure for human life against error, when all are made to behold openly, the secret rites of these men, and the secret orgies which, as their controllers/regulators, they impart to the initiated alone.

And because the seriousness of heretical error—the soteriological or existential threat ("for human life!") posed by the heretics—countenances a comprehensive refutation, Hippolytus finds himself energized as he "labor[s] with entirety of body and soul" (πάσῃ ψυχῇ καὶ σώματι ἐργαζόμενοι).[117] And he performs this toil fully aware of its power to mold his readers and to fashion his own authorial persona.[118] The labor and pain expended by the heresiologists to discern even the most minute of details become emblems of honor: "The endeavor is, then, full of toil and requiring much inquiry. We shall not, however, be lacking [in exertion]; for afterwards it will bring joy."[119] To cement his textual achievement, Hippolytus analogizes his accomplishment to four images of victory: the athlete who secures the champion's crown, the captain who successfully navigates the rough seas, the prophets whose predictions are realized, and the shepherd who tends his flock and reaps its fruit thereafter.[120] Hippolytus's polemical project describes its will to

---

116. Hippolytus, *Ref.* pro. 5.27 (Marcovich 55; altered from ANF). The language of secrecy is a recurrent theme of the *Refutatio*. For the cognates of κρύπτω, see 1.24.2; 5.7.1; 6.9.5–7; 10.12.1; for ἄρρητος (and cognates), see pro. 1, 2, 5; 4.28.6, 34.1, 42.2; 5.7.1, 7.4, 7.19, 7.22, 7.34, 8.5, 8.7, 8.9, 8.26, 8.27, 5.7.4, 5.7.19, 5.7.22, 5.7.34, 5.8.5, 5.8.7, 5.8.9, 5.8.26, 5.8.27, 5.8.40, 5.9.1, 5.12.1, 5.12.1, 5.17.13, 5.24.1; 6.6.1, 6.38.2, 6.40.2, 6.41.4, 6.44.3, 6.46.1, 6.46.4, 6.49.5, 6.50.1; 7.27.4, 7.25.4, 7.26.1; 9.15.2, 17.1; 10.5.1. On secrecy in the *Panarion*, see 21.6.2; 24.5.4, 24.5.5; 25.2.5; 27.2.4, 27.6.9; 30.3.8, 30.5.7, 30.9.5; 31.10.13, 31.21.4; 35.1.7; 40.1.6; 49.3.1; 61.7.4; 66.3.6; 71.1.3; 73.38.2. Irenaeus, *Adv. haer.* 1.2.2, 1.5.6, 1.7.2, 1.9.3, 1.11.3, 1.16.3, 1.18.1, 1.20.2; 2.2.4, 2.4.2, 2.14.1, 2.18.6, 2.21.2; 3.5.1, 3.14.1, 3.15.2.

117. Hippolytus, *Ref.* pro. 6.39 (Marcovich 55; altered from ANF).

118. On orthodoxy and performance, see Virginia Burrus, "'In the Theater of This Life': The Performance of Orthodoxy in Late Antiquity," in *The Limits of Ancient Christianity: Essays in Honor of R. A. Markus*, ed. William Klingshirn and Mark Vessey (Ann Arbor: University of Michigan Press, 1999), 80–96; and Alberto J. Quiroga Puertas, ed., *The Purpose of Rhetoric in Late Antiquity: From Performance to Exegesis* (Tübingen: Mohr Siebeck, 2013). For a parallel of ethnographic performance, see Rosalind Thomas, *Herodotus in Context: Ethnography, Science, and the Art of Persuasion* (New York: Cambridge University Press, 2000), 249–69.

119. Hippolytus, *Ref.* pro. 10.59–60 (Marcovich 56; altered from ANF).

120. Hippolytus, *Ref.* pro. 10.59–64. Epiphanius imagines himself as a field laborer in his opening remarks against the Secundians, though the imagery signals toil rather than triumph (*Pan.* 32.1.1).

victory as it realizes its expository triumph over against the enemy of truth.[121] Textual labor, in short, demonstrates theological and intellectual triumph. Epiphanius similarly contends that the crown of victory follows those who have demonstrated willingness to travail: "For to receive the crown afterwards and continue happy with the crown, the contestant must first engage in the contest, and the toil and other struggles of the contest. Not that the crown comes last; it is there before the bout but is awarded afterwards, for the joy and gladness of him who has worked for it."[122]

Theodoret of Cyrrhus conveys the orthodox triumph over heresy with reference to a series of territorial liberations. The prologue of Book 2 of his *Compendium of Heretical Fables* proclaims (regarding far older heresies) that "cities and rural areas" alike were emancipated from the tares "of Simon, Menander, Cleobius, Dositheus, Gortheus, Adrianus, Satornilus, Basilides, Isidore, Carpocrates, Epiphanes, and others."[123] He further specifies the geographical contours of heretical liberation in Book 3: "The East was totally freed from the Montanists, and the Novatians, and the Quartodecimans and also Egypt and Libya were freed, and the West was liberated from these. Only a small portion of Asia and Pontus still have their tares."[124] And although the work of the heresiologists remains ongoing, the metaphorical images of crowned victory and the territorial retreat of certain heretical parties indicate orthodoxy's exultant incursion into the rhetorical and geographical worlds of heresy. Heresy and orthodoxy are as much theological categories as geographical demarcations. They are the categorical foundations of a new theological topography, one that is both real and imagined. Heresiology thus narrates the exploration, expansion, and ultimately the triumph of orthodox theology in the world.

In describing heresiology in the language of triumph, the heresiologists devise all manner of exposition to extol their supreme achievement. Their acquisition of heretical knowledge—and their willingness to launch themselves into the murky and dangerous abyss of heresy—legitimizes their reputation as the true apostolics of their particular historical moments. As an agent of the Godhead, Hippolytus, for instance, conceives his mission against the heretics as an act of perseverance and preparation "to make for [his] divine benefactor a worthy return."[125] Like John

---

121. On the relationship between ethnography and triumph, see Emma Dench, *Romulus' Asylum: Roman Identities from the Age of Alexander to the Age of Hadrian* (New York: Oxford University Press, 2005), 76–80; and Michael McCormick, *Eternal Victory: Triumphal Rulership in Late Antiquity, Byzantium and the Early Medieval West* (Cambridge: Cambridge University Press, 1986), 80–130.

122. Epiphanius, *Pan.* 80.11.4 (GCS 37:495).

123. Theodoret, *Haer.* 2 pro. (PG 83:388A–B).

124. Theodoret, *Haer.* 3.6 (PG 83:409A).

125. Hippolytus, *Ref.* pro. 6.39–40 (Marcovich 55; altered from ANF). On millennial expectations and God's control over the evolution of creation see Enrico Norelli, "Paix, justice, intégrité de la creation: Irénée de Lyon et ses adversaires," *Irén* 64.1 (1991): 5–43, esp. 40.

the Baptist, who readies the world for the Christ, the heresiologists prepare the world for the eventual eschaton. In casting his treatise as preparation for and assurance of the inevitability of Christ's return, Hippolytus conceives heresiology as an indispensable and obligatory component of the Christianization of the world and its future consummation in the image and will of Christ. As he finds himself mired in the domain of the Elchasaites (in Book 9 of his *Refutatio*), he longs to steady the trajectory of his inquiry: "I shall move on to a demonstration of the doctrine of truth, lest . . . we, piously pushing forward toward the kingdom's crown and believing the truth, be disoriented."[126] It is telling that the image of the athlete's crown (στέφανος, pro. 10.61) now signals the ultimate triumph of the impending kingdom of God. Victory over the heretics is but a small step toward the larger eschatological victory that is yet to come. And while Hippolytus ultimately counteracted the disruptive potency of "contests against all the heretics" (ἀγῶνα τοῦ κατὰ πασῶν αἱρέσεων) with appeal to the fixity of doctrinal truth, he confesses the power of the heretics to confound.[127] As their texts became authoritative codifications of falsity, the heresiologists perceive their problematic creation of a readily intelligible heretical world.[128] In their reflections on the peril of textual permanence (via codification), they try to contain the damage of an endeavor whose very purpose is a necessary contradiction: to describe the very thing whose details have the power to dismantle the pillars of orthodoxy. To constrain the effects of this unveiling, the heresiologists devised rhetorical maneuvers to fortify their theological intentions, intellectual vigor, and dangerous labor.

THE RHETORICS OF HERESIOLOGY: DANGER AND FEAR

The recurrent emphasis on masterful, comprehensive knowledge contains an implicit acknowledgment of the latent effects of knowing and writing the heretics. While the allure of discovery and the indispensability of information drive heresiological inquiry, the repulsion and fear of potentially uncontrollable and deeply ruinous knowledge injects a strain of caution into the investigatory process. During his prolonged discussion of the Gnostics, Epiphanius offers the most salient articulation of the dissociative underpinnings of heresiological writing:[129]

> And I am afraid that I may be revealing the whole of this potent poison, like the face of some serpent's basilisk, to the harm of the readers, rather than to their

---

126. Hippolytus, *Ref.* 9.17.4 (Marcovich 363; altered from ANF).
127. Hippolytus, *Ref.* 9.17.4 (Marcovich 363; altered from ANF).
128. See, for example, Richard Lim, "Christian Triumph and Controversy," in *Late Antiquity: A Guide to the Postclassical World*, ed. G. W. Bowersock, Peter Brown, and Oleg Grabar (Cambridge, Mass.: Harvard University Press, 1999), 196–212.
129. Epiphanius, *Pan.* 26.3.5 (GCS, n. F.,10:279). See also *Pan.* 26.4.5.

correction. Truly it pollutes the ears—the blasphemous assembly of great audacity, the gathering and the interpretation of its dirt, the mucky perversity of the scummy obscenity.

These remarks qualify the advantageous consequences of representing the heretics in texts. Because the heresiologists' investigations of the heretics preserve their theological opinions and ritualistic practices, the rhetorical hesitancy of the *Panarion* captures the tension between heresiology as a conceptual endeavor oriented around creative destruction and the apprehension that heresiology in fact facilitates and fortifies destructive creation or (creations).[130]

While the heresiologist succeeded in revealing and refuting the opinions of the heretics for the benefit of his readers and congregation, he did so at grave risk to himself. By venturing into the abyss of heresy—by becoming immersed in the culture of heresy, as the heresiologist's obligation requires—the heresiologist "risks actually becoming infected with the savagery" he seeks to destroy.[131] Epiphanius expressly articulates the paradox of his competing obligations to expose the heretics on the one hand and to protect his congregation and himself on the other. His fears are as much about the dangers for his congregations as they are about his own personal orthodoxy, the denaturation of his self: "How shall I shake off this filthy burden since I am both willing and unwilling to speak—compelled to, lest I appear to be concealing any of the facts, and yet afraid that by revealing their horrid activities I may soil or wound those who are given to pleasures and lusts, or incite them to take too much interest in this? In any case may I, and all the [body] of the holy catholic church, and all the readers of this book, remain unharmed by such a suggestion of the devil and his mischief!"[132] Epiphanius is worried about the "corrupting influence which the proximity to tabooed [heretical] indecencies can exercise upon even the most rigidly virtuous Christians."[133] Epiphanius's fear stresses one of the central contradictions of ethnographic investigation: the dangers of intimacy, proximity, and understanding. The fears of the heresiologists—born of research, investigation, observation, exchange, and debate—were fears of legitimation, association, collusion, Satanism, and, the most serious, a loss of orthodoxy. Indeed, fear of the heretics was already present, as Irenaeus famously noted, in the earliest decades of the Jesus movement: "The apostles and their disciples had such fear [of

---

130. In Epiphanius see *Pan.* 9.5.1; 26.3.5, 26.9.1, 26.14.4, 26.17.1; 27.4.5; 29.2.1; 50.1.9; 66.43.5–6; 76.7.7; *De fide* 1.4; and Theodoret, *Haer.* 1 pro.; 2 pro.; 4.3.

131. Christopher Herbert, *Culture and Anomie: The Ethnographic Imagination in the Nineteenth Century* (Chicago: University of Chicago Press, 1991), 179.

132. Epiphanius, *Pan.* 26.17.1–2 (GCS, n. F., 10:297). This idea harks back to Aristotle's famous suggestion in *De anima* (431a) that to know is to become or to, at the very least, initiate a literal physiological transformation. On this point, see Richard Sorabji, "Body and Soul in Aristotle," *Philosophy* 49 (1974): 63–89.

133. Herbert, *Culture and Anomie*, 179.

them] that they would not even converse with any of those who adulterated the truth."[134]

Given the theological and institutional ramifications of heretical discourse, a hint of ambivalent caution imposed intellectual distance between writer and object. The vacillations of the heresiologists acknowledge and preemptively avert the impact of disclosing heretical customs and habits. The dutiful veneer that pervades the heresiological project further differentiates the relative position of the author, reader, and textual object. Although Tertullian advocated a wholesale withdrawal from debate and dialogue with the heretics, he did permit, if vaguely, those who desired a Christian education to attach themselves to qualified pedagogues or to journey to the great centers of apostolicity.[135] If heresiology functioned to broaden the availability of knowledge of the diversifying and regenerative problem of heresy—to be employed by the local teachers Tertullian had recommended—its progenitors imagined a privileged barrier between those who sought the knowledge and those who compiled it. Caught between the compulsion to identify the particularities of their opponents' positions and the fear that doing so emboldened those opponents, the heresiologists frequently embraced the tension as an illustration of their intellectual proficiency and skill. It is the precise problem Plutarch identifies in his treatise on curiosity: curiosity serves the very ills it uncovers. "Busybodies," Plutarch insists, "by gleaning and gathering the blunders and errors and solecisms, not of lines of poems, but of lives, carry about with them a most inelegant and unlovely record-box of evils, their own memory."[136] It is the fear of preservation and dissemination that so unnerves both Plutarch and the heresiologists.[137] Conscious of this peril, the heresiologists defined their investigatory efforts in terms that explicitly acknowledged the potential consequences of their revelations. And in so doing, they found a way to transform these unwanted possibilities into triumphant achievements.

The heresiologists undertook these aggressive investigations of foreign, base, and corrupting worlds by appealing "to a discourse which endowed them with incontestable moral authority" over and against heretical populations.[138] They devised a discourse of unimpeachable expertise and pious relentlessness to obviate the concomitant sense of guilt and danger by association.[139] While the anodyne

---

134. Irenaeus, *Adv. haer.* 3.3.4 (SC 211:42).

135. On the relationship between geography and the apostolic tradition in Irenaeus, see Jared Secord, "The Cultural Geography of a Greek Christian: Irenaeus from Smyrna to Lyons," in *Irenaeus: Life, Scripture, Legacy*, ed. Sara Parvis and Paul Foster (Minneapolis: Fortress Press, 2012), 25–33.

136. Plutarch, *Curios.* 520B (LCL 337:498–501).

137. See, for example, Theodoret, *Haer.* 2.11 and 3.6, mentioning extinct heresies, most of which, he relates, were unknown to the vast majority of people.

138. Herbert, *Culture and Anomie*, 158.

139. See Geoffrey S. Smith, *Guilt by Association: Heresy Catalogues in Early Christianity* (New York: Oxford University Press, 2014).

language of obligation and fear may well have functioned as a sort of rhetorical inoculation, the concomitant allure and danger posed by the heretics buoyed the heresiologists' rhetoric of expertise and onerous self-sacrifice. The strategy of full-fledged engagement is precisely what Epiphanius endorses as he concludes his remarks on the Gnostic sect: "So here too . . . I have not avoided the subject, but have shown what this one of the sects which came my way is like. And I could speak plainly of it because of things which I did not do—heaven forbid!—but which [I knew] by learning them in exact detail from persons who were trying to convert me to this and did not succeed."[140] As a reflection either of genuine fear or mere rhetorical opportunism, the emphases on peril and reluctance served to accentuate the investigative reach of the heresiologists' cure. The danger of these texts was a collateral but necessary function of their expansive inquiry, which actually illustrated the genre's procedural successes. Manifested danger revealed investigatory progress. Insofar as masterful comprehension magnified fear of the heretics, the genre built its effectiveness by championing heresy's danger.[141] Only a meticulous analysis of heresy could produce such alarming fear. The fear of nourishing the teachings of the heretics—the corollary of assiduous research—accentuated heresiology's rhetorical vacillations and attested the underlying achievement of the endeavor. It was the rampant success of heresiological inquiry that rendered it such a problematic genre.[142]

In negotiating their roles as defenders of the church and as ethnographers of the Christian οἰκουμένη, the heresiologists crafted a textual tradition designed to edify and heal. With dogged investigatory skills, they fashioned the tools by which Christians could identify the diverse array of heretics throughout the Roman Empire. And although the danger of overintellectualization and the fear of excessive research remained part of the very edifice of heresiology, the rhetoric of humility, expertise, and toil served to counteract these dangerous scholastic overtones. And as much as the reticent tone of heresiology presaged the unintended consequences of its discoveries, it ultimately prioritized another set of possibilities: the precision of heresiology would enable Christians across the Mediterranean to defeat the heretics around them.

Instead of fearing knowledge of the heretics, the *Panarion* compelled its readers to contemplate their lives as mired in the filth of heresy: "For perhaps, if I reveal this pitfall, like the 'pit of destruction,' to the wise, I shall arouse fear and horror in them, so that they will not only avoid this crooked serpent and basilisk . . . but

---

140. Epiphanius, *Pan.* 26.18.1–2 (GCS, n. F., 10:298).

141. On detection and the heretics, see *Pan.* 25.5.4; 26.3.2; 29.9.1, 29.23.2; 31.9.4, 33.2; 36.6.8; 37.1.1; 41.2.1; 42.15.2; 43.1.6, 43.2.1, 43.2.7; 44.2.4; 46.14.4; Hippolytus, *Ref.* 9.13.6; 10.5.1.

142. On destruction and demolition in Epiphanius, see *Pan.* 14.3.1; 25.7.3; 27.8.4.4; 31.29.4, 31.30.1, 31.33.2; 37.8.10; 40.4.1; 41.3.5; 42.10.5; 44.4.2; 63.68.1; in Theodoret, see *Haer.* 1 pro., 1.26; in Hippolytus, see *Ref.* 5.13.1; 6.8.4, 6.16.6.

stone it too, so that it will not even dare to approach anyone."[143] Alongside each sect's coda, in which Epiphanius celebrated his destruction of that heresy, he articulated a hope that the remedy provided by his *Panarion* would function as a call to arms against the heretics.[144] Explaining the symptoms of heresy's disease in the language of contagion and terror served to transform the rhetorical world of the *Panarion* into the lived (and ideally more livable) world of the fourth century.[145] The twofold ethnographic project of heresiology—the description of the heretics' worldviews and the delineation of their customs, habits, and opinions—extrapolated the lived conditions of Christian dissension from the abstract theorization of their genesis. Epiphanius's rhetorical posture amplified his dutiful role as pedagogue, caretaker, and catalyst of Christianity's growth and safety. His task was to make the abstract musings of the heretics an intolerable condition of the quotidian Christian experience. By this metric, the fear of knowing heresy paled in comparison to the danger of living alongside it in ignorance.

CONCLUSION: ENDING DIALOGUE AND CHASING HERESY

"A sound and safe and religious and truth-loving mind," Irenaeus posited, "will readily apply itself to the things God placed within the power of men and granted to our knowledge. It will make progress in them because by daily exercise it will make easy for itself the acquisition of knowledge."[146] Lamenting that scripture induces men to overindulge their curiosities in order to seek the definitive causes of natural phenomena and to test the truths of scripture (Matt. 10.29 and 10.30 serve as his prime examples), Irenaeus repeatedly emphasizes the limits of human rationality and its incapacity to comprehend the fullness of God and his created order. He bemoans the fact that the eagerness of the heretics to rationalize every facet of the natural world propels them to "extol [their] own mind[s] above the

---

143. Epiphanius, *Pan.* 26.3.9 (GCS, n. F., 10:280).

144. See, for example, Epiphanius, *Pan.* 26.18.4-5; 32.7.7-9; 34.22.2 (GCS, n. F., 10:299, 447; GCS 31:38). There is much debate among scholars about the degree to which the vehemence and polemic of Christian rhetoric contributed to violence and intolerance. See Brent D. Shaw, *Sacred Violence: African Christians and Sectarian Hatred in the Age of Augustine* (New York: Cambridge University Press, 2011), 260-347, 421-40; Michael Gaddis, *There Is No Crime for Those Who Have Christ: Religious Violence in the Christian Roman Empire* (Berkeley and Los Angeles: University of California Press, 2005), esp. 124-30, 131-46, 190-93, 251-82; and Thomas Sizgorich, *Violence and Belief in Late Antiquity: Militant Devotion in Christianity and Islam* (Philadelphia: University of Pennsylvania Press, 2009), 108-43.

145. For an analogous discussion of the violence and power relations between Christians, Jews, and heretics in late antiquity, see Susanna Drake, *Slandering the Jew: Sexuality and Difference in Early Christian Texts* (Philadelphia: University of Pennsylvania Press, 2013).

146. Irenaeus, *Adv. haer.* 2.27.1 (SC 294:264).

greatness of the Creator."[147] By deluding themselves into conceptualizing wisdom as the product of inquiry, they collapse the fundamental distinction between humanity and divinity.[148] For Irenaeus, the acquisition of knowledge has become a game of sorts, which engenders dangerous and unsettling repercussions:[149]

> These [heretics], while seeking to explain the scriptures and parables, introduce another, great God above the God who is Creator of the world. Thus, they do not solve the difficulties. How can they? Rather, they attach a greater difficulty to a smaller one and so tie a knot that cannot be untied. They make a collection of foolish discourse that might come to this knowledge, [namely] to know that the Lord indeed came to the baptism of the truth at the age of thirty, but without learning this [i.e., the meaning of baptism], they impiously scorn the very God who is the Creator and who sent the Lord for the salvation of humankind.

Irenaeus fears that the creation of supratextual deities and simultaneous denaturation of divine transcendence will disturb the epistemological hierarchy of the human-divine bond and undercut the mystery of divine creation. When the inquirer believes that "the more that he occupies himself with questions of this sort, and the more he thinks that he has found more than others," he substitutes his own understanding of the created world in place of the transcendent will of the divine.[150] As we have seen, Irenaeus and Tertullian characterize the entire exercise of investigating scriptural and exegetical truth as emblematic of the misplaced inclination to seek uselessly that is endemic to the human condition. For both authors, an inquisitive mentality invariably contests the upper boundaries of human knowledge.[151] To ask or interpret ad infinitum is to become a heretic.[152]

Tertullian and his fellow heresiologists feared that their refutations not only served the interests of the heretics by advancing knowledge that was altogether vainglorious but also supplied the heretics with a legitimating platform. And while debates over the legitimacy of inquiry signified an appreciation of the dangers of certain types of knowledge and methods of inquiry, the heresiologists' discussions of both hesitation and mastery, fear and triumph, humility and exaltation assumed the capacity to undertake and complete such a task. The question of whether heresiology *ought* to be written fed into assertions about what heresiology contained and how its authors created it. The rhetoric of heresiology reflected issues of

---

147. Irenaeus, *Adv. haer.* 2.26.3 (SC 294:262).
148. Irenaeus, *Adv. haer.* 2.26.3–4; 27.1–3.
149. Irenaeus, *Adv. haer.* 2.10.2 (SC 294:88).
150. Irenaeus, *Adv. haer.* 2.26.3 (SC 294:262). I shall return below in chapter 7 to the parallel I see between knowledge of the divine and knowledge of the heretics. Lim, however, in his *Public Disputation*, 149–81, flags the relationship between curiosity and disputation in the late fourth and early fifth centuries.
151. Irenaeus, *Adv. haer.* 2.26.3; 2.27.1; 2.28.3–9.
152. Irenaeus, *Adv. haer.* 2.27.1–2.

pastoral responsibility, dialogical legitimation, heretical (and philosophical) association, and authorial achievement. The oddity or paradox of heresiological inquiry is its repeated emphasis on stanching curiosity. Curiosity fed the appetite to understand the natural world in all its particularity. Inquiry enabled the human sciences to objectify the natural world by deducing its continuity and its rules of operation. I want to suggest, however, that the principle of continuity proved insufficient to orient the task of writing ethnography in the late antique world. Despite their elaborate paradigms of macroscopic analysis, the heresiologists could not manage the knowledge they had accrued. If the apprehensiveness articulated by the heresiologists was the fear of knowing too much, of being too successful as ethnographers—too revealing, too forthcoming!—this oratorical sleight of hand only heightened the problem of textual closure. How did the heresiologists summarize their efforts? How did they articulate their comprehension of the world of heresy and their ability to delineate its borders? How, in other words, did the heresiologists *know* that they had finished and thus succeeded in their ethnographic task? It is these questions—the relationship between ethnographic writing and textual comprehension and closure—that I take up in the next two chapters.

6

The Infinity of Continuity

Epiphanius of Salamis and the Limits of the Ethnographic Disposition

> In the eighteenth century, the continuity of nature is a requirement of all natural history, that is, of any effort to establish an order in nature and to discover general categories within it, whether they be real and prescribed by obvious distinctions or a matter of convenience and quite simply a pattern produced by our imagination. Only continuity can guarantee that nature repeats itself and that structure can, in consequence, become character.
> —MICHEL FOUCAULT

In *The Order of Things*,[1] Michel Foucault describes the emergence of natural history from the end of the seventeenth century and into the nineteenth as the development of a "grid of knowledge" that examines living beings in new spaces and forms.[2] As he explains the protracted effort to establish the sciences of life, Foucault posits that the structuring of living beings in taxonomic tables assumes or requires (or both) an underlying continuity within the natural order.[3] Categories, real or imagined, depend on patterns, and patterns adhere to rules of continuity. "For," as Foucault insists, "*taxonomy* to be possible ... nature must be truly continuous, and in all its plenitude."[4] To describe nature as ordered is to be able to characterize it, define its scope, and fix its operational laws. Systems of continuity likewise enabled the naturalists of the classical age to move from the specific to the general, to comprehend and organize the whole via the part. The late antique heresiologists, as ethnographers of the Christian world, attempted a similar task: to map the Christian world via ethnographic paradigms that organized the totality by

---

1. This chapter's epigraph is quoted from Michel Foucault, *The Order of Things: An Archaeology of the Human Sciences* (New York: Vintage, 1970), 147.
2. Ibid. 128. For more on his theorization of taxonomy, see 71–76.
3. Ibid. 125.
4. Ibid. 159.

positing a continuous stream of heresies. There is, however, an important disjuncture between knowledge and order, which sets these binaries on a collision course. As Foucault himself notes, naturalists and philosophers alike wondered about their ability to classify the rich variety of the natural world into functional taxonomies.[5] Ethnographic models of heresy may well have arranged the heretics into discrete patterns, but such paradigms could not predict or identify the details of their customs, habits, and beliefs. A macroscopic analysis of the heretical world provided organizational but not descriptive clarity. One could trace the genesis of heretical diversification (the genus of heresy) but not necessarily the differences therein (the heretical species). It is the heresiologists' awareness of the discordance between classification, origins, and comprehension that I discuss in these final two chapters.

To illustrate the tension between modeling heresy and knowing heresy, this chapter explores the conceptual and discursive ruminations of Epiphanius of Salamis as he attempts in his *Panarion* to survey and manage the ever-expanding heretical world. To systematize and regularize the origins of heretical parties, Epiphanius articulated a Christian model of ethnographic organization: the heretics were the product of geographical, genealogical, demonogenic, and ethnogenic processes. But the effort to organize this mess of opinions and habits reveals his inability to control the depths of the world of Christian heresy. And his struggle to manage this diversification is a product of his own creation: Epiphanius chose, through the very act of including and excluding certain heresies in his *Panarion*, to regulate—to regularize and naturalize—the precise number of Christian groups identified as heretics.[6] For that reason, heresiological ethnography was not simply a response to Christian diversity but also its manager and creator.[7] Reports about the customs and habits of heretics—as ways of schematizing and classifying the diversity of the Christian world and as representations of diverse ways of Christian life—became meditations on the seemingly limitless but severely limited capacity of Christian authors to comprehend and codify the history of sectarianism. My argument is that the heresiologists, like other ethnographic writers in the ancient world who expressly expounded upon their inability to organize the world and describe the peoples, places, and things within it articulated a rhetoric

---

5. Ibid. 126, 161–62.

6. In entry 59 of the *Panarion*, for example, Epiphanius describes the Purists. At the end of the entry he notes that there is another, similar group in North Africa and Byzicania called the Donatists. Because "they will be refuted by the same arguments as the Navatians, or so-called Purists . . . I therefore do not need to discuss them any further, but have put them together with those who are like them" (59.13.6–7 [GCS 31:378–79]). Cf. Augustine, *Haer.* 41.

7. See J. Rebecca Lyman, "A Topography of Heresy: Mapping the Rhetorical Creation of Arianism," in *Arianism after Arius: Essays on the Development of Fourth Century Trinitarian Conflicts*, ed. Michel R. Barnes and Daniel H. Williams (Edinburgh: T & T Clark, 1993), 45–64.

of expansion that confronted its own inadequacies. A. H. Merrills has observed that "with the development of Christian geographical thought, however, the edges of the world were invested with a new significance. Scriptural assertions that the Word of God would extend throughout the world encouraged Christian writers to demonstrate the parameters of the faith extended far beyond the *limites* of the empire."[8] And while Christian writers, the heresiologists foremost among them, often discovered Christianity at the farthest edges of the world, their geographical and ethnographic discourses were not singularly demonstrations of successful missionary or exploratory activity. The heresiologists' constant invocations of mastery and hegemony or discovery and conquest attested neither ethnographic, nor geographic, nor theological triumph. Rather, they revealed the epistemological deficiencies of ethnographic classification.[9]

As heresiologists ruminated about their ability to see and regulate the world around them, they entrenched the limits of their intellectual ambition by exposing the lacunae of polemical ethnography. But rather than dismiss the rhetorical posturing of these moments of authorial angst, I contend that these moments cement the conceptual parallel between heresiology and ethnography. Above all else, the heresiologists reflect upon the capacity of authors to describe and control the surrounding world *in texts*. Heresiological texts exhibited not a discourse of an orthodox Christian tradition over against heresy but a complex process in which the *possibility* of knowing the heresies is explored through an exposition of the contours of orthodoxy. Even as the heresiologists proclaimed their comprehension of the heretics, they sought to situate the phenomenon of heresy within an increasingly expansive Christian world. While for the sake of Christians throughout the world they wrote heresiologies, the results of which would demonstrate their textual mastery, the lingering intractability of the heresies vitiated any of their claims of textual victory. In the second half of this chapter, I explore the self-conscious qualifications that Epiphanius appends to his ethnographic foray. The rhetoric of the *Panarion* reveals Epiphanius's forthright recognition of his own limitations as an ethnographer. The rhetorical hesitations registered by Epiphanius, Tertullian, Hippolytus, and Irenaeus—the fear that explaining heresy will spawn heresy—

---

8. A. H. Merrills, "Monks, Monsters, and Barbarians: Redefining the African Periphery in Late Antiquity," *JECS* 12.2 (2004): 217–44, at 242.

9. The very same concern attends literature about Rome's rise and geographical and cultural expansion; the issues of containment and mapping are problematic elements of the ideology of triumph. On this last point, see the remarks of Paul Veyne, "*Humanitas*: Romans and Non-Romans," in *The Romans*, ed. Andrea Giardina, trans. Lydia G. Cochrane (Chicago: University of Chicago Press, 1993), 342–69; Emma Dench, *Romulus' Asylum: Roman Identities from the Age of Alexander to the Age of Hadrian* (New York: Oxford University Press, 2005), 55–61; and, most systematically, Clifford Ando, *Imperial Ideology and Provincial Loyalty in the Roman Empire* (Berkeley and Los Angeles: University of California Press, 2000), 277–335.

betrayed their overriding impulse to reveal the fruits of their armchair ethnography. Bracketed by an appeal to expose on the one hand and to combat and cure on the other, writings that studied and refuted the doctrines of the heretics articulated a protracted epistemological negotiation between ethnography and polemic: discovering the secrets and mysteries of the heretics reflected the equivocal desire to know the world that is purportedly Christian and the firm desire to expand the Christian world.

ETHNOGRAPHIC EFFECTS: DISCOVERY, COMPREHENSION, AND THE UNKNOWABLE

In forging territorial models of their surroundings, ancient geographical writers, as Claude Nicolet has incisively observed, developed categories of knowledge to represent the world in their own political and ideological terms.[10] Geographical and ethnographic discourse created a hierarchy of lands, peoples, and societies in which the world and its contents were not only ordered but also moralized.[11] The intellectual mapping of cultures by means of discovery magnified the world's diversity, wonderment, and mystery:[12]

> Like all sciences, it moves cumulatively: all sorts of progress, some empirical and others theoretical, slowly create a body of knowledge, more or less imperfect and more or less accepted by society. But concerning geography, the frontier between the *known* and the *unknown* is first of all traced on a territory, in a space: the world is still a partly unexplored piece of land. Whence the fundamental notions, according to the concepts of that time, of the known and unknown world, of the inhabited or inhabitable earth. Geography—knowledge and representation of the earth—is still at the stage of voyages and discoveries: "inaccessible" spaces still remain. As for what is known, or rather surveyed, the first stage of understanding passes through different *descriptive* methods: such and such a thing in such and such a location, before or after such and such a thing—which is little else than an imaginary voyage.

Just as geography mapped lands, ethnography mapped peoples: the two, taken together, organized the territorial and human contents of the world. Ethnographies and travel writing served as imaginative tools through which rhetoric and

---

10. Claude Nicolet, *Space, Geography, and Politics in the Early Roman Empire*, trans. Hélène Leclerc (Ann Arbor: University of Michigan Press, 1991), 1–84.

11. See Benjamin Isaac, *The Invention of Racism in Classical Antiquity* (Princeton: Princeton University Press, 2004), 1–168; and Elizabeth Rawson, "Geography and Ethnography," in her *Intellectual Life in the Late Roman Republic* (London: Duckworth, 1985), 250–66.

12. Nicolet, *Space, Geography, and Politics in the Early Roman Empire*, 3. See also the recent study of Steven H. Rutledge, *Ancient Rome as Museum: Power, Identity, and the Culture of Collecting* (New York: Oxford University Press, 2012), esp. 193–286.

reality intertwined.[13] In traversing foreign and domestic environments, ancient writers described the world as they saw, wished, and even feared it to be. In creating intellectual and aspirational maps, ethnographers and geographers wrote the world in their own cultural, political, and religious vernaculars. Consider, for example, the *Chorography* of Pomponius Mela. Written in the first century, shortly after the death of Augustus Caesar, Mela's *Chorography* is a tripartite navigation (or *periplous*) of the known world:[14] it takes its readers on a tour of the world, accentuating "anthropological curiosities, natural phenomena, supernatural phenomena, and the lay of the land."[15] Although Mela used his literary map to display his ethnographical, mythological, and geographical knowledge, he also discovers and discusses the impassible and unknowable features of the natural world.

As the *Chorography* or *Description of the World* commences, Mela links the substantive focus of his inquiry—the study of ethnographic and geographic diversity—to the burdens of authorship and personal expenditure: "A description of the known world is what I set out to give, a difficult task and one hardly suited to eloquence, since it consists chiefly in names of peoples and places and in their fairly puzzling arrangement. To trace this arrangement completely is a time-consuming, rather than a welcome, subject, but nevertheless a very worthwhile thing to consider and understand."[16] As he maps the various regions of the world, Mela juxtaposes his tour

---

13. On travel in antiquity, see Mark Handley, *Dying on Foreign Shores: Travel and Mobility in the Late-Antique West* (Portsmouth, R.I.: Journal of Roman Archaeology, 2011); Lionel Casson, *Travel in the Ancient World* (Baltimore: The Johns Hopkins University Press, 1994); Colin Adams and Ray Laurence, eds., *Travel and Geography in the Roman Empire* (New York: Routledge, 2001); Philip A. Harland, ed., *Travel and Religion in Antiquity* (Waterloo, Ont.: Wilfrid Laurier University Press, 2011); and J. L. Lightfoot, "Pilgrims and Ethnographers: In Search of the Syrian Goddess," in *Pilgrimage in Graeco-Roman and Early Christian Antiquity*, ed. Jaś Elsner and Ian Rutherford (New York: Oxford University Press, 2005), 333–52. On late antique travel in particular, see Scott Fitzgerald Johnson, "Travel, Cartography, and Cosmology," in *The Oxford Handbook of Late Antiquity*, ed. Scott Fitzgerald Johnson (New York: Oxford University Press, 2012), 562–94; and Linda Ellis and Frank L. Kidner, eds., *Travel, Communication, and Geography in Late Antiquity: Sacred and Profane* (Burlington, Vt.: Ashgate, 2004).

14. On Mela's text as a type of *periplous*, see Roger Batty, "Mela's Phoenician Geography," *JRS* 90 (2000): 70–94. The *periplous* narrative—a "sailing around"—was a rather technical genre in which territories and waterways, usually in a particular region, were mapped and described in literary form.

15. F. E. Romer, trans., *Pomponius Mela's Description of the World* (Ann Arbor: University of Michigan Press, 2001), 12. For more on Pomponius Mela, see Romer, *Mela's Description of the World*, 1–32; Alain Silberman, ed., *Pomponius Mela: Chorographie* (Paris: Les Belles Lettres, 1998), vii–liv; Kai Brodersen, *Pomponius Mela: Kreuzfahrt durch die alte Welt* (Darmstadt: Wissenschaftliche Buchgesellschaft, 1994); and Batty, "Mela's Phoenician Geography." For Mela's dependence upon earlier geographical texts, see Dmitry A. Shcheglov, "Pomponius Mela's *Chorography* and Hellenistic Scientific Geography," in *The Periphery of the Classical World in Ancient Geography and Cartography*, ed. Alexander V. Podossinov (Leuven: Peeters, 2014), 77–94.

16. Pomponius Mela, *Chor.* 1.1 (Silberman 1). I have used the translation in Romer, *Pomponius Mela's Description of the World*.

of rivers, oceans, and lands with brief but quintessentially ethnographical details. The emphasis on microcosm, at the expense of macroscopic unity, reflects the preoccupation of the chorographers with regional details. Because "the goal of regional cartography" (χωρογραφικόν), according to the second-century Greek geographer Claudius Ptolemaeus (Ptolemy), "is an impression of a part, as when one makes an image of just an ear or an eye," it dwells on particularities without devising an overarching coherence for the whole of the world.[17] The chorographical effect, then, is the presentation of a loose confederation of particularized data that follows a narrative journey, even if the narrative itself contains disparate, unaligned, and contradictory details.

To ponder the effects of prolonged exposure to foreign peoples, places, and customs was, as Mela's *Chorography* demonstrates, an opportunity to reify cultural and communal dispositions.[18] In Book 3, for instance, discussing the lands off the coast of northern Europe, he arrives at the isle of Britain. The island, he reports, is a fertile and generous habitat for sheep, though its terrain is less suitable for human needs. The land does maintain people, "but they all are uncivilized" (*sed sunt inculti omnes*).[19] Removed as they are from the umbrella of civilization, the Britons lack knowledge of "other kinds of wealth, being wealthy only in sheep and land."[20] Like many foreign peoples, they are a population defined by a "strong desire to rule and a strong drive to expand their holdings."[21] Despite Mela's lack of affinity for the Britons, their incivility served a critical rhetorical function for the Roman imperial project of conquest and domination.[22] The ever-growing sphere

---

17. Ptolemy, *Geographia* 1.1.17–19 in *Claudii Ptolemaei Geographia*, vol. 1, ed. C. F. A. Nobbe (1843; repr., Hildesheim: Olms, 1966), 3. For the translation, see *Ptolemy's Geography: An Annotated Translation of the Theoretical Chapters*, trans. J. Lennart Berggren and Alexander Jones (Princeton: Princeton University Press, 2000), 57. "World cartography (γεωγραφία) is an imitation through drawing of the entire known part of the world together with things that are, broadly speaking, connected with it" (*Geog.* 1.1.1 [Nobbe 3]).

18. The rhetoric of global domination by way of study has been carefully mapped by Andreas Alföldi, *Die monarchische Repräsentation im römischen Kaiserreiche* (Darmstadt: Wissenschaftliche Buchgesellschaft, 1970); Pascal Arnaud, "L'image du globe dans le monde romain: Science, iconographie, symbolique," *Mélanges de l'École Française de Rome* 96.1 (1984): 53–116; and Sorcha Carey, *Pliny's Catalogue of Culture: Art and Empire in the "Natural History"* (New York: Oxford University Press, 2003), 36–39.

19. Mela, *Chor.* 3.51 (Silberman 82).

20. Mela, *Chor.* 3.51 (Silberman 82). See the complementary description of the Britons in Tacitus's *Agricola* 21. For Roman techniques of ethnographic translation (in the context of the Britons in particular), see Dench, *Romulus' Asylum*, 82–87; and Katherine Clarke, "An Island Nation: Re-Reading Tacitus' *Agricola*," *JRS* 91 (2001): 94–102.

21. Mela, *Chor.* 3.52 (Silberman 82).

22. See, for example, S. T. James, "'Romanization' and the Peoples of Britain," in *Italy and the West: Comparative Issues in Romanization*, ed. Simon Keay and Nicola Terrenato (Oxford: Oxbow Books, 2001), 187–209.

of Roman occupation—both literal and metaphorical—renders the disposition of these northern islanders both firmly known and readily comprehensible. Mela explains:[23]

> Next, as to what kind of place Britain is and what kind of people it produces, information that is more certain and better established will be stated. The reason is that— lo and behold!—the greatest princeps [first citizen: i.e., Augustus] is opening the long-closed island, and as conqueror of previously unsubdued and previously unknown peoples, the princeps brings with them the proof of his own accomplishments, since he will reveal in his triumph as much as he has laid claim to in war.

The ignorance of the Britons—and their Irish neighbors—was no longer an object of speculation. As Rome expanded its frontiers, ethnographic writing served to stabilize the cultural periphery, including the monstrous peoples of the North, the British and Irish, and those from the South, in and around the Nile.[24] Textual recollections of exploration purported to identify and even to tame the once-unknown and savage. Increased knowledge of the Britons demystified their savagery and demonstrated, according to Mela, Augustus's great triumph over the *orbis terrarum*.

A report from Book 6 of Pliny's *Natural History* about the island of Ceylon (Taprobane or Sri Lanka) similarly captures the enduring power of discovery: "Ceylon, under the name of the Land of the Counterlanders, was long considered to be another world (*alterum orbem terrarum*); but the epoch and the achievements of Alexander the Great supplied clear proof of its being an island."[25] And even though Alexander's exploits confirmed the nation's topography, Taprobane's inaccessibility—it was "banished by nature beyond the confines of the world," Pliny reports—left it a place of profound mystery.[26] During the reign of the emperor Claudius, however, the nation sent four envoys to Rome, from whom Pliny drew his account. He stresses that "Taprobane is a distant reflection of Rome, a reversal but

---

23. Mela, *Chor.* 3.49 (Silberman 81).
24. Pliny, in fact, listed a series of towns—previously unknown—that were destroyed by Aelius Gallus. As Trevor Murphy explains in *Pliny the Elder's "Natural History": The Empire in Encyclopedia* (New York: Oxford University Press, 2004), 130: "In the case of these towns [Negrana, Nestus, Nesca, Magusus, Caminacus, Labaetia, Bariba, and Caripeta], we learn of their presence in the world only after the *Natural History* tells us they no longer exist—their destruction is the necessary precondition of our being informed. That such complete information should be available to the *Natural History* is a consequence of the spread of Roman authority, which has opened up the *orbis terrarum* to expeditions such as that of Aelius Gallus."
25. Pliny, *Nat.* 6.24.81, trans. H. Rackham, LCL 352 (Cambridge, Mass.: Harvard University Press, 1942), 398. See Ernst Badian, "Alexander the Great and the Unity of Mankind," *Historia* 7 (1958): 425–44. On Ceylon, see Stefan Faller, *Taprobane im Wandel der Zeit: Das Śrî Laṅkâ-Bild in griechischen und lateinischen Quellen zwischen Alexanderzug und Spätantike* (Stuttgart: Steiner, 2000).
26. Pliny, *Nat.* 6.24 (LCL 352: 404–5)

analogous image: in geographical terms, the Rome of another hemisphere."[27] The inhabitants of Taprobane shared with the Romans a taste for luxuries.[28] They cherished precious stones, gold, silver, pearls, and tortoiseshell. Pliny also pointedly idealized their political system, which rewarded leaders with temperate dispositions and eschewed hereditary monarchies. As Trevor Murphy notes, the acquisition and refinement of ethnographic knowledge, "provoke the reader to wonder and to speculate, whether about the furthest limits of what human life is permitted by Nature, or the limits of what moral men permit themselves as consumers and users of Nature."[29] For Mela and Pliny, the intellectual fruits of geographical expansion *refined* an ethnographic knowledge and rhetoric about the peoples and places of the οἰκουμένη (the known, inhabited world).[30]

As the seat of political and cultural power shifted from Greece and Rome to the Christian churches of the Mediterranean, heresiological literature translated the peoples at the geographical periphery into the peoples of the theological fringes. In that effort, ethnography proved an essential contribution to the discourse through which Christian writers likewise translated the world into the vernacular of Christian triumph and universalism.[31] Jeremy Schott has persuasively argued that the ethnographic and philosophical emphases in Christian apologetic literature served, alongside other textual ventures such as universal history, as a tool of literary control.[32] For Schott, Greek and Roman philosophers of the early empire harnessed the results of cross-cultural exchange as demonstrations of a broader universal philosophy that strengthened the cultural asymmetry between the Greek and Roman philosophical tradition on the one hand and the peripheral intellectual pursuits of non-Greeks and non-Romans on the other. Ethnography in antiquity, which Schott reads as a method of intellectual collection, discovery, and

---

27. Murphy, *Pliny's the Elder's "Natural History,"* 106.
28. Pliny, *Nat.* 6.24.89 (403–4).
29. Murphy, *Pliny the Elder's "Natural History,"* 95.
30. See Michael Sommer, "ΟΙΚΟΥΜΕΝΗ: longue durée perspectives on ancient Mediterranean 'globality,'" in *Globalisation and the Roman World: World History, Connectivity and Material Culture*, ed. Martin Pitts and Miguel John Versluys (New York: Cambridge University Press, 2015), 175–97; C. R. Whittaker, *Rome and Its Frontiers: The Dynamics of Empire* (New York: Routledge, 2004); Susan P. Mattern, *Rome and the Enemy: Imperial Strategy in the Principate* (Berkeley and Los Angeles: University of California Press, 1999); and Daniela Dueck, "The Augustan Concept of 'an Empire without Limits,'" in *Creating and Representing Sacred Spaces*, ed. Michael Dickhardt and Vera Dorofeeva-Lichtman, Göttinger Beiträge zur Asienforschung 2–3 (Göttingen: Peust and Gutschmidt, 2003), 211–27.
31. See Averil Cameron, *Christianity and the Rhetoric of Empire: The Development of Christian Discourse* (Berkeley and Los Angeles: University of California Press, 1991), 15–46; and Hervé Inglebert, *Interpretatio Christiana: Les mutations des savoirs (cosmographie, géographie, ethnographie, histoire) dans l'Antiquité chrétienne, 30–630 après J.-C.* (Paris: Institut d'Études Augustiniennes, 2001).
32. Jeremy Schott, *Christianity, Empire, and the Making of Religion in Late Antiquity* (Philadelphia: University of Pennsylvania Press, 2008), 166.

appropriation, served to schematize the diversity of the world into a single system of philosophical order. In this way, barbarian wisdom was given value and meaning through Greek and Roman interpretation.[33] Various ancient writers—notably Diodorus Siculus, Hecataeus of Abdera, Posidonius, Numenius, and Plutarch—developed narratives that recounted the history of humanity, often told with philosophical inflection, through their respective lenses of ethnic particularity.[34] These writers sought, as Greg Woolf has demonstrated, to synchronize the history of barbarians within their own indigenous histories.[35] As the boundaries of the world were rapidly expanding, cultural and intellectual centers harnessed these changes to enumerate their enduring influence (cultural, philosophical, militarily, etc.) over and within this enlarged territory.

Following the philosophical, ethnographic, and geographic musings of various Greek authors, Christian apologists articulated an ecumenical system of thought by dismantling the rigid dichotomy between Greeks and barbarians.[36] In their appeal to geography and ethnography, Christian apologetic authors positioned themselves at the center of a new homologous knowledge in contrast to the ethnic plurality of paganism.[37] The creation of this Christian intellectual system, adapted but also distinguished from Greek and Roman quests to identify universal philosophy, bolstered Christianity's universalizing claims. Ethnic and cultural particularity were superseded by the universal truth of Christian as "the only valid philosophy."[38] But as Schott explains, the quest for a transcendent universalism served in fact to solidify difference. The juxtaposition of cultures, ethnicities, nations, and histories produced the effect of a thoroughgoing comprehension of the contents of the world, which ultimately magnified these differences:[39]

> Terms like *Christianismos, Hellenismos, ethne, gentes,* and *nationes,* as well as a host of heresiological appellatives, served as signifiers in a science of local and global control. Working within such a system of knowledge, bishops and imperial officials

---

33. See Schott's first chapter, ibid. 15–51, "Philosophers, Apologists, and Empire," which discusses the historical, ethnographic, and geographical propensities of philosophical rumination and the tension between so-called ethnic histories and the desired synchronicity of an overarching historical ethnographic narrative.

34. Ibid. 16–28. On universal history and cultural formations, see Raoul Mortley, *The Idea of Universal History from Hellenistic Philosophy to Early Christian Historiography* (Lewiston, N.Y.: Edwin Mellen, 1996).

35. Greg Woolf, *Tales of the Barbarians: Ethnography and Empire in the Roman West* (Malden, Mass.: Wiley-Blackwell, 2011), 38–44.

36. Schott, *Christianity, Empire, and the Making of Religion,* 166.

37. On the Christian apologists, barbarian wisdom, and geography, see the incisive analysis of Laura Nasrallah, "Mapping the World: Justin, Tatian, Lucian, and the Second Sophistic," *HTR* 98.3 (2005): 283–314.

38. Schott, *Christianity, Empire, and the Making of Religion,* 32.

39. Ibid. 169.

living well inside the borders of Roman territory could find themselves on the frontier between Christians and others. The discourse of apologetics provided a system of knowledge that structured contact between Christians and the *ethne*.

Just as apologetics refined the terms of imperial comprehension, heresiologies embraced the same rhetoric of ethnographic writing and representation.[40] Through their parallel ethnographic investigations, the apologists and heresiologists clarified their knowledge of the world and its intellectual traditions. They took mountains of particularized knowledge and translated it into evidence of Christian triumph and supremacy.

THE JOURNEY OF HERESIOLOGY

Having painstakingly enumerated the eighty heresies of his *Panarion*, Epiphanius of Salamis concludes with a theological exhortation to the exclusive truth of the catholic church. As this ecumenical epilogue, entitled *De fide*, commences, Epiphanius recollects his experience writing the *Panarion* in order to proclaim his accomplishments.[41] Imagining the classification of the heretics as an act of prolonged and treacherous discovery, Epiphanius casts the production of his text in the symbolic language of travel and return:[42]

> We have discussed the various, multiform, much divided, rash teachings of the crooked counsels of our opponents, have distinguished them by species and genus and, by God's power, have exposed them as stale and worthless. We have sailed across the shoreless sea of the blasphemies of each sect, with great difficulty crossed the ocean of their blasphemous, shameful, repulsive mysteries, given the solutions to their hosts of problems, and passed their wickedness by. And we have approached calm lands of the truth, after negotiating every rough place, enduring every squall, foaming, and tossing of billows, and, as it were, seeing the swell of the sea, and its whirlpools, its shallows none too small, and its place full of dangerous beasts, and experiencing them through words.

The taxonomic endeavor of the heresiologist, here articulated as a system of natural classification ordered by genus and species, is conceptualized as an ethnographic

---

40. See Nasrallah, "Mapping the World," 299–314.
41. Ibid. 293, makes a similar observation about the writings of Justin and Tatian. They present their experiential knowledge, born of their travels and inscribed on their bodies, as an intellectual and cultural map of their world.
42. Epiphanius, *De fide* 1.1–3 (GCS 37:496). For similar invocations of heresiology as a metaphorical or textual journey, see *Pan*. 26.19.1; 59.13.1; 66.88.2; 69.81.1. In addition, Epiphanius repeatedly construes the doctrines and practices of the heretics as obstructing the road of truth: *Pan*. 30.25.14; 42.11.15 *refut*. 40 and 53; 42.12.3 *refut*. 16 and 24; 59.12.2–5; 69.22.1, 69.23.2, 69.49.1. For a similar image of travel, see also Hippolytus, *Ref*. 7.13.1.

excursion born of theological necessity. Travel, as the metaphor of textual production, gave rise to an intellectual and spiritual exhaustion, but this was an expected consequence of an ethnographic effort to stabilize the structure and content of the Christian world. Having sailed across the sea of heresy and contended with "the perils of the deep," Epiphanius and his metaphorical travel companions "recover from all our fear, distress, and illness, as we inhale the mainland breezes with the utmost relief, as we [have come to] safety and won our way to the calm harbor."[43]

The result of this theological journey, with all its uncertainty and injury, is a return to the refuge of orthodoxy. When Epiphanius reconnects with the orthodoxy symbolized in the city of Jerusalem—the journey into darkness has led inexorably to "the holy Jerusalem and Christ's virgin and bride, the firm foundation and rock, our holy mother"—he immediately cherishes the restorative power of the Lord's sanctuary both for its physical and for its spiritual sustenance: "For we have always been in need of him and in every part of these Sects, in our continual encounters with their obscurities."[44] Orthodoxy, figured as holy Jerusalem, blossoms into a vivid metropolis, the wonder and glory of which are made manifest to the faithful and concealed from unbelievers.[45] And yet, while the settled comforts of Jerusalem rehabilitate the exhausted Epiphanius, the journey itself remained fixed in his mind; its disruptive effects did not end with his metaphorical rejuvenation. It is the very act of dislocation that engenders inquiry. As James Clifford has noted, "'Theory' is a product of displacement, comparison, a certain distance. To theorize, one leaves home."[46] Epiphanius's voyage into the violent waters of heresy quite naturally prompted reflection about the destabilizing effects of exploration.

43. Epiphanius, *De fide* 1.5, 1.4 (GCS 37:497).
44. Epiphanius, *De fide* 2.2 (GCS 37:497).
45. Epiphanius, *De fide* 2.9 (GCS 37:498).
46. James Clifford, "Notes on Travel and Theory," *Inscriptions* 5 (1989), 177–88, at 177. On the philosophical, ritualistic, and epistemological evolutions of *theōria*, see the excellent study of Andrea Wilson Nightingale, *Spectacles of Truth in Classical Greek Philosophy: Theoria in Its Cultural Context* (New York: Cambridge University Press, 2004). *Theōria*, Nightingale explains, began as a journey (undertaken by the *theōros*) to witness spectacles, momentous events, and sacred objects. The journey or *theōria*, which incorporated the totality of the experience from the journey away, the sacred viewing, and the return home, emphasized the effects of seeing ritual and sacredness. During the classical era, philosophical inquiry, led by Plato, began to model itself in the image of the *theōria*: the philosophers engaged in activity that enabled them to journey into the universe, the gods, and the world around them and see truths. For my purposes, Nightingale's most useful analysis (63–68) concerns what she calls the domain of "*theoria* as cultural practice," specifically a "journey to foreign lands to see the world" (40, 63). In seeing the world, the *theōros* acquires knowledge and wisdom. *Theōria* could be, as Herodotus illustrates, a fundamentally ethnographic experience. See now Ian Rutherford's *State Pilgrims and Sacred Observers in Ancient Greece: A Study of* Theōria *and* Theōroi (New York: Cambridge University Press, 2013). Cf. Scott Scullion, "'Pilgrimage' and Greek Religion: Sacred and Secular in the Pagan *Polis*," in *Pilgrimage in Graeco-Roman & Early Christian Antiquity: Seeing the Gods*, ed. Jaś Elsner and Ian Rutherford (New York: Oxford University Press, 2005), 111–30.

And it is just as Epiphanius celebrated his textual triumph and safe return that he confronts the illusory foundation of his ethnographic knowledge. For the ethnographers of antiquity, to traverse the world, even if only imaginatively, was to contemplate—literally, "to theorize" (θεωρία means "looking at" or "contemplation")—its wonders, oddities, complexities, and mysteries.

While the language of rhetorical mastery substantiated certain authorial pretensions of the heresiologists, it also unmasked the more profound conceptual perplexity endemic to ethnographic writing and research. Scholars routinely identify Christian heresiology as a site of ecclesiastical or theological authority and imperial control. In my reading, however, the genre of heresiology, rather than illustrating complete mastery, actually reveals the internal tensions and constraints embedded within claims of totalizing knowledge. Indeed, this analytical strain permeates the discourse of ethnography in the ancient world. Even as ethnography erected structures of transcendent knowledge, which defined the periphery in terms of the center and elaborated new interpretive mechanisms of knowledge, it also communicated the underlying limitations of authorial projects of universalizing scope. As both a mode of writing and a manner of thinking, ethnography exists at the intellectual conjunction of epistemological ambition and constraint: How much can we know? How do we express that knowledge? How do we know we have been thorough? The ethnographic disposition is oriented around dissociative binaries: triumph and failure on the one hand and control and disruption on the other. Ethnographers in antiquity defined the problem of textual comprehension and representation not through a distinction between objectivity and subjectivity, as much contemporary anthropological discourse does, but by conveying the impression that the myriad diversity of the world was unquantifiable, truly unknowable, and outside the realm of representation.[47] I call this the "epistemological paradox" of ethnography. The campaign for maximal knowledge not only amplifies the deep, pervasive cleavages within the textual conceit of ethnographic writing but also exposes the authorial inability to manage this newfound cultural, ethnic, and religious knowledge. The discoveries of voyages did not simply produce invaluable knowledge; they became lasting evidence of the struggle, past, present, and future, to fix control over a diverse world. Insofar as the world was simply beyond the command and control of texts, ethnography perpetuated this epistemological double bind.

---

47. On contemporary ethnography and the tension between objective and subjective analysis, see Clifford Geertz, *Works and Lives: The Anthropologist as Author* (Stanford: Stanford University Press, 1988); Bronislaw Malinowski, *A Diary in the Strict Sense of the Term* (Stanford: Stanford University Press, 1989); James Clifford, "On Ethnographic Self-Fashioning: Conrad and Malinowski," in his *The Predicament of Culture* (Cambridge, Mass.: Harvard University Press, 1988), 92–113; and Kevin Dwyer, *Moroccan Dialogues: Anthropology in Question* (Baltimore: The Johns Hopkins University Press, 1982).

KNOWN KNOWNS AND KNOWN UNKNOWNS: EXPLORING THE DEPTHS OF THE WORLD

Ethnographic texts from across the ancient world, despite their effort to systematize the world around them, reveal a weakened control over the classificatory effects of their inquiries.[48] To return to my opening example, as Mela's *Chorography* unfolds, the world he describes slowly exposes the fault lines in the ethnographic gaze. Mela's seemingly expert grasp on the world's contents loosens as he delves into its recesses.[49] It is in the *Chorography*'s Africa, a site of profound cultural and anthropological tension, that the textual constraints of ethnographic analysis are most emphatically on display. Africa, Mela informs his readers, is highly fertile yet largely uninhabited.[50] He reports that it is "inhabited by people socialized according to our custom," while in the interior of the continent "the scarcely human and rather brutish Goat-Pans, Blemyes, Gamphasantes, and Satyrs possess, rather than inhabit, the land. They roam freely everywhere, with no houses and no fixed abode."[51] The Romanized north of the country, which bears the marks of Roman civilization, slowly recedes as readers make their way inland to the southern and western parts of the continent. The nomadic peoples of the interior are known for their "rather uncouth way of life."[52] The people "beyond the desert" are further marked off from the norms of the Roman perspective.[53] The Trogodytae ("Cave Dwellers") "own no resources, and rather than speak, they make a high-pitched sound. They creep around deep in caves and are nurtured by serpents."[54] The Augilae worship the spirits of the dead, while the Gamphasantes forswear clothing and weapons. And as Pomponius rounds out his description of the peoples of Africa, he introduces the most extreme illustrations of the periphery: "The Blemyes lack heads; their face is on their chest. The Satyrs have nothing human except their superficial appearance. The form of the Goat-Pans is celebrated in their name. So much for Africa."[55] As Rhiannon Evans describes it: "As the least well-known part of the known world, Africa's interior functions especially well as a stage for playing out fears about the unexplored reaches of the third

---

48. One can see the hesitancy tied to ethnography in the works of Strabo, Pliny, Herodotus, Tacitus, Lucian, Josephus, and Pausanias, among myriad others.

49. This motif of textual fracture within Mela's *Chorography* is expertly traced by Rhiannon Evans, "Ethnography's Freak Show: The Grotesques at the Edges of the Roman Earth," *Ramus* 28.1 (1999): 54–73.

50. Mela, *Chor.* 1.21 (Silberman 7).

51. Mela, *Chor.* 1.33, 1.23 (Silberman 10, 8).

52. Mela, *Chor.* 1.42 (Silberman 13).

53. Mela, *Chor.* 1.43 (Silberman 13).

54. Mela, *Chor.* 1.44 (Silberman 13). On the Trogodytae and the alternative spelling "Troglodytae," see Romer, *Pomponius Mela's Description of the World*, 47–48 n. 43.

55. Mela, *Chor.* 1.48 (Silberman 14).

continent. It is the Counterworld in Our World, the mirror of the *oikoumene*."[56] But by constructing this inverted realm in such jarringly oppositional terms, Mela inaugurates the first of a series of cracks in the structural integrity of his investigation. Africa becomes an ethnographic paradox precisely because these freaks of nature, in enticing and yet repelling the ethnographic gaze, unhinged the simplicity and coherence of Roman taxonomic discourse.[57] The chaos and disorder of the world itself was codified in Mela's text, as he too struggled to contain his subversive discoveries. Precisely because the Africans of the *Chorography* became known, they had to be explained and contained.

Whereas the uncivilized were dispersed throughout the world in Gaul, Britain, Ireland, Scythia, and India, the monstrous peoples of the *Chorography* are confined to the plains of inland Africa. In narrowing the territorial scope of his fascinations, Pomponius encloses or at least seeks to manage the insatiability of his ethnographic curiosity. But Africa endured as a fixture of the ethnographic gaze insofar as it remained beyond the bounds of absolute understanding. Indeed, for all the talk of the Africans' inhumanity, the region and its inhabitants, Pomponius reports, remained largely unknown:[58]

> Moreover, nothing noteworthy meets those who follow the shores eastward. Everything is a wasteland, defined by desolate mountains, and more a riverbank than an oceanfront. After that, there is a huge tract without inhabitants. For quite a long time it was uncertain whether there was sea beyond and whether the earth had a periphery, or whether, with the seawaters eliminated, Africa extended without end.

Strabo's description of Africa in his *Geography* also emphasized the mystery of its interior regions: "Since several deserts intervene, we do not know all these regions. Similarly the regions above Ammon and the oases as far as Ethiopia are likewise unknown. Neither can we tell the boundaries either of Ethiopia or of Libya, nor yet accurately even those of the country next to Egypt, much less of that which borders on the ocean."[59] And when Pliny, after describing numerous peoples and places throughout Africa, ventures into the desolate recesses of the country, his ethnographic imagination is awakened:[60]

56. Evans, "Ethnography's Freak Show," 60.
57. For Roman attitudes toward the monstrous and grotesque, see Carlin A. Barton, *The Sorrows of the Ancient Romans: The Gladiator and the Monster* (Princeton: Princeton University Press, 1993). Barton's analysis draws from a variety of disciplines, including anthropology, psychoanalysis, art history, literary criticism, and queer studies. See also John Block Friedman, *The Monstrous Races in Medieval Art and Thought* (Syracuse: Syracuse University Press, 2000); and Gordon Lindsay Campbell, *Strange Creatures: Anthropology in Antiquity* (Duckworth: London, 2006).
58. Mela, *Chor.* 3.89 (Silberman 91–92).
59. Strabo, *Geogr.* 17.3.23, trans. Horace Leonard Jones, LCL 267 (Cambridge, Mass.: Harvard University Press, 1932), 208. I have modified the spellings of the place names.
60. Pliny, *Nat.* 6.35.195 (LCL 352:482).

The rest of the country is uninhabited. Then come regions that are purely imaginary: towards the west are the Nigroi, whose king is said to have only one eye, in his forehead; the Wild-beast-eaters, who live chiefly on the flesh of panthers and lions; the Eatalls, who devour everything; the Man-eaters, whose diet is human flesh; the Dog-milkers, who have dogs' heads; the Artabatitae, who have four legs, and rove about like wild animals; and then the Hesperioi, the Perosi and the people we have mentioned as inhabiting the border of Mauretania.

Ignorance prompted Pliny's imagination, which created culture and peoplehood in order to complete the imperial ethnographic map. The desire for total comprehension bred imaginative speculation. The opportunity to define what was previously unknown understandably held great ideological potential. Geographic, ethnographic, and encyclopedic contemplation served the interests of imperial domination. But lurking beneath the comforting illusion of mastery lay the unanticipated consequences not only of discovery but also of theoretical miscalculation. In the struggle to contain subversive discoveries in his text, Mela codified the disorder of the surrounding world. His ethnography created an authorial certainty, which faltered as the known world of his text denatured the fixity of cultural and geographic boundaries. Ethnography lulled its proponents into a false sense of authorial security, which slowly revealed itself as false, as the known world in texts enlarged to include disruptive knowledge.

In point of fact, ethnographic texts, however fantastical,[61] complicated the seemingly straightforward cycle by which discovery begat knowledge and knowledge facilitated certain rhetorical postures of mastery and imperialism. As the *Chorography* illustrates, there is an increasingly vivid sense that knowledge of the world beyond Rome is as likely to disorder the narrative of texts as to support them. The periphery held the very real potential to trap authors in an epistemological and rhetorical imbalance. The puzzling nature of the earth—with its various borders, coasts, interiors, inhabitants, climates, and topographies—is exacerbated at the very start of the treatise, when Pomponius outlines his narrative plan. Describing the shape of the whole world, he reflects briefly on its grand divisions:[62]

---

61. See also, for example, Pliny's discussions of the Arimphaei and Hyperboreans in his *Nat.* 6.34–35 and 4.89, respectively. The *Natural History* catalogues an array of monstrous races at 7.2.9–32. Among those named are: the Arimaspi, who have one eye in the middle of their forehead; men with their feet turned backward behind their legs; an Albanian people who are born with grey eyes and are bald from birth; tribes of androgynes; Illyrians with the evil eye (with double pupils, no less); tribes who have a double pupil in one eye and the image of a horse in the other; an array of odd nations in India, including those who have dog's heads (whose speech is bark); a race whose children are born old; the Monocoli, who only have one leg; the Umbrella-foot tribe (who use their huge feet to shield themselves from the heat); and people without necks, among myriad others.

62. Mela, *Chor.* 1.4 (Silberman 2).

In the same way, the earth also is divided from east to west into two halves, which they term hemispheres, and it is differentiated by five horizontal zones. Heat makes the middle zone unlivable, and cold does so to the outermost seasons, but not at the same time. The Antichthones inhabit one [zone], we the other. The chorography of the former zone is unknown because of the heat of the intervening expanse, and the chorography of the latter is now to be described.

Mela jettisons any consideration of this unknowable zone out of necessity, in an effort "to impose limits on the known world, to package the *oikoumene* in a readable and therefore knowable form."[63] The sense of a radical disjuncture between the two worlds, the one firmly knowable (the οἰκουμένη) and the other altogether concealed, the counterworld, or *Antipodes*,[64] slowly recedes as the existence of an alternative hemisphere becomes too enticing and, indeed, too useful to resist.[65] Mela first marshals the notion of the counterworld to explain the otherwise inexplicable flooding of the Nile.[66] And when this counterworld arises again in Book 3, the reference only heightens its enigmatic character: "Taprobane is said to be either a very large island or the first part of the second world, but because it is inhabited, and because no one reportedly has circumnavigated it, the latter interpretation is as good as true."[67] The intrusion of the counterworld into the realm of the inhabited world irrevocably disturbed the neatly delimited structure of the upper hemisphere. If the antiworld explained the natural laws of the οἰκουμένη, the two regions were fundamentally inseparable domains. To the extent that the lower hemisphere remained unexplored, its explanatory potential was elusive. However, the counterworld's disruptive potential remained intact. Gabriella Moretti has noted: "From an ethnographic point of view ... the Antipodes designate the inhabitants of those

63. Evans, "Ethnography's Freak Show," 68. The digressive observations of much ethnographic writing, from the *Odyssey* to Ammianus Marcellinus's *Res Gestae*, serve as a counterpart to the more narratively structured writings of Mela and the chorographers. The former encapsulate a certain nonempirical tendency of ethnographic writing—these are texts that use ethnographic evidence haphazardly and within a larger generic framework—whereas the latter provide a highly ordered and contained account of lands, waterways, and peoples. Both traditions, however, emphasize fantastical discoveries.

64. For a history of the term in ancient literature (and beyond), see Gabriella Moretti, "The Other World and the 'Antipodes': The Myth of the Unknown Countries between Antiquity and the Renaissance," in *The Classical Tradition and the Americas*, vol. 1, part 1, *European Images of the Americas and the Classical Tradition*, ed. Wolfgang Haase and Meyer Reinhold (New York: de Gruyter, 1994), 241–84, esp. 242–57. See also the excellent studies of Alfred Hiatt, *Terra Incognita: Mapping the Antipodes before 1600* (Chicago: University of Chicago Press, 2008); and Matthew Boyd Goldie, *The Idea of the Antipodes: Place, People, and Voices* (New York: Routledge, 2010).

65. On the Antipodes in early and medieval Christianity, see Valerie I. J. Flint, "Monsters and the Antipodes in the Early Middle Ages and the Enlightenment," *Viator* 15 (1984): 65–80.

66. On the Nile, see also Pliny, *Nat.* 5.9.51. The puzzlement produced by the causes and effects of the Nile extend back into the text of Herodotus, who observed at 2.28 and 2.34 that the river's sources were altogether mysterious.

67. Mela, *Chor.* 3.70 (Silberman 87).

lands which, although postulated theoretically, cannot be met in practice."[68] Mela has created an immensely powerful yet powerfully unknowable tool of exposition. The imperial ambition of the Roman world was now defined by the struggle to constrain and comprehend the permeating counterworld.[69] The distinction between the known world and the unknown world had been unsettled, if not altogether obviated.

While Mela may tell us little about the actual geographical features of the ancient Roman world, his journey through the terrain of the known world illustrates the conjoined peril and opportunity of ethnographic discourse.[70] Like the hybrid peoples of inner Africa, the world as a mass of particularities and complexity defies tidy classification. Evans lucidly summarizes the matter:[71]

> For the Roman geographer, there is a tension between the attempts to close down, secure, and contain the world in text, and the intrusion of the so-called 'outlandish'— the world outside those limits is always creeping in. This text emphasizes the disorientation of the Roman onlooker faced with the zones of the world which remain unseen, unmapped, and, more unnervingly, unmappable.... What Mela's world shows is a fear of boundaries dissolving, structures slipping and the Other World seeping into Our World.

As much as the discovery of previously unknown peoples and places bolstered Roman notions of cultural and military triumph, it indicated the conceptual problem of a world of seemingly unknowable in scope, detail, and design. Ideological desires became conceptual impossibilities, and conceptual impossibilities accentuated practical possibilities, transforming the supposed power of ethnography into a self-deceiving trap of fascination. The ethnographic orientation was defined not exclusively by its capacity to interpret and control, but by an equally profound disquietude about the capacity of authors to identify and demarcate fully the peoples and terrain of the natural world, peoples and places that had been constructed. The *Chorography* displays Mela's inability to control the unpredictability of ethnographic investigation and knowledge acquisition.[72]

---

68. Moretti, "The Other World and the 'Antipodes,'" 245.

69. See ibid. 258.

70. Much of the work on Mela has focused on his imprecision, omissions, and interest in the oddities of the world. See Georg Wissowa, "Die Abfassungszeit der Chorographia des Pomponius Mela," *Hermes* 51 (1916): 89–96; and F. R. D. Goodyear, "Technical Writing," in *The Cambridge History of Classical Literature*, vol. 2, ed. E. J. Kenney and W. V. Clausen (Cambridge: Cambridge University Press, 1982), 667–73.

71. Evans, "Ethnography's Freak Show," 69.

72. See also Sorcha Carey's "The Problem of Totality," *Journal of the History of Collections* 12.1 (2000): 1–13. Much like the heresiologists who feared the effects of exhaustive exposure of the heretics, Pliny, too, as a compiler and cataloguer of the natural world, feared the results of plenary inclusion. Pliny's timidity stems from the fact that encyclopedic narratives necessarily include both the best and worst of the world. For Pliny, the requirement to include knowledge of *luxuria*, the great "perversion of reason (*ratio*) and

Sorcha Carey's incisive work on Pliny's *Natural History* identifies a parallel (and antecedent) effort to catalogue the impossible. In *Pliny's Catalogue of Culture*, she contends that Pliny's battle to control the infinite functions to secure his claims of totality.[73] Writing of the incalculable number of sculptures in Rhodes, Olympia, Delphi, and Athens, Pliny asks: "What mortal could recount them all, or what value can be felt in such information? Still it may give pleasure just to allude to the most remarkable and to name the artists of celebrity, though it would be impossible to enumerate the total number of works of each inasmuch as Lysippus is said to have executed 1500 works of art."[74] The impossibility of the task elevates Pliny's performance. In other words, his struggles evince his exceptional genius: "He can do the impossible—count the uncountable and more besides."[75] As Carey further notes, the evidence of omission within the *Natural History* reflects Pliny's judicious editorial hand, and it insulates him from the charge of failure. The very need to edit establishes his credibility as an omniscient narrator:[76]

> If elsewhere his aim to describe the entire world necessitated omitting certain things, then here too, Pliny impresses us with his skill at juggling irreconcilable opposites. The material for discussion is endless, and yet Pliny is still able to dazzle us with an array of facts and figures—the thousands of statues in a range of Greek cities; the hundreds of statues made by Lysippus alone. A consummate master of his material, equally at home with infinity and totality, Pliny artfully presents his omissions as an expression of authorial concern for both his reader's pleasure and the quality of the knowledge he includes in his work.

A diverse world holds the potential to be decoded and fathomed. Textual and geographical exploration proves an invaluable means by which authors secure their intellectual reputations. But more than that, those who sought to understand the full harmony of the natural world aspired to complete knowledge: "Indeed the power and majesty of the nature of the universe at every turn lacks credence if one's mind embraces parts of it only and not the whole."[77] As Pliny notes, the study

---

Nature," disrupts his stabilized taxonomy of civilization (Carey, *Pliny's Catalogue of Culture*, 76). "The problem of totality" is that it is both a manifestly fraudulent aspiration and a deeply destructive one. These two poles of classification, as I have argued, are conceptually interdependent facets of ethnographic discourse.

73. Carey, *Pliny's Catalogue of Culture*, 22. On collection in Pliny see also Aude Doody, *Pliny's Encyclopedia: The Reception of the "Natural History"* (Cambridge: Cambridge University Press, 2010), 1–39; and Murphy, *Pliny the Elder's "Natural History,"* 105–8.

74. Pliny, *Nat.* 34.17.36-37, trans. H. Rackham, LCL 394 (Cambridge, Mass.: Harvard University Press, 1952), 154.

75. Carey, *Pliny's Catalogue of Culture*, 21.

76. Ibid. 22.

77. Pliny, *Nat.* 7.1.7 (LCL 352:510–11). On collection and the hybridization of knowledge, see the very useful discussion of Andrew S. Jacobs, "Epiphanius of Salamis and the Antiquarian's Bible," *JECS* 21.3 (2013): 437–64.

of the world requires not only maximal knowledge but the compilation of discrete categories. As an ethnographer, geographer, encyclopedist, and historian, Pliny arranges this knowledge to construct a coherent and complex portrait of the natural world.[78] And yet even as he champions the scope of his text, Pliny affirms the limitations of his ethnographic expertise: "About the human race as a whole we have in large part spoken in our account of the various nations. Nor shall we now deal with the manners and customs, which are beyond counting and almost as numerous as the groups of mankind."[79]

Writing of Roman *humanitas* ("humanity," or "state of civilization"), Paul Veyne argued that the Romans well knew that they were not the lone civilized peoples within the vast reaches of the world. Civilization was, in his formulation, a question of discovery, not invention; one found its qualities among foreigners and within nature itself.[80] Thus, despite the fact that Romans repeatedly claimed "that they held sway over the entire the world" and that they had incorporated the domain of the Greeks into their own empire (since "the Greeks had long been telling them that the whole inhabited earth had fallen under their domination"), their totalized vision was admittedly fragmentary.[81] They had dominated only "the known world" (the οἰκουμένη), which was defined in strictly favorable terms. Rome, and Greece before her, had struggled to map the world through an ethnocentric paradigm that narrowed it to comport with tendentious interests and military conquests. At certain textual moments, as we see with Pomponius Mela, the scope of ethnographic knowledge suddenly broadened beyond the borders of the known world.

THE ETHNOGRAPHIC BIND OF HERESIOLOGY

As we saw in the previous chapter, ethnography reflects as it negotiates the dangers of an ideology of unyielding curiosity with the unknown, the secret, and the grotesque. For Christian authors, the heretics were the peoples that most persistently ensnared their ethnographic gaze. The heresies challenged the pastoral expertise of the heresiologists and compelled explanations and refutations of their appearance, diversity, and proliferation.[82] As Epiphanius, paraphrasing Irenaeus before

---

78. See Gian Biagio Conte, "The Inventory of the World: Form of Nature and Encyclopedic Project in the Work of Pliny the Elder," in his *Genres and Readers: Lucretius, Love Elegy, Pliny's Encyclopedia*, trans. Glenn W. Most (Baltimore: The Johns Hopkins University Press, 1994), 67–104.

79. Pliny, *Nat.* 7.1.6 (LCL 352:510–11).

80. Veyne, "*Humanitas*: Romans and Non-Romans," 344.

81. Ibid. 345. See also P. A. Brunt, "Laus Imperii," in *Imperialism in the Ancient World: The Cambridge University Research Seminar in Ancient History*, ed. P. D. A. Garnsey and C. R. Whittaker (Cambridge: Cambridge University Press, 2007), 159–92, esp. 168–72.

82. On the responsibility of the bishop to protect his congregation from the threat of heresy, see Caroline Humfress, *Orthodoxy and the Courts in Late Antiquity* (New York: Oxford University Press, 2007), 228–38.

him, declares: "It is difficult to discover or state all [the doctrines] of the people who are being spawned and sprouting up among them even to this day, and every day find something new to say and delude their converts."[83] And although I have outlined the epistemological gymnastics underlying Mela's drive to explore and explain—the inability, conceptually speaking, to stabilize the world—I have only casually gestured at the parallel concerns within heresiology's conceptual framework. I wish now to delineate specifically how the textual apprehensions of heresiology mirror Mela's own quandaries of ethnographic fascination. In comparing the works of Mela and Epiphanius, I am trying to draw attention to how ancient ethnographic texts articulate the constraints of writing and knowing peoples. The point of this comparison is not to suggest literary dependence. Rather, it is to take note of how Christian heresiology poses many of the same ethnographic paradoxes as Mela's text and translates them into distinctly Christian terms. Although the ethnographic structure of the *Panarion* was clearly grounded in scripture, a tension between the form and the content of the text remained. The desire for an expansive and all-encompassing knowledge undermined the simplicity of scripture's ethnographic categorizations. The heretics destabilized orthodoxy both by means of their particular doctrines and customs and by their very existence: heresy's simultaneous specificity and generality thwarted Epiphanius's—and all the heresiologists'—intellectual dexterity.

When in his concluding paean to the holy catholic church Epiphanius revisits his text's organizational paradigm—an allegorical reading of Song of Songs—he offers a detailed account of its broader ethnographic implications.[84] His attempt to inventory the sectarian realm assumes scripture's infallibility as an organizational principle. And though Epiphanius prizes his investigative skills and techniques, his *Panarion* delimits heresy not by phenomenological or observational data but by textual fiat. Reiterating, first, his textual precedent, he then considers its broader ramifications for his ethnography:[85]

> "There are threescore queens, and fourscore concubines, and maidens without number, but one is *my dove, my* perfect one" [Song 6.8]–with the addition of "my" and "my." For she is *his* "dove" and *his* "perfect one," since the others are said to be and are not, while she herself is named twice. He did not say, "They are *my* eighty concubines," of the others. He awarded the queens their honorable connection with him through the glorious name; but of the concubines he declared their complete foreignness. When I note their numbers I am obliged to investigate the passage by the

---

83. Epiphanius, *Pan.* 36.4.2 (GCS 31:47); Epiphanius is paraphrasing the observations of Irenaeus, *Adv. haer.* 1.21.5.

84. Epiphanius, *De fide* 6.1–13.7 (GCS 37:501–14). The majority of *De fide*, in fact, is devoted to enumerating the additional sects of the world.

85. Epiphanius, *De fide* 3.2–5 (GCS 37:498–99).

anagogical method of spiritual interpretation, so as not to pass them by. . . . For [it is plain] that the number written of each thing in scripture is unalterable, and that nothing which is assigned a number can be without value or reduced in number in the scripture for no good reason.

As a textual restraint upon the ethnographic gaze, scripture's power of foreclosure attested heresiology's new fixation: numbering the heretics. In contrast to the early heresiological treatises of Hippolytus and Irenaeus, which contemplated the philosophical, numerological, and astrological borrowings of the heretics in fairly haphazard structural narratives, later iterations of the genre were systematic and precisely enumerated catalogues of heretical parties.[86] Heresiology was no longer a matter of qualitative identification alone; it had become a repository of quantification. Epiphanius, in fact, by enumerating eighty heresies—by using a specific biblical prooftext—consciously expanded the Christian world. And the very fact that heresiology now fastidiously tallied heresies not only confirms the widened topography of the Christian world but also points toward the genre's more rigid or formal organization. While the scriptural precedent from Song of Songs increased the number of the heretics, it also provided a strict limiting principle. But as Epiphanius would discover, the verse upon which be built his text expressly indicated the infinitude of the heretics. In that sense, scripture both produced and precluded the very idea of heresiological completion and closure.

Epiphanius ventured into the world of the youths (heretics) not only to magnify the grandiloquence of the truth housed within the church but, more telling, to confirm the verisimilitude of Song of Songs 6.8. But the eighty concubines that the *Panarion* names and refutes compose only a small portion of the total volume of known heresies. In an acknowledgment of his text's necessary limits, Epiphanius wonders, just as Pliny had, "Who can count the variety of this world?"[87] There are, in fact, "young girls without number," an expression that denotes "the further philosophies all over the world."[88] Forty-four Greek philosophies are added to the *Panarion*'s tally,[89] along with the seventy-two "repulsive philosophies of the Indian

---

86. While the earlier stages of heresiology, as represented by the works of Hippolytus and Irenaeus, are less systematic and philosophical, the later texts from Augustine, Epiphanius, Filastrius, Theodoret, and Isidore are highly structured, ordered, and enumerated. On the evolution of heresiology, see Brent D. Shaw, "Who Were the Circumcellions," in *Vandals, Romans and Berbers: New Perspectives on Late Antique North Africa*, ed. A. H. Merrills (Burlington, Vt.: Ashgate, 2004), 227–58; J. Rebecca Lyman, "Epiphanius on Orthodoxy," in *Orthodoxy, Christianity, History*, ed. Susanna Elm, Éric Rebillard, and Antonella Romano (Rome: École Française de Rome, 2000), 149–61; and Aline Pourkier, *L'hérésiologie chez Épiphane de Salamine* (Paris: Beauchesne, 1992), 19–75.

87. Epiphanius, *De fide* 9.2 (GCS 37:504).

88. Epiphanius, *De fide* 9.1 (GCS 37:504).

89. Thales of Miletus, Anaximander of Miletus, Anaximenes of Miletus, Anaxagoras of Clazomenae, Archelaus the naturalist, Socrates the ethicist, Pherecydes, Pythagoras of Samos, Xenophanes

nation" (only the gymnosophists, Brahmans, pseudo-Brahmans, corpse eaters, practitioners of obscenity, "and those who are past feeling" are named).[90] Media and Ethiopia are each reputed to have six distinct sects. Epiphanius further reports that in Parthia, Elamitis, Caspia, Germany, and Sarmatia, and among the Persians, Dauni, Zickchi, Amazons, Lazi, Iberians, Bosporenes, Geli, and Chinese, "there are any number of different laws, philosophies and sects and a countless throng of varieties."[91] Outlining his knowledge of the plenitude of cultic mysteries and rites among the Greeks, Egyptians, Persians, Babylonians, and Indians, he pays them inconsistent attention, resigning himself to the opinion that "these people are hopelessly lost."[92] Epiphanius's ethnographic pursuits attest his skills as an ethnographic compiler and, in turn, emphasize his textual achievement. His myriad additions to the heretical pantheon illustrate his active engagement with and knowledge of the world beyond the eighty; they accentuate his relentless push to assimilate and reveal as much knowledge as he can acquire.

In the second century, Irenaeus had already signaled the practical limits of heresiology. He writes of his *Adversus haereses:* "In the present book, we shall build up [our own system] as far as we are able and as time will permit, and we shall overthrow their entire system by main principles."[93] Here Irenaeus suggests that time and ability are the limiting factors of his treatise. The heresiologists further emphasized that many of the lacunae in their text were deliberate efforts to restrict the flow of problematic information. Hippolytus, in his discussion of the Gnostics, explained his decision to omit information about the Gnostics as a matter of intentional excision. It was not his ability that limited his knowledge but rather a sense of protective duty: "There are, however, among the Gnostics diversities of opinion; but we have decided that it would not be worthwhile to enumerate the silly doctrines of these

---

from Colophon, Parmenides the Elean, Zeno of Elea, Melissus the Samian, Leucippus the Milesian, Democritus of Abdera, Metrodorus of Chios, Protagoras of Abdera, Diogenes of Smyrna, Pyrrho of Elis, Empedocles of Agrigentum, Heraclitus of Ephesus, Prodicus, Plato the Athenian, Aristippus of Cyrene, Theodorus the atheist, Hegesias of Cyrene, Antisthenes the Athenian, Diogenes the Cynic, Crates of Boeotian Thebes, Arcesilaus, Carneades, Aristotle the Macedonian (or Thracian), Theophrastus of Ephesus, Strato of Lampsacus, Praxiphanes of Rhodes, Critolaus of Phaselis, Zeno of Citium, Cleanthes, Persaeus, Chrysippus of Soli, Diogenes of Babylon, Panaetius of Rhodes, Posidonius of Apamea, Athenodorus of Tarsus, and Epicurus of Athens (*De fide* 9.5–48).

90. Epiphanius, *De fide* 10.2 (GCS 37:497).
91. Epiphanius, *De fide* 10.3 (GCS 37:497).
92. Epiphanius, *De fide* 11.2 (GCS 37:497). Embracing his role as armchair ethnographer, Epiphanius flaunts a few of the odder, more wondrous, customs that he knows. He reports, for instance, that "Chinese men stay at home and weave, and anoint themselves and do womanly things in readiness for their wives," while "the women cut their hair short, wear men's underclothing, and do all the field labor" (*De fide* 10.4 [GCS 37:497]). Like the Amazons of Herodotus's *Histories*, the Chinese women of *De fide* symbolize cultural difference through normative inversion.
93. Irenaeus, *Adv. haer.* 2 praef. (SC 294:24).

heresies, inasmuch as they are [too] numerous and devoid of reason, and full of blasphemy."[94] The sheer madness and total irrationality of the heretics compelled Hippolytus to wield his ethnographic knowledge steadily and selectively. As the ethnographer of heresy, Hippolytus served as the theological filter for his readers, and this gave him the prerogative to edit.

Epiphanius himself used the discourse of omission to demonstrate further his role as shepherd of his readers. As he builds a wide-ranging knowledge of heresy through literary augmentations, he explains his excisions as a necessary result of limited time and space. When he revisits the philosophical and theological topography of the Christian world in *De fide*, he concedes the impossibility of a comprehensive investigation. He cites in support Hebrews 11.32: "And 'what shall I say? For the time will fail me if I tell' of the countless differences in people's various practices, as well as in their virtue and in their vice."[95] Although Epiphanius openly confessed to the insufficiency of the scope of his text, he crafted this concession around a fundamental distinction between the practical and conceptual constraints of his text. He recast the limitations of his heresiological venture as a justifiable redaction of the facts. But the excision of data reflected, he claimed, a conscious choice, not an underlying failure of intellectual capacity: "But again, I omit the names of many other mysteries, heresiarchs and fomenters of schism whose leaders are called Magusaeans by the Persians but prophets by the Egyptians, and who preside over their shrines and temples."[96] The *Panarion*, despite its omissions, was not a product of ignorance but one of remarkable judgment and restraint. Its precise delineation communicated Epiphanius's firm grasp of a heretical domain, whose expansion and evolution his work not only captured but in fact created. The scope of his heresiological investigation, he implies, does not suffer from a lack of knowledge; instead, it is the fear of incompletion that curbs its grandeur.

While one could read—and, indeed, the heresiologists *did* read—excisions as evidence of comprehensiveness, the menace of the heresies derived from the fact that they ruptured the very notion of boundaries within the known world. The profound ethnographic paradox of heresy was that, on account of its geographical diffusion, it brought the unknown into the known world. Strategic ignorance could theoretically contain the counterworld of Mela, although he himself was unable to avoid going there.[97] For Epiphanius, however, there was no escaping heresy's transcendence of geographical difference. Any one heresy might exist in only

---

94. Hippolytus, *Ref.* 7.26.2 (Marcovich 319). On omission in Epiphanius see *Pan.* 8.7.4; 26.9.1; 27.4.5; 32.3.1.

95. Epiphanius, *De fide* 11.1 (GCS 37:511).

96. Epiphanius, *De fide* 12.5 (GCS 37:497).

97. On the anthropological significance of being there among one's ethnographic objects, see Geertz, *Works and Lives*, 1–24.

one region or territory, but heresy, as a theological and ethnographic category, existed everywhere.[98] The rhetorical universalism of heresiology, epitomized in the famous remark from Book 1, chapter 10, of Irenaeus's *Adversus haereses*, depicted a world without theological borders.[99] Epiphanius laments, in fact, how the very mixture of catholic and heretical opinion disturbs not only theological clarity but also ecclesiastical judgment:[100]

> But others, whose origins are orthodox, seem to behave like "youths" and venture to gather their own congregation contrary to the canons. Moreover, they rebaptize the people who come to them from the Arians . . . without the judgment of an ecumenical council. For because the Arian and the catholic laity are still intermingled, and many are orthodox but are joined with the Arianizers from hypocrisy, the matter, as I said, has not yet been settled by a judgment—not until there can be a separation of the blasphemous sect, and then its sentence will be determined.

The eradication of theological borders created the conceptual conditions by which heretical intransigence transformed the singular world of knowable Christian orthodoxy into a profusion of unknowable and scattered heretical opinion. The ethnographic logic of the *Panarion* perpetuated the dangers of Christian universalism.[101] Epiphanius had sought to peel away temporal structures such as language and replaced them with the symbolic language of a unified church.

For the heresiologists, the ethnographic dilemma was not just a fear of the unknown in the periphery but also a fear of the disruptive proximity of unknowable sectarianism. The endlessly unknowable had taken up residence within the very confines of the voluminous οἰκουμένη. The territorial and theological fluidity of the heretics unraveled the fixity of the known and unknown worlds' distinct boundaries. Because heresy is *terra incognita* brought into the known world—because it is not defined, strictly speaking, by territorial boundaries—its danger was all the more acute. Whereas classical ethnographers could take occasional comfort in the fact that the unknown peoples of the world lived at the geographical fringes, heresy disrupted this idea altogether. Unknown heresies lived among orthodox Christians! The theological fringes resided not at the ends of the earth but rather in the very heart of Christian world. A law from June of 389 C.E. against

---

98. The Jews represent a similar problem insofar as they have spread themselves out across the empire, but there was no sense that the Jews were reproducing sectarian parties at a profoundly disturbing rate. A relevant parallel can be found in René S. Bloch, "Geography without Territory: Tacitus' Digression on the Jews and Its Ethnographic Context," in *Internationales Josephus-Kolloquium, Aarhus 1999*, ed. Jürgen U. Kalms (Münster: Lit, 2000), 38–54; and Rhiannon Evans, "Geography without People: Mapping in Pliny's *Historia Naturalis* Books 3–6," *Ramus* 34.1 (2005): 47–74.

99. Irenaeus, *Adv. haer.* 1.10.2.
100. Epiphanius, *De fide* 13.6–7 (GCS 37:514).
101. Epiphanius, *De fide* 2.6, 3.1, 6.1, 6.6, 6.8, 14.1–4, 21.1, 24.3, 25.1–2.

the Manichaeans, issued by Valentinian, Theodosius, and Arcadius (to Albinus, prefect of the city of Rome), attests the unsettling effects of heresy in the language of geographical unity: "If any person whatever should disturb the world (*mundus*) under the name of Manichaeans, they shall indeed be expelled from the whole world (*orbis terrarum*) but especially from this city [Rome], under threat of judgment."[102] While the law participated in a certain rhetorical extremism, the legal-theological point was to counter the existential tumult of the heretics with an equally forceful punishment. The heretics had exposed the regressive potency of ethnographic and geographic inquiry: the world that had once been known was now teeming with the unknown and unknowable. The multiplying infinitude of the heretics ensured that the desire for a totalized οἰκουμένη was always indefinite and forever unobtainable. The realities of delimited theological and ethnographic control subverted the language of Christian transcendence and universality. If the church was to act as the guarantor of a proper theological identity—just as Rome had conceived itself as the new protector of civilized values, succeeding Greece— comprehensive knowledge (and thus total control) of its domain was the sine qua non of the heresiologists' argument for orthodoxy.[103]

The world of heresy out there, reported and imagined in texts, held seemingly limitless types of peoples of places. Epiphanius's scriptural prooftext, Song of Songs 6.8, instead of strengthening his text's force of closure, broke the totalizing framework completely. The verse, as Epiphanius observes, in fact proclaimed the infinitude of heresy:[104]

> For how many other sects have not also arisen among the Greeks after the four most famous ones that we have mentioned—and further, after those sects and the ones after them, how many individuals and ideas keep arising of themselves, with seeming youth, in accordance with the opinion of each? There are some called Pyrrhonians, for example, and many others. Since I have learned of many I shall give their names and their opinions in order below, but [this] is a fraction of the ones in the world.

In upending the heresiologist's measures of control—via diligent research, divine intervention, and rhetorical bombast—scripture codified the insurmountable

---

102. *CTh* 16.5.18 (*Theodosiani libri XVI cum Constitutionibus Sirmondianis et leges novellae ad Theodosianum pertinentes*, ed. Theodor Mommsen and Paul Martin Meyer, vol. 1, part 2 [Berlin: Weidmann, 1905], 861–62. Translation from Clyde Pharr, *The Theodosian Code and Novels and the Sirmondian Constitutions* [Union, N.J.: Lawbook Exchange, 2001], 453–54).

103. Dench, *Romulus' Asylum*, 50–52.

104. Epiphanius, *De fide* 9.2–3 (GCS 37:504): πόσαι γὰρ ἄλλαι παρ᾽ Ἕλλησι μετὰ τὰς προειρημένας τέτταρας φανερωτάτας οὐκ ἔφυσαν καὶ ἔτι μετὰ τὰς αἱρέσεις ἐκείνας καὶ τὰς μετέπειτα κατὰ τὴν ἑκάστου γνώμην ἐν δοκήσει νεανιότητος καθ᾽ ἑαυτὰς γινόμεναι ψυχαί τε καὶ γνῶμαι. ὡς Πυρρώνειοι καλοῦνταί τινες καὶ ἄλλοι πλείους, ὧν τὰ ὀνόματα καὶ τὰς δόξας καθ᾽ εἱρμὸν ὑποτάξω, πολλῶν μὲν ὄντων τῶν εἰς γνῶσιν ἡμῶν ἐληλυθότων, πολλοστημόριον δὲ [τοῦτο] τῶν ἐν κόσμῳ ὑπαρχόντων. To convey the sense that οὐκ, here, is pleonastic, I have altered Williams's translation to "not also."

propagation of heresy. Epiphanius's attempt to enclose the heretics in a precise and bounded system of ethnographic classification exposed the breaches within the conceptual fabric of the endeavor itself. The heretics turned the so-called authority of Christian orthodox writers, garnered through compositional due diligence, against them. If heresiology was to be measured by its comprehensiveness, it foundered before it had even begun. The danger of exploring the world of heresy was that the very impossibility of the task undercut the veracity and depth of all catholic knowledge about the world. As one of Epiphanius's sources in the *Panarion* phrased it: "It is therefore to be feared that if we attempt to speak of what we cannot, we may no longer be permitted to speak of what we can."[105]

The discursive effort to obtain textual comprehension over against the heretics evinced a highly unstable and indefinite grip on the depths of a rapidly evolving, expansive Christian milieu. As a phenomenological category with seemingly endless variations, the adaptability of heresy stymied production of Christian ethnography.[106] Epiphanius himself labored to comprehend the infinitude of the heretical parties. And by recasting the problem in terms of the unified orthodoxy versus a diversified heretical plurality of heresy, he sought to diminish the need for a complete textual catalogue. It is the contrast alone that sufficiently demonstrates his point. He writes:[107]

> And so, as I have said, the sects I have listed in succession are eighty concubines. But no one need be surprised if each of them has been called by different names in every country (ἄλλοις ὀνόμασιν ἑκάστη τούτων κικλήσκεται ἐν ἑκάστῃ χώρᾳ). What is more, we must observe that each sect in turn has frequently divided into many parts on its own and taken different names. This is no surprise; it is the way things are. But I find eighty-one in all—one more than eighty because of the one who is different from them all, but is the only one allotted to the bridegroom whom he has acknowledge by such a name as "one is my dove," and again, "my perfect one." In other words all the concubines are low-born and not reckoned as harmless, or pure and gentle.

Epiphanius addresses here the essential abnormality of the heretics, which differentiates them from virtually every other known ethnographic or geographic object. The heretics presented a double challenge to their orthodox opponents: not only did they articulate alternative modes of being Christian—with distinct rituals, texts, interpretive strategies, cosmologies, and histories—but they also endlessly adapted their doctrines and habits. In contrast to the Roman and Greek ethnographers who had struggled to describe a world beyond total comprehension, the

---

105. Epiphanius, *Pan.* 73.32.4 (GCS 37:307), where he quotes a sermon by Melitius, bishop of Antioch, delivered in 360 C.E.
106. Epiphanius, *De fide* 9.2 (GCS 37:504).
107. Epiphanius, *De fide* 6.4–6 (GCS 37:502).

heresiologists labored to define a sprawling miasma of theological variation that was mutating before their very eyes. There was no conceptual way to exclude an infinitely vast and forever evolving counterworld of heresy. Despite the fact that his list of named "youths without number" *proved* scripture's veracity as the determinant of the natural order of things, it undermined the heresiological strategies for containing heresy. Even though the path of heresy was shown to follow the letter of scripture, that proof was an altogether irreconcilable discovery.

The desire of the heresiologists to expose the heretics—in the face of massive proliferation of the heretics—governed these textual efforts. But beneath the veneer of textual domination was the paradox of ethnographic obsession. Writing of Roman fixations and fascinations, the historian Carlin Barton has identified the destructive hold of what simultaneously allures and repels.[108] In orienting her remarks around the spectacle of the monstrous, Barton emphasizes the fundamental disjuncture between fascination and regulation:[109]

> It was a great temptation to be fascinated. It was hard to resist, impossible to defeat, because it was born of longing and frustration and loss. The unsightly, the unspeakable—the *obscaenus, deformis,* the *turpis, teater, foedus, immundus*—were things which confounded one. They should be hidden; their sightings should be expiated. At the same time they were *monstra* (like *monstro,* "to indicate, show," from *moneo,* "to warn"), things which spoke a mysterious language calling for decipherment. They carried a message, however unclear. The ambiguous, the paradoxical, the puzzling, the obscure and difficult to categorize—in short, the monster—was the great and fatal temptation. As Plutarch's Mestrius Florus points out in the *Quaestiones conviviales,* "the man who demands to see the logic of each and every thing destroys the wonder in all things." . . . Fascination, he realizes, is not compatible with "the logic of things." . . . To subject something which is uncommon, anomalous, monstrous, to a *sensus communis,* to subject it to a physics, to "naturalize" the "unnatural," to give the absurd a species—in short, to interpret—is to wrest control of, to break the spell and fascination of, the monsters.

---

108. Carlin A. Barton, *The Sorrows of the Ancient Romans,* 86–106.

109. Ibid. 101–2. Consider *Pan.* 27.4.5–7 (concerning the Carpocratians), which quite nicely illustrates the rhetorical bind of Barton's argument and the disruptive force of monstrosity that pervades heresiology: "Again, I am afraid to say what sorts of actions, or I might uncover a trench like a hidden sewer, and some might think that I am causing the blast of foul odor. Still, since I am constrained by the truth to disclose what goes on among the deluded, I am going to make myself speak—with some delicacy and yet without overstepping the bounds of the truth. The plain fact is that these people perform every unspeakable, unlawful thing, which is not right even to say, and every kind of homosexual union and carnal intercourse with women, with every member of the body—and that they perform magic, sorcery and idolatry and say that this is the discharge of their obligations in the body, so that they will not be charged any more or required to do anything else, and for this reason the soul will not be turned back after its departure and go on to another incarnation and transmigration."

The cycle of discovery and decipherment was on the one hand the ceaseless power of ethnographic inquiry and on the other its very ruin. While the acquisition of new knowledge of heresy across the world served heresiological interests, it also held the potential to create new lacunae within the very same textual edifice. The customs and habits of the heretics not only disoriented the supposed norms of orthodox Christianity; they also enveloped the entire history of the church in a cloud of epistemological uncertainty, fear, and impossibility.[110]

As much as discovery begets knowledge, and knowledge buttressed existing models of human diversity (and/or engendered new ethnographic models), there came a recognition point at which the accrued information became too abundant, diverse, and fantastical for the authorial intellect and textual field to hold firm. Attempting to organize the infinitude of the heresies rendered Christian ethnography a monumental, if always partial, effort. By proving the firm grip of scriptural precepts, Epiphanius endorses a model of heresy that is uncontrollably vast and beyond the reach of comprehension, as its own conclusions demonstrate. The weight of heresiological microcosm, its limitless potential, was simply too heavy for any model to bear. "Data . . . seem[ed] to overflow the conceptual frameworks available for classifying" the heretics.[111] Epiphanius's system, designed to hold knowledge of the heretics, collapsed under its own weight. As James Clifford has observed, ethnographers' "obsessive inclusion of data . . . may be seen as a desire to unmake as well as to make whole."[112] The aspiration to map people and their culture through sheer force of data actually created a portrait of incoherence: an abundance of ethnographic data simply overwhelms any sense of cultural coherence. Epiphanius's accumulation of data about the heretics textualized the very same tension between aggregation and intelligibility. The desire to find the core of heresy—the desire "to make whole"—was inhibited by the variety and scope of the evidence he presents.[113]

Epiphanius's reading of Song of Songs, while purporting to contain the world of heresy, infinitely multiplied its dominion. And it was not merely the case that some heresies remained unknown, obscure, or altogether unknowable; certain heresies had yet to come into existence. The history of heresy had not run its course, and its continual metamorphoses eluded textual efforts to comprehend

---

110. This is especially clear in Augustine's *Haer.* epil. 1.1–17; 2.24–27.

111. I have obviously recontextualized the remarks of Christopher Herbert, *Culture and Anomie: The Ethnographic Imagination in the Nineteenth Century* (Chicago: University of Chicago Press, 1991), 242. I have taken Herbert's discussion of the work of Henry Mayhew (1812–87) and analogized it to the *Panarion* of Epiphanius.

112. Clifford, "On Ethnographic Self-Fashioning," 104.

113. On the problem of ethnography, data, and theorization, see Herbert, *Culture and Anomie*, 191–203; and Margaret T. Hodgen, *Early Anthropology in the Sixteenth and Seventeenth Centuries* (Philadelphia: University of Pennsylvania Press, 1964), 207–51.

it.[114] Writing of his own ambivalence as the author of an unsettling yet necessary treatise, Epiphanius contemplates the constraints upon his performance:[115]

> In any case may I, and all the entirety of the holy catholic church, and all the readers of this book, remain unharmed by such a suggestion of the devil and his mischief! For if I were to start [in] again on the other things they say and do—which are like these and as numerous, and still more grave and worse—and if, for a curative drug, I should also wish to match a remedy, like an antidote, with each thing they say, I would make a heavy task of composing this treatise.

Even if he had more time—or the wherewithal to begin anew—the epistemological and conceptual fissures remain firmly embedded within the genre itself. Precisely because there is no escaping, as it were, the endless iterations of heretical generation, the genre represents a failure of ambition and imagination. Its inabilities were its essence. When Epiphanius tries to defend his text's unbridled potential for exhaustive comprehension, he only underscores the scriptural strictures undergirding its production:[116]

> But if I were to describe the woman ecstatics in Memphis and Heliopolis, who bewitch themselves with drums and flutes, and the dancing girls, and the performers at the triennial festival—and the women at Bathys and in the temple of Menuthis who have abandoned shame and womanliness—to what burdens for the tongue, or what a long composition I could commit myself, by adding their countless number itself to the number I have already given! For even though I were to take on the enormous task I would leave our comprehension of these things incomplete, since scripture says that there are "young women without number."

While there is, in the end, no circumventing the investigative and classificatory parameters set down by scripture, the infinitude of the heretics attests the overarching textual paradox of ethnographic inquiry. In the extreme case that is heresy, ethnographic objectification evolves into a vicious cycle of futile pursuit. Heresy's malleability upsets the hyperstructured aim of ethnographic analysis. The diversity of the world does not yield to intellectual regulation born of careful research and investigation. Instead, it is illustrative of the inherent epistemological restraints on the human ability to theorize the world.[117]

Despite the fact that exhaustive discovery is finally revealed to be an ethnographic mirage, Epiphanius concludes his epilogue with a reminder that these

---

114. Augustine, *Haer. epil.* 2.55–57.
115. Epiphanius, *Pan.* 26.17.1–3 (GCS, n. F., 10:297).
116. Song 6.8; Epiphanius, *De fide* 12.1–2 (GCS 37:511–12).
117. See *Pan.* 80.3–4, where Epiphanius laments his human efforts to refute the heretics. Though God's will infuses his quest against heresy, he lacks sufficient knowledge of the heretics because he is not divine. Knowledge of and in the world stands apart from the knowledge of the divine, insofar as the former is subject to human comprehension, discovery, and theorization, whereas the latter is not.

sects, though innumerable, are still youths. That is, they are bound by a certain shared disposition and theological orientation that renders them more alike than they would seem:[118]

> And so, at the close of the entire work, I have said that those who are "young" in their own way, to suit their own tastes, are "without number"—by no means for good, to practice the various forms of wisdom, judgment, courage, prudence and righteousness. Others of these act "young" more arbitrarily, and perversely make themselves [strangers] to the truth, so that there is no number of them. But the one dove herself, the holy virgin, confesses that God is the Father, the Son and the Holy Spirit, a perfect Father, a perfect Son, and a perfect Holy Spirit.

While Epiphanius expects heretical plurality, difference, and mutation, the binary between the plurality of heresy and the singularity of orthodoxy obviates the need for textual perfection.

The heretics, he implies, can be refuted with reference to the condition that they represent as the embodied contradistinction of the ever-stable church of Christ. Their impurity conditions their immateriality. If, as Epiphanius proposed, heresy follows a particular genealogy of error that begins with Serug and Terah, the infinite numbers of heretics are simply additional symptoms of an already diagnosed disease.[119] The rhetorical escape hatch—the way around the problem of ethnographic peril—is to remind readers that heresies are a unity of diversity. As Tertullian proudly proclaims in his *Rule against the Heretics*: "Their very unity is schism" (*scisma est enim unitas ipsa*).[120] Their outward difference was superficial, while inwardly they were the same. They were all manifestations of the same hubristic condition.

CONCLUSION: KNOWABILITY IN HERESIOLOGY

Near the start of the second proem of his *Panarion*—before he unfurls his epic tale of the history of sectarianism—Epiphanius invokes the Lord and Holy Spirit, in a gesture explicitly reminiscent of a Greek author's invocation of the Muse, to strengthen his inadequate and feeble mind as he undertakes a systematic treatment of the heretics.[121] In making his plea to the Christian God, Epiphanius posits an essential distinction between what is knowable and what is not. He writes about the limits of his investigation in terms of temporality and eternality, humanity and divinity, knowability and unknowability:[122]

---

118. Epiphanius, *De fide* 13.9 (GCS 37:514).
119. Epiphanius, *Pan.* 3.3.1–10.
120. Tertullian, *Praescr.* 42.6 (SC 46:149).
121. Epiphanius, *Pan.* pro. 2.1.3–5.
122. Epiphanius, *Pan.* pro. 2.2.1–3 (GCS, n. F., 10:170).

To a person reading a work on any question the aim [of the treatise] ought to be [clear]—the discoveries which training enables my small mind to grasp lie in the temporal realm, and I certainly do not proclaim knowledge of everything in the world (πάντων τῶν ἐν τῷ κόσμῳ). There are things which cannot be uttered, and things which can. There are things untold (ἀμύθητα), beyond counting (ἐν ἀριθμῷ μὴ καθιστάμενα), inaccessible so far as man is concerned, and known only to the Lord of all. But we are dealing with variance of opinions and kinds of knowledge, with [proclaimed] faith in God and unbelief, with sects, and with heretical human opinion which misguided persons have been sowing in the world from man's formation on earth till our own day.

The dichotomy Epiphanius posits is clear: knowable and utterable things (φατά) belong to the human mind and the temporal realm, while unknowable and unutterable things (ἄφατα) are the province of God alone. But the details of these epistemological categories are left unspecified, save for his insistence that the sectarianism belongs to the temporal realm. These are heretical human opinions, which have been sowed by misguided men. Although Epiphanius forthrightly acknowledges the limitations of his investigation—what we might call the known unknowns of divine matters—he is adamant that the heretics fall well within the category of knowability. Heresy is a product of the laws of the natural world *and* the operations of the supernatural order. As Tertullian remarks, heretical doctrines are "the doctrines of humans *and* demons, birthed for ears by the ingenuity of worldly wisdom which the Lord calls foolishness, and he chose the foolish things of the world to confuse even philosophy itself."[123] Heresy, as a product of both the world of men and the world of God, problematizes Epiphanius's dichotomy. And as he himself acknowledges, the seemingly incalculable proliferation of the heretics undermines the coherence of his grander narrative. Epiphanius's insistence that those things that are beyond counting remain squarely outside the human realm of understanding undercuts the epistemological framework through which he navigates and combats the heretical plurality: the heretics are an elusive object of knowledge. That elusiveness, like the problem of Mela's counterworld, does not simply diminish the heresiologists' textual control over their world, but it renders the very effort an ethnographic impossibility.

Defined though it was by the words of scripture, Epiphanius's numerical ordering of the heretics emanated both from his exhaustive yet still incomplete knowledge of the world of heresy: "I mean that I have composed a description and refutation of [eighty] sects, and at the same time, as far as my human frailty permitted, revealed what goes on in each. For this is the end of my full account of the origins and causes of the eighty sects I have been told of, and whose number and names

---

123. Tertullian, *Praescr.* 7.1 (SC 46:96; my translation).

I know, and the formularies, proof-texts and positions of some of them."[124] Because heresiology was an attempt, above all else, to manage the unmanageable, its rigid codification produces a complex matrix of epistemological and textual limitations. A careful evaluation of the full rhetorical scope of the *Panarion* reveals less an unvarnished ideology of domination than a tenuous grasp of the burgeoning world of heresy. Heresiological ethnography is at once descriptive and aspirationally prescriptive. It is aspirational precisely because, as Edward Peters usefully observes, "the infinite variety of creation was a lesson to man—as were monsters—of the limitless and inexhaustible power of God."[125] And while Epiphanius was acutely aware of his "human frailty," his inability to understand the mysteries of creation raised a troubling possibility: "If the variety of the world . . . existed to demonstrate to man the power of his Creator, then failure to encounter that variety might be considered a failure in religious duty."[126] Epiphanius's limitations thus became indelible demonstrations of his inability to protect pious Christians across the Mediterranean from the full range of heretics in the world. Failure may not have been an option for Epiphanius, but it seems, ultimately, to have been his only option.

As the form and content of the genre attract the heresiologist's scrutiny, fault lines of ethnographic representation and imposition readily emerge and harden. Epiphanius does not simply register (or feign) his nervousness about the protracted exposition and, by implication, promotion of heretical doctrine. Rather, he advances a far more striking realization: his texts are as much illustrations of the chasms in Christian knowledge about the world as they are instantiations of it. The point is that Epiphanius expressly recognizes and reflects upon his ignorance and the limits of his text in decidedly ethnographic terms. The fact that Epiphanius uses the coda to his *Panarion* to contemplate his own limitations as an ethnographer attests the intractability of this textual and epistemological conundrum. And by evoking the fears and triumphs of the discovery and accumulation of knowledge, he situates his own discourse within that of the geographers and chorographers from across the centuries of Mediterranean history. And yet, by venturing to catalogue the heretical infinitude, Epiphanius succumbs to the very same error that marks Mela's foray into the world and the absurdity, as Barton noted, of Plutarch's interlocutor: How does one organize the infinite and unknown, what allures precisely because of its continually evolving—and thus elusive—nature?

---

124. Epiphanius, *Pan.* 80.10.1–2. (GCS 37:497).
125. Edward Peters, "The Desire to Know the Secrets of the World," *JHI* 62.4 (2001): 593–610, at 603.
126. Ibid. 604.

7

From Ethnography to List

Transcribing and Traversing Heresy

> However, although I had set off on the adventure with enthusiasm, it left me with a feeling of emptiness. I had wanted to reach the extreme limits of the savage; it might be thought that my wish had been granted, now that I found myself among these charming Indians whom no other white man had ever seen before and who might never be seen again. After an enchanting trip upriver, I had certainly found my savages. Alas! They were only too savage. Since their existence had only been revealed to me at the last moment, I was unable to devote to them the time that would have been essential to get to know them. . . . There they were, all ready to teach me their customs and beliefs, and I did not know their language. They were as close to me as a reflection in a mirror; I could touch them, but I could not understand them. I had been given, at one and the same time, my reward and my punishment.
>
> —CLAUDE LÉVI-STRAUSS

Augustine's *De haeresibus*,[1] like the *Recapitulations* of the *Panarion* (the epitome of the *Panarion* written later by pseudo-Epiphanius) before it, stands in marked contrast to the heresiological ethnographies of Hippolytus, Irenaeus, Tertullian, and Epiphanius.[2] There are no digressions, excursions, or detailed (polemical) descrip-

---

1. The epigraph to this chapter is cited from Claude Lévi-Strauss, *Tristes tropiques*, trans. John Weightman and Doreen Weightman (New York: Penguin, 2012), 332–33.

2. The general attitude of scholars towards *De haeresibus*, which I will discuss in some detail, is fairly lackluster. The text lacks, so its critics argue, any of Augustine's impressive intellectual talents; instead, it presents itself as a stark and unoriginal amalgamation of sources. By my reckoning there is not a single essay in the entire history of the journal *Augustinian Studies* devoted to *De haeresibus*. Even G. Bardy's classic essay on Augustine's sources, "Le 'De haeresibus' et ses sources," in *Miscellanea Agostiniana: Testi e Studi* . . . , ed. G. Morin and A. Casamassa, vol. 2 (Rome: Tipografia Poliglotta Vaticana, 1931), 397–416, assumes the text's recapitulative nature. For slightly less critical assessments, see Liguori G. Müller, *The De Haeresibus of Saint Augustine: Translation, with Introduction and Commentary* (Washington, D.C.: Catholic University of America Press, 1956); and Francesca Tasca, "'Ecce Panis Haereticorum': Diversità alimentari ed identità religiose nel 'De haeresibus' di Agostino," *Aug* 50.1 (2010): 233–53.

tions in Augustine's text. There are no lengthy forays into Gnostic sexual acts or lengthy citations from the hands of the heretics. His treatise neither discusses nor presents any of the heretics within a cultural model of the whole—there is no web of affinities elucidating the individual habits and doctrines of the heretics into parts of a larger structure. Augustine is explicit that in this, the first part of his imagined but uncompleted two-part work, he will not attempt a definition of the genus heresy. "In the second part there will be a discussion of what makes one a heretic," he writes, despite his earlier explanation that "what it is, then, that makes one a heretic, in my opinion, either cannot at all, or can only with difficulty, be grasped in a definition in accord with rules."[3] Augustine wonders if the diversity of the species precludes the very existence of a common genus. *De haeresibus* by necessity, then, "is about the heresies which arose against the teaching of Christ after his coming and ascension, insofar as we could get knowledge about them."[4] It attempts to identify the various heresies in an orderly and mundane manner, explaining them, more often than not, in terms of their names. Augustine's prose is restrained, flat, and largely devoid of polemic. There are no theories of heretical origins and devolution. There are just short, pithy entries on eighty-eight different heresies. Though Augustine eschews any sort of macroscopic ethnographic theorization, he does acknowledge his struggle to translate ethnographic information about the heretics into pertinent, accurate, and usable knowledge. In terms of its form, Augustine's *De haeresibus* renders the expansive heresiological genre into a succinct, ready-to-use handbook. It is, in formal terms, a theological list that works to essentialize heretical groups into discrete textual units. *De haeresibus* is an overt attempt to streamline ethnographic knowledge "so that," as Augustine hopes, "every heresy—both known and unknown (*et quae nota est et quae ignota*)—can be avoided and so that any that may become known can be correctly assessed."[5]

But even Augustine's efforts to reduce the heresies to less vexing problems by confining them to discrete textual units could not avoid the intractable and, indeed, inescapable dilemma of ethnographic representation and translation. The move from ethnography to list—the condensation of ethnographic knowledge—does not simplify the task of the heresiologist. Instead it magnifies the genre's conceptual plan to map the whole of the heretical world. The desired finitude of catalogues of the heretics entangles the heresiologists in the vicissitudes of a world

---

3. Augustine, *Haer.* praef. 7.111–12, 7.100–104. I have followed the Latin text of Augustine, *De Haeresibus*, in *S. Aurelii Augustini*, part 13, ed. R. Vander Plaetse and C. Beukers, CCSL 46 (Turnhout: Brepols, 1969), 286–345. In addition, I have more or less adhered to the translation in *Arianism and Other Heresies*, ed. John E Rotelle, trans. Roland J. Teske, vol. 1, part 18 of *The Works of St. Augustine: A Translation for the 21st Century* (Hyde Park, N.Y.: New City Press, 1995), 15–77.

4. Augustine, *Haer.* praef. 7.109–11.

5. Augustine, *Haer.* praef. 7.96–98 (CCSL 46:289).

whose very scope and shape render it an elusive object of inquiry. Augustine is confronted with a world that demands unceasing attention. And yet that very attention—his ethnographic gaze—forces him to contemplate the conceptual and practical impediments to his task. Doubts about the very possibility of the heresiological enterprise—"insofar as we could get knowledge about them" (*et utcumque nobis innotescere potuerunt*)—induce Augustine to pose a series of questions about his capacity to research, write, and comprehend the heretical *orbis*. This chapter explores Augustine's reflections and uncertainties about the ability of the heresiologist to *be* a heresiologist. The content of *De haeresibus* contains ruminations not only about the difficulties of using the written word to convey contextually distinct knowledge (by way of armchair ethnographic research) but also about the problem of writing as an outsider, the limitations of time and skill, translating foreignness, and, more generally, the failure to arrive at a comprehensive understanding of both any one heresy and all the heresies out there in the world. *De haeresibus* is marked by a profound ethnographic hesitation that circumvented one set of ethnographic problems, magnified others, and raised still others. A text of straightforward design, *De haeresibus* is nonetheless remarkable for its sophisticated engagement with techniques of classification. It is a text, despite its overt simplicity, that reveals a far more complex awareness of its conceptual limitations and analytical fissures. As Dominic Keech has put it, "*De haeresibus* is a remarkable work . . . for revealing Augustine at his least comfortable and poised."[6]

This chapter will proceed along two interrelated lines of inquiry. In order to situate Augustine's ruminations about the limits of heresiology and the management of knowledge within its proper textual and literary context, it is necessary to consider the methods and sources he employed to construct his text. I begin with a discussion of his text as a condensation of heresiological knowledge—or of how, in other words, his text functions as a type of literary list. I then turn to a consideration of the manner in which Augustine performatively edits his text as he progresses through his eighty-eight heresies. In emphasizing the fact that *De haeresibus* is simply a recapitulation of earlier heresiological sources, scholars have more or less ignored the fact that he enacts for his reader, Quodvultdeus, the deacon of Carthage (and all others who might read his text), the process by which he has composed his treatise. Augustine, like heresiologists before and after him, harnessed the power of libraries, informants, personal experience, and divine intervention to keep his catalogue current.[7] To the extent that the success and viability of the genre was dependent upon continuously updating its content, heresiology remained in a state of constant flux. While the heresiologists maintained that the fixity and precision of their

---

6. Dominic Keech, *The Anti-Pelagian Christology of Augustine of Hippo, 396–430* (New York: Oxford University Press, 2012), 34.

7. See Augustine, *Haer.* praef.

works were elusive though assiduously pursued ideals, they likewise portrayed their persistent need to edit as evidence of their genre's adaptability and strength. Augustine's text illustrates, in the most explicit terms of any of the late antique heresiologies, the paradox of heresiological knowledge: it is seemingly limitless and yet always requires careful and persistent monitoring. The move to condense heresiological knowledge pinpoints the discursive feedback loop of heresiological investigation and production. His text is trying to remain active in the world. It is trying to be relevant. But Augustine's appeal to these authoritative sources did not cement his control over the heresies of his world; rather, it exacerbated his awareness of his text's myriad shortcomings. It is, paradoxically, through the performative invocation of mastery that Augustine's project confronts its analytical limits.

In the second part of this chapter, I consider the implications of Augustine's description of the process of compilation in order to pose broader questions about the conceptual foundations of his heresiology. Because there is a cyclical relationship between fissures within heresiology's conceptual framework and textual efforts to minimize these breaks, I explore Augustine's text as it displays, organizes, and explores the depths of its knowledge. And although Augustine's editing of earlier heresiological texts solved certain problems, it created others. I will argue that Augustine, in the process of updating the genre of heresiology, used his handbook as a background against which he could opine about the relationship between textual representation and reality, collectors and collections, and knowledge and ignorance. The way that Augustine translated the world of heresy into a specific textual form illustrates that the underlying logic of his intellectual mapping was quintessentially ethnographic. Augustine is aware, as Talal Asad has put it, that "the anthropologist's translation is not merely a matter of matching sentences in the abstract, but of *learning to live another form of life* and to speak another kind of language."[8] Augustine is aware that he does not and cannot live "another form of life" without himself becoming a heretic. The "paradox of intimacy"—the need to associate with, investigate, and yet also repudiate the heretics—only complicates his relation to his objects of inquiry.[9] To that end, Augustine's reflections about his work are not simply stylistic or rhetorical. They are deeply unsettling questions about the ability of authors to describe and control the world around them *in texts*, both to manage the disruptive potential of ethnographic excursion and to produce a coherent ethnographic object. In the latter instance, Augustine meditates, quite

---

8. Talal Asad, "The Concept of Cultural Translation in British Social Anthropology," in *Writing Culture: The Poetics and Politics of Ethnography*, ed. James Clifford and George E. Marcus (Berkeley and Los Angeles: University of California Press, 1986), 141–64, at 149.

9. Christopher Herbert, *Culture and Anomie: The Ethnographic Imagination in the Nineteenth Century* (Chicago: University of Chicago Press, 1991), 157.

unsettlingly, on the inherent problem of words, language, and authorial subjectivity in his quest to write the heretics.

DISTILLING ETHNOGRAPHY: THE NATURE OF THE LIST

When Epiphanius composed his *Panarion,* in the late fourth century, after nearly a century and a half during which no heresiological catalogues were composed, his text's discourse was articulated through the language of medicine. And to make his curative all the more effective, he emphasized his precise enumeration of the heretics.[10] Because this later stage of heresiology catalogued a significantly larger quantity of heresies, it explicitly ordered the heresies by number.[11] As collections of heretical names, the works of these later heresiologists, Epiphanius, Filastrius, Augustine, and Theodoret, advanced a heresiological rubric built upon the highly structured identification and exposition of heresies.[12] And even if a reader could still get lost in the digressive prose of the *Panarion,* the text, unlike earlier iterations of the genre, offered an enumerated superstructure. In later heresiological literature, the analysis of the heretics was contained within discrete, numbered textual sections.

In late 427, Quodvultdeus, a deacon at Carthage and later the city's bishop, wrote to Augustine requesting his pedagogical guidance.[13] He inquired if the bishop of Hippo might compose a treatise to instruct "both the learned and the uneducated, for those with leisure and for those who are busy," how to navigate a world overrun by heresy:[14]

---

10. See Aline Pourkier, *L'hérésiologie chez Épiphane de Salamine* (Paris: Beauchesne, 1992), 84–114.

11. The effects of this turn are well evidenced in Tia M. Kolbaba's *The Byzantine Lists: Errors of the Latins* (Chicago: University of Illinois Press, 2000), which studies Greek medieval lists of Western heretics and errors.

12. J. Rebecca Lyman, "Epiphanius on Orthodoxy," in *Orthodoxy, Christianity, History,* ed. Susanna Elm, Éric Rebillard, and Antonella Romano (Rome: École Française de Rome, 2000), 149–61, makes this point expressly.

13. Quodvultdeus is a somewhat enigmatic figure. See the summary in Thomas Macy Finn, trans., *Quodvultdeus of Carthage: The Creedal Homilies,* ACW 60 (Mahwah, N.J.: Paulist Press, 2004), 1–3.

14. Quodvultdeus, *Epist.* 221.3.42–43 (CCSL 46:274). On Augustine's role as respondent/teacher in his letters, see Jennifer Ebbeler, *Disciplining Christians: Correction and Community in Augustine's Letters* (New York: Oxford University Press, 2012). On Augustine and his world more generally, Peter Brown's bibliography in *Augustine of Hippo,* rev. ed. (Berkeley and Los Angeles: University of California Press, 2000) remains indispensable, as does James J. O'Donnell, *Augustine: A New Biography* (New York: Harper Perennial, 2005); and Brent D. Shaw, *Sacred Violence: African Christians and Sectarian Hatred in the Age of Augustine* (New York: Cambridge University Press, 2011). The recently published *A Companion to Augustine,* ed. Mark Vessey (Malden, Mass.: Wiley-Blackwell, 2012) is also an invaluable resource for all things Augustinian.

The following block quotation is translated from Quodvultdeus, *Epist.* 221.2.20–30 (CCSL 46:273).

I, therefore, beseech Your Goodness to deign to explain, from the time that the Christian religion received the name of the heritage it promised, what heresies existed and now exist, what errors they introduced and now introduce, what they have held and now hold in opposition to the catholic church concerning the faith, the Trinity, baptism, penance, Christ as man, Christ as God, the resurrection, the Old and New Testaments, and absolutely every point on which they disagree with the truth.

The shift toward the use of lists in the later stage of heresiological literature reflects the desire to impose order upon an unruly, chaotic field of inquiry; orderly enumeration sought to naturalize the scope and contents of this evolving branch of learning. Although Quodvultdeus conceded that the task had been undertaken previously, by Augustine himself, no less, he nonetheless insisted that his request was different: "I ask that you briefly, succinctly, and summarily set forth the opinions of each heresy and add what the catholic church holds in opposition to them, *in a single handbook*, as it were, drawn from all of them, to the extent that it suffices for instruction."[15] Those seeking more detailed answers could scour "the extensive and magnificent volumes" of Augustine and the other heresiologists.[16] Above all else, it was brevity that the deacon wanted.

Brent Shaw summarizes the tactical and stylistic developments of later heresiology as signifying a move away from protracted investigation and toward ease of identification: "Rather than the extensive and detailed theological treatise, therefore, it is the 'heresy list' that is the characteristic document of this second age.... The lists were meant to provide quick 'identity profiles' by which interested believers could recognize any one of the variegated host of enemies that the orthodox faced."[17] These lists, this argument runs, with Augustine's *De haeresibus* as the example par excellence, lacked intellectual heft and ingenuity. As an assemblage of sources—a work of editing rather than erudition—Augustine's text is, in Shaw's estimation, "a turgid list that lacks the verve and genius of the author, and which betrays on every page that it is not much more than a re-canned work quickly put together from other existing sources."[18] Although Shaw's general characterization of later heresiology ought to be tempered, his remarks do usefully foreground the turn toward heretical listing.[19] But unlike Shaw, who associates the banality of

---

15. Quodvultdeus, *Epist.* 221.3.34–38 (CCSL 46:274); emphasis added. On handbooks of heresy, see Judith McClure, "Handbooks against Heresy in the West, from the Late Fourth to the Late Sixth Centuries," *JTS* 30 (1979): 186–97

16. Quodvultdeus, *Epist.* 221.3.40 (CCSL 46:274).

17. Brent D. Shaw, "Who Were the Circumcellions," in *Vandals, Romans and Berbers,* ed. A. H. Merrills (Burlington: Ashgate, 2004), 227–58, at 233.

18. Ibid. 238.

19. However one judges the literary and intellectual qualities of heresiology's listing tradition, it is important to consider—as Shaw does—the ways in which the list's content was altered and modified.

heresiology with its penchant for devising lists, I contend that the list as a form perfectly captures the paradox of heresiological exactitude and the rhetoric of containment. As a heresiological handbook, Augustine's *De haeresibus* functions as a list—or perhaps more accurately as an incomplete catalogue—written to provide structure, in terms of both its form and content, for the proliferation of heretics.[20] It seeks to provide order over and against the inherent disorder of the heretics.

If writing can be "a locational sorting device," lists memorialize, enumerate, account, and order through classification.[21] A list arranges peoples, things, or concepts by "defining a 'semantic field,' since it includes some items and excludes others."[22] The list presents information through an organized system or principle by which readers locate and retrieve data readily (the reference function) or grasp meaning through the fact of arrangement (a specific impression).[23] The nonliterary list, governed by its utilitarian or pragmatic function, presents information in a practically ordered form. The literary list, which may contain "an inner logic of form" and leave it unexpressed, unfolds at the whims and imaginings of its author.[24] It induces speculation about its possible significance and hypotheses about its organizing principle; it is less a search for specific knowledge than an opportunity for its readers to devise meaning and purpose. The literary list, unmoored from obligations of exactitude, holds the potential to fashion and refashion itself as it unfolds. The dual nature of the list, wherein it holds contents and the contents hold the list together, attenuates the fixity of the list by eliding form and function. Because "the list is simultaneously the sum of its parts and the individual parts

---

Shaw suggests that the form of the list—its literary clarity and adaptability—eased the reception of Augustine's modifications (about the Circumcellions). That is, in hewing to the character of an externally produced genre (from Epiphanius, Filastrius, and the *Indiculus*) Augustine can update the list without, so it seems, any sense of disruption.

20. On Greek and Roman handbooks, see William Harris Stahl, "The Systematic Handbook in Antiquity and the Early Middle Ages," *Latomus* 23.2 (1964): 311–21; and George A. Kennedy, "The Earliest Rhetorical Handbooks," *AJP* 80.2 (1959): 169–78.

21. Jack Goody, *The Domestication of the Savage Mind* (New York: Cambridge University Press, 1977), 103–4; William Gass, "And," in *Voicelust: Eight Contemporary Fiction Writers on Style*, ed. Allen Wier and Don Hendrie, Jr. (Lincoln: University of Nebraska Press, 1985), 101–25; Lucie Doležalová, ed., *The Charm of a List: From the Sumerians to Computerised Data Processing* (Newcastle-upon-Tyne: Cambridge Scholars Press, 2009); and Robert E. Belknap, *The List: The Uses and Pleasures of Cataloguing* (New Haven: Yale University Press, 2004).

22. Goody, *The Domestication of the Savage Mind*, 103.

23. Belknap, *The List*, 3. Ivan M. Havel, "Time in Lists and Lists in Time," in Doležalová, *The Charm of a List*, 9–11, identifies six characteristics typical of lists: (1) *artificiality* (they are constructed); (2) *significance* (they hold meaning); (3) "the existence of a *carrier*" (its medium of transmission) (4) ordering; (5) *dynamics* (the features of adaptability), which includes six subtypes: insertion, deletion, modification, sorting, combining, and splitting; and (6) *accessibility* of its items based on enumeration or naming, content, or position (10).

24. Belknap, *The List*, 5.

themselves," the association between terms imbues the list's members with an additional meaning that only the whole list can supply.²⁵ The list, then, signifies a complex whole: it articulates a culture of classification.

The eighty-eight heresies of Augustine's *De haeresibus* represent the individual terms of a list and comprise in toto the whole of the list's meaning. His treatise subsumes the identification of the particularity of each heresy—that is, a particular heretical species—under the unity of the heretical genus. There are eighty-eight independent heresies, which Augustine has grouped into a single document, the text that holds them together as a genus. As Robert Belknap notes: "By accretion, the separate units cohere to fulfill some function as a combined whole, and by discontinuity the individuality of each unit is maintained as a particular instance, a particular attribute, a particular object or person."²⁶ The heresiologists' knowledge of the particularities of each sectarian group evinces their microscopic accretions, whereas the structure of their texts, born of collation and collection, defines their macroscopic field of inquiry. Augustine has attempted to fashion an ordered world of heresy from his catholic vantage point. If, as Belknap has phrased it, "the list form is the predominant mode of organizing data relevant to human functioning in the world," Augustine's determination to list the heresies bespeaks an effort to manage the content of Christianity's counterworld.²⁷ *De haeresibus* is a text that aspires to orient the Christian within a world of enemies through negation and antitypology.

To the extent that the list's adaptability governs the general structure of later iterations of heresiological literature, it complements the genre's persistent claims of ever-improving comprehension. The history of heresiology reveals the compositional process by which the genre's authors refined and expanded its polemical trajectory. But even as textual additions and subtractions served to improve a text's precision and comprehensiveness, they also revealed the genre's earlier shortcomings.²⁸ The adaptability of the heretics undercut any pretense of heresiological mastery. As Augustine himself conceded, he was no expert heresiologist. His work was but his limited interpretation of the state of the world as he knew it. Indeed, the very need for adaptation—the very fact that Augustine wrote his text in dialogue

25. Ibid. 15.
26. Ibid.
27. Ibid. 8. See also Havel, "Time in Lists and Lists in Time."
28. See János M. Bak, "Lists in the Service of Legitimation in Central European Sources," in Doležalová, *The Charm of a List*, 34–45. The problematic nature of listing—the ability to introduce error—is explicitly considered by Epiphanius at the outset of the *Panarion*. As a precursor to the full-fledged enumeration of the Christian heresies, Epiphanius comments in the second proem of his *Panarion* on the requisite exactitude of a particular list. In the midst of his presentation of the age of Judaism in the *Panarion*, Epiphanius acclaims his correction of a mistake within a genealogical list that validates Christ's genealogy and the infallibility of scripture. See *Pan.* 8.7.7–8.4.

with his sources—acknowledged that the tradition of heresiology was not in fact fixed but evolving and contingent. However much Epiphanius and others had tried, the rhetoric of exactitude and medical truth could not and did not foreclose its field of knowledge. The rhetoric of compilation mapped the partial accumulations and ruptures within the author's presentation of comprehensive knowledge. It conceded that the genre of heresiology had always been partial and would remain so. To try to order knowledge of the heretics was, as Augustine discovered, to trace an illusion of seemingly infinite varieties.

DE HAERESIBUS: ETHNOGRAPHY TRANSFORMED

Although Quodvultdeus had impressed Augustine because his "brilliant mind both thirsts for the truth about so many things and insists upon brevity out of fear of a surfeit," Augustine initially refused the deacon's request to produce a handbook of heresy.[29] He proposed instead that Quodvultdeus consult the work of Filastrius of Brescia or undertake a Latin translation of Epiphanius's *Panarion*.[30] And even though Quodvultdeus acknowledged that the works of Filastrius and Epiphanius had "escaped [his] notice," he refused to withdraw his request.[31] He pointedly suggested to Augustine that the works of Epiphanius and Filastrius would fail his test of brevity. He further conjectured that each of these authors had lacked skill, and their texts lacked scope: "I still do not think that they have observed such care and diligence that they added responses and included the practices contrary to each and every opinion ... added to this is the fact that some heresies are found to have arisen after their deaths."[32] In arguing that both Filastrius and Epiphanius had failed to array the total extent of the heresies, Quodvultdeus pressed Augustine to become the genre's foremost expert. The need to protect the feeble from the onslaught of the heresies, it seems, persuaded Augustine to undertake the task.[33] Separating "wrong belief from right doctrine" was, as Caroline Humfress has emphasized, the duty of the bishops themselves.[34] They had devoted themselves to their congregations. Heresy threatened not only to divide

---

29. Augustine, *Haer.* praef. 4.47–49 (CCSL 46:287).
30. Augustine, *Epist.* 222.2.8–32.
31. Quodvultdeus, *Epist.* 223.2.17 (CCSL 46:278).
32. Quodvultdeus, *Epist.* 223.2.18–21 (CCSL 46:278–79).
33. The threat is aptly summarized in James J. O'Donnell's essay "The Authority of Augustine," *AugStud* 22 (1991): 7–35: "One need only read Augustine's *De Haeresibus*, the catalogue he compiled late in life (based on a Greek source) [sic] of all the heresies known to him to get a sense of how fragile and threatened was his sense of church unity: so many ways to go wrong, such fine points leading to such disastrous error" (26 n. 7).
34. Caroline Humfress, *Orthodoxy and the Courts in Late Antiquity* (New York: Oxford University Press, 2007), 229.

communities into factions but also to undermine the bishops' work in shepherding the souls of their congregants.[35] As Augustine ultimately admitted: "We cannot, after all, abandon such people in their troubles, for they are not only our tenants but—what is more—our brothers, and come under our care in the love of Christ."[36]

Augustine was acutely aware of the heresiological resources at his disposal, having suggested some to Quodvultdeus in his initial reply. He composed his *De haeresibus* in consultation with four heresiological sources: pseudo-Epiphanius's *Recapitulations*;[37] Eusebius's *Ecclesiastical History*; Filastrius of Brescia's *Catalogue of Diverse Heresies* (*Diversarum haereseon liber*); and, most likely, pseudo-Jerome's *Catalogue of Heresies* (*Indiculus de haeresibus*).[38] He openly admitted and discussed his reliance upon three of these works, mentioning Epiphanius by name on twenty-six occasions, Filastrius on nine, and Eusebius on four.[39] Indeed, ethnography, as the anthropologist Stephen A. Tyler usefully notes, "is actually a complex intertextual practice, ranging from overt citation of other texts to allusion by failure to mention what ought to be mentioned."[40] At times parroting these textual antecedents and at times correcting and supplementing their data, Augustine dutifully enumerated his eighty-eight heresies.[41] Augustine's effort to streamline the genre's form—to maximize its utility—worked to synthesize the divergences in the earlier source material into an authoritative whole of his own creation. While the *Recapitulations* supplied nearly 65 percent of Augustine's evidence, he did not treat it as an unalterable authority. Rather, as Augustine emphatically insisted, it was subject to augmentation, supplementation, wholesale rejection, and reinterpretation:[42]

---

35. Ibid. 260.
36. Augustine, *Epist.* 224.3.41–44 (CCSL 46:281).
37. On the author of the *Anacephalaeoses*, see Müller, *The De Haeresibus of Saint Augustine*, 23–25.
38. On the question of pseudo-Jerome, see Teske's introduction in Rotelle, *Arianism and Other Heresies*, 23 n. 22; and G. Bardy, "L' 'Indiculus de haeresibus' du pseudo-Jérôme," *RevScRel* 19 (1929): 385–405. The text of the *Indiculus* is found in PL 81:636–44. Augustine also shows familiarity with the works of Irenaeus of Lyons in his treatise *Against Julian, an Unfinished Work* (at 4.72–73).
39. For more on Augustine and his sources see Bardy, "Le 'De haeresibus' et ses sources," 397–416.
40. Stephen A. Tyler, "Ethnography, Intertextuality and the End of Description," *American Journal of Semiotics* 3.4 (1985), 83–98, at 84.
41. Chapters 1–57 of *De haeresibus* are largely dependent upon the *Anacephalaeoses*; chapters 42 and 43, for example, are Latin translations of the Greek text. Chapters 58–80 correspond to heresies found in Filastrius's work. Augustine's total of eighty-eight is eight more than Epiphanius's total and sixty-eight less than Filastrius, who lists twenty-eight heresies before Christ and one hundred-twenty-eight after.
42. Augustine, *Haer.* 57.21–26 (CCSL 46:326).

In listing (*in commemorandis*) the heretics, I have not followed his manner, but his order, for I have from other sources added some things that he did not have, and I have omitted some things that he did have. Hence, I have explained some points more fully than he, and I have also explained others more briefly, and in some cases I kept to the same brevity governing everything according to the demands of the plan I had in mind.

With his ambition to supersede Pseudo-Epiphanius's (whom Augustine regarded as Epiphanius) textual constraints—"for you will see how much the work produced by the above-mentioned bishop falls short in comparison to the work you want me to produce"—Augustine, mimicking Quodvultdeus's dissatisfaction, rationalized his editorial alterations as improvements.[43] He excised all the pre-Christian heresies, "list[ing] these heresies which arose after Christ was glorified against the doctrine of Christ and under the cloak of Christ's name."[44] He further moved to correct Epiphanius's wrongful divisions and unions of heretical parties: "I listed two as one where I could find no difference. Again, where he wanted to make one out of two, I listed each of them under their own numbers. But I ought also to mention those heresies I found in other authors or which I myself recall. And so, I now add those which Filastrius listed and Epiphanius did not."[45] Having thus "incorporate[d] fifty-seven [heresies] from Epiphanius's work into my own" and twenty-three from Filastrius, Augustine added eight of his own: Luciferians,[46] Jovinianists,[47] Arabian heretics,[48] Helvidians,[49]

---

43. Augustine, *Haer.* praef. 6.91–93 (CCSL 46:288). From Filastrius, Augustine adds twenty-three sects to his editions of Epiphanius, which, at that point in *De haeresibus*, gave him a running total of eighty.

44. Augustine, *Haer.* 57.57.32–34 (CCSL 46:327). Augustine also excludes three of Epiphanius's Christian entries: the Lucianists, the Marcellians, and the Collyridians. In addition to these outright exclusions, Augustine differentiates and combines two other heretical clans.

45. Augustine, *Haer.* 57.57.35–40 (CCSL 46:327). Augustine combines and differentiates two other heretical groups. He combines the Tatians and Encratites (despite the fact that Epiphanius "call[ed] the Encratites schismatics from Tatian") into one heresy, insisting, instead, that the Tatians "are also called Encratites" (*Haer.* 25.1, 8–9 [CCSL 46:301]). He also distinguishes the Artotyrites from the Pepuzians.

46. Augustine's knowledge of the Luciferians, he tells us, comes from "a certain author, whose work does not bear his name" (*Haer.* 81.4–5, [CCSL 46:336]). The subsequent citation about the inheritance and nature of the soul corresponds exactly to the words of the *Indiculus de haeresibus* 38 (*PL* 81:642). Owing to the exactitude of the citation, Bardy, "Le 'De haeresibus' et ses sources," 408–11, argued that Augustine consulted and cited the *Indiculus* itself. Given the lack of affirmative evidence, Müller, *The De Haeresibus of Saint Augustine*, 28, posited that Augustine and the *Indiculus* could well have shared the same source.

47. Although Augustine reports that he gleaned knowledge of the Jovinianists in the same anonymous author of *Haer.* 81 (see the parallel at *Indiculus* 35 [*PL* 81:641]), he tells us that, unlike the Luciferians, of whom he appears to have been wholly ignorant, he already possessed knowledge of the Jovinianists (*Haer.* 82.16–17).

48. Knowledge of the Arabian heretics comes from Eusebius of Caesarea, *Hist. eccl.* 6.37.

49. His knowledge of Helvidius, whose followers were called Antidicomarites, appears to come from Jerome's *Adversus Helvidium de Mariae virginitate perpetua*. The name caused some confusion

Paternians,⁵⁰ Tertullianists, Abeloim, and Pelagians.⁵¹ Both from his careful study of the works of earlier heresiologists and from his own experiences combatting various North African heretics, he knows that the works before his had failed, as Quodvultdeus also emphasized, to grasp any number of heresies.

Augustine wrote his *De haeresibus* to correct the mistakes and fill in the holes in the heresiologists' knowledge about the heretics—to produce a better ethnography of heresy—as well as to present this abundance of ethnographic knowledge in the form of an ethnographic handbook.⁵² And while *De haeresibus* preserves a certain underlying ethnographic logic, it noticeably moves away from any discussion of macroscopic ethnographic paradigms. This codification of a heretical catalogue deemphasized the organizational structure of ethnographic theorization and instead focused on the microscopic data of heretical customs and habits. Writing about the identification of Jews in the Greco-Roman world, Shaye Cohen asks in his *The Beginnings of Jewishness*: "How, then, did you know a Jew in antiquity when you saw one?"⁵³ While Cohen concludes that Jews were not readily identifiable by name, dress, or phenotype, his answer does not dispute the fact that the Jews were perceived by non-Jewish writers to *behave* differently. They had dietary restrictions, observed unique rituals, and held different theological opinions. In the same way, Augustine produced his text to differentiate the heretics in broadly identifiable and distinctly Christian terms. Augustine's *De haeresibus* was an attempt to render the heretics phenomenologically knowable or, in other words, to answer the question: How did you know a heretic in antiquity when you saw or heard one?

Many of the heretics Augustine described were distinguished by their opinions, whether cosmological, theodicean, Christological, Trinitarian, angelologic,

---

for Augustine, since Epiphanius identified a sect of Antidicomarites at *Pan.* 78.1.3, though, as Augustine noted, the *Panarion* did not mention their association with Helvidius. Augustine appears to have combined these two accounts. On the specifics of the problem, see Bardy, "Le 'De haeresibus' et ses sources," 411 and Teske's introduction in Rotelle, *Arianism and Other Heresies*, 19, 23 n. 29, 76 nn. 218 and 219.

50. On the possible sources of the Paternians, see Augustine's *Against Julian* 5.7.26, which quotes Julian of Eclanum on the Paternians. See Mathijs Lamberigts, "A Short Note on the Paterniani," *RÉAug* 31 (1985): 270–74.

51. When describing the Abeloim and Pelagians, Augustine mentions the fact that the former reside "in our countryside," while the latter "began in our time": Augustine, *Haer.* 87.26–29; 88.1.1–4 (CCSL 46:339, 340).

52. Richard Flower, "'The Insanity of the Heretics Must Be Restrained': Heresiology in the Theodosian Code," in *Theodosius II: Rethinking the Roman Empire in Late Antiquity*, ed. Christopher Kelly (New York: Cambridge University Press, 2013), 172–94, emphasizes this point about Augustine's self-conceptualization of his task.

53. Shaye J. D. Cohen, *The Beginnings of Jewishness: Boundaries, Varieties, and Uncertainties* (Berkeley and Los Angeles: University of California Press, 2001), 67.

demonologic, and so on. The broad aim of his treatise was to reduce the heretics to these doctrinal, ritualistic, and behavioral elements. Among the descriptive markers Augustine associated with the heretics were alimentary matters, sexual behavior, marriage practices, dress, gender, idolatry, Jewish Law, ritualistic conduct, and bodily practices. In his depictions of the irreducible essence of eighty-five of eighty-eight heresies, Augustine emphasizes not only foundational figures—"the Saturninians are named after a certain Saturninus"—but also essential practices and doctrines.[54] The fact that Augustine incorporated into his treatise eleven unnamed heresies, including those who claimed that "the souls of the wicked turn into demons and into certain animals according to their merits," demonstrates that, in these cases, the doctrines and practices of the heretics functioned in place of a name.[55] In Augustine's system of heresiological classification a heresy could be known as much for the name of its founder as for its theology and its rituals.

Indeed, the etymological roots of the heretics often lead back to practices rather than people. The Ascitae, Augustine writes (in what constitutes the entirety of his entry on them), "are named after wineskins, for ἀσκός means 'wineskin' in Greek. They are reported to carry one around, inflated and open, reveling as if they were the new wineskins of the Gospel filled with new wine."[56] The Gnostics, Ophites, Cainites, Sethians, Archontics, Atrotyrites, Tessarescedecatites, Alogi, Cathari, Angelics, Apostolics, Antidicomarites, Metangismonites, Passalorynchites, and Aquarians all owe their names to their adherence to certain practices, their prioritization of certain ideas (such as knowledge, purity, or vessels), or their worship of certain biblical figures (such as Cain or Seth).[57] And if many of the heretics whom Augustine includes are identified on the basis of theological principles—such as the Cerinthians' angel-based theory of creation, the Valentinians' thirty aeons, the Colorbasians' insistence that humans are dependent on the seven stars, the Cerdonians' and Apellites' dualism, the Theodotians' docetism, the Origenists' denial of the resurrection of the dead, and the Coluthians' denial of God-created evil—a great many other heretics are identified by their conduct.[58] The unnamed sixty-eighth heresy, for instance, consists of those "who always walk with bare feet,"

---

54. Augustine, *Haer.* 3 (CCSL 46:291). The entries on the Pelagians, Donatists, Manicheans, and Sabellians are longer, but compared with the earlier heresiologies, they are still quite short. Augustine's entry on the Sabellians (*Haer.* 41) is different insofar as it is a discussion devoted entirely to a question of their various names and offshoots, and their relationship, more broadly, with Noetus and the Noetians. There is almost no discussion whatsoever of the habits or doctrines of the Sabellians themselves.

55. Augustine, *Haer.* 78 (CCSL 46:335).
56. Augustine, *Haer.* 62 (CCSL 46:329).
57. Augustine, *Haer.* 6; 17–20; 28–30; 38–40; 56; 58; 63; 64.
58. Augustine, *Haer.* 8; 11; 15; 21; 23; 33; 43; 65.

following literally God's command at Exodus 3.5.[59] The Valesians "castrate themselves and their guests,"[60] and the Cataphrygians and Pepuzians "are reported to have gruesome sacraments (*sacramenta funesta*), for they are said to confect their eucharist from the blood of a year-old infant, which they squeeze from tiny punctures all over its body; they mix it with wheat and make bread from it."[61] The historicity of these pronouncements is less interesting than their function as taxonomic indications of heretical behavior and belief. In moving away from the tomes of Epiphanius and Filastrius and embracing the structure of the abbreviated *Anacephalaeoses*, Augustine ventured to define the heretics succinctly, and more often than not by a single distinguishing opinion or practice (or both). Although the heretics, like the Jews of the second Temple Period, may well have blended seamlessly into their environs, Augustine sought to make them easier to identify by simplifying the taxonomy of identification.

In agreeing to undertake Quodvultdeus's request to produce a streamlined heresiological handbook, Augustine reflects on the difficulty of brevity, not the difficulty of the subject itself. At the outset of the project, it is form and not content that most concerns him. He asks both himself and Quodvultdeus "whether I ought now to begin this work and send you a part of it so that you might see that its difficulty is greater in proportion to the brevity with which you want me to carry it out."[62] However, Augustine's sense of the difficulty of the task was compounded by his desire to produce the most comprehensive heresiology ever written. As he firmly declared at the outset of his investigation, "I want even more" (*quanto magis quod ego*).[63] Not only did he seem to believe, upon reflection, that he could exceed the labors of his heresiological predecessors, but perhaps he agreed to undertake the task in order to prove that very point. But in wanting or searching for more, Augustine would come to a very different realization: it was content as much as form that curtailed his scholastic ambitions. In the process of constructing this polemical list, Augustine exhibited a specialized knowledge of the circumstances, practices, and opinions of the heretics. But in the very act of composing his treatise, he discovered that his perception of the heretical world was limited by factors both within and beyond his control. As such, his knowledge of the heresies out there was not only incomplete but forever destined to be inadequate.

---

59. Augustine, *Haer.* 67 (CCSL 46:330).
60. Augustine, *Haer.* 37 (CCSL 46:306).
61. Augustine, *Haer.* 26.11–15 (CCSL 46:302). On this gruesome ritual, see Susanna Elm, "'Pierced by Bronze Needles': Anti-Montanist Charges of Ritual Stigmatization in Their Fourth-Century Context," *JECS* 4.4 (1996): 409–39.
62. Augustine, *Epist.* 224.1.5–7 (CCSL 46:280).
63. Augustine, *Haer.* praef. 6.93 (CCSL 46:288).

WRITING AND TRANSLATING HERESY: THE LIMITS OF KNOWLEDGE AND EXPERIENCE

Augustine's concluding remarks in *De haeresibus* reveal a man pondering the epistemological conditions that inform his attempt to write coherently about the heretics. While Augustine had expressed some hesitations during his exchange with Quodvultdeus about the feasibility of such an endeavor, he returned at the end of his treatise, in its epilogue, to express his limitations as an author and ethnographer.[64] Augustine learned only through the activity of writing itself the constraints of his work as an armchair ethnographer. His compilation became, in addition, a meditation on the ethnographer's tenuous understanding of the world and the peoples he attempts to study. Like contemporary ethnographers who examine their own role—and its ideological effects—in producing their ethnographies, Augustine interrogated his participation in the ethnographic *traditio haereticorum*.[65] He articulated his knowledge of the heretics in both positive and negative terms. On the one hand, he possessed real, tangible, articulable knowledge about heresy: the eighty-eight heretics had customs, habits, and opinions that could be and were described in writing. Like Hippolytus, Irenaeus, Tertullian, Filastrius, and Epiphanius before him, Augustine knew the heretics both via the writings of his fellow Christians and through his own encounters. To write heresiology, then, was to merge scholastic knowledge with experiential familiarity. On the other hand, textual lacunae gestured at the more unsettling problem of trying to bring his heresiology to a close. As Epiphanius had admitted in the *Panarion*: "It is difficult to discover or state all the [doctrines] of the people who are being spawned and sprouting up among them even to this day, and every day they find something new to say and delude their converts."[66] This unknowable aspect of the heretics necessitated an explanation, and like Epiphanius, Augustine attempted one. He offered three reasons to account for this epistemological chasm. The first I have

---

64. For a fairly comprehensive treatment of Augustine's theory of linguistic (or verbal) epistemology, see Marcia L. Colish, *The Mirror of Language: A Study in the Medieval Theory of Knowledge* (Lincoln: University of Nebraska Press, 1983), 7–54.

65. By contemporary ethnographic examination (or more accurately, self-examination), I mean the process by which anthropologists and sociologists—in reaction, perhaps, to the postmodern turn—reflect upon their own, irreversible ideological interpretation of fieldwork and research. Unlike earlier anthropologists of the late nineteenth and early to mid-twentieth century, who claimed simply to report the facts about a given people and place, recent ethnographers have apprehended (if not abandoned) the fallacious dangers embedded in such claims. See, for example, Gabrielle Schwab, *Imaginary Ethnographies: Literature, Culture, and Subjectivity* (New York: Columbia University Press, 2012); Charlotte Aull Davies, *Reflexive Ethnography: A Guide to Researching Selves and Others*, 2nd ed. (New York: Routledge, 2008); and Paul Rabinow, *Reflections on Fieldwork in Morocco* (Berkeley and Los Angeles: University of California Press, 1977).

66. Epiphanius, *Pan.* 36.4.2 (GCS 31:10), which is a paraphrase of Irenaeus *Adv. haer.* 1.21.5.

already discussed briefly, related to the problem of intertextual collection, comparison, and archiving: it is an editorial problem. Second, there was the conceptual problem of abundant and persistent heretical metamorphosis, which hindered efforts both to essentialize the heretics and to delineate their sphere of influence. And third, Augustine noted that his authorial position, outside the world of heresy per se, erected a barrier between himself as ethnographer and his object of study. Augustine identified the cultural, linguistic, and religious divide that all ethnographic research and writing must traverse.

The epistolary exchange between Quodvultdeus and Augustine conceived *De haeresibus* as a work of explicitly utilitarian design. It was an occasion for Augustine to unveil his investigative skill and transform heresiological dissonance into a uniform and comprehensive handbook. In combing through various resources to capture the full portrait of heretical plurality, he mined layers of textual material. But editing, collating, and collecting could supply Augustine only a partial knowledge:[67]

> You see how many heresies we have mentioned, and we still have not fulfilled your request. How could I mention all "the heresies which have arisen," to use your words, 'from the time the Christian religion received the name of the inheritance promised it," since I could not get knowledge of all of them (*qui omnes nosse non potui*)? I think that the reason is that no one of those whose writings I have read has recorded them all. At times I found in one author heresies that I did not find in another. I have listed more than they did, because I have gathered heresies from all of them, though I did not find all of them in each author. Moreover, I added those which I myself recall, but could not find in any of those authors. Hence, I am right in believing that I could not record all the heresies, both because I could not read all the authors who have written on this topic and because I do not see that any of them whom I have read have recorded them all.

Augustine's point here is that aspiring to completeness imposes certain impossible literary and editorial demands. Not only does the deacon's desire for an exhaustive heresiology strain Augustine's scholastic aptitude, but his desire for a handbook compounds this impossibility: "Who can fail to see the amount of work and the number of books this request would demand?"[68] Even as Augustine openly performed his editorial handiwork—his incorporation and modification of Filastrius, Epiphanius, and Eusebius—he was well aware that he had only just scratched the surface. He knew that his performative editing did not result in comprehensive knowledge.[69] His work emphatically proved, in fact, that heresiology was a genre of

---

67. Augustine, *Haer.* epil. 1.1–14 (CCSL 46:343).
68. Augustine, *Haer.* epil. 3.43–44 (CCSL 46:344).
69. Augustine similarly tries to transfer the manifest shortcomings of his heresiological handbook to the heretics, whose failure to comprehend their own divergences and abundance of error

known unknowns. There were heretics and references he knew he did not know: "I have heard that the saintly Jerome has written something on heresies, but we could not find his work in our library, and we do not know where to get it."[70] But even if Quodvulteus were to discover Jerome's work on this subject, the problem of incompletion remained: "I do not think that even he, although a very learned man, could track down all the heresies."[71] If ever Ecclesiastes 12.12 could capture Augustine's predicament, here was its moment: "Of making many books there is no end."[72]

In an essay entitled "And," which begins as an examination of the conjunction and evolves into an analysis of literary organizing principles, the novelist William Gass describes the underlying logic of terminological sequences. Because, as he insists, "every addition implies that somewhere there's a sum," chains of information assume a point of culmination.[73] Enumeration, moreover, not only implies completion; it also assumes the stability of its terms: "You can't add one number to another—8 to 4—if the 8 has disappeared by the time the 4 has come round to be counted."[74] Gass's observations highlight the two facets of organizational structures that destabilize their clarity and function: continuity and completion. If "a list is able to fill a gap in our knowledge," what about a list with no end?[75] How does a seemingly infinite repository of knowledge influence efforts to circumscribe knowledge within a text?[76] How does an author confront a list or catalogue whose components are always changing? Does the instability of the terms make investigation altogether impossible? I suggest that by describing his text as the most recent and thorough iteration of heresiology, Augustine ultimately transposed an inquiry about the *process* of textual collation into a question about its telos: Where and how does heresiology end? Not only had laborious research failed to produce a complete account of the heretical world; the process gave rise to Augustine's unsettling conclusion: "Even if I did perhaps record all of them, which I do not think is the case, I certainly do not know that these are all of them. Hence, that

---

seemingly acquits Augustine's failure: "Those who compose empty tales that are long and complicated are so full of many false teachings that they themselves could not count them or could do so only with great difficulty" (*Haer.* epil. 3.38–41 [CCSL 46:344]). The observation, perhaps, frees him from the burden of comprehension, for when the contours of heresy are beyond description, both its definition and its ascertainment become logical impossibilities.

70. Augustine, *Haer.* epil. 2.18–20 (CCSL 46:343).
71. Augustine, *Haer.* epil. 2.24–27 (CCSL 46:343): *quamvis nec ipsum, licet hominem doctissimum, omnes haereses arbitrer indagare potuisse.*
72. *Faciendi plures libros nullus est finis* in the Vulgate.
73. Gass, "And," 101–25, at 108.
74. Ibid. 108.
75. Tavas Visi, "A Science of Lists?," in Doležalová, *The Charm of a List*, 12–33, at 26.
76. For strategies of information management, see Ann M. Blair, *Too Much to Know: Managing Scholarly Information before the Modern Age* (New Haven: Yale University Press, 2011).

which you want me to put down in my writing I cannot even grasp with my mind, for I cannot know them all" (*non saltem potest me cognoscente comprehendi quia omnia scire non possum*).[77] Knowledge of the heretics was not simply a matter of exhaustive labor: it may very well have been, as Augustine himself suggests, beyond the bounds of human reason. To the extent that Augustine had shed his original fears as to how to distill the heretics into a brief catalogue, he apprehended a new set of textual and epistemological problems. For him, the fear of knowing the heretics too well or too completely—in essence, the fear of becoming a heretic or a heretical apologist—had morphed into the problem of never being able to *really* know the heresies at all. Although Epiphanius had mused about heretical infinitude in his *De fide*, he had only gestured at the source of this quandary.[78] Augustine confronted and ultimately reasoned through the problem directly. He realized, in language far less sanguine than Epiphanius, the impossibility of his genre's potency. If earlier heresiology was marked by its digressive polemics, the ordered succession of later heresiology gave way to a discourse of unsettling self-reflection. As Augustine reminds Quodvultdeus, his treatise was just a sampling of the heretical world, since "other heresies which are not mentioned in this book of ours can exist or come to exist."[79]

In denying the force of orthodox closure over against the heretics, Augustine's embrace of an epistemological chasm within his heresiological writing solidified *not* control and mastery but rather imperfection, fragility, and incompleteness.[80] Irenaeus, two centuries earlier, had emphatically declared the human mind's inability to apprehend the fullness of divine truth. And although the mystery of creation existed to be discovered and understood, it too was ultimately beyond definitive explanation:[81]

> We, however, precisely inasmuch as we are inferior to God's Word and his Spirit, have need of a knowledge of his mysteries. It should be no surprise if, in matters spiritual and heavenly and such as need to be revealed, we experience this, because even matters that are at our feet—I mean, that are in this creation, and that we can touch and see that are with us—many of these matters escape our knowledge, and we leave these to God.... What happens when we try to explain the reason for the rise of the Nile? We give many answers, perhaps plausible, perhaps not, but what actually is true, certain, and secure is in God's keeping.

77. Augustine, *Haer. epil.* 1.14–17 (CCSL 46:343).
78. The problems of collection and counting are most explicitly addressed, though not altogether substantively, at *De fide* 6.5, 9.1–4, 10.1–2, 11.1, 12.4–5.
79. Augustine, *Haer. epil.* 2.55–57 (CCSL 46:344).
80. This had the added benefit of undercutting the association between heretical hubris and (orthodox) theological engagement.
81. Irenaeus, *Adv. haer.* 2.28.2 (SC 294:270–72).

Although the wonders of the natural world—the rising of the Nile, the migration patterns of birds, the ebb and flow of the tides, weather patterns, and the stations of the moon—could be subjected to rational, predictable explanation, it was "God alone, who made them," and he alone "can declare their truth."[82] Insofar as human models of the observable phenomena of creation remained mere theory, the innate truths of the divinely ordered universe were shrouded in an aura of mystery, wonder, and transcendence. There were some matters, Irenaeus reasoned, that fell well within the purview of the human mind, whereas others belonged solely to the realm of the divine. And although the things before our eyes, in our hands, and at our feet eluded precise understanding, it was, at least, subject to observation and investigation. Orthodox Christians recognized their humility before God. By contrast, the heretics embraced an epistemological hubris, which drove them to speculate wildly about the invisible, supercelestial, and spiritual matters of the cosmos.[83] As Hippolytus lamented, all those heretics who "name themselves Gnostics in this peculiar way . . . they alone have gulped down the marvelous knowledge of the perfect and good."[84] The Gnostics and those who followed them drove individuals away from the observable phenomena of the physical world. In refusing to accept the mystery of divine creation, they created elaborate cosmologies and theories of knowledge. They, like Augustine, wanted more.

For Irenaeus, the abiding mystery of creation demanded humanity's dependence on God. To leave the lacunae of scripture unanswered—how and from where God created matter, why he produced it, why some of his creations sinned against him and yet others remained loyal, what drives the nature of the sinner, and so forth—was not, as the heretics thought, mistake. "As long as we live in the form of this world," Irenaeus explained, "we should leave perfect knowledge and such questions to God."[85] Because humanity conceded the limits of its wisdom, it essentially bound itself to an incomplete temporal existence, "so that God may always teach and man may always learn from God."[86] The promise of eternal glory in the kingdom of heaven *preserved* the possibility of acquiring perfect knowledge. In the present, however, humans must embrace, as Tertullian advocated in his *De prae-*

---

82. Irenaeus, *Adv. haer.* 2.28.2 (SC 294:272).

83. See W. C. van Unnik, "Theological Speculation and Its Limits," in *Early Christian Literature and the Classical Intellectual Tradition*, ed. William R. Schoedel and Robert L. Wilken (Paris: Éditions Beauchesne, 1979), 33–44. See also Kristoffel Demoen, "Incomprehensibility, Ineffability and Untranslatability: The Poverty of Language and the Abundance of Heresy in Fourth-Century Greek Patristic Thought," in *Heretics and Heresies in the Ancient Church and in Eastern Christianity: Studies in Honour of Adelbert Davids*, ed. Joseph Verheyden and Herman Teule (Leuven: Peeters, 2011), 105–26.

84. Hippolytus, *Ref.* 5.23.3 (Marcovich 199); translation altered from ANF.

85. Irenaeus, *Adv. haer.* 2.28.8 (SC 294:290).

86. Irenaeus, *Adv. haer.* 2.28.3 (SC 294:274).

scriptione, a life of humility and even ignorance.[87] By admonishing his readers to "keep order in your knowledge, and ... go not beyond God himself," Irenaeus sought not simply to tame the hubristic heretical mentality but to preserve the underlying mystery of Christian doctrine and salvation.[88]

Epiphanius, in his panegyric to the catholic church, also discussed his inability to articulate fully the nature and visage of the Christian God. And though his praise for God's earthly institution provides some degree of mediation between the human and the divine, his praise alone could not overcome the mystery of divine transcendence:[89]

> As you go through the whole work, or even parts of it, pray for me and make request that God will give me a portion in the holy and only catholic and apostolic church and the true, life-giving and saving [faith], and deliver me from every sect. And if, in my humanity, I cannot reach the full measure of the incomprehensible and ineffable Godhead, but am still pressed to offer its defense and compelled to speak for God in human terms, and have been led by daring [to do so], you yourselves, pardon me, for God does.

The juxtaposition here between the redemption from heresy (by way of faith) and the ineffability of God elucidates a fundamental distinction between the knowable and the unknowable. Knowledge of and in the world stood apart from knowledge of the divine, insofar as the former was subject to human comprehension, discovery, and theorization, whereas the latter was not. Moreover, Epiphanius's remarks allude to the very start of his *Panarion*, where he articulated the trajectory of his inquiry:[90]

> There are things untold, beyond counting, inaccessible so far as man is concerned, and known only to the Lord of all. But we are dealing with variance of opinions and kinds of knowledge, with faith in God and unbelief, with sects, and with heretical *human* opinion which misguided persons have been sowing in the world from man's formation on earth till our own day.

The human condition enabled him to comprehend and refute heretical opinions because they were *human* opinions. For the same reason, he could not attain complete comprehension of the Godhead. The unreachable chasm—the unknowability of God—produced the space for faith *in* God.[91] Though Epiphanius

---

87. See also Irenaeus, *Adv. haer.* 2.26.1.

88. Irenaeus, *Adv. haer.* 2.25.4 (SC 294:254–56). See Richard Norris, "The Transcendence and Freedom of God: Irenaeus, the Greek Tradition and Gnosticism," in Schoedel and Wilken, *Early Christian Literature*, 87–100.

89. Epiphanius, *De fide* 20.3–4 (GCS 37:521). See also *Pan.* 76.54.17 for a description of how one heretical group, the Anomoeans, articulated its knowledge of God as tangible, objective knowledge.

90. Epiphanius, *Pan.* pro. 2.2.2–3 (GCS, n. F., 10:170); emphasis added.

91. On faith as the space in which God and humanity unite, see Carol Harrison's *Augustine: Christian Truth and Fractured Humanity* (New York: Oxford University Press, 2000), 15–40; and Paul

insisted that temporal and divine knowledge were radically distinct, the diverse profusion of the heretics suggested that this boundary was not so neatly determined.[92]

Augustine recognized that a similar epistemological disjuncture undergirded his understanding of the heretics: "Even if I knew all of them, I still am not able to do what your letters hold, 'that we state entirely all those things on which the heretics dissented from the truth.' Far less can I do, since I am not able to know all of them."[93] In bemoaning the gap in his knowledge, Augustine defined his relationship to the heretics as one of perpetual inadequacy. The limitations Augustine discovered in his own writing and cognition reflected a deeper awareness of the limitations of language and thought. As Marcia Colish writes: "There always remains an opaque residuum of inexpressibility when a man tries to signify verbally his internal states of being. In the face of the ineffable mystery of God, human language labors under crushing limitations."[94] What Colish ascribes to Augustine's self-interrogation in his *Confessions* likewise applies to his interrogation of the heretics. The world of heresy, like God himself, could never be known in full, nor could any single heresy be thoroughly comprehended.[95] Although the incarnation had bestowed humankind with a redeemed speech, which functioned as a "mirror through which men may know God in this life by faith," Augustine's Christian eloquence could not circumvent the epistemological constraints of his humanity.[96]

Heresiology was an illustration of the larger Christian discourse that, in the words of Averil Cameron, "attempt[ed] to express the paradoxical, to describe in language what is by definition indescribable."[97] The heretics, like God himself, were shrouded in an essential mystery. They were a paradox of representation and

---

L. Gavrilyuk, *The Suffering of the Impassable God: The Dialectics of Patristic Thought* (New York: Oxford University Press, 2004).

92. Looming over the entire edifice of heresiological discourse was the assumption that any effort to comprehend the specifics of any one of or all the heresies—the process of classifying these sectarian groups—*presupposed* a foundational understanding of heresy itself. Even before Augustine undertook his full-fledged editorializing of Filastrius and Epiphanius, he framed the task, in his first response to Quodvultdeus, as a definitional problem. See *Epist.* 222.2.11–28 and, again, *Haer.* epil. 3. See also the essays of Gerald Bonner, "*Dic Christi Veritas Ubi Nunc Habitas:* Ideas of Schism and Heresy in the Post-Nicene Age," in *The Limits of Ancient Christianity: Essays on Late Antique Thought and Culture in Honor of R. A. Markus,* ed. William E. Klingshirn and Mark Vessey (Ann Arbor: University of Michigan Press, 1999), 63–79.

93. Augustine, *Haer.* epil. 1.14–17 (CCSL 46:343). See R. A. Markus, "Christianity and Dissent in Roman North Africa: Changing Perspectives in Recent Work," in *Schism, Heresy and Religious Protest,* ed. Derek Baker (Cambridge: Cambridge University Press, 1972), 21–36.

94. Colish, *The Mirror of Language,* 25.

95. Hippolytus, *Ref.* pro. 5.27 (Marcovich 55; translation altered from ANF).

96. Colish, *The Mirror of Language,* 26.

97. Averil Cameron, *Christianity and the Rhetoric of Empire: The Development of Christian Discourse* (Berkeley and Los Angeles: University of California Press, 1991), 156.

classification. Because heresy, Augustine reasons, "is very difficult to define," it imposes a treacherous burden on those who attempt to systematize it through its essential ambiguity:[98] "We should, therefore, be cautious, when we try to count them all so that we do not omit some, though they are heresies, and include others, though they are not."[99] Augustine's acknowledgment of gradations of heretical existence further complicated the task of classifying the heretics. A coherent definition of heresy would have, at the very least, provided guidance for future heresiologists and Christians in their efforts to steer clear of heresy. As Augustine wrote, to "inquire into what makes one a heretic so that, in avoiding that with the Lord's help, we may avoid the poison of heresies, not only of those which we know but also of those we do not know, whether they already actually exist or merely could exist."[100] But the heretics, like nature, evolved and thus evaded ready detection and precise rationalization. Although this constant metamorphosis influenced the heresiologists' models of heresy, it was nonetheless clear that the macroscopic theorization of heretical generation could lead the heresiologist only so far. The construction of a comprehensive system did not, however, provide descriptions and refutations of each new part of the system. A theory of the heretics' evolution and development did not explain the precise nature of each newly created heresy but rather provided an explanation only for *why* new heresies continued to develop.

CROSSING THE ETHNOGRAPHIC CHASM

In Book 3 of his *Confessions*, Augustine recounted his eager embrace, as a student at Carthage, of a Ciceronian maxim from the (now-lost) *Hortensius*. The Roman rhetorician and politician was adamant that one ought "not to study one particular sect but to love and seek and pursue and hold fast and strongly embrace wisdom itself, whatever it may be."[101] Although Augustine delighted in Cicero's dictum and credits the *Hortensius* with kindling his love for *philosophia*, he nonetheless

---

98. In acknowledging at the outset that "not every error is a heresy; yet, since every heresy involves a defect, a heresy could only be a heresy by reason of some error," Augustine sought to impose some semblance of order upon his admittedly partial knowledge (*Haer.* praef. 7.98–100 [CCSL 46:289]). In effect, the perpetual cycling of heresies in and out of existence condenses Epiphanius's universal history into a problem of definitional uniformity. Augustine's task was thus doubly undercut by terminological incoherence: the heretics themselves were not simply growing and changing, but their so-called opponents had never had a coherent rubric by which to identity them!

99. Augustine, *Epist.* 222 2.28–32 (CCSL 46:277). Bonner, "*Dic Christi Veritas Ubi Nunc Habitas*," remarks of this passage: "This last observation was crucial: heresy can exist in the mind of the inquisitor rather than in the intention of the heretic" (73).

100. Augustine, *Haer.* epil. 2.58–62 (CCSL 46:344–45).

101. Augustine, *Conf.* 3.4.8.29–31 (CCSL 27:30; altered from Chadwick): *quod non illam aut illam sectam, sed ipsam quaecumque esset sapientiam ut diligerem et quaererem et assequerer et tenerem atque amplexarem fortiter.*

turned away from Cicero, since he was not a Christian.[102] Because he had "with his infant heart . . . piously drunk in with my mother's milk" the name of the Savior, Augustine possessed a deep if scarcely conscious memory of Christ.[103] This lingering memory provoked in him a seemingly irreconcilable aversion to the writings of the philosophers: "Any book which lacked this name [Christ], however well written or polished or true, could not entirely grip me. I therefore decided to give attention to the holy scriptures and to find out what they were like."[104] His devotion to the Bible, however, proved disappointing. He encountered a text that "seemed . . . unworthy in comparison to the dignity of Cicero."[105] And because scripture was "lowly to the beginner but, on further reading, of mountainous difficulty and enveloped in mystery," it was only from his ecclesiastical perch decades later that its depth of meaning revealed itself to him.[106] Augustine's failure to apprehend the profundity and potentiality of scripture, which paradoxically stemmed from his judgment that the Bible lacked the "dignity of Cicero," precipitated a prolonged period of waywardness from Christianity:[107]

> My inflated conceit shunned the Bible's restraint, and my gaze never penetrated to its inwardness. Yet the Bible was composed in such a way that as beginners mature, its meaning grows with them. I disdained to be a little beginner. Puffed up with pride, I considered myself a mature adult. That explains why I fell in with men proud of their slick talk, very earthly-minded and loquacious. In their mouths were the devil's traps and a birdlime compounded of a mixture of the syllables of your name, and that of the Lord Jesus Christ, and that of the Paraclete, the Comforter, and the Holy Spirit. These names were never absent from their lips; but it was no more than sound and noise in their tongue. Otherwise their heart was empty of truth.

His turn toward the teaching of the Manichaeans, which he describes as a period of wandering and separation from God in Books 3, 4, and 5 of the *Confessions*, began as an effort to fill a theological void. It was born of his own hubris, his "inflated conceit that shunned the Bible's restraint."[108]

Augustine, as *Confessions* makes abundantly clear, was a man in search of answers, and the Manichaeans were eager, on the surface, to supply them.[109] But, as

---

102. Augustine, *Conf.* 3.4.8.15–26.
103. Augustine, *Conf.* 3.4.8.34–5 (CCSL 27:30).
104. Augustine, *Conf.* 3.4.8.36–5.9.2 (CCSL 27:30–31).
105. Augustine, *Conf.* 3.5.9.6–7 (CCSL 27:30).
106. Augustine, *Conf.* 3.5.9.3–4 (CCSL 27:31).
107. Augustine, *Conf.* 3.5.9.7–6.10.6 (CCSL 27:31).
108. Augustine, *Conf.* 3.5.9 (CCSL 27:31).
109. Augustine, *Conf.* 3.7.12.3. On separation from God, see *Conf.* 3.6.11.44–45. The most recent and comprehensive treatment of Augustine's affiliation with Manichaeism is (a projected three-volume effort, of which the first two have been published) Jason BeDuhn's *Augustine's Manichaean Dilemma*, vol. 1, *Conversion and Apostasy, 373–388 C.E.* (Philadelphia: University of Pennsylvania Press, 2009);

he explains, unable to find a better alternative, he settled upon his affiliation with the Manichaeans: "My position was that I had not found anything more satisfactory than that into which I had somehow fallen."[110] Augustine later realized that his infatuation with the customs and theology of the Manichaeans was misguided—that they offered "splendid hallucinations" (*phantasmata splendida*) rather than theological truth—because it privileged the fruits of the earth, the stars, and his own sensuality.[111] Indeed, his association with the Manichaeans, although it lasted for roughly nine years, came to a rather abrupt end after his engagements with the esteemed Manichaean bishop Faustus proved disappointing.[112] Faustus, who was praised as the intellectual luminary of the Manichaeans, seemed incapable of answering Augustine's myriad questions: "So the renowned Faustus . . . had begun to loosen the bond by which I had been captured."[113]

Though Augustine never explicitly mentions his personal ties to the Manichaeans in *De haeresibus*, the sheer amount of detail he expends enumerating their customs and doctrines surely stemmed from his intimate familiarity with the heresy.[114] His entry on the Manichaeans comprises nearly a quarter of the treatise. There is an unavoidable sense, given not just the abnormal length of the entry but also the range of the issues discussed, that his lived experiences with the Manichaeans enabled him to say more. Augustine, in fact, insists that the ability to say more—to weigh in with some sense of authority and authenticity—was the true measure of the heresiologist. In his essay "On Ethnographic Authority," James Clifford identifies an early and deceptively straightforward mentality of ethnographic authority: "Ethnographic writing enacts a specific strategy of authority. This strategy has classically involved an unquestioned claim to appear as the purveyor of

---

and *Augustine's Manichaean Dilemma*, vol. 2, *Making a "Catholic" Self, 388–401 C.E.* (Philadelphia: University of Pennsylvania Press, 2012). For other useful essays and discussions, see Johannes van Oort, "Young Augustine's Knowledge of Manichaeism: An Analysis of *Confessiones* and Some Other Relevant Texts," *VC* 62 (2008): 441–66; and his "Manichaean Christians in Augustine's Life and Work," *Church History and Religious Culture* 90 (2010): 505–546; J. Kevin Coyle, "Part Four: Manichaeism and Augustine of Hippo," in his *Manichaeism and Its Legacy* (Leiden: Brill, 2009), 209–328; and Elizabeth A. Clark, "Vitiated Seeds and Holy Vessels: Augustine's Manichean Past," in *Images of the Feminine in Gnosticism*, ed. Karen L. King (Philadelphia: Fortress Press, 1988), 367–401.

110. Augustine, *Conf.* 5.7.13.30–1 (CCSL 27:63).
111. Augustine, *Conf.* 3.6.10.20 (CCSL 27:31).
112. Augustine, *Conf.* 5.6.10.1.
113. Augustine, *Conf.* 5.7.13.33–34 (CCSL 27:64).
114. Augustine, *Epist.* 222.3, does contain a brief inquiry about a certain Theodosius who revealed some Manichees in Carthage. *Haer.* 46.9 further emphasizes the *current* infestation of Manichaeans within the African Christian community. See Johannes van Oort, "Mani and Manichaeism in Augustine's *De haeresibus*: An Analysis of *haer.* 46.1," in *Studia Manichaica: IV. Internationaler Kongress zum Manichäismus*, ed. Ronald E. Emmerick, Werner Sundermann, and Peter Zieme (Berlin: Akademie Verlag, 2000), 451–63.

truth in the text."[115] By implicitly using his former way of life to enumerate a pithy if still detailed explanation of the Manichaean people, Augustine could circumvent the twin problems of ethnographic translation and ethnographic foreignness that threatened to collapse his entire textual endeavor.[116] He sought to represent himself as a purveyor of truth. It was his lived fieldwork that magnified not only his ethnographic knowledge but also his ethnographic authority. By contrast, Augustine's unfamiliarity with nearly all the other heretics of the world lingered in his mind as a seemingly intractable problem.

Augustine made a point of noting his personal familiarity with certain heresies. In his descriptions of the Tertullianists, Abeloim (or Abelians), and Pelagians, he emphasized the contemporaneity of these sects and his personal knowledge of them.[117] He averred, for example, that the Tertullianists were "gradually dying out toward our time" and that in fact, upon his last visit to the city of Carthage, "they were completely gone."[118] While Augustine's personal familiarity with certain heresies and his diligent research into others supplied his text with a modicum of ethnographic authority, he knew that his text remained fragmentary despite all his efforts. Whereas Epiphanius had mused about heretical infinitude by way of biblical allegory, Augustine articulated a simple yet unmistakably ethnographic cognizance of the constraints of his position as a *foreign* author. As he recounted his plan to comprehend the full range of heretical parties, opinions, and practices, he parlayed the achievement of his *De haeresibus*—the most accurate, systematic, and dutifully researched account yet of the heretics—into an illustration of his a-priori failure as an ethnographic author: "Nor can any heresy be so readily known to any outsider as [it is] by its own members; hence, I acknowledge that I have not stated and have not learned all the teachings of those heresies which I mentioned."[119] His admission demonstrated the acuity of his ethnographic mindset. Augustine was simply unable to inhabit the world of heresy and hence unable to describe it fully.

---

115. James Clifford, "On Ethnographic Authority," in his *The Predicament of Culture: Twentieth-Century Ethnography, Literature, and Art* (Cambridge, Mass.: Harvard University Press, 1988), 21–54, at 25.

116. For a useful discussion of the Christian treatment of the Manichaeans as foreign peoples, see Guy G. Stroumsa, "Philosophy of the Barbarians: On Early Christian Ethnological Representations," in his *Barbarian Philosophy: The Religious Revolution of Early Christianity* (Tübingen: Mohr Siebeck, 1999), esp. 78–83.

117. On Augustine's characterization of and relationship to the Abeloim, see Gian Ackermans, "Einige rechtliche und theologische Fragen zu den Abeloitae in Augustins *De Haresibus*," in *Augustine, Manichaeism and Other Gnosticism: Studies for Johannes van Oort at Sixty*, ed. Jacob Albert van den Berg et al. (Leiden: Brill, 2011), 123–38. For a sense of the magnitude of Augustine's engagement, both in writing and in person, with specific errors, doctrines, and sects, see Caroline Humfress, "Controversialist: Augustine in Combat," in *A Companion to Augustine*, ed. Mark Vessey (Malden, Mass.: Blackwell, 2012), 323–35.

118. Augustine, *Haer.* 86.2–3, 5–6 (CCSL 46:338).

119. Augustine, *Haer. epil.* 3.41–43 (CCSL 4:344): *Nec ulli alieno ulla haeresis facile sic innotescit ut suis; unde nec earum quas commemoravi omnia dogmata me dixisse vel didicisse profiteor.*

Augustine lacked the time to acclimate himself fully to the particularities of the heretics; he lacked the resources, textual and otherwise, to produce a comprehensive heresiology; and above all else he lacked the insider status necessary to know what it was that heretics did, said, and believed. In standing apart from the heretics, Augustine gained only superficial knowledge. His foreignness precluded genuine understanding. In giving expression to sentiments of ethnographic failure and limitation, Augustine articulated the paradox and problems of his desire for more. As Clifford Geertz notes in his *Works and Lives*:[120]

> Confronted, in the academy, by a sudden explosion of polemical prefixes (neo-, post-, meta-, anti-) and subversive title forms (*After Virtue, Against Method, Beyond Belief*), anthropologists have had added to their "Is it decent?" worry (Who are *we* to describe *them*) an "Is it possible?" one (Can Ethiopian love be sung in France?), with which they are even less prepared to deal. How you know you know is not a question they have been used to asking in other than practical, empiricist terms: What is the evidence? How was it collected? What does it show? How words attach to the world, texts to experience, works to lives, is not one they have been used to asking at all.

Indeed, it was not just the ethnographers of the modern academy who contemplated the impossibility of ethnographic representation. Augustine too wondered how his *polemical* descriptions could ever serve as accurate depictions from which orthodox refutations would be constructed. He could not supply his congregants with authentic knowledge. Even with their manifestly different interests, both modern and ancient authors knew that ethnographic writing was an endeavor defined by translational, conceptual, and epistemological divides. Though the heresiologists' rhetoric of exposure was tempered by the fear of digging too deeply—a fear unrecognizable to an anthropologist such as Lévi-Strauss or Geertz—in both times and places the persistent desire to discover and uncover endured, despite reservations. There was no effort to bury the complexities of the worlds they sought to inhabit; they were embraced as the consequences of the human condition. The difficulty of the ethnographer's perspective could not simply be circumvented or ignored. It was a problem immanent within the activity itself.

CONCLUSION: CONSTRUCTING LACUNAE

Augustine's abbreviated heresiology conceived heretical errata as more than historical or theological phenomena to be refuted in texts. Heretics became ethnographic and thus textual dilemmas by virtue of their variable identities. Even in the cases where orthodox authors included heresies that they reported as extinct,

---

120. Clifford Geertz, *Works and Lives: The Anthropologist as Author* (Stanford: Stanford University Press, 1988), 135.

identified only in passing, or failed to name, heresiological inquiry was driven by the desire for comprehensive knowledge. While Augustine stopped at eighty-eight heresies, Epiphanius had enumerated eighty, and Filastrius had proposed one hundred fifty-six.[121] The world of heresy was not a stable entity with irreducible parameters. Beneath the veneer of infallibility, totality, unyielding investigation, exposure, and refutation, there was an equivocal awareness of the incompleteness and impossibility of the heresiologists' project. In openly acknowledging the elusive quality of the heretics and heretical knowledge, Augustine tried, instead, to theorize the fissures in his knowledge. The excessively possible—the hubristic rhetoric of exposure and the language of endless discovery—mutated into an explicit meditation on the possibility of the endeavor itself.

The disjuncture he observed between the many heretics with all their microscopic particularities and his position outside their world remained intact because of the conceptual fissure of the ethnographic gaze. The fact that Augustine's accounts of the most recent heresies—the Manichaeans, Tertullianists, Pelagians, Donatists, and Priscillianists—make up such a disproportionate volume of the text only reinforced the rifts of ethnographic gaze. His knowledge of the heretics, even when it appears altogether comprehensive, was necessarily partial. The sheer volume of heretics, known and unknown, present and future, laid an impossible burden upon the heresiologist. Though troubled by the implications of his incomplete knowledge, he refused to gloss over or ignore the limitations of his ethnographic expertise. Augustine's self-reflections worked in precisely the opposite manner of what Stephen Tyler describes as ethnographic projection: "Ethnographers project their fragmentary and incomplete experience of exotic cultures in a rhetorical form that creates the illusion of a comprehensive and coherent whole, and readers, by prior acquaintance with this form, fill in missing parts, creating in their imaginations what is not given but must be there by implications drawn from the form itself."[122] There was no effort on Augustine's part to create the illusion of a complex whole of heresy. The very flexibility of the list format made the appearance of the complex whole only all the more elusive. Far from inducing clarity about the heretics, Augustine's list perpetuated a paradox. On the one hand, a list must have a final entry and thus an ending. On the other hand, the form was eminently adaptable. The form itself facilitated and perhaps even cemented Augustine's ethnographic hesitations.

Heresiological authors sought, as the writings of Hippolytus, Epiphanius, and Theodoret demonstrated, to classify a seemingly chaotic world of unknowable disruption by anchoring heresy's essential function to the divine narrative of sacred

---

121. See *Filastrii Episcopi Brixiensis Diversarum Hereseon Liber*, ed. F. Heylen, CCSL 9 (Turnhout: Brepols, 1957), 207–324.

122. Tyler, "Ethnography, Intertextuality and the End of Description," 88.

history. Ethnographic master narratives ordered the disruption and centralized its remedy within the church. But while master narratives systematized the production and perpetuation of heretical diversity, they did not (and could not) explain the particularities of each new generation of heresy. Models of the heretics' development were not the same as an actual understanding of the heretics. Microscopic data, by contrast, described peoples but did not theorize them. These twin pillars of the ethnographic project—the macroscopic theorization and the microscopic collection of data—were mutually reinforcing; the one supplied the lacunae for the other. Augustine, however, disambiguated this twofold understanding of heresy. His "confusion of feeling" over the scope of his ethnographic project prompted his realization that there was no coherent structure that could elucidate the world of heresy. Through his investigation of the heretics, Augustine captured the paradox of Christian universalism: to proclaim Christianity as an ur-culture was to confront and ultimately defy the labile condition of culture itself. Stephen Greenblatt's comments about cultural formation and exportation in early modern Europe nicely illuminate the bind of an early Christian ideology of expansion and comprehension:[123]

> Cultures are inherently unstable, mediatory modes of fashioning experience. Only as a result of the social imposition of an imaginary order of exclusion—through the operation of what in the discussion that follows I will call "blockage"—can culture be invoked as a stable entity within which there are characteristic representations that are ordered, exported, accommodated. Such blockage occurs constantly—an infinite, unrestricted, undifferentiated circulation would lead to the collapse of cultural identity altogether—but it is never absolute.

Precisely because the world of heresy was a diffuse and diverse body, its very expansiveness, liminality, and mutation confounded the ethnographic gaze. Heretics contested the fabric of Christian ecumenical culture by exposing its thoroughgoing ignorance of the world around it. Neither macroscopic analysis nor microscopic travel could circumvent the limitations of ethnography and ethnographic classification. The internal rhetoric of heresiological texts at best complicated and at worst subverted the triumphalist, expansive discourse of Christian orthodoxy. The heresies were not simply a disruption within sacred history; they challenged the very foundations of narration, comprehension, and human understanding of the world that they had permeated. Insofar as Christian ethnography could never fully map, and by extension unite the world it studied, the world given to Adam by God was perhaps not so easily governed, named, and ordered as Genesis had promised.

---

123. Stephen Greenblatt, *Marvelous Possessions: The Wonder of the New World* (Chicago: University of Chicago Press, 1991), 121.

Epilogue

The Legacy of Heresiology

In 1947, the Argentinean writer and essayist Jorge Luis Borges published a short story entitled "The Theologians" ("Los teólogos") about a series of fictional theological controversies.[1] It is a story that treats debates over heresy and its extermination as contests over expertise, innovation, intellectualism, betrayal, fear, legitimation, and memorialization. For Borges, heresy and heresiology formed a mutually reinforcing, dependent, and ultimately comical discourse. The story begins with a massive conflagration of books. A group of Huns, we are told, set the library of a monastery ablaze because they were "fearful perhaps that the letters of the books might harbor blasphemies against their god, which was a scimitar of iron."[2] Despite the Huns' best efforts, a text survived—"the twelfth book of the *Civitas Dei*, which says that in Athens Plato once taught that at the end of time all things will return again to where they once were"—and on account of its seemingly miraculous survival, it "came to enjoy a special veneration" by Christians.[3] That veneration, however, was the product of a misunderstanding. For those who "read and reread [the twelfth book] in that remote province came to forget that the author put forth the doctrine only in order more roundly to refute it."[4] Heresiology became, despite its express intention to be the opposite, a mouthpiece of the heretics. It had given rise and credence to a *Christian* interpretation of Plato's blasphemous theory: a "newborn sect called the *Monotoni* (also the *Annulari*)" claimed that history was a cir-

---

1. Jorge Luis Borges, "The Theologians," in *Collected Fictions*, trans. Andrew Hurley (New York: Penguin, 1998), 201–7.
2. Ibid. 201.
3. Ibid.
4. Ibid.

cle, "and that all things that exist have existed before and will exist again."⁵ In failing to destroy the library completely, the Huns had produced an even more devastating event in the history of Christianity. Not only had they unwittingly caused the rise of the heresy of the Monotoni, the Huns had proved, paradoxically, the impossibility of their aspirations: heresy was indestructible. And the impossibility of its eradication would be felt most acutely not by the Huns but by the very people whom the Huns had sought to destroy. The Huns would ultimately get their wish: Christians would destroy Christians.

Fear of the Annulari, the narrator of the story reports, "gripped all men's hearts, yet all were comforted by the rumor that John of Pannonia . . . was preparing to refute this abominable heresy."⁶ A lone voice of dissent and despair, however, arose out of this seemingly welcome turn of events. Aurelian, bishop-coadjutor of Aquileia, "knew that in theology, there is no novelty without danger, then he reflected that the notion of circular time was too strange, too shocking, for the danger to be very serious."⁷ Aurelian sensed, as had Tertullian before him, that engaging with the Annulari was to transform an outré, bizarre, worthless opinion and group into a full-fledged, sanctioned, heretical foe. There was no reason to make them into an object worthy of engagement, for "the heresies we ought to fear are those that can be confused with orthodoxy."⁸ There was nothing remotely orthodox, according to Aurelian, about the Monotoni. To emphasize their teachings was to raise their profile, to amplify the destructive handiwork of the Huns. And although Aurelian knew better than to legitimize the enemy—he knew better, he implies, than John—ultimately he could not remain silent. His ego provoked and in due time overcame his restraint. Indeed, Aurelian "was pained most of all by the intervention—the intrusion—of John of Pannonia. Two years before, John's verbose treatise *De septima affectione Dei sive de aeternitate* had trespassed upon Aurelian's own field of expertise."⁹ Unable to resist an opportunity to outshine his theological rival, Aurelian seized the moment and undertook his own refutation of the Monotoni. When Aurelian finally read a copy of John's refutation of the Monotoni, he "looked at it with contempt. . . . John's treatise was limpid, universal; it seemed written not by a particular person, but by any man—or perhaps all men."¹⁰ There was no style to John's treatise, no effort to make it his own. It was utterly unsurprising, then, that the Council of Pergamon chose the measured words of John and not the erudite rhetoric of Aurelian to serve as the church's official refutation of the heresy of the Monotoni.

5. Ibid.
6. Ibid.
7. Ibid.
8. Ibid.
9. Ibid. 201–2.
10. Ibid. 203.

As Aurelian continued his "invisible" duel with John, "another tempestuous heresy spread. . . . the sect soon infested the eastern provinces, and sanctuaries were built in Macedonia, Carthage, and Trèves. It seemed to be everywhere."[11] The heresy, which Aurelian called the Histrioni, a name "they defiantly adopted for themselves," interpreted scripture to prove fallaciously "that the earth influences heaven."[12] "Contaminated," however, "by the Monotoni, they imagined that every man is two men and the real one is the other one, the one in heaven."[13] Humans had two forms, one earthly the other heavenly. These two modes of existence were in diametric opposition to each other, such that "if we [on earth] fornicate, the other man [in heaven] is chaste."[14] Upon death, the earthly form was subsumed by the heavenly appearance, and humans became a united, composite, coherent entity. Like most good heretics, of course, the Histrioni were a diverse lot. They were known by many names, including Speculari, Abysmali, Cainitae, Simulacra, Forms, and Nebuchadnezzars, and were distinguished by another theological doctrine. A second group of Histrioni "believed that the world would end when the number of its possibilities was exhausted."[15] It was only by performing every conceivable action and set of actions—by doing and saying everything imaginable, no matter how seemingly profane—that humans could prompt the eschaton.

The heresiologists of "The Theologians" revile the Histrioni not just for their devious theological opinions but equally for their base ways of life: "There is no heresiologue who does not express shock as he recounts their wild customs."[16] It is reported that many Histrioni practiced asceticism and bodily mutilation ("others put out their own eyes"); some even lived underground in sewers, while others went so far as to graze "on grasses like the oxen."[17] Certain communities were known to tolerate homicide, theft, sodomy, incest, and bestiality. They wrote their own sacred texts and theorized about the nature of history. Those who believed that the world would end only when "the number of its possibilities was exhausted; since there can be no repetitions, the righteous are duty-bound to eliminate (commit) the most abominable acts so that those acts will not sully the future and so that the coming of the kingdom of Jesus may be hastened."[18] The Histrioni shared only one attribute across their polyphonic mess of customs, habits, and opinions: "All were blasphemous."[19] "The Histrioni wove many, and diverse mythologies;

11. Ibid. 204.
12. Ibid.
13. Ibid. 205.
14. Ibid.
15. Ibid.
16. Ibid. 204.
17. Ibid.
18. Ibid. 205.
19. Ibid. 204.

some preached asceticism, others license—all preached confusion."[20] They were, like the Messalians of the *Panarion*, a blasphemous confusion.

In a report to the authorities at Rome about the state of his diocese, Aurelian mentioned the heresy of the Histrioni. He struggled, however, to put into words "the horrible thesis that no two moments are the same."[21] His gift for words failed him until a short description of this horrible doctrine suddenly came to him. While he wrote the words down furiously—in a fit of inspired joy, we are told—shortly thereafter he sensed that they were not his own. The words, his library confirmed, belonged to John of Pannonia, who had written them to combat the heresy of the Annulari. John had unwittingly declared himself to be a Histrion before the Histrioni had even existed! Aurelian was wracked by indecision, knowing full well the enormity of the implications behind John's words. "To alter or omit those words was to weaken the force of the statement; to let them stand was to plagiarize a man he detested; to indicate the source was to denounce him."[22] When Aurelian began pleading for divine intercession, his guardian angel proposed a compromise. Aurelian "kept the words, but set this disclaimer before it: *That which the heresiarchs howl today, to the confusion of the faith, was said during this century, with more levity than blameworthiness, by a most learned doctor of the church.*"[23] Aurelian's qualification, however, did little to blunt the ramifications of his discovery: "John of Pannonia was accused of professing heretical opinions."[24]

Hauled before a panel of judges, John was unwilling to recant his position: "Time and again he repeated that to deny his proposition was to fall into the pestilential heresy of the Monotoni."[25] What John had failed to realize was that the Monotoni and their heresy were now forgotten. John was sentenced to be burned at the stake. And so, like the books of the monastery destroyed by the Huns, he was consumed by flames. In the wake of John's fiery demise, Aurelian himself sought out the desert, where "he rethought the complex accusations against John of Pannonia and for the millionth time he justified the verdict."[26] And while he went to the desert for contemplative solitude, the desert had alternative plans: it took his life. Aurelian met his death when a lightning bolt set the wooded forest of his monastic cell ablaze. Like John, Aurelian was burned alive.[27] The shared manner of their deaths was, in fact, the culmination of their connected lives; it demonstrated the essential correspondence between heresy and orthodoxy. As the narrator of the

20. Ibid. 205.
21. Ibid. 206.
22. Ibid.
23. Ibid.
24. Ibid.
25. Ibid.
26. Ibid. 207.
27. Ibid.

story explains in its very last lines, with an almost sardonic sense of glee, "in paradise, Aurelian discovered that in the eyes of the unfathomable deity, he and John of Pannonia (the orthodox and the heretic, the abominator and the abominated, the accuser and the victim) were a single person."[28] In the end, the Histrioni were right: orthodoxy and heresy were one and the same.

In a mere seven pages, Borges captures the dilemma at the core of heresiological inquiry that I have described over the course of the previous seven chapters. Heresiology was an endeavor constructed not simply through competition—as much between heretics and heresiologists as among the heresiologists themselves—but through contradiction and limitation. Because the foundation on which heresiology rested was never secure, it unwittingly contained and created the seeds of its own obsolescence and destruction. Heresy was a fluid concept not simply for those proclaiming heresy and those seeking its destruction but, in fact, for all those who played a role in its birth, death, transformation, and afterlife. It was as theological ethnography—as a way of *writing* and *memorializing* heretical peoples—that heresiology's destructive capacity shook the theological foundations of Christianity. Insofar as the very act of managing heresy became, with time, heresy itself, the heresiologist was destroyed by his very allegiance to the church. The church demanded responses, and those responses required responses as the terrain of heresy changed. John's zeal to combat the heretics was the source of his own demise. Orthodoxy was a theological mirage, and heresiology was an ethnographic mirage. What John had failed to appreciate—and what he could never have appreciated—was that the contours of heresy defied predictability, continuity, and order. Although Theodoret's typological model of heresy had emphasized the contradictory nature of heretical opinion—owing to the fact that Satan tried to supplant orthodoxy by trial and error—it did not confront the fact that heresy was only strengthened by efforts to refute it.

While the heresy of Borges's Histrioni was a contingent phenomenon born of a particular moment in time, a particular crisis within the church—John's plea during his trial fell on deaf ears precisely because no one remembered the Monotoni—it was a symptom of an incurable disease endemic to Christianity. Particular heresies may come *and* go, but heresy itself always comes. The heresiologists understood that the history of heresy was an endless cycle of shifting theological frontiers. The Monotoni were right: their existence proved that history did unceasingly repeat itself. Because the refutation of the Monotoni was the heresy of the Histrioni, heresiology operated as a font of heresy. Orthodox condemnations opened the floodgates for strategic appropriation by heretics and heresy's demonic supporters: "The heresies we ought to fear are those that can be confused with

28. Ibid.

orthodoxy."²⁹ The history of heresy, as the heresiologists understood it, was germinated and perpetuated by heresiological inquiry: heresy was an unstoppable, inescapable facet of a now–theologically defined world. The orthodox commitment to studying and dismantling heresy was as much the problem as the solution. To study heresy was, at best, to destroy orthodoxy and, at worst, to reveal heresy and orthodoxy to be one and the same. Heresy destroys. Heresiology destroys. As Irenaeus laments of the heretics: "They seize the weak and entice them, by imitating our words in order to make them come [and listen] more often."³⁰

I have suggested that to describe heresiology is to identify a form of theological ethnography marked by contradictory and competing rhetoric. Heresiology propagates a discourse of anxiety, fear, and irresolution on the one hand and a discourse of discovery, conquest, and expertise on the other. It is the oscillation between these two poles—and the failure of either to emerge "victorious"—that has shaped my reading of heresiology over the course of the preceding chapters. Heresiology was a paradoxical field of study dedicated to a paradoxical enemy, an enemy at once natural and yet contrived, particular and yet universal, destructive yet worthless, human and yet supernatural. The imaginative universe of the heresiologists—even into the eighteenth century, as the works of Thomas Edwards and Ephraim Pagitt illustrate—was born of a series of theological contradictions, conceptual paradoxes, and discursive uncertainties.³¹ Heresiological catalogues expanded and contracted under the weight of their own innovation and upon the realization that the world was, perhaps, beyond description and understanding. Heresiological writing, in all its variations, transmitted unstable knowledge through unstable forms. Reading heresiology as ethnography has, I hope, emphasized the epistemological fractures, fissures, and self-reflection within the genre and among those who viewed themselves as its caretakers and practitioners. Indeed, what stands out is the Sisyphean quality to heresiological investigation: the way in which, as a type of polemical ethnography, it cracks under the weight of its own aspirations. It is an endless cycle of creative destruction and destructive creation. And the heresiologists knew it.

In positing a discursive consonance between ethnographic writing and heresiology, I have drawn particular attention to the problems of comprehension, repre-

29. Ibid. 201.
30. Irenaeus, *Adv. haer.* 3.15.2 (SC 211:280).
31. One can see this rhetorical hesitation in Thomas Edwards, *Gangraena; or, A Catalogue and Discovery of Many of the Errours, Heresies, Blasphemies and Pernicious Practices of the Sectaries of This Time, Vented and Acted in England in These Four Last Years* . . . (London, 1646), as well as Ephraim Pagitt's two heresiologies, *Christianography; or, The Description of the Multitude and Sundry Sorts of Christians in the World, Not Subject to the Pope: With Their Unity, and How They Agree with the Protestants in the Principall Poynts of Difference between Them and the Church of Rome* . . . (London, 1635); and *Heresiography; or, A Description of the Hereticks and Sectaries of These Latter Times* (London, 1645).

sentation, and textual closure. The heresiologists struggled immensely to map the boundless depths of the heretical world precisely as they attempted to depict the heretics "down to [their] last constituent element."[32] As they contemplated the heretics' profusion in terms that problematized their ability to translate people into words, Epiphanius and Augustine, in particular, struggled to comprehend the heretical profusion in its entirety. The heresiologists desired to identify the "complex whole" of heresy, to uncover the wholeness that the conjunction of "beliefs, customs, moral values, and so forth . . . somehow creates or makes manifest."[33] For the heresiologists, of course, their effort to understand the heretics' culture was motivated by a desire to dismantle it. And so the heretics' customs, habits, rituals, doctrines, dispositions, and geographies were described and invariably attacked in language that at once posited a coherent heretical wholeness and yet denied them any sense of order. The heretics were given coherence as part of a culture with its own systems of knowledge, ritual, and doctrine even as they were denied coherence, order, and clarity. Heresy was at once a complex whole made up of various parts (and parties) *and* an utterly incoherent mess of seemingly infinite difference and diversity. Heresiologists saw in the heretics a culture of unrestrained desire born of their theological hubris and demonic temptation. Theirs was a culture—at times manifestly clear and at other times utterly incoherent—to be avoided, rejected, and destroyed.

In the eras of uncritical ethnography, ethnographers characterized peoples, cults, and nations by a certain attitude toward themselves, the cosmos, and natural world. Edward Said famously argued that the orientalist projects into the world he studies a desire for schematization: "to make out of every observable detail a generalization and out of every generalization an immutable law about the Oriental nature, temperament, mentality, custom, or type; and, above all, to transmute living reality into the stuff of texts."[34] Insofar as foreign peoples across various times and places were represented and explained by principles, regardless of their truth, they were, as Said notes, denied their full humanity and their histories.[35] They were made into objects seemingly without agency by the missionaries, travelers, and academics who crafted them. The work of both orientalists and heresiologists reflects an effort to articulate a textual worldview, to conflate rhetoric and reality,

---

32. Claude Lévi-Strauss, *Tristes tropiques*, trans. John Weightman and Doreen Weightman (New York: Penguin, 2012), 333.

33. Christopher Herbert, *Culture and Anomie: The Ethnographic Imagination in the Nineteenth Century* (Chicago: University of Chicago Press, 1991), 4, 5.

34. Edward W. Said, *Orientalism* (New York: Vintage, 1978), 86.

35. On the denial of humanity and the colonial, postcolonial, and orientalist projects, see Catherine Hall, *Civilising Subjects: Metropole and Colony in the English Imagination, 1830–1867* (Chicago: University of Chicago Press, 2002); and Andrew Zimmerman, *Anthropology and Antihumanism in Imperial Germany* (Chicago: University of Chicago Press, 2002).

and to produce the very structures, themes, and comparative values that solidify their moral and religious centrality. Both projects were firmly tied to the discourse of Christianity as the only *vera religio* and as the intellectual place from which judgments about religion and irreligion were rendered. Even though I have investigated the ways in which the early Christian heresiologists developed their own powerful ethnographic discourse, there remains much to be said about the effects of the Christian coalescence of comparative ethnography and comparative theology in the history of ethnographic writing and in the history of religion. How did early Christian discourses about heretical worship, belief, and practice shape—beyond the commonly recognized etymological transformation of *religio* and *superstitio*—the modern discourse of religion or religions as both a part of and apart from notions of cultural and ethnic difference?[36] As the anthropologist Mary Louise Pratt has argued, ethnography's appeal to legitimacy via its scientific orientation, "over and against older, less specialized genres, such as travel books, personal memoirs, journalism, and accounts by missionaries, settlers, colonial officials, and the like ... blinds itself to the fact that its own discursive practices were often inherited from these other genres and are still shared with them today."[37]

Insofar as comparative theology was among the influential antecedents to the discipline of anthropology generally, and anthropology of religion specifically, notions of heresy and sectarianism held enormous influence over the discourse of religion.[38] As the necessary counter term to claims of Christian religiosity, the discourse of heresy became especially commonplace in and central to the writings of missionaries, early modern ethnographers, and comparative theologians. But to write heresy and heretical people—and by extension to write religion and religious people—was complicated by the fact that heresy was and would continue to be a protean, tenuous category. The discourse of heresy was never stable, uniform, or systematic, precisely because the indicia and criteria of orthodoxy were themselves variable. The genealogy of heresy must, then, account for the evolutions and opacity of the term—it must account for its ethnographic qualities—in relation to corresponding notions of religiosity, community, culture, civility, and savagery. Studies of heresy that attend to how the production of the discourse of heresy paralleled and shaped the formation and maintenance of "religion as a discrete cate-

---

36. See, for instance, Timothy Fitzgerald, *Discourse on Civility and Barbarity: A Critical History of Religion and Related Categories* (New York: Oxford University Press, 2007); Peter Harrison, *"Religion" and the Religions in the English Enlightenment* (New York: Cambridge University Press, 1990); and Talal Asad, "Medieval Heresy: An Anthropological View," *Social History* 11.3 (1986): 345–62.

37. Mary Louise Pratt, "Fieldwork in Common Places," in *Writing Culture: The Poetics and Politics of Ethnography*, ed. James Clifford and George E. Marcus (Berkeley and Los Angeles: University of California Press, 1986), 27–50, at 27.

38. Tomoko Masuzawa, *The Invention of World Religions; or, How European Universalism Was Preserved in the Language of Pluralism* (Chicago: University of Chicago Press, 2005), 14–21.

gory of human experience" reveal the mutual fluidity and interdependence of this terminological dyad.[39] How has the discourse of heresy—the *traditio haereticorum*—expressly shaped efforts to define the category of religion and the boundaries of religious knowledge? How did heresy as a pejorative theological category facilitate and disrupt the classification of religious knowledge, religious peoples, and religious places?

In the preceding chapters, I have maintained that the Christian heresiologists of late antiquity fashioned a style of theological ethnography and ethnographic investigation in order to construct and navigate the contours of their expanding Christian world. The process of creating what Averil Cameron has called Christianity's "intellectual and imaginative universe" was, at its most basic level, an exercise in ethnographic reasoning and writing.[40] It was a method of classifying the contents of the known world into an ordered theological schema in which heresy and sectarianism loomed especially large.[41] But the process of creating discourses for Christianity—rhetorics of education, biography, historiography, suffering, violence, and law, among myriad others, which advanced Christian theological, political, and intellectual interests—was not simply an exercise in fashioning a Christian culture:[42] it was a far grander undertaking, a protracted endeavor to create the conditions for a decidedly Christian world. As Cameron notes:[43]

> Out of the framework of Judaism, and living as they did in the Roman Empire and in the context of Greek philosophy, pagan practice, and contemporary social ideas, Christians built themselves a new world. They did so partly through practice—the evolution of a mode of living and a communal discipline that carefully distinguished them from their Jewish and pagan neighbors—and partly through a discourse that was itself constantly brought under control and disciplined.

---

39. Seth Schwartz, *Imperialism and Jewish Society, 200 B.C.E to 640 C.E.* (Princeton: Princeton University Press, 2004), 179.

40. Averil Cameron, *Christianity and the Rhetoric of Empire: The Development of Christian Discourse* (Berkeley and Los Angeles: University of California Press, 1991), 6.

41. Elizabeth Castelli, *Martyrdom and Memory: Early Christian Culture Making* (New York: Columbia University Press, 2004), has rightly championed the idea of early Christian culture making, which denotes the forging of a Christian framework for producing culture via the collective memory of suffering and martyrdom. With the notion of world making, as one fundamental aspect of ethnographic writing, I am gesturing at a conceptual endeavor related to culture making. Christian culture was being formed in conjunction with a deeper desire to read the entire world's content and history as part and parcel of a Christianizing gaze.

42. The polyphony of these writings—what Cameron calls the "elasticity" of early Christian discourse (*Christianity and the Rhetoric of Empire*, 9, 106, 113)—demonstrates the struggle not only to fashion coherent narratives about Christian history and tradition but also to emphasize the potential of the Christian intellectual tableau. Late antique Christianity was growing in the world as its elites were writing its texts and history.

43. Ibid. 21.

I have argued that in the late antique world, defined by remarkable religious and political change, the preoccupation to organize and systematize the world bound the aspiration to unite the world under the mantle of Christianity to ethnography and ethnographic investigation. Ethnographies of heresy functioned as theological imaginings of the world's Christians while also casting the wider world in theological language defined by the ideas of truth and falsity. The world existed not simply to be classified and discovered but to be revealed as fundamentally and irreversibly Christian. But the crucial question about heresiological classification is how Christians *managed* the knowledge they found and, in many cases, created.[44] How did they make sense of their fellow humans, both Christian and not? How did they fit them into a narrative of Christian sacred history? And what happened when authors looked beyond the limitations of the Bible? What happened when this foundational ethnological text failed to provide sufficient ethnographic resolution?

The overarching claim of *Classifying Christians* has been that Christians constructed an apparatus of classification through the development of Christian ethnographic discourses and dispositions. Principles of ethnographic writing enabled Christians to set the terms for the study of the world's people. In producing ethnographies, the heresiologists were asking and answering a series of questions about the process and effects of representing heretics in texts:[45]

> How were the ways of life of other peoples to be described? What items in their behavior were to be regarded as worthy of description and incorporation in a collection? What, in short, was a "manner" or a "custom"? And what words or images were to be called up by the members of a describing culture to communicate their views of the cultures under description?

In writing the heretics, the Christian heresiologists made decisions not only about what constituted heresy but also about how the heretics were to be described, represented, and circumscribed. Through discussions of the heretics' rituals, opinions, dress, diet, sexual practices, and a host of other attributes, the heresiologists developed their own distinctly ethnographic disposition. The preceding pages have been an attempt to examine how the heresiologists operated as ethnographers and thus as assemblers of the Christian world—how, in other words, the heresiologists created their own ethnographic language and discourse. And while the process of writing the heretics created and naturalized the contours of Christian knowledge about the world, it also permanently altered the trajectory of eth-

---

44. For a detailed study about knowledge management in the premodern era, see Ann M. Blair, *Too Much to Know: Managing Scholarly Information before the Modern Age* (New Haven: Yale University Press, 2010).

45. Margaret T. Hodgen, *Early Anthropology in the Sixteenth and Seventeenth Centuries* (Philadelphia: University of Pennsylvania Press, 1964), 166.

nographic writing. The infusion of Christian theology into ethnographic writing fundamentally transformed the landscape for thinking about the peoples of the world. Human unity and difference were recast in the language of theological doctrine, practice, and behavior. Surveying the world now meant mapping the contours of orthodoxy and heresy.

BIBLIOGRAPHY

SELECTED PRIMARY SOURCES

Aristotle. *Metaphysics*. 2 vols. Ed. and trans. Hugh Tredennick. LCL 271, 317. Cambridge, Mass.: Harvard University Press, 1933-35.

———. *On the Soul.* [*De anima.*] In *Aristotle*, vol. 8, ed. and trans. W. S. Hett, LCL 288:8-203. Cambridge, Mass.: Harvard University Press, 1936.

Athanasius. *Orations against the Arians.* [*Orationes contra Arianos.*] In *The Orations of St. Athanasius according to the Benedictine Text*, ed. William Bright. Oxford: Clarendon Press, 1870. Trans. *NPNF*, ser. 2, 4:306-447.

Augustine. *Against Faustus, a Manichee.* [*Contra Faustum Manichaeum.*] PL 42:207-518. Trans. Roland J. Teske, *Answer to Faustus, a Manichean*, in *The Works of Saint Augustine: A Translation for the 21st Century*, vol. 1, part 20, ed. Boniface Ramsey, 69-431. Hyde Park, N.Y.: New City Press, 2007.

———. *Catholic and Manichaean Ways of Life.* [*De moribus ecclesiae catholicae* and *De moribus Manichaeorum.*] PL 32:1309-78. Trans. Donald A. Gallagher and Idella J. Gallagher, *Saint Augustine: The Catholic and Manichaean Ways of Life*, FC 56. Washington, D.C.: Catholic University of America Press, 1966.

———. *Confessions.* In *Augustinus: Opera*, vol. 1, part 1, ed. Martin Skutella and Lucas Verheijen, CCSL 27. Turnhout: Brepols, 1990. Trans. Henry Chadwick, *Saint Augustine: Confessions*. New York: Oxford University Press, 1998.

———. *Letters 221* and *223. See under* Quodvultdeus.

———. *Letters 222* and *224*. In *S. Aurelii Augustini*, part 13, ed. R. Vander Plaetse and C. Beukers, CCSL 46:276-77, 280-81. Turnhout: Brepols, 1969. Trans. Roland J. Teske in *Arianism and Other Heresies*, vol. 1, part 18 of *The Works of Saint Augustine: A Translation for the 21st Century*, ed. John E. Rotelle, 25-26 and 27-28. Hyde Park: New City, 1995.

———. *On Genesis and Against the Manicheans*. [*De Genesis contra Manichaeos*.] In *Augustinus: De Genesis contra Manichaeos*, ed. Dorothea Weber, CSEL 91. Vienna: Verlag der Österreichischen Akademie der Wissenschaften, 1998.

———. *On the Heresies*. [*De haeresibus*.] In *S. Aurelii Augustini*, part 13, ed. R. Vander Plaetse and C. Beukers, CCSL 46:286–345. Turnhout: Brepols, 1969. Trans. Ronald J. Teske in *Arianism and Other Heresies*, vol. 1, part 18 of *The Works of Saint Augustine: A Translation for the 21st Century*, ed. John E Rotelle, 15–77. Hyde Park, N.Y.: New City Press, 1995.

Borges, Jorge Luis. "The Theologians." In *Collected Fictions*, trans. Andrew Hurley, 201–7. New York: Penguin, 1998.

Codex Theodosianus. [*Theodosian Code*.] Text in *Theodosiani libri XVI cum Constitutionibus Sirmondianis et leges novellae ad Theodosianum pertinentes*, ed. Theodor Mommsen and Paul Martin Meyer. Berlin: Weidmann, 1905. Trans. Clyde Pharr, *The Theodosian Code and Novels and the Sirmondian Constitutions*. Union, N.J.: Lawbook Exchange, 2001.

Diodorus Siculus. *Library of History*. 12 vols. Ed. and trans. C. H. Oldfather et al. LCL 279, 303, 340, 375, 377, 384, 390, 399, 409, 422, 423, 489. Cambridge, Mass.: Harvard University Press, 1933–67.

Edwards, Thomas. *Gangraena; or, A Catalogue and Discovery of Many of the Errours, Heresies, Blasphemies and Pernicious Practices of the Sectaries of This Time, Vented and Acted in England in These Four Last Years . . .* London, 1646.

Epiphanius. *Panarion*. Vol. 1, *Ancoratus and Panarion, Haer. 1–33*, ed. Karl Holl et al., GCS, n. F., 10. Boston: de Gruyter, 2013; vol. 2, *Panarion, Haer. 34–64*, ed. Karl Holl and Jürgen Dummer, GCS 31. Berlin: Akademie-Verlag, 1980; vol. 3, *Panarion, Haer. 65–80, and De fide*, ed. Karl Holl and Jürgen Dummer, GCS 37. Berlin: Akademie-Verlag, 1985; vol. 4, *Register zu den Bänden I–III*, ed. Karl Holl et al. New York: de Gruyter, 2006. Trans. Frank Williams, *The* Panarion *of Epiphanius of Salamis: Book I, Sects 1–46*, 2nd ed. Boston: Brill, 2009; and *The* Panarion *of Epiphanius of Salamis: Books II and II and De Fide*. 2nd ed. Boston: Brill, 2013.

Eusebius of Caesarea. *Ecclesiastical History*. 2 vols. Ed. and trans. Kirsopp Lake and J. E. L Oulton. LCL 153, 265. Cambridge, Mass.: Harvard University Press, 1926–32.

Filastrius. *Catalogue of Diverse Heresies*. [*Diversarum haereseon liber*.] In *Filastrii Episcopi Brixiensis Diversarum Hereseon Liber*, ed. F. Heylen, CCSL 9:207–324. Turnhout: Brepols, 1957.

Herodotus. *The Histories*. 4 vols. Ed. and trans. A. D. Godley. LCL 117–20. Cambridge, Mass.: Harvard University Press, 1920–25.

Hippolytus. *Refutation of All the Heresies*. [*Refutatio omnium haereseon*.] Ed. Miroslav Marcovich. Berlin: de Gruyter, 1986. Trans. ANF 5:9–153.

Irenaeus. *Against All Heresies*. [*Adversus haereses*.] Text and French translation in *Contre les hérésies*, ed. Adelin Rousseau, Louis Doutreleau, et al., 10 vols., SC 100.1, 100.2, 152, 153, 210, 211, 263, 264, 293, 294. Paris: Éditions du Cerf, 1969–2002. English trans. ANF 1:315–567; and Dominic J. Unger et al. in *St. Irenaeus of Lyons: Against the Heresies, Books 1–3*, 3 vols., ACW 55, 65, 64. Mahwah, N.J.: Paulist Press, 1992–2012.

Jacoby, Felix, ed. *Die Fragmente der griechischen Historiker*. [*FGrHist*.] 3 vols. Berlin: Weidmann, 1923–59.

Jerome. *Against Helvidius concerning the Perpetual Virginity of Mary*. [*Adversus Helvidium de Mariae virginitate perpetua*.] PL 23:193–216. Trans. NPNF 6:334–46.

John Cassian. *The Institutes.* [*De institutis coenobiorum.*] In *Iohannis Cassiani De institutis coenobiorum et De octo principalium vitiorum remediis libri XII*, ed. Michael Petschenig, CSEL 17:2–231. Vienna: apud C. Geroldi Filium, 1888. Trans. Boniface Ramsey, *John Cassian: The Institutes*, ACW 58. Mahwah, N.J.: Paulist Press, 2000.

———. *On the Incarnation.* [*De incarnatione Domini contra Nestorium libri VII.*] In *Iohannis Cassiani De institutis coenobiorum et De octo principalium vitiorum remediis libri XII*, ed. Michael Petschenig, CSEL 17:239–391. Vienna: apud C. Geroldi Filium, 1888. Trans. *NPNF*, ser. 2, 11:551–621.

Josephus. *Against Apion.* [*Contra Apionem.*] In *Josephus*, vol. 1, ed. and trans. H. St. J. Thackeray, LCL 186. Cambridge, Mass.: Harvard University Press, 1926.

Lucian of Samosata. A True Story [*Vera historia*]. In *Lucian*, vol. 1, *A True Story*, ed. and trans. A. M. Harmon, LCL 14:247–357. Cambridge, Mass.: Harvard University Press, 1913.

Manilius. *Astronomica.* Ed. and trans. G. P. Goold. LCL 469. Cambridge, Mass.: Harvard University Press, 1977.

Montaigne, Michel de. *Essays.* Trans. J. M. Cohen. New York: Penguin, 1993.

Müller, Carl, ed. *Fragmenta Historicorum Graecorum.* [*FHG.*] 5 vols. Paris: Firmin Didot, 1841–70.

———. *Geographi Graeci Minores.* [*GGM.*] 3 vols. Paris: Firmin Didot, 1855–61.

Nicander. *Theriaca.* In *Nicander: The Poems and Poetical Fragments*, ed. A. S. F. Gow and A. F. Scholfield, 28–93. London: Bristol Classical Press, 1997.

Pagitt, Ephraim. *Christianography; or, The Description of the Multitude and Sundry Sorts of Christians in the World Not Subject to the Pope: With Their Unity, and How They Agree with the Protestants in the Principall Poynts of Difference between Them and the Church of Rome . . .* London, 1635.

———. *Heresiography; or, A Description of the Hereticks and Sectaries of These Latter Times.* London, 1645.

Pausanias. *Description of Greece.* 5 vols. Ed. and trans. W. H. S, Jones, H. A. Ormerod, and R. E. Wycherley. LCL 93, 188, 272, 297, 298. Cambridge, Mass.: Harvard University Press, 1918–35.

Pliny. *Natural History.* 10 vols. Ed. and trans. H. Rackham et al. LCL 330, 352, 353, 370, 371, 392–94, 418, 419. Cambridge, Mass.: Harvard University Press, 1938–52.

Plutarch. *On Being a Busybody.* [*De curiositate.*] In *Moralia*, vol. 6, ed. and trans. W. C. Helmbold, LCL 337:471–517. Cambridge, Mass.: Harvard University Press, 1939.

Pomponius Mela. *Chorography.* In *Chorographie*, ed. Alain Silberman. Paris: Les Belles Lettres, 1998. Trans. F. E. Romer, *Pomponius Mela's Description of the World* (Ann Arbor: University of Michigan Press, 2001).

Posidonius. *Fragments.* Vol. 1, *The Fragments*, 2nd ed., ed. L. Edelstein and I. G. Kidd. New York: Cambridge University Press, 2005); vol. 2, *The Commentary, Parts 1 and 2*, and vol. 3, *The Translation of the Fragments*, trans. I. G. Kidd. New York: Cambridge University Press, 2004.

Pseudo-Jerome. *Indiculus de haeresibus.* PL 81:636–44.

Ptolemy. *Geography.* In *Claudii Ptolemaei Geographia*, ed. C. F. A. Nobbe, 3 vols. reprint, Hildesheim: Olms, 1966. Trans. J. Lennart Berggren and Alexander Jones, *Ptolemy's Geography: An Annotated Translation of the Theoretical Chapters.* Princeton: Princeton University Press, 2000.

———. *Tetrabiblos.* Ed. and trans. F. E. Robbins. LCL 435. Cambridge, Mass.: Harvard University Press, 1940.

Purchas, Samuel. *Purchas His Pilgrimage; or, Relations of the World and the Religions Observed in All Ages and Places Discovered, from the Creation unto This Present.* London: William Stansby, 1617.

Quodvultdeus. *Creedal Homilies.* In *Opera Quodvultdeo Carthaginiensi Episcopo Tributa,* ed. Réné Braun, CCSL 60:305–6. Turnhout: Brepols, 1976. Trans. Thomas Macy Finn, *Quodvultdeus of Carthage: The Creedal Homilies,* ACW 60. Mahwah, N.J.: Paulist Press 2004).

———. *Letters 221 and 223.* In *S. Aurelii Augustini,* part 13, ed. R. Vander Plaetse and C. Beukers, CCSL 46:273–75 and 278–79. Turnhout: Brepols, 1969. Trans. Ronald J. Teske in *Arianism and Other Heresies,* vol. 1, part 18 of *The Works of Saint Augustine: A Translation for the 21st Century,* ed. John E Rotelle, 24–25 and 26–27. Hyde Park, N.Y.: New City Press, 1995.

Sextus Empiricus. *Against the Professors.* Ed. and trans. R. G. Bury. LCL 382. Cambridge, Mass.: Harvard University Press, 1949.

Strabo. *Geography.* 8 vols. Ed. and trans. Horace Leonard Jones. LCL 49, 50, 182, 196, 211, 223, 241, 267. Cambridge, Mass.: Harvard University Press, 1917–32.

Tacitus. *Germania.* In *Germania: Translated with Introduction and Commentary,* ed. and trans. James B. Rives. Oxford: Clarendon Press, 1999.

———. *The Histories* and *The Annals.* 4 vols. Ed. and trans. C. H. Moore and J. Jackson. LCL 111, 249, 312, 322. Cambridge, Mass.: Harvard University Press, 1925–37.

Tertullian. *Against Hermogenes.* [*Adversus Hermogenem.*] Ed. A. Kroymann in *Tertullianus,* CCSL 1:395–436. Turnhout: Brepols, 1954.

———. *Against Marcion.* [*Adversus Marcionem.*] Ed. A. Kroymann and E. Evans in *Tertullianus,* CCSL 1:437–730. Turnhout: Brepols, 1954.

———. *Against Praxeas.* [*Adversus Praxean.*] Ed. A. Kroymann in *Tertullianus,* CCSL 2:1157–1206. Turnhout: Brepols, 1954.

———. *Against the Valentinians.* [*Adversus Valentinianos.*] Ed. A. Kroymann in *Tertullianus,* CCSL 1:751–78. Turnhout: Brepols, 1954.

———. *On the Soul.* [*De anima.*] Ed. J. H. Waszink in *Tertullianus,* CCSL 2:779–870. Turnhout: Brepols, 1954.

———. *Rule against the Heretics.* [*De praescriptione haereticorum.*] In *Traité de la prescription contre les hérétiques,* ed. and trans. R. F. Refoulé, SC 46. Paris: Éditions du Cerf, 1957. Trans. S. L. Greenslade, *Early Latin Theology: Selections from Tertullian, Cyprian, Ambrose, and Jerome,* 25–64. Louisville: Westminster John Knox Press, 1956.

Theodoret of Cyrrhus. *Compendium of Heretical Fables.* [*Haereticarum fabularum compendium.*] PG 83:336–556. Trans. Glenn Melvin Cope, "An Analysis of the Heresiological Method of Theodoret of Cyrus in the 'Haereticarum fabularum compendium,'" 74–356. Ph.D. dissertation, Catholic University of America, 1990.

SECONDARY SOURCES

Ackermans, Gian. "Einige rechtliche und theologische Fragen zu den Abeloitae in Augustins *De Haresibus.*" In *Augustine, Manichaeism and Other Gnosticism: Studies for Johannes van Oort at Sixty*, ed. Jacob Albert van den Berg, Annemaré Kotzé, Tobias Nicklas, and Madeleine Scopello, 123–38. Leiden: Brill, 2011.

Adams, Colin, and Ray Laurence, eds. *Travel and Geography in the Roman Empire*. New York: Routledge, 2001.

Adler, Patricia A., and Peter Adler. "Of Rhetoric and Representation: The Four Faces of Ethnography." *The Sociological Quarterly* 49 (2008): 1–30.

Adler, William. "The Origins of the Proto-Heresies: Fragments from a Chronicle in the First Book of Epiphanius' *Panarion*." *JTS* 41.2 (1990): 472–501.

Alcock, Susan E., John F. Cherry, and Jaś Elsner, eds. *Pausanias: Travel and Memory in Roman Greece*. New York: Oxford University Press, 2001.

Alföldi, Andreas. *Die monarchische Repräsentation im römischen Kaiserreiche*. Darmstadt: Wissenschaftliche Buchgesellschaft, 1970.

Almagor, Eram, and Joseph E. Skinner, eds. *Ancient Ethnography: New Approaches*. New York: Bloomsbury, 2013.

Ameling, Walter. "Ethnography and Universal History in Agatharchides." In *East & West: Papers in Ancient History Presented to Glen Warren Bowersock*, ed. T. Corey Brennan and Harriet I. Flower, 13–59. Cambridge, Mass.: Harvard University Press, 2008.

Anderson, Benedict. *Imagined Communities: Reflections on the Origin and Spread of Nationalism*. New York: Verso, 1983.

Ando, Clifford. *Imperial Ideology and Provincial Loyalty in the Roman Empire*. Berkeley and Los Angeles: University of California Press, 2000.

Aragione, Gabriella, and Enrico Norelli, eds. *Des évêques, des écoles et des hérétiques: Actes du colloque international sur la "Réfutation de toutes les hérésies," Genève, 13–14 juin 2008*. Lausanne: Éditions du Zèbre, 2011.

Armayor, O. Kimball. *Herodotus' Autopsy of the Fayoum: Lake Moeris and the Labyrinth of Egypt*. Amsterdam: Gieben, 1985.

Arnaud, Pascal. "L'image du globe dans le monde romain: Science, iconographie, symbolique." *Mélanges de l'École Française de Rome* 96.1 (1984): 53–116.

Asad, Talal. "The Concept of Cultural Translation in British Social Anthropology." In *Writing Culture: The Poetics and Politics of Ethnography*, ed. James Clifford and George E. Marcus, 141–64. Berkeley and Los Angeles: University of California Press, 1986.

———. "The Construction of Religion as an Anthropological Category." In his *Genealogies of Religion: Discipline and Reasons of Power in Christianity and Islam*, 27–54. Baltimore: The Johns Hopkins University Press, 1993.

———. "Medieval Heresy: An Anthropological View." *Social History* 11.3 (1986): 345–62.

Aujac, Germaine. *Claude Ptolémée, astronome, astrologue, géographe: Connaissance et représentation du monde habité*. Paris: Editions du CTHS, 1993.

Ayres, Lewis. *Nicaea and Its Legacy: An Approach to Fourth-Century Trinitarian Theology*. New York: Oxford University Press, 2004.

———, ed. *The Question of Orthodoxy*. Baltimore: The Johns Hopkins University Press. [Special issue, *JECS* 14.4 (2006).]

Badian, Ernst. "Alexander the Great and the Unity of Mankind." *Historia* 7 (1958): 425–44.

Bailey, Alan. *Sextus Empiricus and Pyrrhonean Scepticism*. New York: Oxford University Press, 2002.

Bak, János M. "Lists in the Service of Legitimation in Central European Sources." In *The Charm of a List: From the Sumerians to Computerised Data Processing*, ed. Lucie Doležalová, 34–45. Newcastle-upon-Tyne: Cambridge Scholars Press, 2009.
Bakhtin, Mikhail. "The Problem of Speech Genres." In his *Speech Genres and Other Late Essays*, ed. Caryl Emerson and Michael Holquist, trans. Vern W. McGee, 60–102. Austin: University of Texas Press, 1986.
———. *Problems of Dostoevsky's Poetics*. Ed. and trans. Caryl Emerson. Minneapolis: University of Minnesota Press, 1984.
Bardy, G. "Le 'De haeresibus' et ses sources." In *Miscellanea Agostiniana: Testi e Studi*, ed. G. Morin and A. Casamassa, vol. 2, 397–416. Rome: Tipografia Poliglotta Vaticana, 1931.
———. "L'‘indiculus de haeresibus' du pseudo-Jérôme." *RevScRel* 19 (1929): 385–405.
Barnard, Laurette. "The Criminalisation of Heresy in the Later Roman Empire: A Sociopolitical Device?" *Journal of Legal History* 121 (1995): 121–46.
Barnes, Timothy David. *Tertullian: A Historical and Literary Study*. Rev. ed. Oxford: Clarendon Press, 1985.
Barth, Fredrik, Andre Gingrich, Robert Parkin, and Sydel Silverman, eds., *One Discipline, Four Ways: British, German, French, and American Anthropology*. Chicago: University of Chicago Press, 2005.
Barton, Carlin A. *The Sorrows of the Ancient Romans: The Gladiator and the Monster*. Princeton: Princeton University Press, 1993.
Barton, Tamsyn. *Ancient Astrology*. New York: Routledge, 1994.
———. *Power and Knowledge: Astrology, Physiognomics, and Medicine under the Roman Empire*. Ann Arbor: University of Michigan Press, 2002.
Batty, Roger. "Mela's Phoenician Geography." *JRS* 90 (2000): 70–94.
Bauer, Walter. *Orthodoxy and Heresy in Earliest Christianity*. Ed. Robert A. Kraft and Gerhard Kroedel. Trans. Philadelphia Seminar on Christian Origins. 2nd ed. Philadelphia: Fortress, 1971.
Baumgarten, Albert I. *The Flourishing of Jewish Sects in the Maccabean Era: An Interpretation*. Leiden: Brill, 1997.
Beard, Mary, John North, and Simon Price. *Religions of Rome*. 2 vols. New York: Cambridge University Press, 1998.
BeDuhn, Jason. *Augustine's Manichaean Dilemma*. Vol. 1, *Conversion and Apostasy, 373–388 C.E.*; vol. 2, *Making a "Catholic" Self, 388–401 C.E.* Philadelphia: University of Pennsylvania Press, 2009–12.
Belknap, Robert E. *The List: The Uses and Pleasures of Cataloguing*. New Haven: Yale University Press, 2004.
Bentley, Jerry H. *Old World Encounters: Cross-Cultural Contacts and Exchanges in Pre-Modern Times*. New York: Oxford University Press, 1993.
Bergjan, Silke-Petra. *Theodoret von Cyrus und der Neunizänismus: Aspekte der altkirchlichen Trinitätslehre*. New York: de Gruyter, 1994.
Bertelli, Lucio. "Hecataeus: From Genealogy to Historiography." In *The Historian's Craft in the Age of Herodotus*, ed. Nino Luraghi, 67–95. New York: Oxford University Press, 2001.
Berzon, Todd S. "The Double Bind of Christianity's Judaism: Law, Language, and the Incoherence of Late Antique Discourse." *JECS* 23.3 (2015): 445–80.

———. "Heresiology as Ethnography: Theorising Christian Difference." In *Religious Competition in the Third Century CE: Jews, Christians, and the Greco-Roman World*, ed. Jordan D. Rosenblum, Lily C. Vuong, and Nathaniel P. DesRosiers, 180–92. Göttingen: Vandenhoeck & Ruprecht, 2014.
Bickerman, Elias J. "Origines Gentium." *CP* 47.2 (1952): 65–81.
Blair, Ann M. *Too Much to Know: Managing Scholarly Information before the Modern Age*. New Haven: Yale University Press, 2010.
Bloch, René S. *Antike Vorstellungen vom Judentum: Der Judenexkurs des Tacitus im Rahmen der griechisch-römischen Ethnographie*. Stuttgart: Steiner, 2002.
———. "Geography without Territory: Tacitus' Digression on the Jews and Its Ethnographic Context." In *Internationales Josephus-Kolloquium, Aarhus 1999*, ed. Jürgen U. Kalms, 38–54. Münster: Lit, 2000.
Blumenberg, Hans. "Curiositas und Veritas: Zur Ideengeschichte von Augustin, Confessiones X 35." *StPatr* 6 (1962): 294–302.
Boas, Franz. *The Mind of Primitive Man*. Rev. ed. New York: MacMillan, 1938.
———. *Race, Language, and Culture*. Chicago: University of Chicago Press, 1940.
Bonner, Gerald. "*Dic Christi Veritas Ubi Nunc Habitas:* Ideas of Schism and Heresy in the Post-Nicene Age." In *The Limits of Ancient Christianity: Essays on Late Antique Thought and Culture in Honor of R. A. Markus*, ed. William E. Klingshirn and Mark Vessey, 63–79. Ann Arbor: University of Michigan Press, 1999.
Bowlus, Charles E. "Ethnogenesis: The Tyranny of a Concept." In *On Barbarian Identity: Critical Approaches to Ethnicity in the Early Middle Ages*, ed. Andrew Gillet, 241–56. Turnhout: Brepols, 2002.
Boyarin, Daniel. "Apartheid Comparative Religion in the Second Century: Some Theory and a Case Study." *JMEMS* 36.1 (2006): 3–34.
———. *Border Lines: The Partition of Judaeo-Christianity*. Philadelphia: University of Pennsylvania Press, 2004.
Brakke, David. "Canon Formation and Social Conflict in Fourth-Century Egypt: Athanasius of Alexandria's Thirty-Ninth *Festal Letter*." *HTR* 87.4 (1994): 395–419.
———. *Demons and the Making of the Monk: Spiritual Combat in Early Christianity*. Cambridge, Mass.: Harvard University Press, 2006.
———. *The Gnostics: Myth, Ritual, and Diversity in Early Christianity*. Cambridge, Mass.: Harvard University Press, 2010.
———. A New Fragment of Athanasius's Thirty-Ninth *Festal Letter*: Heresy, Apocrypha, and the Canon." *HTR* 103.1 (2010): 47–66.
Brantlinger, Patrick. *Taming Cannibals: Race and the Victorians*. Ithaca: Cornell University Press, 2011.
Brent, Allen. "Diogenes Laertius and the Apostolic Succession." *JEH* 44.3 (1993): 367–89.
———. *Hippolytus and the Roman Church in the Third Century: Communities in Tension before the Emergence of a Monarch-Bishop*. New York: Brill, 1995.
Brodersen, Kai. *Pomponius Mela: Kreuzfahrt durch die alte Welt*. Darmstadt: Wissenschaftliche Buchgesellschaft, 1994.
Brown, Peter. *Augustine of Hippo*. Rev. ed. Berkeley and Los Angeles: University of California Press, 2000.

———. *Power and Persuasion in Late Antiquity: Towards a Christian Empire.* Madison: University of Wisconsin Press, 1992.
Brubaker, Rogers. *Ethnicity without Groups.* Cambridge, Mass.: Harvard University Press, 2004.
Bruce, Scott G. "Hagiography as Monstrous Ethnography: A Note on Ratramnus of Corbie's Letter concerning the Conversion of the Cynocephali." In *Insignis Sophiae Arcator: Medieval Latin Studies in Honor of Michael Herren on His 65th Birthday,* ed. Gernot R. Wieland, Carin Ruff, and Ross G. Arthur, 45–56. Turnhout: Brepols, 2006.
Brunt, P. A. "Laus Imperii." In *Imperialism in the Ancient World: The Cambridge University Research Seminar in Ancient History,* ed. P. D. A. Garnsey and C. R. Whittaker, 159–92. Cambridge: Cambridge University Press, 2007.
Buell, Denise Kimber. *Making Christians: Clement of Alexandria and the Rhetoric of Legitimacy.* Princeton: Princeton University Press, 1999.
———. *Why This New Race: Ethnic Reasoning in Early Christianity.* New York: Columbia University Press, 2005.
Burkert, Walter. *Ancient Mystery Cults.* Cambridge, Mass.: Harvard University Press, 1987.
Burridge, Kenelm. *Encountering Aborigines: A Case Study—Anthropology and the Australian Aboriginal.* Elmsford, N.Y.: Pergamon, 1973.
Burrus, Virginia. "Equipped for Victory: Ambrose and the Gendering of Orthodoxy." *JECS* 4.4 (1996): 461–75.
———. "The Heretical Woman as Symbol in Alexander, Athanasius, Epiphanius, and Jerome." *HTR* 84.3 (1991): 229–48.
———. "'In the Theater of This Life': The Performance of Orthodoxy in Late Antiquity." In *The Limits of Ancient Christianity: Essays on Late Antique Thought and Culture in Honor of R. A. Markus,* ed. William Klingshirn and Mark Vessey, 80–96. Ann Arbor: University of Michigan Press, 1999.
———. *The Making of a Heretic: Gender, Authority, and the Priscillianist Controversy.* Berkeley and Los Angeles: University of California Press, 1995.
Buzard, James, and Joseph Childers, eds. *Victorian Ethnographies.* Bloomington: Indiana University Press, 1998. [Special issue, *Victorian Studies* 41.3 (1998).]
Byron, Gay L. *Symbolic Blackness and Ethnic Difference in Early Christian Literature.* New York: Routledge, 2002.
Callataÿ, Godefroid de. "La géographie zodiacale de Manilius (*Astr.* 4, 744–817), avec une note sur l'Énéide virgilienne." *Latomus* 60 (2001): 35–66.
Cameron, Averil. *Christianity and the Rhetoric of Empire: The Development of Christian Discourse.* Berkeley and Los Angeles: University of California Press, 1991.
———. *Dialoguing in Late Antiquity.* Washington, D.C.: Center for Hellenic Studies, 2014.
———. "Enforcing Orthodoxy in Byzantium." *SCH* 43 (2007): 1–24.
———. "How to Read Heresiology." *JMEMS* 33.3 (2003): 471–92.
Campbell, Gordon Lindsay. *Strange Creatures: Anthropology in Antiquity.* London: Duckworth, 2006.
Campbell, Mary Baine. *The Witness and the Other World: Exotic European Travel Writing, 400–1600.* Ithaca: Cornell University Press, 1988.
Caner, Daniel. *Wandering, Begging Monks: Spiritual Authority and the Promotion of Monasticism in Late Antiquity.* Berkeley and Los Angeles: University of California Press, 2002.

Cannell, Fenella, ed. *The Anthropology of Christianity*. Durham: Duke University Press, 2006.
Capps, Walter H. *Understanding the New Religions*. New York: Seabury, 1978.
Carey, Sorcha. *Pliny's Catalogue of Culture: Art and Empire in the "Natural History."* New York: Oxford University Press, 2003.
———. "The Problem of Totality." *Journal of the History of Collections* 12.1 (2000): 1–13.
Casson, Lionel. *Travel in the Ancient World*. Baltimore: The Johns Hopkins University Press, 1994.
Castelli, Elizabeth A. *Martyrdom and Memory: Early Christian Culture Making*. New York: Columbia University Press, 2004.
Castelli, Emanuele. "The Author of the *Refutatio omnium haeresium* and the Attribution of the *De universo* to Flavius Josephus." In *Des évêques, des écoles et des hérétiques: Actes du colloque international sur la "Réfutation de toutes les hérésies," Genève, 13–14 juin 2008*, ed. Gabriella Aragione and Enrico Norelli, 219–31. Lausanne: Éditions du Zèbre, 2011.
Cerrato, J. A. *Hippolytus between East and West: The Commentaries and the Provenance of the Corpus*. New York: Oxford, 2002.
Chidester, David. *Empire of Religion: Imperialism and Comparative Religion*. Chicago: University of Chicago Press, 2014.
———. *Savage Systems: Colonialism and Comparative Religion in Southern Africa*. Charlottesville: University of Virginia Press, 1996.
Clark, Elizabeth A. *The Origenist Controversy: The Cultural Construction of an Early Christian Debate*. Princeton: Princeton University Press, 1992.
———. "Vitiated Seeds and Holy Vessels: Augustine's Manichean Past." In *Images of the Feminine in Gnosticism*, ed. Karen L. King, 367–401. Philadelphia: Fortress, 1988.
Clark, Gillian. "Can We Talk? Augustine and the Possibility of Dialogue." In *The End of Dialogue in Antiquity*, ed. Simon Goldhill, 117–34. New York: Cambridge University Press, 2008.
Clarke, Katherine. *Between Geography and History: Hellenistic Constructions of the Roman World*. New York: Oxford University Press, 1999.
———. "An Island Nation: Re-Reading Tacitus' *Agricola*." *JRS* 91 (2001): 94–102.
Clifford, James. "Introduction: Partial Truths." In *Writing Culture: The Poetics and Politics of Ethnography*, ed. James Clifford and George E. Marcus, 1–26. Berkeley and Los Angeles: University of California Press, 1986.
———. "Notes on Travel and Theory." *Inscriptions* 5 (1989): 177–88.
———. "On Ethnographic Allegory." In *Writing Culture: The Poetics and Politics of Ethnography*, ed. James Clifford and George E. Marcus, 98–121. Berkeley and Los Angeles: University of California Press, 1986.
———. "On Ethnographic Authority." In his *The Predicament of Culture: Twentieth-Century Ethnography, Literature, and Art*, 21–54. Cambridge, Mass.: Harvard University Press, 1988.
———. "On Ethnographic Self-Fashioning: Conrad and Malinowski." In his *The Predicament of Culture: Twentieth-Century Ethnography, Literature, and Art*, 92–113. Cambridge, Mass.: Harvard University Press, 1988.
Cohen, Shaye J. D. *The Beginnings of Jewishness: Boundaries, Varieties, and Uncertainties*. Berkeley and Los Angeles: University of California Press, 2001.

———. *From the Maccabees to the Mishnah*. 2nd ed. Louisville: Westminster John Knox, 2006.

Coleman, John E., and Clark A. Walz, eds. *Greeks and Barbarians: Essays on the Interactions between Greeks and Non-Greeks in Antiquity and the Consequences for Eurocentrism*. Bethesda, Md.: CDL Press, 1997.

Colish, Marcia L. *The Mirror of Language: A Study in the Medieval Theory of Knowledge*. Lincoln: University of Nebraska Press, 1983.

Conte, Gian Biagio. *Genres and Readers: Lucretius, Love Elegy, Pliny's Encyclopedia*. Trans. Glenn W. Most. Baltimore: The Johns Hopkins University Press, 1994.

Conybeare, Catherine. *The Irrational Augustine*. New York: Oxford University Press, 2006.

Cooper, John M. *Pursuits of Wisdom: Six Ways of Life in Ancient Philosophy from Socrates to Plotinus*. Princeton: Princeton University Press, 2012.

Countryman, L. William. "Tertullian and the *Regula Fidei*." *SecCent* 2 (1982): 208–27.

Coyle, John Kevin. *Manichaeism and Its Legacy*. Leiden: Brill, 2009.

———. "Saint Augustine's Manichaean Legacy." *AugStud* 34 (2003): 1–22.

Crapanzano, Vincent. "Hermes' Dilemma: The Masking of Subversion in Ethnographic Description." In *Writing Culture: The Poetics and Politics of Ethnography*, ed. James Clifford and George E. Marcus, 51–76. Berkeley and Los Angeles: University of California Press, 1986.

Davies, Charlotte Aull. *Reflexive Ethnography: A Guide to Researching Selves and Others*. 2nd ed. New York: Routledge, 2008.

Dechow, Jon. *Dogma and Mysticism in Early Christianity: Epiphanius of Cyprus and the Legacy of Origen*. Macon, Ga.: Mercer University Press, 1988.

Decret, François. *Aspects du manichéisme dans l'Afrique romaine: Les controverses de Fortunatus, Faustus et Felix avec saint Augustin*. Paris: Institut d'Études Augustiniennes, 1970.

Demoen, Kristoffel. "Incomprehensibility, Ineffability and Untranslatability: The Poverty of Language and the Abundance of Heresy in Fourth-Century Greek Patristic Thought." In *Heretics and Heresies in the Ancient Church and in Eastern Christianity: Studies in Honour of Adelbert Davids*, ed. Joseph Verheyden and Herman Teule, 105–26. Leuven: Peeters, 2011.

Demont, Paul. "Figures of Inquiry in Herodotus's *Inquiries*." *Mnemosyne* 62 (2009): 179–205.

Dench, Emma. "Ethnography and History." In *A Companion to Greek and Roman Historiography*, ed. John Marincola, 493–503. Malden, Mass.: Blackwell, 2007.

———. *Romulus' Asylum: Roman Identities from the Age of Alexander to the Age of Hadrian*. New York: Oxford University Press, 2005.

Denzey Lewis, Nicola. "*Apolytrosis* as Ritual and Sacrament: Determining a Ritual Context for Death in Second-Century Marcosian Valentinianism." *JECS* 17.4 (2009): 525–61.

———. *Cosmology and Fate in Gnosticism and Graeco-Roman Antiquity: Under Pitiless Skies*. Boston: Brill, 2013.

Doležalová, Lucie, ed. *The Charm of a List: From the Sumerians to Computerised Data Processing*. Newcastle-upon-Tyne: Cambridge Scholars Press, 2009.

Doody, Aude. *Pliny's Encyclopedia: The Reception of the "Natural History."* Cambridge: Cambridge University Press, 2010.

Drake, H. A. *Constantine and the Bishops: The Politics of Intolerance*. Baltimore: The Johns Hopkins University Press, 2000.

Drake, Susanna. *Slandering the Jew: Sexuality and Difference in Early Christian Texts*. Philadelphia: University of Pennsylvania Press, 2013.

Dueck, Daniela. "The Augustan Concept of 'an Empire without Limits.'" In *Creating and Representing Sacred Spaces*, ed. Michael Dickhardt and Vera Dorofeeva-Lichtman, 211–27. Göttingen: Peust and Gutschmidt, 2003.

Dunderberg, Ismo O. *Beyond Gnosticism: Myth, Lifestyle, and Society in the School of Valentinus*. New York: Columbia University Press, 2008.

———. "The School of Valentinus." In *A Companion to Second-Century "Christian Heretics,"* ed. Antti Marjanen and Petri Luomanen, 64–99. Boston: Brill, 2008.

Dunn, Geoffrey D. *Tertullian*. New York: Routledge, 2004.

———. "Tertullian's Scriptural Exegesis in *De praescriptione haereticorum*." *JECS* 14.2 (2006): 141–55.

Dunn, James D. G. *Unity and Diversity in the New Testament: An Inquiry into the Character of Earliest Christianity*. Philadelphia: Westminster, 1977.

Dwyer, Kevin. *Moroccan Dialogues: Anthropology in Question*. Baltimore: The Johns Hopkins University Press, 1982.

Ebbeler, Jennifer. *Disciplining Christians: Correction and Community in Augustine's Letters*. New York: Oxford University Press, 2012.

Ehrman, Bart D. *The Orthodox Corruption of Scripture: The Effect of Early Christological Controversies on the Text of the New Testament*. New York: Oxford University Press, 1993.

Elders, Leo J. "The Greek Christian Authors and Aristotle." In *Aristotle in Late Antiquity*, ed. Lawrence P. Schrenk, 111–42. Washington, D.C.: Catholic University of America Press, 1996.

Ellis, Linda, and Frank L. Kidner, eds., *Travel, Communication, and Geography in Late Antiquity: Sacred and Profane*. Burlington, Vt.: Ashgate, 2004.

Elm, Susanna. "'Pierced by Bronze Needles': Anti-Montanist Charges of Ritual Stigmatization in Their Fourth-Century Context." *JECS* 4.4 (1996): 409–39.

———. "The Polemical Use of Genealogies: Jerome's Classification of Pelagius and Evagrius Ponticus." *StPatr* 33 (1997): 311–18.

Elm, Susanna, Éric Rebillard, and Antonella Romano, eds. *Orthodoxie, christianisme, histoire*. Rome: École Française de Rome, 2000.

Eshleman, Kendra. "Becoming Heretical: Affection and Ideology in Recruitment to Early Christianities." *HTR* 104.2 (2011): 191–216.

———. *The Social World of Intellectuals in the Roman Empire: Sophists, Philosophers, and Christians*. New York: Cambridge University Press, 2012.

Evans, Rhiannon. "Ethnography's Freak Show: The Grotesques at the Edges of the Roman Earth." *Ramus* 28.1 (1999): 54–73.

———. "Geography without People: Mapping in Pliny's *Historia Naturalis*, Books 3–6." *Ramus* 34.1 (2005): 47–74.

Evans-Pritchard, E. E. "Religion and the Anthropologists." In his *Essays in Social Anthropology*, 29–45. New York: Free Press of Glencoe, 1963.

Fabian, Johannes. *Time and the Other: How Anthropology Makes Its Object*. New York: Columbia University Press, 2002.

Faller, Stefan. *Taprobane im Wandel der Zeit: Das Śrî Laṅkâ-Bild in griechischen und lateinischen Quellen zwischen Alexanderzug und Spätantike*. Stuttgart: Steiner, 2000.

Feldman, Louis H. *Jew and Gentile in the Ancient World*. Princeton: Princeton University Press, 1993.
Ferguson, Everett. "Tertullian, Scripture, Rule of Faith, and Paul." In *Tertullian and Paul*, ed. Todd D. Still and David Wilhite. 22–33. New York: T & T Clark, 2013.
Ferreiro, Alberto. *Simon Magus in Patristic, Medieval and Early Modern Traditions*. Leiden: Brill, 2005.
Fitschen, Klaus. *Messalianismus und Antimessalianismus: Ein Beispiel ostkirchlicher Ketzergeschichte*. Göttingen: Vandenhoeck und Ruprecht, 1998.
Fitzgerald, Timothy. *Discourse on Civility and Barbarity: A Critical History of Religion and Related Categories*. New York: Oxford University Press, 2007.
Flint, Robert. "Christianity in Relation to Other Religions." In *The Faiths of the World: A Concise History of the Great Religious Systems of the World*, 335–64. London: William Blackwood and Sons, 1882.
Flint, Valerie I. J. "Monsters and the Antipodes in the Early Middle Ages and the Enlightenment." *Viator* 15 (1984): 65–80.
Floridi, Luciano. *Sextus Empiricus: The Transmission and Recovery of Pyrrhonism*. New York: Oxford University Press, 2002.
Flower, Richard. "Genealogies of Unbelief: Epiphanius of Salamis and Heresiological Authority." In *Unclassical Traditions*, vol. 2, *Perspectives from East and West in Late Antiquity*, ed. Christopher Kelly, Richard Flower, and Michael Stuart Williams, 70–87. Cambridge: Cambridge University Press, 2011.
———. "'The Insanity of the Heretics Must Be Restrained': Heresiology in the *Theodosian Code*." In *Theodosius II: Rethinking the Roman Empire in Late Antiquity*, ed. Christopher Kelly, 172–94. New York: Cambridge University Press, 2013.
Fornara, Charles. *The Nature of History in Ancient Greece and Rome*. Berkeley and Los Angeles: University of California Press, 1998.
Foucault, Michel. *The Archaeology of Knowledge*. Trans. A. M. Sheridan Smith. New York: Pantheon, 1972.
———. *The Order of Things: An Archaeology of the Human Sciences*. New York: Vintage, 1970.
Fowler, Robert L. "Genealogical Thinking, Hesiod's *Catalogue*, and the Creation of the Hellenes." *Proceedings of the Cambridge Philological Society* 44 (1998): 1–19.
Frankfurter, David. "Comparison in the Study of Religions of Late Antiquity." In *Comparer en histoire des religions antiques: Controverses et propositions*, ed. Claude Calame and Bruce Lincoln, 83–98. Liège: Presses Universitaires de Liège, 2012.
Fredriksen, Paula. *Augustine and the Jews: A Christian Defense of Jews and Judaism*. New York: Doubleday, 2008.
Frend, W. H. C. "Heresy and Schism as Social and National Movements." In *Schism, Heresy and Religious Protest*, ed. Derek Baker, 37–56. Cambridge: Cambridge University Press, 1972.
Friedman, John Block. *The Monstrous Races in Medieval Art and Thought*. Syracuse: Syracuse University Press, 2000.
Gaddis, Michael. *There Is No Crime for Those Who Have Christ: Religious Violence in the Christian Roman Empire*. Berkeley and Los Angeles: University of California Press, 2005.

Galvão-Sobrinho, Carlos R. *Doctrine and Power: Theological Controversy and Christian Leadership in the Later Roman Empire*. Berkeley and Los Angeles: University of California Press, 2013.
Gass, William. "And." In *Voicelust: Eight Contemporary Fiction Writers on Style*, ed. Allen Wier and Don Hendrie, Jr., 101–25. Lincoln: University of Nebraska Press, 1985.
Gavrilyuk, Paul L. *The Suffering of the Impassable God: The Dialectics of Patristic Thought*. New York: Oxford University Press, 2004.
Geertz, Clifford. "Ethos, World View, and the Analysis of Sacred Symbols." In his *Interpretation of Cultures: Selected Essays by Clifford Geertz*, 126–41. New York: Perseus, 1973.
———. "Religion as a Cultural System." In his *The Interpretation of Cultures: Selected Essays by Clifford Geertz*, 87–125. New York: Perseus, 1973.
———. "Thick Description: Toward an Interpretive Theory of Culture." In his *The Interpretation of Cultures: Selected Essays by Clifford Geertz*, 3–30. New York: Perseus, 1973.
———. *Works and Lives: The Anthropologist as Author*. Stanford: Stanford University Press, 1988.
Gibbons, Kathleen. "Who Reads the Stars? Origen's Critique of Astrological Geography." In *The Routledge Handbook of Identity and the Environment in the Classical and Medieval Worlds*, ed. Rebecca Futo Kennedy and Molly Lewis-Jones, 230–46. New York: Routledge, 2015.
Ginzburg, Carlo. "The Inquisitor as Anthropologist." In his *Clues, Myths, and the Historical Method*, trans. John Tedeschi and Anne C. Tedeschi, 156–64. Baltimore: The Johns Hopkins University Press, 1989.
Goldie, Matthew Boyd. *The Idea of the Antipodes: Place, People, and Voices*. New York: Routledge, 2010.
González, Justo L. "Athens and Jerusalem Revisited: Reason and Authority in Tertullian." *CH* 43 (1991): 17–25.
Goodrum, Matthew R. "Biblical Anthropology and the Idea of Human Prehistory in Late Antiquity." *History and Anthropology* 13.2 (2002): 69–78.
Goody, Jack. *The Domestication of the Savage Mind*. New York: Cambridge University Press, 1977.
Goodyear, F. R. D. "Technical Writing." In *The Cambridge History of Classical Literature*, vol. 2, ed. E. J. Kenney and W. V. Clausen, 667–73. Cambridge: Cambridge University Press, 1982.
Grafton, Anthony. *Defenders of the Text: The Traditions of Scholarship in an Age of Science, 1450–1800*. Cambridge, Mass.: Harvard University Press, 1991.
Grafton, Anthony, April Shelford, and Nancy Siraisi, eds. *New Worlds, Ancient Texts: The Power of Tradition and the Shock of Discovery*. Cambridge, Mass.: Harvard University Press, 1995.
Green, Steven J. *Disclosure and Discretion in Roman Astrology: Manilius and His Augustan Contemporaries*. New York: Oxford University Press, 2014.
Greenblatt, Stephen. *Marvelous Possessions: The Wonder of the New World*. Chicago: University of Chicago Press, 1991.
Gribomont, Jean. "Le dossier des origines du messalianisme." In *Epektasis: Mélanges patristiques offerts au Cardinal Jean Daniélou*, ed. Jacques Fontaine and Charles Kannengiesser, 611–25. Paris: Beauchesne, 1972.

Gruen, Erich S. *Rethinking the Other in Antiquity.* Princeton: Princeton University Press, 2011.
Gurevich, Aron. *Historical Anthropology of the Middle Ages.* Chicago: University of Chicago Press, 1992.
Hadot, Pierre. *Philosophy as Way of Life: Spiritual Exercises from Socrates to Foucault.* Ed. Arnold I. Davidson. Trans. Michael Chase. Malden, Mass.: Blackwell, 1995.
———. *What Is Ancient Philosophy?* Trans. Michael Chase. Cambridge, Mass.: Belknap Press, 2004.
Hahm, David E. *The Origins of Stoic Cosmology.* Columbus: Ohio State University Press, 1977.
Hall, Catherine. *Civilising Subjects: Metropole and Colony in the English Imagination, 1830–1867.* Chicago: University of Chicago Press, 2002.
Hall, Jonathan M. *Ethnic Identity in Greek Antiquity.* New York: Cambridge University Press, 1997.
———. *Hellenicity: Between Ethnicity and Culture.* Chicago: University of Chicago Press, 2002.
Handley, Mark. *Dying on Foreign Shores: Travel and Mobility in the Late-Antique West.* Portsmouth, R.I.: Journal of Roman Archaeology, 2011.
Hardwick, Charles. *Christ and Other Masters: An Historical Inquiry into Some of the Chief Parallelisms and Contrasts between Christianity and the Religious Systems of the Ancient World.* 2 vols. 2nd ed. Cambridge: Macmillan, 1863.
Harland, Philip A., ed. *Travel and Religion in Antiquity.* Waterloo, Ont.: Wilfrid Laurier University Press, 2011.
Harmless, William J. *Desert Christians: An Introduction of the Literature of Early Monasticism.* New York: Oxford University Press, 2004.
Harper, Kyle. *From Shame to Sin: The Christian Transformation of Sexual Morality in Late Antiquity.* Cambridge, Mass.: Harvard University Press, 2013.
Harrington, D. J. "The Reception of Walter Bauer's *Orthodoxy and Heresy in Earliest Christianity* during the Last Decade." *HTR* 73 (1980): 289–98.
Harrison, Carol. *Augustine: Christian Truth and Fractured Humanity.* New York: Oxford University Press, 2000.
Harrison, Peter. "Curiosity, Forbidden Knowledge, and the Reformation of Natural Philosophy in Early Modern England." *Isis* 92.2 (2001): 265–90.
———. *"Religion" and the Religions in the English Enlightenment.* New York: Cambridge University Press, 1990.
Hartog, François. *The Mirror of Herodotus: The Representation of the Other in the Writing of History.* Trans. Janet Lloyd. Berkeley and Los Angeles: University of California Press, 1988.
Havel, Ivan M. "Time in Lists and Lists in Time." In *The Charm of a List: From the Sumerians to Computerised Data Processing,* ed. Lucie Doležalová, 9–11. Newcastle-upon-Tyne: Cambridge Scholars Press, 2009.
Hegedus, Tim. *Early Christianity and Ancient Astrology.* New York: Peter Lang, 2007.
Hegeman, Susan. "Franz Boas and Professional Anthropology: On Mapping the Borders of the 'Modern.'" In *Victorian Ethnographies,* ed. James Buzard and Joseph Childers, 455–83. Bloomington: Indiana University Press, 1998. [Special issue, *Victorian Studies* 41.3 (1998).]

Helleman, Wendy E. "Tertullian on Athens and Jerusalem." In *Hellenization Revisited: Shaping a Christian Response within the Greco-Roman World,* ed. Wendy E. Helleman, 361–82. Lanham, Md.: University Press of America, 1994.

Herbert, Christopher. *Culture and Anomie: The Ethnographic Imagination in the Nineteenth Century.* Chicago: University of Chicago Press, 1991.

Herzfeld, Michael. *Anthropology through the Looking-Glass: Critical Ethnography in the Margins of Europe.* New York: Cambridge University Press, 1987.

Hiatt, Alfred. *Terra Incognita: Mapping the Antipodes before 1600.* Chicago: University of Chicago Press, 2008.

Hilhorst, A. ed., *The Apostolic Age in Patristic Thought.* Leiden: Brill, 2004.

Hodgen, Margaret T. *Early Anthropology in the Sixteenth and Seventeenth Centuries.* Philadelphia: University of Pennsylvania Press, 1964.

Hodges, Horace Jeffrey. "Gnostic Liberation from Astrological Determinism: Hipparchan 'Trepidation' and the Breaking of Fate." *VC* 51.4 (1997): 359–73.

Honigmann, John J. *The Development of Anthropological Ideas.* New York: Dorsey, 1976.

Hopkins, Keith. "Christian Number and Its Implications." *JECS* 6.2 (1998): 185–226.

Hübner, Wolfgang. *Zodiacus Christianus: Jüdisch-christliche Adaptionen des Tierkreises von der Antike bis zur Gegenwart.* Königstein: Beiträge zur Klassischen Philologie, 1983.

Hughes, Ann. *Gangraena and the Struggle for the English Revolution.* New York: Oxford University Press, 2004.

———. "Thomas Edwards's *Gangraena* and Heresiological Traditions." In *Heresy, Literature, and Politics in Early Modern English Culture,* ed. David Loewenstein and John Marshall, 137–59. New York: Cambridge University Press, 2009.

Humfress, Caroline. "Controversialist: Augustine in Combat." In *A Companion to Augustine,* ed. Mark Vessey, 323–35. Malden, Mass.: Wiley-Blackwell, 2012.

———. *Orthodoxy and the Courts in Late Antiquity.* New York: Oxford University Press, 2007.

Hunter, David G. *Marriage, Celibacy, and Heresy in Ancient Christianity: The Jovinianist Controversy.* New York: Oxford University Press, 2007.

Hymes, Dell, ed. *Reinventing Anthropology.* New York: Vintage, 1974.

Inglebert, Hervé. "L'histoire des hérésies chez les hérésiologues." In *L'historiographe de l'Église des premiers siècles,* ed. B. Pouderon and Y.-M. Duval, 105–26. Paris: Beauchesne, 2001.

———. *Interpretatio Christiana: Les mutations des saviors (cosmographie, géographie, ethnographie, histoire) dans l'antiquité chrétienne, 30–630 après J.-C.* Paris: Institut d'Études Augustiniennes, 2001.

Iricinschi, Eduard, and Holger M. Zellentin. "Making Selves and Marking Others: Identity and Late Antique Heresiologies." In *Heresy and Identity in Late Antiquity,* ed. Eduard Iricinschi and Holger M. Zellentin, 1–27. Tübingen: Mohr Siebeck, 2008.

Isaac, Benjamin. *The Invention of Racism in Classical Antiquity.* Princeton: Princeton University Press, 2004.

Jacob, Christian. *Géographie et ethnographie en Grèce ancienne.* Paris: Armand Colin, 1991.

Jacobs, Andrew S. "Epiphanius of Salamis and the Antiquarian's Bible." *JECS* 21.3 (2013): 437–64.

———. *Remains of the Jews: The Holy Land and Christian Empire in Late Antiquity.* Stanford: Stanford University Press, 2004.

Jacoby, Felix. "Über die Entwicklung der griechischen Historiographie und den Plan einer neuen Sammlung der griechischen Historikerfragmente." *Klio* 9 (1909): 80–123.

James, S. T. "'Romanization' and the Peoples of Britain." In *Italy and the West: Comparative Issues in Romanization*, ed. Simon Keay and Nicola Terrenato, 187–209. Oxford: Oxbow, 2001.

Johnson, Aaron P. *Ethnicity and Argument in Eusebius' "Praeparatio Evangelica."* New York: Oxford University Press, 2006.

———. *Religion and Identity in Porphyry of Tyre: The Limits of Hellenism in Late Antiquity*. New York: Cambridge University Press, 2013.

Johnson, Scott Fitzgerald. "Travel, Cartography, and Cosmology." In *The Oxford Handbook of Late Antiquity*, ed. Scott Fitzgerald Johnson, 562–94. New York: Oxford University Press, 2012.

Johnson Hodge, Caroline E. *If Sons, Then Heirs: A Study of Kinship and Ethnicity in the Letters of Paul*. New York: Oxford University Press, 2007.

Johnston, Anna. "The Strange Career of William Ellis." *Victorian Studies* 49.3 (2007): 491–501.

Jones, A. H. M. "Were the Ancient Heresies National or Social Movements in Disguise?" *JTS* 10 (1959): 280–98.

Jones, Christopher P. "Ἔθνος and Γένος in Herodotus." *CQ* 46.2 (1996): 315–20.

———. *Kinship Diplomacy in the Ancient World*. Cambridge, Mass.: Harvard University Press, 1999.

Kaldellis, Anthony. *Ethnography after Antiquity: Foreign Lands and Peoples in Byzantine Literature*. Philadelphia: University of Pennsylvania Press, 2013.

Kaufman, Peter Iver. "Tertullian on Heresy, History, and the Reappropriation of Revelation." *CH* 60.2 (1991): 167–79.

Keech, Dominic. *The Anti-Pelagian Christology of Augustine of Hippo, 396–430*. New York: Oxford University Press, 2012.

Kelley, Nicole. "Astrology in the Pseudo-Clementine *Recognitions*." *JEH* 59.4 (2008): 607–29.

Kennedy, George A. "The Earliest Rhetorical Handbooks." *AJP* 80.2 (1959): 169–78.

Kessler, Andreas, Thomas Ricklin, and Gregor Wurst, eds. *Peregrina curiositas: Eine Reise durch den Orbis antiquus zu Ehren von Dirk van Damme*. Göttingen: Vandenhoeck & Ruprecht, 1994.

Khanmohamadi, Shirin A. *In Light of Another's Word: European Ethnography in the Middle Ages*. Philadelphia: University of Pennsylvania Press, 2014.

Kidd, Colin. *The Forging of Races: Race and Scripture in the Protestant Atlantic World, 1600–2000*. New York: Cambridge University Press, 2006.

Kidd, Douglas. *Aratus: Phaenomena*. New York: Cambridge University Press, 1997.

Kim, Young Richard. *Epiphanius of Cyprus: Imagining an Orthodox World*. Ann Arbor: University of Michigan Press, 2015.

———. "Epiphanius of Cyprus and the Geography of Heresy." In *Violence in Late Antiquity: Perceptions and Practices*, ed. H. A. Drake, 235–52. Burlington, Vt.: Ashgate, 2006.

———. "Reading the *Panarion* as Collective Biography: The Heresiarch as Unholy Man." *VC* 64 (2010): 382–413.

King, Karen L. "Factions, Variety, Diversity, Multiplicity: Representing Early Christian Differences for the 21st Century." *MTSR* 23 (2011): 216–37.

———. "Social and Theological Effects of Heresiological Discourse." In *Heresy and Identity in Late Antiquity*, ed. Eduard Iricinschi and Holger M. Zellentin, 28–49. Tübingen: Mohr Siebeck, 2008.

———. *What Is Gnosticism?* Cambridge, Mass.: Belknap Press, 2003.

———. "Which Early Christianity?" In *The Oxford Handbook of Early Christian Studies*, ed. Susan Ashbrook Harvey and David G. Hunter, 66–84. New York: Oxford University Press, 2008.

King, Richard. *Orientalism and Religion: Postcolonial Theory, India and 'The Mystic East.'* New York: Routledge, 1999.

Klawans, Jonathan. "Heresy without Orthodoxy: Josephus and the Rabbis on the Dangers of Illegitimate Jewish Beliefs." *JJMJS* 1 (2014): 99–126.

———. *Josephus and the Theologies of Ancient Judaism*. New York: Oxford University Press, 2013.

Kolbaba, Tia M. *The Byzantine Lists: Errors of the Latins*. Urbana: University of Illinois Press, 2000.

Koschorke, Klaus. *Hippolyt's Ketzerbekämpfung und Polemik gegen die Gnostiker: Eine tendenzkritische Untersuchung seiner "Refutatio omnium haeresium."* Wiesbaden: Harrassowitz, 1975.

Kraemer, Ross S. "Ecstasy and Possession: The Attraction of Women to the Cult of Dionysus." *HTR* 72.1–2 (1979): 55–80.

Krausmüller, Dirk. "Aristotelianism and the Disintegration of the Late Antique Theological Discourse." In *Interpreting the Bible and Aristotle in Late Antiquity: The Alexandrian Commentary Tradition between Rome and Baghdad*, ed. Josef Lössl and John W. Watt, 137–50. Burlington, Vt.: Ashgate, 2011.

Krueger, Derek. "Typological Figuration in Theodoret of Cyrrhus's *Religious History* and the Art of Postbiblical Narrative." *JECS* 5.3 (1997): 393–419.

Kuklick, Henrika. *The Savage Within: The Social History of British Anthropology, 1885–1945*. New York: Cambridge University Press, 1991.

Lamberigts, Mathijs. "Julian of Eclanum and Augustine on the Origin of the Soul." *Augustiniana* 46 (1996): 243–60.

———. "A Short Note on the Paterniani." *RÉAug* 31 (1985): 270–74.

Larsen, Timothy. *The Slain God: Anthropologists and the Christian Faith*. New York: Oxford University Press, 2014.

Le Boulluec, Alain. *La notion d'hérésie dans la littérature grecque, IIe–IIIe siècles*. 2 vols. Paris: Études Augustiniennes, 1985.

Lestringant, Frank. "The Euhemerist and the European Perception and Description of the American Indians." In *The Classical Tradition and the Americas*, vol. 1, part 1, *European Images of the Americas and the Classical Tradition*, ed. Wolfgang Haase and Meyer Reinhold, 173–88. New York: de Gruyter, 1994.

Lévi-Strauss, Claude. *Tristes tropiques*. Trans. John Weightman and Doreen Weightman. New York: Penguin, 2012.

Lightfoot, J. L. "Pilgrims and Ethnographers: In Search of the Syrian Goddess." In *Pilgrimage in Graeco-Roman and Early Christian Antiquity*, ed. Jaś Elsner and Ian Rutherford, 333–52. New York: Oxford University Press, 2005.

Lim, Richard. "Christians, Dialogues and Patterns of Sociability in Late Antiquity." In *The End of Dialogue in Antiquity*, ed. Simon Goldhill, 149–81. New York: Cambridge University Press, 2008.
———. "Christian Triumph and Controversy." In *Late Antiquity: A Guide to the Postclassical World*, ed. G. W. Bowersock, Peter Brown, and Oleg Grabar, 196–212. Cambridge, Mass.: Harvard University Press, 1999.
———. *Public Disputation, Power, and Social Order in Late Antiquity*. Berkeley and Los Angeles: University of California Press, 1995.
Lipsius, Richard Adelbert. *Zur Quellengeschichte des Epiphanios*. Vienna: Braumüller, 1865.
Livingstone, David N. *Adam's Ancestors: Race, Religion, and the Politics of Human Origins*. Baltimore: The Johns Hopkins University Press, 2011.
Lloyd, G. E. R. *The Ambitions of Curiosity: Understanding the World in Ancient Greece and China*. New York: Cambridge University Press, 2002.
Luttikhuizen, Gerard P. "Elchasaites and Their Books." In *A Companion to Second-Century "Christian Heretics,"* ed. Antti Marjanen and Petri Luomanen, 335–64. Boston: Brill, 2008.
Lyman, J. Rebecca. "2002 NAPS Presidential Address: Hellenism and Heresy." *JECS* 11.2 (2003): 209–22.
———. "Epiphanius on Orthodoxy." In *Orthodoxy, Christianity, History*, ed. Susanna Elm, Éric Rebillard, and Antonella Romano, 149–61. Rome: École Française de Rome, 2000.
———. "A Topography of Heresy: Mapping the Rhetorical Creation of Arianism." In *Arianism after Arius: Essays on the Development of Fourth-Century Trinitarian Conflicts*, ed. Michel R. Barnes and Daniel H. Williams, 45–64. Edinburgh: T & T Clark, 1993.
Maas, Michael. "'Delivered from Their Ancient Customs': Christianity and the Question of Cultural Change in Early Byzantine Ethnography." In *Conversion in Late Antiquity*, ed. Anthony Grafton and Kenneth Mills, 152–88. Princeton: Princeton University Press, 2009.
MacDonald, Scott. "The Paradox of Inquiry in Augustine's *Confessions*." *Metaphilosophy* 39.1 (2008): 20–38.
Maier, Harry O. "Dominion from Sea to Sea: Eusebius of Caesarea, Constantine the Great, and the Exegesis of Empire." In *The Calling of the Nations: Exegesis, Ethnography, and Empire in a Biblical-Historic Present*, ed. Mark Vessey, Sharon V. Betcher, Robert A. Daum, and Harry O. Maier, 149–75. Toronto: University of Toronto Press, 2011.
Maldonado-Rivera, David. "Encyclopedic Trends and the Making of Heresy in Late Ancient Christianity." Ph.D. dissertation, Indiana University, 2016.
Malinowski, Bronislaw. *A Diary in the Strict Sense of the Term*. Stanford: Stanford University Press, 1989.
Mansfeld, Jaap. *Heresiography in Context: Hippolytus' Elenchos as a Source of Greek Philosophy*. New York: Brill, 1992.
Marincola, John. *Authority and Tradition in Ancient Historiography*. New York: Cambridge University Press, 1997.
Marjanen, Antti, and Petri Luomanen, eds. *A Companion to Second-Century Christian "Heretics."* Boston: Brill, 2005.
Markus, R. A. "Christianity and Dissent in Roman North Africa: Changing Perspectives in Recent Work." In *Schism, Heresy and Religious Protest*, ed. Derek Baker, 21–36. Cambridge: Cambridge University Press, 1972.

Martin, Dale B. *Inventing Superstition: From the Hippocratics to the Christians.* Cambridge, Mass.: Harvard University Press, 2004.
Masuzawa, Tomoko. *The Invention of World Religions; or, How European Universalism Was Preserved in the Language of Pluralism.* Chicago: University of Chicago Press, 2005.
Mattern, Susan P. *Rome and the Enemy: Imperial Strategy in the Principate.* Berkeley and Los Angeles: University of California Press, 1999.
Matthews, John F. *Laying Down the Law: A Study of the Theodosian Code.* New Haven: Yale University Press, 2000.
Maurice, Frederick Denison. *The Religions of the World and Their Relations to Christianity, Considered in Eight Lectures Founded by the Right Hon. Robert Boyle.* London: John W. Parker, 1847.
McClure, Judith. "Handbooks against Heresy in the West, from the Late Fourth to the Late Sixth Centuries." *JTS* 30 (1979): 186–97.
McCormick, Michael. *Eternal Victory: Triumphal Rulership in Late Antiquity, Byzantium and the Early Medieval West.* Cambridge: Cambridge University Press, 1986.
McLennan, John F. *Primitive Marriage: An Inquiry into the Origin of the Form of Capture in Marriage Ceremonies*, ed. Peter Rivière. Chicago: University of Chicago Press, 1970.
McLynn, Neil B. *Ambrose of Milan: Church and Court in a Christian Capital.* Berkeley and Los Angeles: University of California Press, 1994.
Meeks, Wayne A. *The First Urban Christians: The Social World of the Apostle Paul.* 2nd ed. New Haven: Yale University Press, 2003.
——. *The Origins of Christian Morality: The First Two Centuries.* New Haven: Yale University Press, 1993.
Mejer, Jørgen. "Diogenes Laertius and the Transmission of Greek Philosophy." *ANRW* 2.36.5 (1992): 3556–3602.
Mena, Peter Anthony. "Insatiable Appetites: Epiphanius of Salamis and the Making of the Heretical Villain." *StPatr* 67 (2011): 257–63.
Merrills, A. H. "Monks, Monsters, and Barbarians: Re-Defining the African Periphery in Late Antiquity." *JECS* 12.2 (2004): 217–44.
Miles, Richard. "'Let's (Not) Talk about It': Augustine and the Control of Epistolary Dialogue." In *The End of Dialogue in Antiquity*, ed. Simon Goldhill, 135–50. New York: Cambridge University Press, 2008.
Milner, Vincent. *Religious Denominations of the World: Comprising a General View of the Origin, History and Condition of the Various Sects of Christians, the Jews, and Mahometans, as well as the Pagan Forms of Religion Existing in the Different Countries of the Earth.* Philadelphia: Bradley, Garreston, 1860.
Mitchell, Margaret M. *Paul and the Rhetoric of Reconciliation: An Exegetical Investigation of the Language and Composition of 1 Corinthians.* Louisville: Westminster John Knox, 1992.
Molendijk, Arie L., and Peter Pels, eds. *Religion in the Making: The Emergence of the Sciences of Religion.* Boston: Brill, 1998.
Moretti, Gabriella. "The Other World and the 'Antipodes': The Myth of the Unknown Countries between Antiquity and the Renaissance." In *The Classical Tradition and the Americas*, vol. 1, part 1, *European Images of the Americas and the Classical Tradition*, ed. Wolfgang Haase and Meyer Reinhold, 241–84. New York: de Gruyter, 1994.

Mortley, Raoul. *The Idea of Universal History from Hellenistic Philosophy to Early Christian Historiography*. Lewiston, N.Y.: Edwin Mellen, 1996.

Most, Glenn W, ed. *Collecting Fragments/Fragmente sammeln*. Göttingen: Vandenhoeck & Ruprecht, 1997.

Müller, Liguori G. *The "De Haeresibus" of Saint Augustine: Translation, with Introduction and Commentary*. Washington, D.C.: Catholic University of America Press, 1956.

Munier, Charles. "Analyse du traité de Tertullien De Praescriptione Haereticorum." *RevScRel* 59 (1985): 12–33.

Munson, Rosaria Vignolo. *Telling Wonders: Ethnographic and Political Discourse in the Work of Herodotus*. Ann Arbor: University of Michigan Press, 2001.

———, ed. *Herodotus*. Vol. 1, *Herodotus and the Narrative of the Past*; vol. 2, *Herodotus and the World*. New York: Oxford University Press, 2013.

Murphy, Trevor. *Pliny the Elder's "Natural History": The Empire in the Encyclopedia*. New York: Oxford University Press, 2004.

Murray, Oswyn. "History." In *Greek Thought: A Guide to Classical Knowledge*, ed. Jacques Brunschwig and Geoffrey E. R. Lloyd, trans. Catherine Porter, 328–37. Cambridge, Mass.: Belknap Press, 1996.

Nasrallah, Laura. *An Ecstasy of Folly: Prophecy and Authority in Early Christianity*. Cambridge, Mass.: Harvard University Press, 2003.

———. "Mapping the World: Justin, Tatian, Lucian, and the Second Sophistic." *HTR* 98.3 (2005): 283–314.

Nicolet, Claude, *Space, Geography, and Politics in the Early Roman Empire*. Trans. Hélène Leclerc. Ann Arbor: University of Michigan Press, 1991.

Nightingale, Andrea Wilson. *Spectacles of Truth in Classical Greek Philosophy: Theoria in Its Cultural Context*. New York: Cambridge University Press, 2004.

Norelli, Enrico. "Paix, justice, intégrité de la creation: Irénée de Lyon et ses adversaires." *Irén* 64.1 (1991): 5–43.

Norris, Richard. "The Transcendence and Freedom of God: Irenaeus, the Greek Tradition and Gnosticism." In *Early Christian Literature and the Classical Intellectual Tradition*, ed. William R. Schoedel and Robert L. Wilken, 87–100. Paris: Éditions Beauchesne, 1979.

O'Donnell, James J. *Augustine: A New Biography*. New York: Harper Perennial, 2005.

———. "The Authority of Augustine." *AugStud* 22 (1991): 7–35.

O'Gorman, Ellen. "No Place Like Rome: Identity and Difference in the *Germania* of Tacitus." *Ramus* 22.2 (1993): 135–54.

Olender, Maurice. *The Languages of Paradise: Race, Religion, and Philology in the Nineteenth Century*. Trans. Arthur Goldhammer. Cambridge, Mass.: Harvard University Press, 2009.

O'Loughlin, Thomas. "The Development of Augustine the Bishop's Critique of Astrology." *AugStud* 30.1 (1999): 83–103.

Olster, David M. "Classical Ethnography and Early Christianity." In *The Formulation of Christianity by Conflict through the Ages*, ed. Katherine B. Free, 9–31. Lewiston, N.Y.: Edwin Mellen, 1995.

Oort, Johannes van. "Mani and Manichaeism in Augustine's *De Haeresibus*: An Analysis of *Haer*. 46.1." In *Studia Manichaica: IV. Internationaler Kongress zum Manichäismus*, ed. Ronald E. Emmerick, Werner Sundermann, and Peter Zieme, 451–63. Berlin: Akademie-Verlag, 2000.

——. "Manichaean Christians in Augustine's Life and Work." *Church History and Religious Culture* 90 (2010): 505–46.

——. "Young Augustine's Knowledge of Manichaeism: An Analysis of *Confessiones* and Some Other Relevant Texts." *VC* 62 (2008): 441–66.

Osborn, Eric F. *Irenaeus of Lyons*. New York: Cambridge University Press, 2001.

——. "Reason and the Rule of Faith in the Second Century AD." In *The Making of Orthodoxy: Essays in Honour of Henry Chadwick*, ed. Rowan Williams, 40–61. New York: Cambridge University Press, 1989.

Pagels, Elaine. "Irenaeus, the 'Canon of Truth,' and the 'Gospel of John': 'Making a Difference' through Hermeneutics and Ritual." *VC* 56.4 (2002): 339–71.

——. *The Origins of Satan: How Christians Demonized Jews, Pagans, and Heretics*. New York: Vintage, 1995.

Paschoud, François. "Deux études sur Manilius." In *Romanitas, Christianitas: Untersuchungen zur Geschichte und Literatur der römischen Kaiserzeit*, ed. Gerhard Wirth, 125–53. Berlin: de Gruyter, 1982.

Pássztori-Kupán, István. *Theodoret of Cyrus*. New York: Routledge, 2006.

Patterson, Thomas C. *A Social History of Anthropology in the United States*. New York: Berg, 2001.

Perrin, Michel-Yves. "The Limits of the Heresiological Ethos in Late Antiquity." In *Religious Diversity in Late Antiquity*, ed. David M. Gwynn and Susanne Bangert, 201–27. Leiden: Brill, 2010.

Peters, Edward. "The Desire to Know the Secrets of the World." *JHI* 62.4 (2001): 593–610.

Pollmann, Karla. "Unending Sway: The Ideology of Empire in Early Christian Latin Thought." In *The Calling of the Nations: Exegesis, Ethnography, and Empire in a Biblical-Historic Present*, ed. Mark Vessey, Sharon V. Betcher, Robert A. Daum, and Harry O. Maier, 176–99. Toronto: University of Toronto Press, 2011.

Popkin, Richard H. *Isaac La Peyrère (1596–1676): His Life, Work and Influence*. New York: Brill, 1987.

Pourkier, Aline. *L'hérésiologie chez Épiphane de Salamine*. Paris: Beauchesne, 1992.

Pratt, Mary Louise. "Fieldwork in Common Places." In *Writing Culture: The Poetics and Politics of Ethnography*, ed. James Clifford and George E. Marcus, 27–50. Berkeley and Los Angeles: University of California Press, 1986.

Puertas, Alberto J. Quiroga, ed. *The Purpose of Rhetoric in Late Antiquity: From Performance to Exegesis*. Tübingen: Mohr Siebeck, 2013.

Qureshi, Sadiah. *Peoples on Parade: Exhibitions, Empire, and Anthropology in Nineteenth-Century Britain*. Chicago: University of Chicago Press, 2011.

Raaflaub Kurt A., and Richard J. A. Talbert, eds. *Geography and Ethnography: Perceptions of the World in Pre-Modern Societies*. Malden, Mass.: Wiley-Blackwell, 2013.

Rabinow, Paul. *Reflections on Fieldwork in Morocco*. Berkeley and Los Angeles: University of California Press, 1977.

Rapp, Claudia. *Holy Bishops in Late Antiquity: The Nature of Christian Leadership in an Age of Transition*. Berkeley and Los Angeles: University of California Press, 2005.

Rawson, Elizabeth. *Intellectual Life in the Late Roman Republic*. London: Duckworth, 1985.

Redfield, James. "Herodotus the Tourist." *CP* 80.2 (1985): 97–118.

Reed, Annette Yoshiko. "Retelling Biblical Retellings: Epiphanius, the Pseudo-Clementines, and the Reception-History of *Jubilees*." In *Tradition, Transmission, and Transformation from Second Temple Literature through Judaism and Christianity in Late Antiquity*, ed. Menahem Kister, Hillel Newman, Michael Segal, and Ruth Clements, 306–21. Leiden: Brill, 2015.

Richter, Daniel. *Cosmopolis: Imagining Community in Late Classical Athens and the Early Roman Empire*. New York: Oxford University Press, 2011.

———. "Plutarch on Isis and Osiris: Text, Cult, and Cultural Appropriation." *TAPA* 131 (2001): 191–216.

Riddle, Joseph E. *The Natural History of Infidelity and Superstition in Contrast with Christian Faith*. London: J. W. Parker, 1852.

Riggsby, Andrew M. *Caesar in Gaul and Rome: War in Words*. Austin: University of Texas Press, 2006.

———. "Guides to the Wor(l)d." In *Ordering Knowledge in the Roman Empire*, ed. Jason König and Tim Whitmarsh, 88–107. New York: Cambridge University Press, 2007.

Robinson, Thomas. *The Bauer Thesis Examined: The Geography of Heresy in the Early Christian Church*. Lewiston, N.Y.: Edwin Mellen, 1988.

Roller, Duane W. *Through the Pillars of Herakles: Greco-Roman Exploration of the Atlantic*. New York: Routledge, 2006.

Romm, James S. *The Edges of the Earth in Ancient Thought: Geography, Exploration, and Fiction*. Princeton: Princeton University Press, 1992.

Rosaldo, Renato. "From the Door of His Tent: The Fieldworker and the Inquisitor." In *Writing Culture: The Poetics and Politics of Ethnography*, ed. James Clifford and George E. Marcus, 77–97. Berkeley and Los Angeles: University of California Press, 1986.

Rothschild, Clare K. "Christ the Foolish Judge in Tertullian's *On the Prescription of Heretics*." In *Tertullian and Paul*, ed. Todd D. Still and David Wilhite, 34–44. New York: T & T Clark, 2013.

Royalty, Robert M., Jr. *The Origin of Heresy: A History of Discourse in Second Temple Judaism and Early Christianity*. New York: Routledge, 2013.

Rutherford, Ian. *State Pilgrims and Sacred Observers in Ancient Greece: A Study of* Theōriā *and* Theōroi. New York: Cambridge University Press, 2013.

———. "Tourism and the Sacred: Pausanias and the Traditions of Greek Pilgrimage." In *Pausanias: Travel and Memory in Roman Greece*, ed. Susan E. Alcock, John F. Cherry, and Jaś Elsner, 40–60. New York: Oxford University Press, 2001.

Rutledge, Steven H. *Ancient Rome as Museum: Power, Identity, and the Culture of Collecting*. New York: Oxford University Press, 2012.

Sacks, Kenneth S. *Diodorus Siculus and the First Century*. Princeton: Princeton University Press, 1990.

Said, Edward W. *Orientalism*. New York: Vintage, 1978.

Schepens, G. "Jacoby's *FGrHist*: Problems, Methods, Prospects." In *Collecting Fragments/ Fragmente sammeln*, ed. Glenn W. Most, 144–72. Göttingen: Vandenhoeck & Ruprecht, 1997.

Schillbrack, Kevin. "Religion, Models of, and Reality: Are We Through with Geertz?" *JAAR* 73.2 (2005): 429–52.

Scholten, Clemens. "Die Funktion der Häresienabwehr in der alten Kirche." *VC* 66 (2012): 229–68.

Schor, Adam. *Theodoret's People: Social Networks and Religious Conflict in Late Roman Syria*. Berkeley and Los Angeles: University of California Press, 2011.
Schott, Jeremy. *Christianity, Empire, and the Making of Religion in Late Antiquity*. Philadelphia: University of Pennsylvania Press: 2008.
———. "Heresiology as Universal History in Epiphanius's *Panarion*." ZAC 10.3 (2006): 546–63.
Schwab, Gabrielle. *Imaginary Ethnographies: Literature, Culture, and Subjectivity*. New York: Columbia University Press, 2012.
Schwartz, Seth. *Imperialism and Jewish Society, 200 B.C.E. to 640 C.E.* Princeton: Princeton University Press, 2004.
Scott, Alan. *Origen and the Life of the Stars: A History of an Idea*. New York: Oxford University Press, 1991.
Scott, James M. "On Earth as in Heaven: The Apocalyptic Vision of World Geography from Urzeit to Endzeit according to the *Book of Jubilees*." In *Geography and Ethnography: Perceptions of the World in Pre-Modern Societies*, ed. Kurt Raaflaub and Richard J. A. Talbert, 182–96. Malden, Mass.: Wiley-Blackwell, 2010.
Scullion, Scott. "'Pilgrimage' and Greek Religion: Sacred and Secular in the Pagan *Polis*." In *Pilgrimage in Graeco-Roman & Early Christian Antiquity: Seeing the Gods*, ed. Jaś Elsner and Ian Rutherford, 111–30. New York: Oxford University Press, 2005.
Secord, Jared. "The Cultural Geography of a Greek Christian: Irenaeus from Smyrna to Lyons." In *Irenaeus: Life, Scripture, Legacy*, ed. Sara Parvis and Paul Foster, 25–33. Minneapolis: Fortress, 2012.
———. "Medicine and Sophistry in Hippolytus' *Refutatio*." StPatr 65 (2011): 217–24.
Shaw, Brent D. "Bad Boys: Circumcellions and Fictive Violence." In *Violence in Late Antiquity: Perceptions and Practices*, ed. H. A. Drake, 179–97. Burlington, Vt.: Ashgate, 2006.
———. *Sacred Violence: African Christians and Sectarian Hatred in the Age of Augustine*. New York: Cambridge University Press, 2011.
———. "Who Were the Circumcellions?" In *Vandals, Romans and Berbers: New Perspectives on Late Antique North Africa*, ed. A. H. Merrills, 227–58. Burlington, Vt.: Ashgate, 2004.
Shaw, Teresa M. "Ascetic Practice and the Genealogy of Heresy: Problems in Modern Scholarship and Ancient Textual Representation." In *The Cultural Turn in Late Ancient Studies*, ed. Dale B. Martin and Patricia Cox Miller, 213–36. Durham: Duke University Press, 2005.
Shcheglov, Dmitry A. "Pomponius Mela's *Chorography* and Hellenistic Scientific Geography." In *The Periphery of the Classical World in Ancient Geography and Cartography*, ed. Alexander V. Podossinov, 77–94. Leuven: Peeters, 2014.
Shoemaker, Stephen J. "Epiphanius of Salamis, the Kollyridians, and the Early Dormition Narratives: The Cult of the Virgin in the Fourth Century." JECS 16.3 (2008): 371–401.
Sillett, Helen. "Orthodoxy and Heresy in Theodoret of Cyrus' *Compendium of Heresies*." In *Orthodoxy, Christianity, History*, ed. Susanna Elm, Éric Rebillard, and Antonella Romano, 261–73. Rome: École Française de Rome, 2000.
Simon, Marcel. "From Greek Hairesis to Christian Heresy." In *Early Christian Literature and the Classical Intellectual Tradition*, ed. William R. Schoedel and Robert L. Wilken, 101–16. Paris: Éditions Beauchesne, 1979.

Sizgorich, Thomas. *Violence and Belief in Late Antiquity: Militant Devotion in Christianity and Islam*. Philadelphia: University of Pennsylvania Press, 2009.

Skinner, Joseph E. *The Invention of Greek Ethnography: From Homer to Herodotus*. New York: Oxford University Press, 2012.

Smith, Geoffrey S. *Guilt by Association: Heresy Catalogues in Early Christianity*. New York: Oxford University Press, 2014.

Smith, Jonathan Z. "Sacred Persistence: Toward a Redescription of Canon." In *Imagining Religion: From Babylon to Jonestown*, 36–52. Chicago: University of Chicago Press, 1982.

Smith, Wilfred Cantwell. *The Meaning and End of Religion*. Reprint, Minneapolis: Fortress, 1991.

Smyth, Thomas. *The Unity of the Human Races*. New York: Putnam, 1850.

Sommer, Michael. "OIKOYMENH: Longue Durée Perspectives on Ancient Mediterranean 'Globality.'" In *Globalisation and the Roman World: World History, Connectivity and Material Culture*, ed. Martin Pitts and Miguel John Versluys, 175–97. New York: Cambridge University Press, 2015.

Sorabji, Richard. "Body and Soul in Aristotle." *Philosophy* 49 (1974): 63–89.

Spencer, Herbert. *The Principles of Sociology*. 3 vols. 3rd ed. London: Williams and Norgate, 1897–1906. Reprint, Westport: Greenwood, 1975.

Sponsler, Claire. "Medieval Ethnography: Fieldwork in the European Past." *Assays* 7 (1992): 1–30.

Staden, Heinrich von. "Haireseis and Heresy: The Case of the *haireseis iatrikai*." In *Jewish and Christian Self-Definition*, vol. 3, *Self-Definition in the Greco-Roman World*, ed. Ben F. Meyer and E. P. Sanders, 76–100. Philadelphia: Fortress, 1982.

Stahl, William Harris. "The Systematic Handbook in Antiquity and the Early Middle Ages." *Latomus* 23.2 (1964): 311–21.

Stewart, Columba. *"Working the Earth of the Heart": The Messalian Controversy in History, Texts, and Language to A.D. 431*. Oxford: Clarendon Press, 1991.

Stocking, George W., Jr. "Franz Boas and the Culture Concept in Historical Perspective." *American Anthropologist* 68 (1966): 867–82.

———. *Race, Culture, and Evolution: Essays in the History of Anthropology*. Chicago: University of Chicago Press, 1982.

———. *Victorian Anthropology*. New York: Free Press, 1991.

———, ed. *A Franz Boas Reader: The Shaping of American Anthropology, 1883–1911*. Chicago: University of Chicago Press, 1989.

Stowers, Stanley. "The Concept of 'Community' and the History of Early Christianity." *MTSR* 23 (2011): 238–56.

Stroumsa, Guy G. *A New Science: The Discovery of Religion in the Age of Reason*. Cambridge, Mass.: Harvard University Press, 2010.

———. "Philosophy of the Barbarians: On Early Christian Ethnological Representations." In *Barbarian Philosophy: The Religious Revolution of Early Christianity*, ed. Guy G. Stroumsa, 57–84. Tubingen: Mohr Siebeck, 1999.

———. "Religious Contacts in Byzantine Palestine." *Numen* 36.1 (1989): 16–42.

Stuckrad, Kocku von. "Jewish and Christian Astrology in Late Antiquity: A New Approach." *Numen* 47 (2000): 1–40.

Sulimani, Iris. *Diodorus' Mythistory and the Pagan Mission: Historiography and Culture-Heroes in the First Pentad of the "Bibliotheke."* Leiden: Brill, 2011.
Tasca, Francesca. "'Ecce Panis Haereticorum': Diversità alimentari ed identità religiose nel 'De haeresibus' di Agostino." *Aug* 50.1 (2010): 233–53.
Tasinato, Maria. *La curiosità: Apuleio e Agostino.* Milan: Luni, 2000.
Thomas, Richard F. *Lands and Peoples in Roman Poetry: The Ethnographical Tradition.* Cambridge: Cambridge Philological Society, 1982.
Thomas, Rosalind. *Herodotus in Context: Ethnography, Science and the Art of Persuasion.* New York: Cambridge University Press, 2000.
———. *Oral Tradition and Written Record in Classical Athens.* New York: Cambridge University Press, 1989.
Tiele, C. P. *Outlines of the History of Religion to the Spread of Universal Religions.* Trans. J. Estlin Carpenter. 7th ed. London: Kegan Paul, Trench, Trübner, 1905.
Tilley, Maureen A. "When Schism Becomes Heresy in Late Antiquity: Developing Doctrinal Deviance in the Wounded Body of Christ." *JECS* 15.1 (2007): 1–21.
Torchia, Joseph N. *Restless Mind: Curiositas and the Scope of Inquiry in St. Augustine's Theology.* Milwaukee, Wisc.: Marquette University Press, 2013.
Townsend, Philippa Lois. "Another Race? Ethnicity, Universalism, and the Emergence of Christianity." Ph.D. dissertation, Princeton University, 2009.
Tyler, Stephen A. "Ethnography, Intertextuality and the End of Description." *American Journal of Semiotics* 3.4 (1985): 83–98.
Unnik, W. C. van. "Theological Speculation and Its Limits." In *Early Christian Literature and the Classical Intellectual Tradition*, ed. William R. Schoedel and Robert L. Wilken, 33–44. Paris: Éditions Beauchesne, 1979.
Urbainczyk, Theresa. *Theodoret of Cyrrhus: The Bishop and the Holy Man.* Ann Arbor: University of Michigan Press, 2002.
Vallée, Gerard. *A Study in Anti-Gnostic Polemics: Irenaeus, Hippolytus, and Epiphanius.* Waterloo, Ont.: Wilfrid Laurier University Press, 1981.
Van Maanen, John. *Tales of the Field: On Writing Ethnography.* 2nd ed. Chicago: University of Chicago Press, 2011.
Vergin, Wiebke. *Das Imperium Romanum und seine Gegenwelten: Die geographisch-ethnographischen Exkurse in den "Res Gestae" des Ammianus Marcellinus.* Berlin: de Gruyter, 2013.
Verheyden, Joseph. "Epiphanius of Salamis on Beasts and Heretics: Some Introductory Comments." *Journal of Eastern Christian Studies* 60 (2008): 143–73.
Vessey, Mark, ed. *A Companion to Augustine.* Malden, Mass.: Wiley-Blackwell, 2012.
Veyne, Paul. "*Humanitas*: Romans and Non-Romans." In *The Romans*, ed. Andrea Giardina, trans. Lydia G. Cochrane, 342–69. Chicago: University of Chicago Press, 1993.
Visi, Tavas. "A Science of Lists?" In *The Charm of a List: From the Sumerians to Computerised Data Processing*, ed. Lucie Doležalová, 12–33. Newcastle-upon-Tyne: Cambridge Scholars Press, 2009.
Volk, Katharina, *Manilius and His Intellectual Background.* New York: Oxford University Press, 2009.
Walsh, P. G. "The Rights and Wrongs of Curiosity (Plutarch to Augustine)." *GR* 35.1 (1988): 73–85.

Warren, James. "Diogenes Laërtius, Biographer of Philosophy." In *Ordering Knowledge in the Roman Empire*, ed. James König and Tim Whitmarsh, 133–49. New York: Cambridge University Press, 2007.

Wessel, Susan. *Cyril of Alexandria and the Nestorian Controversy: The Making of a Saint and of a Heretic*. New York: Oxford University Press, 2004.

White, Hayden. "The Forms of Wildness: Archaeology of an Idea." In his *Tropics of Discourse: Essays in Cultural Criticism*, 150–82. Reprint, Baltimore: The Johns Hopkins University Press, 1986.

Whittaker, C. R. "Ethnic Discourses on the Frontiers of Roman Africa." In *Ethnic Constructs in Antiquity: The Role of Power and Tradition*, ed. Ton Derks and Nico Roymans, 189–206. Amsterdam: Amsterdam University Press, 2009.

———. *Rome and Its Frontiers: The Dynamics of Empire*. New York: Routledge, 2004.

Wilhite, David E. *Tertullian the African: An Anthropological Reading of Tertullian's Context and Identities*. New York: de Gruyter, 2007.

Williams, John. *A Narrative of Missionary Enterprises in the South Sea Islands*. London: Snow, 1837.

Willis, Geoffrey G. *Saint Augustine and the Donatist Controversy*. London: SPCK, 1950.

Wiseman, T. P. "Legendary Genealogies in Late-Republican Rome." *GR* 21.1 (1974): 153–64.

Wissowa, Georg. "Die Abfassungszeit der Chorographia des Pomponius Mela." *Hermes* 51 (1916): 89–96.

Wolf, Eric R. *Europe and the People without History*. 2nd ed. Berkeley and Los Angeles: University of California Press, 2010.

Woolf, Greg. *Tales of the Barbarians: Ethnography and Empire in the Roman West*. Malden, Mass.: Wiley-Blackwell, 2011.

Young, Frances M. "Did Epiphanius Know What He Meant by 'Heresy'?" *StPatr* 17 (1982): 199–205.

Zimmerman, Andrew. *Anthropology and Antihumanism in Imperial Germany*. Chicago: University of Chicago Press, 2002.

INDEX

Abeloim, Augustine on, 229, 242
Abraham (the patriarch), children of, 141
Acacius (abbot), Epiphanius's advice to, 42, 130
Academic culture, Christianity and, 163–64
Adam (the patriarch), 4n16; curiosity of, 157; disobedience of, 132; in Justinus, 118; world given to, 245
Adamians (heretics), 70
Aetius, Bishop: Epiphanius on, 172, 173
Africa: in Mela's *Chorography*, 198–99; the monstrous in, 199; Pliny on, 199–200; as unknowable, 199
Alföldi, Andreas, 191n18
Alogi (sect), 131
Anacephalaeoses (*Recapitulations*): Augustine's use of, 227n41, 231; authorship of, 227n37
ancestral worship, 135–36; and communal identity, 136
ancestry, ethnographic validation of, 41
Anderson, Benedict: on shared culture, 75
angels, in Justinus's cosmology, 118–19
Anomoeans: Epiphanius on, 172–73; on knowledge of God, 237n89
anthropology: astrological, 111–12; authority of, 54; biblical, 3–4, 19, 20, 90; Boas's contributions to, 1–2; Christianity and, 2–3, 142n75; and colonialism, 87; early modern, 4; fieldwork in, 22, 232n65; human unity in, 5n21; negotiation of uncertainty, 56; objective reality in, 5n21; signature and discourse in, 56;

study of non-Western world, 19; theological, 5, 171
anthropology, Victorian, 30; armchair, 19, 20, 58, 87; heresiology and, 60; on human diversity, 87; on mentalities, 86–87; missionary purpose of, 23n89; on non-Western religions, 18; pioneers of, 18n67; sources for, 23n89; taxonomy of, 19
Antidicomarites, Epiphanius on, 228n49
antiethnography, rhetoric of, 25, 92n72, 160
Antipodes: in Christianity, 201n65; in Mela, 201–2. *See also* counterworld
antiquity: astrology in, 101n12; curiosity in, 35, 156–57; human unity in, 125; incoherent coherence in, 79n101; similarities among peoples, 29n7. *See also* ethnography, ancient
Apollonius Molon, 36n39
apologists, Christian, 193, 194; particularized knowledge of, 195
apolytrosis, deathbed, 64
apostolic succession, 140, 140n62, 163; heretics' incompatibility with, 151
Arateans, astrology of, 109–10
Aratus, *Phaenomena,* 114
Aristotle: on curiosity, 156–57; ethnography of, 90; on inquiry, 163; on knowledge, 180n132. Works: *Metaphysics*, 157; *Politics,* 90
Arius: intellectual lineage of, 147; as polemical tool, 77; Theodoret on, 147
Artemon (heretic), 147

INDEX

Asad, Talal, 63, 87, 221
asceticism: development of, 72; heretical disposition toward, 80–85; orthodoxy and, 81n111; true/false, 81–82, 84–85, 94
Ascitae, Augustine on, 230
astrogeography, 104, 105–6; Manilius's, 105n24
astrology: in antiquity, 101n12; Chaldean, 104, 111, 112; challenge to God's omnipotence, 110, 113; in Christian dogma, 104; and climatology, 106–7; delegitimization of, 115; early Christian attitudes toward, 101n12; emanated universe of, 113n64; false powers of, 114; and free will, 110, 113; genethlialogical, 107, 111, 113; Greco-Roman, 104–9; heretical, 24; human diversity in, 104, 105n24, 112, 116; as knowledge system, 114, 116; macrocosm of, 106, 113, 114, 124; Manilius on, 104–7; microcosmic, 106, 113; mundane, 107; and physiognomy, 107; prescience of, 110; as system of governance, 109; *technē* of, 110; terminology of, 113. *See also* determinism, astrological; horoscopes; zodiac
astrology, ethnographic, 104, 105, 106, 107; Hippolytus on, 109–16; reasoning of, 112; suppositions of, 115
Athanasius of Alexandria, *Orations against the Arians*, 66
Audians, Epiphanius on, 174–75
Augilae, Mela on, 198
Augustine of Hippo: affiliation with Manichaeans, 240–42; on argumentation, 170; on avoidance of heresy, 239; comprehension of heresy, 220; on curiosity, 157; ethnographic failures of, 242–43; definition of heretics, 219; devotion to Bible, 240; dislike of dialogic form, 164; engagement with error, 242n117; ethnographic authority of, 242; ethnographic gaze of, 220; and Faustus, 70–71, 241; as foreign author, 242, 243; heresiology of, 6, 227; on intellectual openness, 161; knowledge of heresy, 220, 232; linguistic epistemology of, 232n64; lived fieldwork of, 242; love of Cicero, 239–40; on Manichaeans, 70; memory of Christ, 240; polemical descriptions of, 243; as purveyor of truth, 242; on reading of scripture, 240; on scope of ethnography, 245; self-conceptualization of, 229n52; on Simonians, 146n89; as teacher, 222n14; on totalizing knowledge, 10
—*Against Faustus, a Manichee*, 70–71
—*Confessions*, self-interrogation in, 238
—*De haeresibus*, 43n70; Abeloim in, 229, 242; Adamians in, 70; aim of, 230; antecedents of, 26; antitypology of, 225; armchair research in, 220, 232; on Ascitae, 230; authorial position of, 233; on Cataphrygians, 231; classification in, 220, 230; collection in, 235n78; comprehension of heresy in, 234n69; condensation in, 219, 221, 227; conduct of heretics in, 230–31; correction of errors, 229; currency of, 220; customs in, 68; definitional problem of, 238; desire for comprehensiveness in, 231; dialogic form of, 225–26; differentiation of heresiologies, 218–19, 228n45; enumeration of heretics, 16, 69–70, 119, 222, 225, 227, 228–30; epistemology of, 232, 235, 238; on ethnographers' understanding, 232; ethnographic foreignness in, 242; ethnographic hesitation in, 220, 232, 244; ethnographic logic of, 229; ethnographic mapping in, 221; ethnographic representation in, 219; etymology in, 230; foundational figures in, 230; as handbook, 219, 224, 229; Helvidians in, 228; on heresiological knowledge, 220, 221; impediments for, 220; incompleteness of, 219, 231, 238, 242–43, 244; interrogation of heretics, 238; invocation of mastery, 221; on Jovianists, 228; knowledge management in, 220; limits of, 26, 221; listing in, 219, 223, 224, 244; literary units of, 69; Luciferians in, 228; Manichaeans in, 241; Messalians in, 73–74; omissions from, 229; partial knowledge in, 233, 239n98; particularity in, 225; Pelagians in, 229, 242; on Pepuzians, 231; performative editing of, 233; the phenomenologically knowable in, 229; as polemical palimpsest, 26; prose of, 219; Quodvultdeus's request for, 44, 69, 220, 222–23, 226, 231, 232, 233; on Sabellians, 230n54; Saturninians in, 230; scholarship on, 218n2, 220; shortcomings of, 233n69; sources of, 220, 223, 226, 227–28, 232, 233; state of heretical world in, 225; Tertullianists in, 242; textual aspects of, 234, 235; theological principles of, 230; totalizing aspirations of, 26; transformation of ethnography in, 226–31; unity in, 225; the unknowable in, 232–33; unnamed heresies in, 230; updating of, 224n19; usable knowledge in, 219; use of *Anacephalaeoses*, 227n41, 231; use of Epiphanius, 228, 233, 238n92; use of Filastrius, 228, 233, 238n92; use of Irenaeus, 227n38; use of *Recapitulations*, 227; utilitarian design of, 233; ways of life in, 72
Augustus (emperor of Rome), triumph over world, 192

authors, ancient: ethnic particularity of, 193, 194; ethnographic disposition of, 24
authors, ethnographic, 23, 24, 159; objectivity of, 41; preconceptions of, 55; textual choices of, 39; travels of, 6n22, 37, 87
authorship: anthropological, 56; writing and, 56
autopsy, ethnographical, 37, 41; discursive choice of, 38; in heresiology, 43n70

Babel (angel), 118
Babel, tower of, 134, 135
Babylonian exile, 137–38
Bakhtin, Mikhail, 7
baptism: in Donatist controversy, 69n45; jeopardy of heresy to, 68
barbarians, wisdom of, 194
Barbarism (foundational heresy), 132, 133, 143
Bardy, G., 228n46
Barthes, Roland: "From Work to Text," 56
Barton, Carlin A., 199n57, 212, 217
Barton, Tamsyn: on astrology, 104, 107n32
Baruch (paternal angel), 118–19
Bauer, Walter: theory of heresy, 13–14, 14n17
Baumgarten, Albert I., 48n94
behavior, human: in heresiological ethnography, 99; heretical, 21, 61, 116–20; Messalian, 80
Belknap, Robert, 225
Berossus, *Babyloniaka*, 34
bishops, responsibilities of, 204n82, 226, 227
Boas, Franz, 22; contributions to anthropology, 1–2; definition of culture, 2; *The Mind of Primitive Man*, 1
Borges, Jorge Luis: "The Theologians," 247–51; book burning in, 247–50; fictional sects in, 247–51; fictitious theologians in, 248–51; heresiologists of, 249
Bourdieu, Pierre, 77
Boyarin, Daniel, 22; on Christian identity, 59; on Council of Nicaea, 158; on heresiology, 93
Brakke, David, 14, 51n111; on discourse of heresy, 78
Brubaker, Rogers, 77–78; on categories, 27–28
Buddhism, Western ethnography on, 45
Burridge, Kenelm, 2; *Encountering Aborigines*, 5n21, 23n89

Caesar, Julius: ethnography in, 33–34, 90
Cain, fratricide of, 133
Callataÿ, Godefroid de, 105n24
Callinicium, anti-Valentinian violence at (388), 91
Callistus, Bishop: controversy with Hippolytus, 102; school of, 120n96

Calvert, James, 89
Cameron, Averil, 23; on Christian dialectic, 159; on Christian universe, 255; "How to Read Heresiology," 14–16; on the indescribable, 238
Caner, Daniel: on Epiphanius, 84; on Messalians, 75, 79n100
Carey, Sorcha: *Pliny's Catalogue of Culture*, 203
Carpocratians, Epiphanius on, 88, 212n109
Cassian, John: heresiological discourse of, 171
Castelli, Elizabeth: on Christian culture making, 255n41
catalogues, heresiological, 6n23, 7, 10, 14, 206, 211; elusiveness in, 219–20; innovation in, 252
Cataphrygians, blood sacrifice of, 231
categories: Foucault on, 186; heresiologists' use of, 27–28, 78; Pliny's, 204; rules of continuity for, 186; in theology, 28. *See also* classification
Ceylon: embassy to Rome, 192; in Mela, 201; Pliny on, 192–93
Chaldeans, astrology of, 104, 111, 112
charity, Godly disposition toward, 82
Chidester, David, 23, 125; on human diversity, 86; on pagan gods, 150n113; on Satanic structuralism, 150
chorographers, ethnography of, 201n63
Christ: accessible wisdom of, 165; atemporal finality of, 144; injunction on inquiry, 165–67; memory of, 240; pedagogical fulfillment of, 167; revelation of, 166; single truth of, 164–65
Christianity: academic, 158n19; and Academic culture, 163–64; anthropology and, 2–3, 142n75; boundaries between sects, 11; categorization of world, 116; as city of believers, 97; colonialism and, 87; community identity in, 59; competition within, 14, 17; construction of narratives about, 255n42; continuity in, 153–55; cosmological superstructure of, 119; counterworld of, 225; curiosity in, 153–55; disunity in, 12, 12nn38,40–41, 14, 154; effect of heresy on, 91; episcopal, 158n19; epistemological limits of, 161, 213; ethnographic ordering of, 139; genealogical, 141, 120n98; heresiological care of, 56; heresy in definition of, 8; in hierarchy of religions, 19; identity-formation model of, 14; ideology of expansion, 245; imaginative universe of, 255; inward gaze of, 53; orders of church, 94; paganism and, 71; pedagogical institutions of, 120, 129; as philosophy, 66n32; pluralism of, 7; procreative language of, 120n98; production of, 23; relationship to temporal world,

Christianity *(continued)*
  81n112; restoration of order, 93; restraint of, 90; reunification of, 125; self-definition in, 14; self-mastery in, 72; semantic universe of, 63; shared humanity in, 125; spiritual exercises of, 72; state power behind, 91; transformative, 164; true way of life, 81n112; as ur-culture, 245; as *vera religio*, 254; world unity and, 256; written word in, 64. *See also* ethnography, Christian; knowledge, Christian; *oikoumenē*, Christian; orthodoxy
Christology: Ebion's, 149; errors in, 145; fifth-century controversies of, 152–53; Tertullian's, 167
Cicero: Augustine's love for, 239–40; on human unity, 125; on *religio*, 63
civility, and theological truth, 88–89
civilization: contradictions in, 88n148; degradation by heresy, 143; discovery in, 204; Roman protection of, 210; taxonomies of, 203n72
classification: culture of, 225; heresiologists', 9, 47, 239; scriptural parameters of, 214; of the unknowable, 244. *See also* categories
classification, ethnographic: ancient, 23, 29, 37, 198; Augustine's, 220, 230; continuity in, 155; Epiphanius's, 211; epistemological deficiencies of, 188; limitations of, 245; of natural world, 202; through Christian ethnography, 256
Clement of Alexandria, 72
Clifford, James, 23, 54–55; on displacement, 196; on ethnographic data, 213; "On Ethnographic Authority," 241–42
Cohen, Shaye: *The Beginnings of Jewishness*, 229
Colish, Marcia, 238
Collyridians, rites of, 61
colonialism: and anthropology, 87; denial of humanity, 253n35; destruction of indigenous cultures, 92n172; ethnography of, 93
Colossians, baptismal formula of, 132
communities: division by heresy, 222–27; errors within, 136; pre-Christian concepts of, 61–62, 76n84; sectarianism of, 138; in theology, 78n92
comparison: analytical practice of, 28–29
completion, in organizational structure, 234
comprehension, human: ethnographic effects of, 189–95; limits of, 57
constellations, Aratean interpretation of, 114. *See also* astrology; zodiac
continuity: in organizational structure, 234; systems of, 186
control, imperial discourse of, 10

Cooper, John M.: *Pursuits of Wisdom*, 66
Cope, Glenn Melvin, 146n94
Corinth, Christian disunity at, 12n40
cosmology: Aratus's, 114; of book of Jubilees, 133n26; Christian allegorical, 114; ethnographic causation in, 106, 109, 113; explanatory capacity of, 105; Gnostic, 174; heretical, 24, 102, 103, 116–20; in Herodotus, 117; Ptolemy's, 107–8; and study of geography, 105–6; understanding of natural world in, 109
Council of Nicaea, orthodoxy following, 158
counterworld: Christian, 225; disruptive potential of, 201–2; of heresy, 212; Mela's, 199, 201, 208, 216
creation: causes of, 122; evolution of, 178n125; Gnostics on, 236; mystery of, 235, 236; observable phenomena of, 236. *See also* cosmology
culture: Boas's definition of, 2; center and periphery in, 29; ethnographic reification of, 191; hierarchies of, 1, 4; production of texts, 55; transience of, 142; typologies of, 1
culture, heretical: appropriations of, 98–99, 115; and orthodox wholeness, 94–97; particularity of, 100
curiosity: about Christian *oikoumenē*, 162–64; about natural world, 185; in antiquity, 156–57; Aristotle on, 156–57; Christian, 153–55; and Christian truth, 157, 168; and disputation, 184n150; disruptive potential of, 17; ethnographic, 145; excessive, 136, 157; in heresiology, 17, 99, 155; in heresy, 164; and necessity, 161; regulation of, 162; Tertullian on, 25, 165, 168, 184; in testing of scripture, 183. *See also* inquiry, theological
Cyril of Alexandria, controversy with Nestorius, 152

decay, religious: human arrogance and, 143n80
deception, heretical, 160n27
degeneration: ethnography and, 148n104; heresiology on, 153; through heresy, 93n176
demography, Christian, 12n37
demons: gods as, 150n113; role in heresy, 52, 149–52, 251
Dench, Emma, 32, 36, 53
Denzey, Nicola Lewis, 64
determinism: climatic, 108; environmental, 108n41
determinism, astrological, 103, 105–6; among Gnostics, 104n17; Christian debates over, 114; and climatalogical determinism, 106–7; cosmic order in, 115; ethnographic theory of,

110; Hippolytus on, 112; human order in, 115; Ptolemy's, 107. *See also* astrology; horoscopes; zodiac
devolution, religious: human division in, 148
dialectic, ancient, 163n40; philosophical tradition of, 169
dialectic, Christian: in Epiphanius, 44, 172–73; with heretics, 168–70; opposition to, 159; orthodoxy and, 159n24; problems of, 159–70; in Tertullian, 163–65, 168
Didascalia apostolorum, 82–83
difference: Christian, 7; geographical, 208–9; religious and ethnological, 3
difference, human, 2; alternative models of, 103; in ancient ethnography, 31, 39; causes of, 41; as Christian difference, 153; ethnographic study of, 6, 10, 29, 124; extrapolation from, 127; in heresiology, 7–8, 9, 16, 22; heretical, 128; orthodox thought on, 4; sectarian theories of, 99; in theological doctrine, 257. *See also* diversity
Diodorus Siculus: *Library of History*, 61; Ethiopians in, 38–39; ethnography in, 34; use of textual precedents, 39
Diogenes Laertius, 22, 48n94
Dionysus, cult of, 50
discovery: in civilization, 204; ethnographic effects of, 189–95; struggle in, 197; subversive, 200
diversity: of non-Christian peoples, 59; sectarian, 86; unity of, 121. *See also* difference, human
diversity, Christian, 59, 60, 95; assessment of, 73; ethnographic modeling of, 187; predictability of, 153; and Satanic structuralism, 150; theorizations of, 11
diversity, human: astrological account of, 104, 105n24, 112, 116; cause and effect in, 40; and Christian diversity, 48–49; Christian structuring of, 93; cognitive control over, 86; comparative religion and, 86; early anthropologists on, 87; ethnographic narrative of, 125, 128; in Genesis, 59; in heresiology, 7–8, 24, 101, 103, 116, 127–28; macroscopic analysis of, 24; making of gods in, 135; and sectarianism, 49; theological theorization of, 48
divination, Hippolytus on, 112
domination, Roman imperial, 191–92
Donatists: Epiphanius on, 187n6; in *Theodosian Code*, 53
Dunderberg, Ismo, 50
Dunn, Geoffrey D., 166n54, 167

The East, liberation from heresy, 178
Ebion (heretic): Christology of, 149; offshoots of, 150; typology of, 146
Echidna: creation of, 118; relations with Heracles, 116–17
Edem (female creative principle), 117–18; angelic agents of, 118
Edwards, Thomas, 252, 252n31
Elchasaites: astrology of, 109–10; Hippolytus on, 179
Ellis, William, 89, 93
Elohim (the Father), 117–18; captivity of, 119; punishment of, 118n89
empire, imaginative ethnography and, 56n144. *See also* Roman Empire
Epiphanius of Salamis: advice to churchmen, 130; as armchair ethnographer, 207n92; authorial ambivalence of, 214, 217; authority of, 172n91; awareness of his shortcomings, 26; comparative methodology of, 96; defeat of Ptolemy, 171; divine will infusing, 214n117; ethnographic disposition of, 74, 89; experience with Gnostics, 88, 182; fondness for study, 42; investigative skills of, 205; limitations as ethnographer, 26, 188, 215, 216, 217; literary predecessors of, 88n145; oppositional mentality of, 89; as pedagogue, 130, 183; as voice of his era, 130
—*De fide*, 148; authors' accomplishments in, 195; catholic church in, 96; Chinese women in, 207n92; Christian life in, 95, 97; conceptual restraints of, 208; discourse of omission, 208; heretical infinitude in, 235; human and divine in, 237; monks in, 95; orthodoxy in, 95, 96, 97; Sabbath celebration in, 94; sects in, 205n84; unified Christian culture in, 95, 96; virginity in, 72n65, 94
—*Panarion*, 43–45, 195–97; Abraham in, 141; Adamic past in, 132, 140, 142; Aetius in, 172, 173; ages of man in, 133–36; ancestral worship in, 135–36; Anomoeans in, 172–73; on Antidicomarites, 228n49; apostolic tradition in, 140; asceticism in, 81–85, 94–95; assimilation of data, 43, 207; Assyrians in, 138; Audians in, 174–75; Augustine's use of, 73, 228, 233, 238n92; autopsy in, 43; behaviors in, 80; biblical prooftexts of, 44; Carpocratians in, 88, 212n109; catholic church in, 140, 143, 205; chain of heterodoxy in, 139; Christian conduct in, 81; on Christian truth, 80; Christian unity in, 96, 142; circularity in, 80; classification system of, 85–86, 93, 148,

—*Panarion (continued)*
211; comparative ethnography of, 84, 97; on comprehensiveness, 214; creation in, 131; cultural knowledge in, 96; cultural transience in, 142; customs in, 65, 68; destruction in, 182–83; dialectic in, 44, 172–73; on diet, 69; discourse of barbarism, 88; on Donatists, 187n6; enumeration of heretics, 16, 130–31, 187, 195, 211, 216–17, 244; epistemological categories of, 216; erasure of ethnographical knowledge, 172; ethnogenesis in, 136, 138; ethnography of, 45, 61, 65, 86–87, 119, 130, 143, 144, 205, 209; on excessive curiosity, 136; exhaustiveness of, 171; extremism in, 74n76; fear of heresy in, 65; feminizing language of, 135n42; foundational heresies in, 132–35, 139, 142, 143; fundamentals of heresiology in, 16; genealogy of, 44, 130–37, 141, 142, 145; on Genesis, 142; gentile nations in, 121; Gnostics in, 88, 163n39, 179, 182; on Greek philosophy, 206; heresiological literature in, 120n96; heresy in, 43, 61, 86, 119, 127, 129, 131, 178, 179–80, 205, 213; hyperbole in, 15; idolatry in, 136–37; innovation in, 139; on intellectual speculation, 136; knowable/unknowable dichotomy in, 215–16; knowledge gaps in, 217; knowledge system of, 97; laborer imagery of, 177n120; language of contagion, 183; language of *ethnē*, 172; language of therapy, 130n10; language of travel in, 195–97; the lost in, 207; macroscopic theorization of, 143; Mani in, 77n89; on manual labor, 81–82; Marcionites in, 68–69; master narrative of, 132, 142, 143; medical imagery of, 85n133; Melchizedekians in, 140; Messalians in, 24, 74–85, 88n145, 90, 92–95, 132, 250; mockery in, 171n87; models for, 15; monks in, 83–84, 94, 95; monogenism in, 141–42, 144; mythology in, 134–35, 137; omissions in, 208; on orthodoxy, 81–82, 96, 143, 153; pedagogical purpose of, 130; on philosophy, 137; physiognomics in, 83; plan of, 130, 131, 187; polemical ethnography of, 79, 82, 85, 94; polyvocality of, 43, 44; pre-Christian error in, 132–36; predecessors of, 131; on presectarian religiosity, 137; *Proems*, 131, 215, 225n28; on proliferation of heresies, 232; on Purists, 187n6; reductionism in, 77, 85, 92; refutation in, 171; religious devolution in, 148; religious rites in, 65; remedy in, 183; renunciatory impulse in, 75; request for, 44; rhetorical devices of, 26; rhetorical hesitation in, 17n65, 179–80, 188; rhetorical integrity of, 171; rhetoric of medicine, 93; rhetoric of science, 15; sacred time in, 144; Samaritans in, 137, 138; Satan in, 150n112; scope of, 171–72, 208; secession of lineages in, 144; sectarianism in, 86, 129, 130, 131, 132n25, 135, 136, 137–44, 150n112, 153, 171; seeing motif in, 44; Sethians in, 151; Simonians in, 90; on Simon Magus, 51–52, 139; sociological writing in, 142; Song of Songs in, 132n24, 140, 205–6, 210, 213; on the soul, 69; sources of, 42–43, 44, 88, 211; tautologies in, 84; teachings in, 65; textual achievement of, 207; textual restraints on, 228; Theodoret's *Compendium* and, 147–48; theological opinions of, 44, 65, 196; therapeutic ethnography of, 130, 144; time of Adam in, 68; totality of human history in, 25; on transmission of error, 134, 137; the universal in, 85, 239n98; the unknowable in, 237; on the unspeakable, 212n109; use of Irenaeus, 204–5; on vastness of heresy, 213; world history in, 140

errors: astrological, 116; Augustine on, 229, 242n117; competing, 137; diversity of, 11; Epiphanius on, 132–36, 137; genealogy of, 215; pre-Christian, 132–36; process of, 139; transmission of, 134, 137

Eshleman, Kendra, 99; *The Social World of Intellectuals in the Roman Empire*, 6n23

ethnogenesis: ancient and medieval, 129n5; genealogy of, 132; and human religiosity, 135

ethnography: as academic discipline, 30; allegorical possibilities of, 40n57; analytical, 100, 175; anthropological, 5, 87; aporetic core of, 26; appeal to legitimacy, 254; aspirational, 67, 94; associative bonds in, 41; authority of, 241–42; circularity in, 80; colonial, 93; comparative, 254; contractually determined, 54; critical, 2; cultural didacticism of, 127; of cultural exchange, 47; didactic, 28; dispositional, 80, 89; early modern, 12; and empire, 56n144; epistemological divides in, 243; expressive speech of, 54; field observation in, 39n51; fissures in, 12; forms of, 28; heuristic function of, 28–29; hierarchies of, 189; historically determined, 54; incompleteness in, 244; institutionally determined, 54; interpretive expertise of, 46; intertextual practices in, 227; and manuscript reading, 42; mapping of peoples, 189; multifaceted, 24; multiple meanings of, 40n57; negotiation in, 91, 189; on non-Christian peoples, 58; objective/subjective analysis in, 197n47; para-

INDEX   291

doxes of, 197; performative spectacle of, 54; polemical, 25, 79, 82, 131, 160, 188; politically determined, 54; predictive, 80; production of text, 55; reception of, 54; rhetoric of, 54, 56, 172n89; rhetoric/reality mix in, 189–90; scientific orientation, 254; self-reflection in, 35n35; study of religious customs, 61; subject and object in, 54; subjectivity in, 55; systems of relationships, 54; theoretical decisions in, 37; therapeutic, 130, 144; totality/particularity in, 11; triumph and, 178n121; uncritical, 3, 93, 127, 253; and universal history, 34n32; use in religion, 3–4; vernaculars of, 190; writing of customs in, 8n29

ethnography, ancient, 30–36, 54n133; of Africa, 198–200; analysis in, 32; in ancient genres, 8n29, 34; armchair, 9, 39; in astrological discourse, 104, 105, 106, 107; authorial objectives of, 36; center and periphery in, 197; of chorographers, 201n63; Christian appropriation of, 116; Christian classification in, 9, 47; and Christian ethnography, 24; Christianization of, 25–26; civilizing discourse of, 57; classification in, 23, 29, 37, 198; communities in, 5; comparison in, 28–9; constraints on, 205; creation of cultural hierarchies, 32–33, 40; customs in, 5; data collection in, 32, 41; in defeat of Christian plurality, 48; descriptive content of, 33; destabilizing qualities of, 23; detail in, 29; disposition for, 24; disruptive knowledge in, 200; diverse techniques of, 35; diversity of world in, 193–94; essentializing discourse of, 36; explanatory paradigms of, 40, 41; fictive kinship in, 41; form of, 33; fragmentary, 30; functions of, 23; genealogy in, 40–41; geographic, 33, 40–41; heresiology and, 22–23, 57, 205; hesitancy in, 198n48; as heuristic category, 28–29; as historical writing, 31; human difference in, 31, 39; ideological power of, 32; as independent tradition, 34n33; institutions in, 5; interpretive strategies of, 32, 39; investigation of peoples, 5; in late antique Christianity, 37; as literary process, 29; lost texts of, 30, 34; macroscopic, 24, 25; microscopic, 24; negotiation in, 37; observation in, 40; on origins, 41; origins of, 31n15; paradoxes of, 23; parodies of, 35n36; peoplehood in, 37, 56; periegetic tradition of, 33n26, 56; peril/opportunity in, 202; in Ptolemy, 107–8; reflective disposition of, 32; relationship to history, 32; rhetorics of, 172; on Roman frontiers, 192, 193; Roman techniques of, 191n20; scholarship on, 30–33; second-order data in, 39n51; self-reflective, 53; sources of, 6n22, 24, 37; speculation in, 200; stages of, 33; textual constraints of, 198; textual construction of, 36, 37; textual precedents for, 37, 39; *theōria* in, 197; theorization in, 6, 39, 40; tradition of, 31n18; the unknowable in, 200, 209; the unknown in, 204; validation of ancestry, 41; writing process for, 41

ethnography, Christian, 3, 47, 85–93; Augustine's transformation of, 226–31; charges of heresy against, 4; chasm in, 239–45; of Christian *oikoumenē*, 182; and classical ethnography, 24; coherence in, 10; comparative theology of, 60, 65; competing rhetorics of, 252; conceptual paradigms of, 6; consonance with heresy, 161; in construction of Christian *oikoumenē*, 255; dangers of, 91; data for, 213; disruptive potential of, 221; distillation of, 222–26; epistemology of, 6; heresiology as, 23, 42–54, 57, 252; heretics' paradigms of, 24; human difference in, 6, 10, 124; idealism of, 61; limitations of, 57, 245; macroscopic, 7–8, 101; master narratives of, 245; microscopic, 24, 60–61, 102; and missionary activity, 128n3; mission of church in, 126; of morals, 97n193; ordering of heresy, 129; organizational structure of, 229; orthodoxy in, 99; outgrowth from classical culture, 60; paradoxical nature of, 25; partial nature of, 213; perpetuation of heresy, 129; polemical, 25; reasoning in, 65–66; religious Empire in, 9; and sacred history, 128n3; as salvational enterprise, 88; selectivity in, 98; self-interest in, 98; separation of theology from, 60; theology in, 5, 48, 59, 82, 257; theorization of diversity, 128; *traditio haereticorum* of, 232; vernacular of, 24, 37

ethnography, contemporary: on impossibility of representation, 243; interpretation of fieldwork, 232n65; and Victorian ethnography, 23

ethnography, heresiological, 8n29, 27, 255; care of Christian tradition, 56; Christian knowledge in, 54; classification in, 28; description of peoples, 48n93; descriptive, 69, 217; discourse of control in, 10; heretics' customs in, 183; human behavior in, 99; inquiry in, 158; limits of, 57; logic of, 124; management of diversity, 187; material consequences of, 92; paradigms of, 100; paradox of, 90, 91; polemical, 57, 71, 99; prescriptive, 69, 73, 217; proscriptive, 69,

ethnography, heresiological *(continued)* 73; rhetoric of, 195; tautologies in, 89; Tertullian's, 67–68; theological, 37, 75, 255; ways of life in, 66–73. *See also* heresiology

ethnography, macroscopic, 115–16, 128; aggregation of knowledge, 129; ancient, 24, 25; Christian, 100, 101; heretics', 100–101; human unity in, 125; order through, 154

ethnography, Victorian, 45; civilization/primitivism in, 89; and contemporary ethnography, 23; normative culture in, 95; oppositional mentality of, 89; pollution metaphors of, 91; totalization in, 10

ethnology: biblicism of, 2; evolutionist, 1–2; nineteenth-century British, 19n75, 20; pioneers of, 87; study of social life, 22

Euchitai. *See* Messalians

eugenics, in anthropology, 1, 2

euhemerism, 134, 135n41

Europe, modern: social structure of, 19n69

Eusebius of Caesarea, *Historia ecclesiastica,* 13n44, 227

evangelism, anthropology and, 87

Evans, Rhiannon, 198–99, 202

Eve (matriarch): curiosity of, 157; in Justinus, 118

expertise: ethnographic: 10, 40, 54, 198, 204, 244; heresiological: 10, 22, 42–47, 130, 158, 169, 181–82, 225–26, 248, 252

Faustus (Manichaean bishop): Augustine and, 70–71, 241; on schism, 71

Feldman, Louis, 36

fieldwork: ethnographic, 39n51; self-other dilemma of, 55–56

Filastrius of Brescia, 6n24, 72; Augustine's use of, 228, 233, 238n92; *Catalogue of Diverse Heresies,* 227; enumeration of heretics, 16, 244

Flint, Robert, 19

Flower, Richard, 172

Fornara, Charles, 33

Foucault, Michel: on categories, 186; on epistemes, 46, 47. Works: *Archaeology of Knowledge,* 46; *The Order of Things,* 155, 186, 187; "What Is an Author," 56

Frankfurter, David, 28–29

free will: astrology and, 110, 113; 2 Timothy on, 151

Gallus, Aelius: destruction of towns, 192n24

Gamphasantes, Mela on, 198

Gass, William, 234

Geertz, Clifford, 23, 42, 129; definition of religion, 87; *Works and Lives,* 55–56, 243; on world views, 100n8

genealogy: in ancient ethnography, 40–41; of Christian knowledge, 25; of divine knowledge, 142; in Epiphanius, 44; of error, 215; ethnographic paradigms of, 142; of Genesis, 4–5, 140, 142; of godliness, 141; in heresiology, 99, 116, 120–21; of heresy, 254; in Hippolytus, 120–24; Homeric, 41; intellectual, 120–24; in Irenaeus, 99; ranked relationships in, 141; in Theodoret, 25

Genesis: gaps in, 12; genealogy in, 4–5, 140, 142; human diversity in, 59

gentile nations: distinction from Christians, 120; Epiphanius on, 121; in Hippolytus, 121–23, 124, 126; ignorance of Christ, 166; pedagogical contributions of, 123; theological ignorance of, 123

geography: and the apostolic tradition, 181n135; aspirational maps of, 190; hierarchies of, 189; limits of, 188; the unknowable in, 189. *See also* Mela, Pomponius; Ptolemy

Ginzburg, Carlo, 160

Gnostics: astrological determinism among, 104n17; cosmology of, 174; curiosity of, 157; diversity of opinions among, 207; on divine creation, 236; Epiphanius on, 88, 163n39, 179, 182; heresiologists on, 84–85; kinship among, 74n77; sexual perversions of, 61; theological speculation of, 163n39

Goat-Pans, 198

God: antediluvian devotees of, 121; creative power of, 121–22, 174n101; Greek ignorance of, 122; human dependence on, 236, 237; human hierarchy with, 184; human understanding of, 158; ineffability of, 237; mercy of, 143n80; omnipotence of, 100, 110, 113, 174; singularity of, 167, 174n101; transcendent will of, 184; unknowability of, 237

godliness: genealogy of, 141; progression of, 140

gods: as demons, 150n113; human creation of, 140; human relations with, 62

Goodrich, Charles A., 143n80

Grafton, Anthony, 4

Greece, in hierarchy with Egypt, 40

Greenblatt, Stephen, 38

Greenslade, S. L., 162n34

Gribomont, Jean, 79n100

groupism: heretical, 78–79; intellectual, 8n29; theological, 60

INDEX 293

groups, reification of, 77–78
Gruen, Erich S., 142n74

Hadot, Pierre, 67, 72
Hagar, descendants of, 141
hairesis (choice), semantic transformation of, 20n78
handbooks: Greco-Roman, 224n20; of heresy, 219, 223n15, 224, 229
Harrison, Peter, 157, 164n43; on curiosity, 158
Hartog, François: *The Mirror of Herodotus*, 172n89
Havel, Ivan M., 224n23
Hecataeus of Miletus: Jacoby on, 31n15; *Periēgēsis*, 33
Hegedus, Tim, 101n12, 114n71
Hegesippus, *Hypomnēmata*, 146n94
Hellanicus of Lesbos, 34
Hellenism (foundational heresy), 132, 133; cultural development in, 135; endurance of, 144; error of, 139, 142; ethnic particularities of, 139; idolatry in, 136; making of gods in, 135
Helvidians, Augustine of Hippo on, 228
Heracles, relations with Echidna, 116–17
Herbert, Christopher, 10, 23, 45; on cultural wholeness, 95–96; *Culture and Anomie*, 89; on Ellis, 93; on Mayhew, 213n111
heresiologists: as antiethnographic ethnographers, 160; armchair ethnography of, 145n84, 189; assembling of Christian world, 256; authorial achievements of, 185; categorization of the world, 27–28, 256; as Christian therapists, 94; and colonial missionaries, 60; construction of knowledge, 46; control measures of, 10, 188, 210, 216; as defenders of church, 182; on definition of heresy, 256; dissemination of heresy, 181; distance from object of study, 181; epistemological dilemmas of, 53; as ethnographical interpreters, 46, 256; ethnographic disposition of, 88, 212; ethnographic problems of, 29; fear of corruption, 180; hermeneutical expertise of, 46; imaginative universe of, 252; intellectual elitism of, 161, 170; intellectual proficiency of, 179, 181; language of ethnic reasoning, 48n93; language of rhetorical mastery, 197; mapping of world, 186–87, 253; moral authority of, 181; pastoral expertise of, 204; rhetoric of expansion, 187; rhetoric of humility, 182; risks to, 180, 181; taxonomies of, 195–96; textual worldview of, 253
heresiology: adaptability of, 153, 221; agendas of, 15; aggregation in, 7; and ancient ethnography, 22–23, 57, 205; authority in, 26, 197; binaries of, 14n47, 58, 78, 85, 91, 197; center and periphery in, 22; chains of utterance in, 7; Christian behavior in, 61; Christian knowledge in, 256–57; Christian/non-Christian sources of, 28–29; and civility, 85–93; claims to tradition, 11; in classes of knowledge, 129; classification in, 9, 47, 239, 244; closure in, 185, 206, 232, 234–35; and colonial ethnography, 93; comparative ethnography of, 63; comparative theology of, 59–60, 63; competition in, 251, 252; comprehension of world through, 57; comprehensiveness of, 211, 239; confession in, 63; consensus/dissensus in, 158; construction of lacunae, 243–45; continuity in, 44n74, 153–55; control through texts, 188, 216; cross-cultural contact in, 17; curiosity in, 17, 99, 155; dangers of, 19, 25, 57, 159, 179–83; definition of Truth, 22; on degeneration, 153; description in, 174; destructive capacity of, 251, 252; development of genre, 6n23; difference/unity in, 86; discourse of Christian knowledge, 16; discursive unity of, 174n104; disputation in, 63; earliest, 6n23; early modern, 7; elusiveness of, 57; encyclopedism and, 129n4; epistemological scope of, 143; and ethnography, 23, 25, 73, 42–54, 57, 188, 129, 204–15, 232–33, 235, 254, 251, 256; evolution of, 206n86; eyewitness testimony in, 43n70; facilitation of creative destruction, 180; failures of, 187, 214; fear in, 179–83; fissures in, 214, 221; form and content in, 16; gap between heresy and, 10; genealogy in, 99, 116, 120–21; genre of, 28, 29; goal for heretics, 45; guilt by association in, 17; historiographical impulse of, 132n22; human difference in, 9, 16, 22; human diversity in, 7–8, 24, 101, 103, 116, 127–28; imposition of order, 154; intellectual tradition of, 7, 16, 128–29; interdependence in, 43n70; internal rhetoric of, 245; knowability in, 215–17, 232; knowledge-experience mix in, 232; labels in, 77; later, 42, 223, 235; limits of, 16, 17, 26, 217, 220, 251; listing tradition of, 222–26; literary language of, 7, 16; macroscopic, 7–8, 53, 102, 153, 185, 187, 239, 245; management of the unmanageable, 217; mastery in, 170–79; microscopic, 7–8, 60–61, 74, 225, 245; the monstrous in, 212n109; naming of heresies, 175; as natural history, 154; negotiation in, 69, 189; obsolescence of, 251; ongoing work of, 178; orthodoxy and, 13–14, 17, 21–22, 124; in

heresiology *(continued)*
other genres, 9; paradox of, 10, 17–8, 23, 59, 185, 208, 221, 224, 238–39; partial character of, 226; pastoral duties and, 185; and pedagogy, 129; performative texts of, 15–16; perpetuation of uncertainty, 160; poetics of, 15; polemical, 6n23, 21, 22, 24, 47, 61, 160, 235, 252; pollution metaphors of, 91; preparation for eschaton, 179; problems of completeness, 233–34; protracted discovery in, 170; quantification in, 206; rationalizing aspects of, 49; reading of, 11–18; refutation in, 63, 171, 174; reification in, 78; reimagination of Christian theology, 37; on religious custom, 22; rhetorics of, 56, 92, 170–83, 224, 243; scholarship on, 6n23; Second Sophistic and, 6n23; self-destructiveness in, 251; self-mastery in, 171; self-reflection in, 235; as simplistic, 15; Sisyphean quality of, 252; sociology of knowledge, 15; survey of Christian *oikoumenē*, 22; techniques of, 8; tensions within, 44n74, 197; Theodoret's expansion of, 145; theological variation in, 193, 212; totalizing, 10, 26; triumph in, 170–79; tropes of investigation, 158; tropes of travel, 195–97; true interpretation in, 44; typological theory of, 25, 129, 144–53; unintended consequences of, 182; and universal history, 99, 129; the unknown in, 208, 233–34, 235; use of scripture, 174; use of theology, 64, 66, 125n129, 255; viability of, 220; vulnerabilities of, 10; worldview of, 9, 15. *See also* ethnography, heresiological

heresy: adaptability of, 129, 211, 213–14; alteration of tradition, 13; as alternative Christianity, 211; with alternative Christologies, 145; with alternative creators, 145; analysis of customs, 128; and ancient philosophy, 163–65; astrological error in, 116; authoritative interpretations of, 28; as behavioral difference, 21, 61; as choice, 20–21; consonance with Christian ethnography, 4, 161; contradictions in, 79n101; corruption of scripture, 99; counterworld of, 212; cultural manifestations of, 21; curiosity in, 164; dangers of ignorance about, 183; decipherment of, 213; in definition of Christianity, 8; degeneration through, 93n176; as degraded civilization, 143; delineation of borders, 185; demons in, 52, 149–52, 251; derivative opinions of, 120; detection of, 182n141; developmental theory of, 7, 245; diagnoses of, 171; as disease, 88; diversification of, 124, 176, 245; division of communities, 222–27; doctrinal history of, 148; effect on Christianity, 91; elusive character of, 10–11; entrenchment of, 153; as episteme, 46–47, 53; error processes in, 116, 139; ethnographic investigation of, 58, 126, 160, 187, 254; evolving, 217, 254; failed, 150; fascination with, 212; feminized language of, 135n42; fluidity of, 209, 251; as foolishness, 76; as foreignness, 63–64; forms of renunciation in, 75n78; foundational, 132–35; gap between heresiology and, 10; genealogy of, 116, 254; generative explanation of, 139, 147; handbooks of, 219, 223n15, 224, 229; heresiologists' dissemination of, 181; human comprehension of, 152, 237; on human evolution, 125; human frailty in, 151; hybridity and, 99n3; impact on human history, 22; incomplete knowledge of, 238; the indescribable in, 238; indestructible, 248, 252; infinitude of, 211, 213, 215, 235, 238; influence on religious formation, 254–55; instability of, 12–13, 244, 254; interaction with orthodoxy, 47, 53, 148, 159, 188, 205, 251–52; interdependence with religion, 255; intractability of, 188; jeopardy to baptism, 68; knowledge systems of, 10, 13, 97; lack of boundaries, 26, 209; layered meaning of, 42; legal discourses on, 125; legitimation of, 180, 184; macroscopic theories of, 7–8, 53, 102, 153, 185; master narratives of, 102–9; means for study of, 28; means of overcoming, 66; modeling versus knowing, 187; models of reality, 99; modern discourse of, 58; monolithic, 86; multiple names of, 16n58, 131n13; mutability of, 148, 233, 239n98, 245; as natural phenomenon, 139; natural/supernatural dichotomy of, 216; opposition to Christian norms, 67; ordering by ethnography, 129; origins of, 28, 133n28; particularities of, 128, 139; periodized history of, 130–37; perpetual cycling of, 239n98; perpetuation by ethnography, 129; persistence of, 152; philosophical error in, 98–99, 116; philosophy and, 163–65; as plurality, 21n83; and poisonous beasts, 15n56; power to confound, 179; pre-Christian, 228; proliferation of, 175, 212, 216, 232, 233; protean nature of, 147; protection from, 226; rationalization of, 152, 163; redemption from, 237; reproduction of, 140; restructuring of truth, 13; rhetorical creation of, 89; sacred history and, 244–45; schism and, 71n57; scholarship on, 13–14; science of, 46; as scriptural tool,

20, 167; similarity in, 74; as Siren song, 120; specificity of, 205; succession in, 147, 148; taxonomies of, 153, 187, 231; textualization of, 47; in *Theodosian Code*, 52–53; theological causes of, 59; theological deviation in, 122–23, 145; theological topology of, 178; through social deviation, 65; transcendence of geographical difference, 208–9; translation to text, 221, 232–39; trickery in, 173; typology of, 25, 129, 144–53; uninterrupted history of, 132; universal narrative of, 175–76; in writing of peoples, 23. *See also* sectarianism

heretics: abnormality of, 211; alternative world views of, 101, 102; Arabian, 228; arrogance of, 67–68, 99, 140; astrological theories of, 24; attacks on truth, 67; Augustine's definition of, 219; behavior of, 21, 61; betrayal of apostolic tradition, 83, 123; blackness of, 139n59; changes among, 145; cosmology of, 102, 103; cultural appropriations of, 98–99, 115; cultural kinship among, 78; cultural particularity of, 100; debates with Christians, 168–70; defeat through heresiology, 182; demonic temptation of, 52, 149; detection of, 239; as deviants from norm, 128; dispositional kinship among, 74, 90; effect on ethnographic tropes, 24; as emblems of error, 48; enumeration of, 16, 69–70, 146–47, 187, 195, 206–7, 211, 216–17, 222, 225, 227, 228–30, 244; epistemological relationship with God, 121; escape from scrutiny, 176; ethnography of, 24, 27, 79, 90, 91, 101–2, 243; ethnoracial language against, 139n59; etymologies of, 230; evolution of, 239; explanatory potential of, 47; expulsion of, 210; grouping of, 75; hubris of, 48, 90, 175, 215, 235n80; as hybridized Christians, 98–99; ideas of order, 100; incompatibility with apostolic succession, 151; on inquiry, 165–66; intellectual inheritance of, 147, 176; irrationality of, 92–93; lack of consensus, 121; naming of, 77; ontology of, 174; pagans and, 100; paradox of intimacy with, 221; polemical caricatures of, 10; prevention of contact with, 47; pride of, 175; relentless inquiry of, 165–66; self-definition of, 28; sexual excesses of, 85n133; theology of, 47, 64, 74; undermining of God's omnipotence, 100; unknowable aspects of, 232; use of alien philosophy, 98–99, 116, 122–24; use of macroscopic ethnography, 100–101; use of scripture, 20, 167, 168–69; violence against, 91; ways of life, 66–73

Hermogenes (heretic), 162n36

Herodotus: cosmic creation in, 117; on custom, 29; ethnography in, 33; Lydian-Milesian war in, 38; on the Nile, 201n66; peoples of, 33n29; on Scythians, 117n79; use of witnesses, 38

hierarchy, divine: invention of, 146

Hippolytus of Rome, 48n94, 177n120; as agent of Godhead, 178; amassing of knowledge, 173; authorial persona of, 177; enumeration of heretics, 16; heresiology of, 6, 126; historical, 102n14; macroscopic ethnography of, 115–16; participation in theological controversies, 102; protective duty of, 207; rhetorical hesitancy of, 188

—*Refutation of All the Heresies*, 24; advice on heretics, 120; astrological ethnography in, 102, 103–4, 109–16; attack on alternative narratives, 24; authorship of, 102n14; Christian *oikoumenē* in, 121; on cultural appropriations, 115; divination in, 112; on divine creativity, 121–22; doxographical record of, 98n2; Elchasaites in, 179; ethnography of, 102, 109–16; fear of omission in, 176; genealogy of, 145; gentile nations in, 121–23, 124, 126; on Gnostics, 207, 236; Greek philosophy in, 122–24, 176; on heretics appropriations, 98n2; on heretics' disorder, 121; history of error in, 99; horoscope in, 110–11; human difference in, 25, 103, 112, 116; on ignorance of heresy, 176; intellectual genealogy in, 120–24; on Justin (pseudo-Gnostic), 119; on Marcosians, 64; master narrative of, 120–24; mythography in, 102, 103, 119–20; Naasseni in, 116; nation of worshippers in, 123; omissions in, 207–8; opening of, 131; orthodoxy in, 153; Peratae in, 104, 116; polemical project of, 177–78; proem of, 122; on Pythagoreans, 123; sectarianism in, 143; Sethians in, 116; on Simon Magus, 146n89; soteriological threat in, 177; true Christianity in, 103; use of Sextus Empiricus, 102, 103, 111, 113; on Valentinians, 124; victory in, 177, 178, 179; zodiac in, 111–12

—*Syntagma*, 42–43

historical ethnography, 194n33

historiography, ancient: capacious character of:, 31

history, human: as Christian history, 153; theological shaping of, 154

history, universal, 86; and cultural formations, 194n34; ethnography and, 34n32; heresiology and, 99, 129

Holy Spirit: dialectic and, 164n43; guide to believers, 167

Homer: genealogies of, 41; Phaeacians of, 90
Hopkins, Keith, 9n31, 59
horologes (gongs), 111
horoscopes: fixing of, 111–12; Hippolytus on, 110–11. *See also* astrology; determinism, astrological; zodiac
hubris: of heretics, 48, 90, 175, 215, 235n80; subversion of divine authority, 17
humanitas, Roman, 204
humanity: ages of, 133–36; dependence on God, 236; ethnogenic divisions of, 136; faith in God, 237; hierarchy with the divine, 184; introduction of wickedness to, 133; limits of, 193, 236; prefallen, 70; reunification of, 126, 141; universal history of, 86. *See also* difference, human; diversity, human; unity, human
Humfress, Carolina, 92, 226, 242n117

identity, Christian: heresy and, 59
ideology, Christian: justification of, 9n31
idolatry, rupturing of human lineage, 136–37
Ignatius, on Christian identity, 59
information management, strategies of, 234n76
inquiry: professional, 169; relentless, 163, 165–66
inquiry, theological: ancient philosophy and, 163–65; concept of, 160; corruption of truth, 165; heretics on, 165–66; legitimacy of, 161; pastoral duties and, 158, 159; problems of, 159–70; self-indulgence in, 164–65; Tertullian on, 162–70; unrestricted, 160. *See also* curiosity
intellect, excessive freedom of, 136
Irenaeus of Lyons: amassing of knowledge, 173–74; Augustine's use of, 227n38; on diversity of error, 11; forging of truth, 175n109; heresiology of, 6, 157–58
—*Adversus haereses*, 42–43; on acquisition of knowledge, 184; on curiosity, 99, 183, 184; divine mystery in, 235, 237; effectiveness of, 174; enumeration of heretics, 16; Epiphanius's use of, 204–5; genealogy in, 99; on Gnostic cosmology, 174; on heretics' appropriations, 99; on heretics' followers, 252; on heretics' pride, 175; on human understanding, 236; on inquiry, 168; instability of heresy in, 13; Marcosians in, 49–51, 64; mythography in, 99; on natural world, 236; orthodoxy in, 153; on overthrow of heretics, 207; plan of, 131; predecessors' errors in, 174; on proto-orthodoxy, 14; on rationality, 183–84; refutation in, 174, 175; rhetorical distinctions in, 13; on supratextual deities, 184; universalism of, 209; on Valentinians, 150n113, 173–74, 176
Isaac, Benjamin: *The Invention of Racism*, 17n64; on physiognomics, 83n123
Isis (goddess), in Greek ethnography, 40
Israel, divisive opinions within, 138

Jacoby, Felix: *Die Fragmente der griechischen Historiker*, 31; study of ancient ethnography, 30–33
Jacobs, Andrew: 8n30, 172n91, 203n77
Jerome, on heresy, 234; *Indiculus de haeresibus*, 228n46
Jews: in ancient ethnography, 35–56; presence across empire, 209n28; recognition of, 229; sectarianism of, 48n94
John the Baptist, 178–79
Jones, A. H. M., 47
Josephus, 36n39; as eyewitness, 38; heresiology of, 59n6; historiographical method of, 38
—*Jewish Antiquities*, 61
—*Jewish War*, ethnography of, 8n29
Jovianists, Augustine of Hippo on, 228
Jubilees (apocryphal book), 133
Judaism, as *superstitio*, 62n14
Judaism (foundational heresy), 132, 134, 142; cultural development in, 135; endurance of, 144; ethnic particularities of, 139; proliferation of, 135; rejection of idolatry, 137
Justin Martyr: on Christian identity, 59; travels of, 195n41
Justinus (pseudo-Gnostic): *Baruch*, 116–20; angels in, 118–19; cosmology of, 117–20; origins of Christianity in, 117

Keech, Dominic, 220
Kelley, Nicole, 114
Keturah, descendants of, 141
Kidd, Colin, 3–4; on Genesis, 4–5
Kim, Young Richard, 78n93, 131 n17, 140n61
King, Karen L., 13n46, 14, 58; on discourse of heresy, 78; on Gnostics, 84–85; on heresiology, 65, 86
King, Richard, 64
kinship: among Gnostics, 74n77; among heretics, 74, 78, 90, 148; fictive, 41
knowledge: astrological, 114, 116; categorization of, 158; Christian culture of, 95; collection of, 158; conceptual problem of, 56; discursive formation of, 46; disjuncture from order, 187; as game, 184; heretics' search for, 157–58; hybridization of, 203n77; interpretive mecha-

nisms of, 197; nineteenth-century forms of, 18n69; perfect, 236; pious and impious, 159; professionalism of, 137, 170; proper transmission of, 120; theorization of, 158; through observation, 17; through travel, 17; transformative, 180n132; upper boundaries of, 184
knowledge, Christian: boundaries of, 255; chasms in, 217; classification of, 9, 10, 11; effect of astrology in, 104; expounding of, 159; genealogy of, 25; in heresiology, 16, 256–57; imperial ideologies in, 9; limits of, 57; management of, 256; production of, 16; refraining from, 159; role of empire in, 125; versus theological exploration, 167; theorization of, 161
knowledge, divine, 119; genealogy of, 142; and human knowledge, 237; and knowledge of heretics, 184n150
knowledge, ethnographic, 100; Augustine's, 26, 219; heresiological periodization of, 129, 130–37; heretics', 101–2; organization of, 40; problem of, 54–57; scope of, 41
knowledge, heresiological: acquisition of, 178; condensation of, 221; dangers of, 159, 179–83, 185; destabilizing, 160; display of, 172; instability in, 252; limits of, 232; paradox of, 221; particularity of, 225; scope of, 170–71; uncontrollable, 179; usable, 219
knowledge, heretical: dangers of, 17; search for, 157–58; types of, 13
knowledge management, premodern, 256n44
knowledge production, vernacular of, 56
known world: classification of, 202; harmony of, 203; human nature and, 11; operational laws of, 186; puzzle of, 200; taxonomies of, 187; the unknowable in, 201–2; wonders of, 236. See also *oikoumenē*
Kolbaba, Tia M.: *The Byzantine Lists*, 222n10

Lactantius, on *religio*, 62–63, 64
language: classificatory, 155; heretical, 128n2; proliferation of, 138; representative capacity of, 11
La Peyrère, Isaac, 20; charges of heresy against, 4; *Prae-Adamitae*, 4
law: against Manichaeans, 209–10; biblical, 134; divine, 140; heresy in, 52; of Moses, 138
Lévi-Strauss, Claude, 98n1, 126, 243
Lim, Richard, 160n26, 169; on Augustine, 161; on curiosity, 184n150; on Tertullian, 165
Lipsius, Richard Adelbert, 42n68
lists: adaptability of, 225; changing, 234; characteristics of, 224n23; in culture of classification, 225; heresiological, 222–26, 244; introduction of errors, 225n28; literary/nonliterary, 224; organizing principles of, 224; updating of, 225
literature, ancient: ethnographic disposition in, 35, 36–41
literature, Roman: fear of foreigners in, 17n64
Livingstone, David, 3
Lucian of Samosata, *True Stories*, 35n36
Luciferians, 228

Manetho, *Aigyptiaka*, 34
Mani (heretic): Messalians and, 77n89; teachings of, 70
Manichaeans: in African Christian community, 241n114; Augustine's affiliation with, 240–42; dualism of, 70; as foreign peoples, 242n115; laws against, 209–10; in *Theodosian Code*, 53
Manilius: *Astronomica*, 104–7; astrogeography of, 105n24; climatic determinism in, 108; ethnographic difference in, 108–9; human diversity in, 105n24, 106; zodiac in, 106–7
manuscripts, as textual relics, 42
Marcion (heretic): body and soul in, 69; dualism of, 162n36; interpretation of scripture, 68; on reincarnation, 68–69
Marcionites, Epiphanius on, 68–69
Marcosians, 49–51; claims of perfection, 50; cosmology of, 50, 51, 64–65; as cult society, 50; death rites of, 49n96, 51, 64; differences among, 51; libertinism of, 50; redemptive practices of, 51; rituals of, 49; use of spurious writings, 50; women, 49
Marcovich, Miroslav, 102n13, 122n110
Marcus (heretic), 49–50; cosmology of, 50; faux Eucharist of, 49; as receptacle of Silence, 49
Marincola, John, 60–61
Masuzawa, Tomoko, 3, 30, 58n2; on Christian truth, 143; on divisions in Christianity, 95; *The Invention of World Religion*, 18; on Purchas, 21; on religious diversity, 60; on Victorian ethnography, 45
Matthew 7.7, inquiry in, 25, 165–66
Mayhew, Henry, 213n111
Mela, Pomponius: *Chorography*, 190–92; Africa in, 198–99; *Antipodes* in, 201–2; Britain in, 191, 192; Ceylon in, 201; as *periplous*, 190; counterworld of, 199, 201, 208, 216; the disruptive in, 201; ethnography in, 190; the periphery in, 200; scholarship on, 202n70; stabilization in, 205; subversive discoveries in, 200; textual fracture within, 198n49; the unknowable in, 190; unpredictability in, 202

Melchizedekians, 140, 147
Melitius (bishop of Antioch), 211n105
Menander (heretic), 147
Merrills, A. H., 188
Messalians, 73–79, 132; abstention from labor, 74, 80, 81, 83–84; associates of, 73, 77n89; Christian, 76, 80–81; commonality of, 75, 77; contentiousness of, 75, 80–85; determinative essence of, 85; dress of, 82–83; in Epiphanius, 24, 74–85, 88n145, 90, 92–95, 132, 250; essence of, 84; estrangement of, 80; extreme piety of, 75; hair of, 82–83; historical, 79n100, 85; immoderacy of, 80, 81; inconsistency of, 76, 77, 85; language of groupism for, 78–79; libertinism of, 84, 90n155, 92–93; Mesopotamian antecedents of, 83–84, 94; multiple identities of, 80; offshoots from, 76n86; pagan, 76, 81; purification of souls, 73–74; scholarship on, 73n67; *superstitio* of, 74; unceasing prayer of, 73, 74, 76, 81, 95
millennialism, 178n125
Milner, Vincent: *Religious Denominations of the World*, 58n2
missionary activity, 93; ethnography and, 8, 87, 128n3; heresiologists and, 60; robbing of agency, 253
Monad, divine, 49
monasticism, 72
monks, Mesopotamian: Messalians and, 83–84, 94
monogenism, 4, 90n158, 144; in Epiphanius, 141–42
the monstrous: in Africa, 199; in heresiology, 212n109; Pliny on, 200n61
Montaigne, Michel de: "On Cannibals," 127
Moretti, Gabriella, 201
Müller, Carl, 30–31
Murphy, Trevor, 192n24, 193
mythography: cosmological, 103, 124; Hippolytus on, 102, 103; in Irenaeus, 99
mythology: Christian allegorization of, 119; disrupting influence of, 119–20; hereticizing of, 116–20

Naas (maternal angel), 118–19
Naasseni, heresy of, 116
Nag Hammadi texts, 101n11
Nasrallah, Laura, 195n41
natural sciences: curiosity about, 157; eighteenth-century, 18n69; the monstrous in, 200n61
Nestorian controversies, Theodoret and, 152
New Testament, heresy in, 4–5, 6n23, 69, 72

Nicander, *Theriaka*, 15
Nicolet, Claude, 189
Nightingale, Andrea Wilson, 196n46
Nile, flooding of, 201
Nimrod, practice of astrology, 133

O'Donnell, James J.: "The Authority of Augustine," 226n33
Odysseus, and the Sirens, 120
oikoumenē: counterworld of, 199; Roman, 204; totalized, 210; zones of, 201. *See also* natural world
oikoumenē, Christian: boundaries of, 208; creation of conditions for, 255; curiosity about, 162–64; ethnography of, 182, 196; expansion of, 188, 255; heresiological survey of, 22, 126, 186–87, 253; in Hippolytus, 121; intellectual regulation of, 214; as nation of worshippers, 123; ordering of, 154; pagan philosophy and, 119; redescription of, 126; theological governance of, 154; topography of, 206; ungovernability of, 245; the unknowable in, 209, 244
Old Testament, ethnicity in, 3–4. *See also* Genesis
omnipotence, divine: astrological challenge to, 110, 113; heretics' undermining of, 100
Orientalism, 18, 30; schematization in, 253; study of non-Western world, 19
Origen, 72
orthodoxy: asceticism and, 81n111; cataloguing of world through, 21; criteria for, 254; dialectic and religious, 159n24; emergence of, 57; ethnographical models of, 99; heresiology and, 13, 17, 21–22, 124; heretical descriptions in, 153; as history of world, 142; humility before God, 236; identity formation in, 16; interaction with heresy, 47, 48n95, 53, 148, 159, 188, 205, 251–52; as Jerusalem, 196; modern discourse of, 58; Nicene, 143, 158; performance and, 177n118; porous boundaries of, 160n26; singularity of, 215; strengthening by temptation, 146; as theological mirage, 251; theological topology of, 178; travel metaphors of, 196; triumph of, 178, 245; wholeness of, 94–97
otherness, rhetoric of, 172n89

Pagitt, Ephraim, 252
Paul (presbyter), 42
Paul, apostle: on Christian unity, 12, 158, 168n72
Paul of Chalcis, Epiphanius's advice to, 130
Pausanias, 22
pedagogy, Christianity, 120, 129–30, 134, 183, 222

Pelagians, Augustine on, 229, 242
peoples, translation into texts, 40n57
peoples, foreign: Christian knowledge of, 47
peoples, primitive: ethnographic study of, 45, 89. *See also* anthropology; primitivism
Pepuzians, blood sacrifice of, 231
Peratae (heretics), 116; astrology of, 104, 109–10
periēgēsis texts, 33n26
periplous narratives, 33n26; Mela's, 190. *See also* geography; travel writing
Perrin, Michel-Yves, 47; on heresiological ethos, 160n27
Peters, Edward, 17
philosophy, ancient: Augustine's love of, 239; and Christian inquiry, 163–65; Christian *oikoumenē* and, 119; Epiphanius on, 206; heresy and, 163–65; Hippolytus on, 176; legitimate processes of, 137; theistic speculation in, 137; *theōria* in, 196n46; as way of life, 66, 67
Phrygians, in *Theodosian Code*, 53
physiognomics, Christian, 83
piety, extreme, 75
Plato: riddles of, 122n109; *theōria* of, 196n46
Pliny: ethnographic imagination of, 200; fears of inclusion, 202n72; as omniscient narrator, 203
—*Natural History*, 61; Africa in, 199–200; categories of, 204; Ceylon in, 192–93; destroyed towns in, 192n24; diversity in, 203; the impossible in, 203; *luxuria* in, 202n72; the monstrous in, 200n61; omission within, 203; taxonomy of civilization in, 203n72
Plutarch: *De curiositate*, 156, 157, 181; on fascination, 212; *On Isis and Osiris*, 40
Polemo of Laodicea, 107
Polynesia, Western ethnography on, 45, 89
Popkin, Richard, 4n16
Pourkier, Aline, 42n68, 131n17
power relations, Christian, 183n145
praescriptio (precept), 162n34
Pratt, Mary Louise, 254
Priapus (the Good One), in Justinus, 117, 118, 119
Prichard, James Cowles, 19–20, 87
primitivism: ethnography of, 45, 89; and promiscuity, 80n103; racial/cultural concept of, 1
Priscillianists, in *Theodosian Code*, 53
Prodicus (heretic), 147
promiscuity, sexual: primitive mentality and, 80n103
prose, Greek: genres of, 31

pseudo-Clement, *Recognitions*, 114–15
pseudo-Epiphanius, *Recapitulations*, 68, 218, 227–28
pseudo-Jerome, *Catalogue of Heresies*, 227
Ptolemy, on regional cartography, 191
—*Tetrabiblos*, 107–9; determinism in, 107; ethnography in, 107–9; tripartite cosmology of, 107–8
Purchas, Samuel: *Purchas His Pilgrimage*, 21; on religious plurality, 21n83
Pythagoreans, 123

Quodvultdeus (deacon of Carthage), 228, 234, 235; Augustine's reply to, 226, 227, 238; request to Augustine, 44, 69, 220, 222–23, 226, 231, 232, 233

race: in anthropology, 1, 2; typologies of, 1
rationalism, European, 18
reality: Christian, 100; heretics', 99
reasoning: ethnic, 48n93; heretical, 52
religio: Christian connotation of, 62, 63–64; Cicero on, 63; Roman concept of, 62
religion: as category of human experience, 254–55; hierarchies of, 4, 19; interdependence with heresy, 255; local versus transcendent, 20; presectarian, 137; taxonomies of, 3; use of ethnography, 3–4; in Western intellectual tradition, 63
religion, comparative: apartheid, 93; human diversity and, 86
Religionwissenschaft, nineteenth century, 19
Rives, James, 33, 34, 36
Roman Empire: Christianity in, 125; containment issues in, 188n9; cross-cultural exchange in, 193; domination project of, 191–92; Jews of, 209n28; knowledge of other civilizations, 204; peripheries of, 192, 193, 200; as protector of civilization, 210; totalized vision of, 204; triumph in, 202
Royalty, Robert M.: *The Origin of Heresy*, 5n19, 6n23

Sabellins, Augustine on, 230n54
Said, Edward, 253
Samaritans: genesis of, 138; rejection of idolatry, 137
Satanism: heresiologists' fear of, 180; structuralist, 150
Satanists (Messalian offshoot), 76n86
Saturninians, Augustine on, 230
schism, heresy and, 71n57

scholasticism, Christian: limits of, 159–61, 231–33
Schott, Jeremy, 9–10, 23; on apologetic literature, 193; on ethnic histories, 194n33; on ethnogenic linkage, 135; on Purchas, 21; on *religio*, 62–63; on universalism, 194–95
scripture: Christian truth in, 165; classificatory parameters of, 214; corruption by heresy, 99; curiosity concerning, 183; heresiologists' use of, 174; heretics' use of, 20, 167, 168–69; infallibility of, 225n28; mystery of, 240; organizational principles of, 205; power of foreclosure, 206; Tertullian on, 163, 164, 166n54
Scythianism (foundational heresy), 132, 133; genealogy of godliness in, 141; making of gods in, 135–36
Scythians, ethnography of, 117
Second Sophistic, heresiology and, 6n23
sectarianism: codification of, 187; of communities, 138; diversity of, 9; etiology of, 135; historical pattern of, 140; and human diversity, 49; in human history, 124; influence on religious discourse, 254; intellectual trajectory of, 102; Jewish, 48n94, 137; limited comprehension of, 53; pre-Christian, 129; Samaritan, 137; in study of world religions, 58n2; underlying causes of, 138; unknowable, 209; warnings about, 12. *See also* heresy
sects, as new nations, 137–44, 154
Seneca, on human unity, 125
Sethians, heresy of, 116, 151
Sextus Empiricus: *Against the Astrologers*, 103–4; on Chaldean astrology, 111; Hippolytus's use of, 102, 103, 111, 113
Shaw, Brent, 206n86, 223
signs, astrological. *See* astrology; horoscope; zodiac
Sillett, Helen, 145
Simonians: cosmology of, 52; Epiphanius on, 90; mysteries of, 51–52
Simon Magus, 51–52, 90, 139, 145–46; offshoots of, 146–47, 150; typology of, 146, 153
Sirens, song of, 120
Smith, Geoffrey S.: *Guilt by Association*, 6n23, 101n11
Smith, Jonathan Z., 126n130
Smyth, Thomas: *The Unity of the Human Races*, 20
social sciences, nineteenth-century, 18
Song of Songs, influence on Epiphanius, 132n24, 140, 205–6, 210, 213

Stocking, George, Jr., 3, 87; on monogenism, 4; *Victorian Anthropology*, 19n70
Stoics, universalism of, 125
Strabo: Africa in, 199; astronomy in, 109; ethnography of, 90
Strousma, Gedaliahu (Guy) G., 63n20
superstitio: Judaism as, 62n14; of Messalians, 74; objects of worship, 62; Roman concept of, 62

tables of contents, ancient, 130n11
Tacitus: on Britain, 191n20
—*Germania*, 33; ethnography in, 90
—*Histories*: ethnographic analysis in, 35n37; Jews in, 35–36
Taprobane. *See* Ceylon
tares, parable of, 146
Tatian, travels of, 195n41
taxonomies: of civilization, 203n72; of heresiologists, 195–96; of identification, 231; of religions, 3; Roman, 199; Theodoret's, 145
temptation, demonic, 52, 149
Tertullianists, Augustine on, 242
Tertullian of Carthage: on choice, 159; on Christian pedagogy, 181; on Christian unity, 159; ethnographic disposition of, 66; exegetical techniques of, 167; heresiology of, 6; inward-looking faith of, 165–66; on philosophy, 161, 169; rhetorical hesitancy of, 188; transformative Christianity of, 164
—*Adversus Hermogenem*, 162
—*Adversus Marcionem*, 162
—*Adversus Praxean*, 162
—*Adversus Valentinianos*, 162
—*Rule against the Heretics*: abstention from analysis, 162; on Aristotle, 163; catechumens in, 67; Christology of, 167; on curiosity, 25, 165, 168; customs in, 68; on debate with heretics, 168–70, 181; on dialectic, 163–65, 168; on epistemological humility, 168; on false exegesis, 168; heresiological ethnography in, 67–68; on heretical arrogance, 67–68; on heretical reasoning, 175; on heretics' appropriations, 99; human experience in, 164; humility in, 236; on inquiry, 162–70, 167–68; *regula fidei* in, 167–68; on revelation of Christ, 166; rhetorical structure of, 162n35; on scriptural investigation, 163, 164, 166n54; testing by faith in, 163; unity of heresies in, 215; on universality of Gospels, 166n60; ways of life in, 66

INDEX   301

texts, author-saturated/author-evacuated, 55
Theodoret of Cyrrhus: enumeration of heretics, 16, 146–47; heresiology of, 6, 251; scholarship on, 145n84; sources of, 43n70
—*Compendium of Divine Doctrines,* 144, 148; cosmic struggle in, 149; protreptic language of, 149
—*Compendium of Heretical Fables:* Arius in, 147; Artemon in, 147; Christian diversity in, 150; Christological controversies in, 152, 153; classification in, 148; cosmic struggle in, 150; demonic intrusion in, 149–52; doctrinal lineages in, 145; enumeration of heresies, 146–47; expansion of heresiology, 145; genealogy of, 25, 145, 146–47, 148; heretical liberation in, 178; heretical origins in, 129; intellectual inheritance in, 147; language of succession, 147, 151; master narrative of, 144–53; Melchizedekians in, 147; Messalians in, 74n75; orthodox doctrine in, 148, 149, 153; *Panarion* and, 147–48; response to Nestorian controversies, 152; taxonomies of, 145; on theological errors, 146–47; triumph over heresy in, 178; typology of, 25, 129, 144–53
—*Discernment of Lies and Truth,* 144–45
Theodosian Code: book burning in, 92n172; discursive logic of, 53; heresy in, 52–53
Theodosius II, Emperor: heresy law of, 52
theology: categorization in, 28; as classification tool, 66; community in, 78n92; degeneration and, 148n104; eradication of borders, 209; as ethnographic device, 59, 63, 82; false reasoning in, 52; heresiologists' use of, 64, 66, 125n129; heretics', 47, 64, 74
theology, comparative, 66; as Christian ethnography, 59–66
theory: displacement through, 196; ethnographic experience of, 196n46
thiasos (cultic association), 49–50
thought: relationship to action, 67; as totality of life, 66–67
time, sacred: eschatological moment of, 144
traditions: apostolic, 83, 123, 140; invention of, 100
travel, disruptive effects of, 196
travel writing, rhetoric/reality mix in, 189–90
Trinity, nature of, 162n36
triumph: containment in, 188n9; in heresiology, 170–79; of orthodoxy, 178, 245
Trogodytae, Mela on, 198

truth, Christian: continuous struggle of, 132; corruption by inquiry, 165; curiosity and, 157, 168; discernment of, 152; Epiphanius on, 80; ethic of, 97; ethnic argumentation in, 63; ethnographic definition of, 256; falsity and, 17n64; heresiologists on, 88; heretical mutilation of, 13, 67, 123; innovation of, 63; monovocality of, 158; never-ending investigation of, 167n64; Rule of, 175; in scripture, 165; travelers' accounts of, 21; unity of, 143
Tyler, Stephen A., 87, 227, 244

unity, Christian, 90, 96, 158; descent from Adam, 142; ethnographic investigation of, 256; fragility of, 226n33
unity, heretical, 176
unity, human, 5n21, 19n75, 20, 124–26, 143; in antiquity, 125; Christian longing for, 25; in macroscopic ethnography, 125; as religious unity, 20; in theological doctrine, 257
universalism, Christian, 125; dangers to, 209, 210; difference in, 194; role of ethnography in, 193
universality: heretical, 28, 209; and particularity, 9
universe, creative agents of, 117–20. *See also* cosmology
the unknowable: in ancient ethnography, 200, 209; in Augustine, 232–33; classification of, 244; concerning heretics, 232; in Epiphanius, 237; ethnographic effects of, 189–95; in geography, 189; of God, 237; in Mela, 190; in natural world, 201–2; in sectarianism, 209

Valentinian III, Emperor: heresy law of, 52
Valentinians: creation beliefs of, 151; ethics of extremes, 84; Hippolytus on, 124; inexact comprehension of, 173–74; Irenaeus on, 150n113, 173–74, 176; and other Christians, 51n111; Tertullian on, 162n36; violence against, 91
Valentinus (teacher of Marcus), 49, 147
Valesians, castration of, 61
Veyne, Paul, 125, 204
violence: against heretics, 91; contribution of Christian rhetoric to, 183n144
virginity, Christian, 94
Volk, Katharina, 105, 106

White, Hayden: on human unity, 143, 154–55; "The Forms of Wildness," 90–91
Williams, John, 89, 96
witnesses, ethnographical, 37

Woolf, Greg, 36, 142n74; on astrology, 104; on ethnographic knowledge, 100; on explanatory paradigms, 40–41
world. *See* natural world; *oikoumenē*

Xanthus the Lydian, *Lydiaka*, 34

Zephyrinus, Bishop: controversy with Hippolytus, 102
zodiac: anthropological effects of, 111–12; deterministic potential of, 111–12; Manilius on, 106–7; Ptolemy on, 107–8. *See also* astrology; horoscopes

www.ingramcontent.com/pod-product-compliance
Lightning Source LLC
Chambersburg PA
CBHW030523230426
43665CB00010B/744